MANAGEMENT SYSTEMS

MANAGEMENT SYSTEMS

Thomas B. Glans
International Business Machines Corporation

Burton Grad
International Business Machines Corporation

David Holstein
International Business Machines Corporation

William E. Meyers
Rich Products Corporation, Buffalo

Richard N. Schmidt
State University of New York at Buffalo

Holt, Rinehart and Winston, Inc.

New York   Chicago
San Francisco   Atlanta
Dallas   Montreal
Toronto   London

To: Hester Ann, Pauline, Anita, Betty, and Mildred

Copyright © 1968 by Holt, Rinehart and Winston, Inc.
Library of Congress Catalog Card Number: 68-28177

03-068970-8

Printed in the United States of America

0123   22   987654

7-8-86

Preface

The life cycle of a management system consists of three stages: (1) the study and design of the system, (2) its implementation as a new system, and (3) its operation within the organization for which it was designed.

Most of the literature concerning management systems has heretofore concentrated on the second and third stages of the life cycle, thus leaving the first stage relatively untouched. There are two reasons for this concentration. First, computers promise substantial benefits and, once the decision to go ahead is made, there is typically great urgency to get them installed and into some kind of productive operation. Much of the available literature is a response to this pressing need. The second reason for the concentration on the second and third stages is the considerable difficulty there has been in drawing together an appropriately tested body of knowledge encompassing the study and design of systems. While writers widely acknowledge the importance of the study and design stage, there has been, until recently, a paucity of recorded information concerning the procedural details to system development. This situation is now changing and there is a greater understanding of both the abstract and applied implications of information processing systems in a computer environment.

The purpose of our book is to present a thorough, detailed treatment of the first stage in the life cycle of a management system—its study and design. The material is given comprehensive treatment in order to provide a source for beginning students in systems design. Experienced practitioners may want to use our book selectively to avoid the planned redundancy and emphasis on detailed case studies.

Although the material we present implies that computer-based systems are to be developed, the concepts can also be applied to manual and semiautomated methods, often part of the resources that are used in any business system.

Our book is therefore recommended for:

1. A systems course for students of business, computer science, economics, engineering, and management.
2. Use in the professional and technical training of systems analysts, systems engineers, systems and procedures personnel, programmers, and for others interested in systems.
3. Use by systems and programming personnel.
4. Use by management and systems design personnel in developing "Management Information Systems."
5. Use as a reference by supervisory and management personnel in commercial, educational, governmental, industrial, medical, and other organizations.

We have divided the book into four parts. Part 1 outlines a general method for studying and designing a system from an organizational point of view. We explain the concept of three phases to cover the study and design of systems. These phases are discussed in detail in subsequent Parts 2, 3, and 4. Part 2, the first phase in the study and design of a system, is *understanding the present system.* In this part we cover techniques for determining organization goals and for gathering data and organizing it into a management report describing the present system. Part 3, the second phase in the study and design of a system, is the *determination of the requirements for the new system.* Here we show how goals, objectives, and activities can be translated into definitions of system inputs and system outputs, and how these determine the requirements of the system. An important aspect of this phase is the consideration of those present or planned resources of men and data processing equipment that will need to be part of the new system. The major report containing the results of the findings in Phase II can be described as a systems requirements specification. The third phase in the study and design of a system is the actual *design of the new system.* In Part 4 we describe the factors needed in designing a new system. Fundamentally, a set of alternative designs must be considered so that the final decision for a particular design will include proper handling of activity requirements, equipment configuration, costs, implementation, and conversion. Part 4 concludes with the final report on a new system plan.

To make more systematic the work of designing systems, we present several documentation forms that serve useful purposes—for the analysts who make the study and for management who review the reports.

The examples, ideas, and illustrations provided are adapted from actual case studies in which the methodology presented in our book was employed. Names, identifying locations, and products have been changed, but the substance of the material quoted is taken from the reports produced in selected studies. We make specific reference to nine studies by name. They are: *Atlantic Distributors,* a

Michigan-based warehouse chain; *Associated Retailers, Inc.,* a department store in Florida; *Butodale Electronics,* a 15-year-old Massachusetts corporation specializing in analog computers; *Collins, McCabe and Company,* a stock brokerage firm in Texas; *Custodian Life Insurance Company,* once a stock company, now a mutual company in Illinois; *National Bank of Commerce,* a moderate-sized bank in Kansas; *Supersonic Airlines, Inc.,* an international passenger and freight carrier with headquarters in New York; *Typical State,* a state well-known for its use of computers; and *Worthington Hardware,* a family-held wholesaling organization in California. The Butodale case study is used extensively to illustrate the three major reports mentioned above.

A glossary is provided to familiarize the student with technical terms in the area of computers, data processing, and systems.

We wish to acknowledge the assistance of the International Business Machine Corporation in making available to us various published and unpublished material, and we thank them for their kind permission to use it in this book. The concepts underlying our book were first published by IBM under the name "Study Organization Plan"; these were contained in IBM manuals and covered in certain courses.

Credit is also given to those companies, who must remain nameless, that participated in the evaluation of our approach to system studies and provided the basis for the various illustrations, examples, and case studies.

We also wish to thank the many individuals who contributed to the ideas expressed through planning, using, writing, teaching, and preparing the material. Two of our closest associates have died since the original material was formulated; Lee H. Baker of IBM and Robert R. Smith, a private consultant, were members of the team that created and tested these concepts. We have sorely missed their good counsel.

We particularly want to acknowledge the special efforts of Frank T. Dolen and Robert F. Walleck, both of IBM, who were instrumental in applying the concepts to smaller businesses and in preparing educational material. Sincere thanks are also due to Mrs. Eleanor S. Harris who typed many drafts of the original work and to L. Kenneth Heath, Ray W. Oldham, William C. Tumelty, Harold W. Leffingwell, and Walt M. Whitmyre, all of IBM, who used and evaluated this approach with various firms. Richard G. Canning, a private consultant, helped initiate the work.

White Plains, New York	T.B.G.
White Plains, New York	B.G.
White Plains, New York	D.H.
Buffalo, New York	W.E.M.
Buffalo, New York	R.N.S.
September 1968	

Contents

PART

OVERVIEW OF MANAGEMENT SYSTEMS

Part 1 comprises an overview of the main concepts in the study and design of management systems. We define three stages in the life cycle of a system: (1) its study and design, (2) its implementation and installation, and (3) its operation, evaluation, and modification with the passage of time. Our aim being to concentrate on the first stage, we will cover only the study and design of a new system.

The objective of Part 1 is to provide a general coverage of this study and design stage. The first chapter introduces the main terms and concepts, such as the meaning of goals and the overall approach. The second chapter provides the specific coverage of three phases defined for the study and design stage of a management system. These three phases are: (1) understanding the present system, (2) determining the requirements of the new system, and (3) designing the new system. For each phase, we explain the general form and contents of a management report containing the findings presented by the team that is studying the organization and designing the new system.

In the third chapter we present some general topics that the analysts who form the study team should consider in planning and carrying out a systems study.

Thus, Part 1 is a broad conceptual framework, designed to give the reader a comprehensive picture of general aspects of a systems study and design without the details which might obscure the overall picture. The subsequent three parts of our book develop these concepts more fully.

CHAPTER

INTRODUCTION

1.1 ORGANIZATION—MANAGEMENT SYSTEM

Every organization has a management system. These two key terms—organization and management system—are used extensively throughout the book and we begin by defining them.

Organization generally means any business, enterprise, firm, establishment, or institution formed for some purpose. Parts of organizations may also be considered as organizations in themselves if needed for a definite purpose.

Management system means the methods by which an organization plans, operates, and controls its activities to meet its goals and objectives by utilizing the resources of money, people, equipment, materials, and information.

We extend the use of the term "management system" to include any aspect in the life of an organization to which management personnel devote their attention. Consequently, the reader should keep in mind the larger picture of the organization and its management systems. Because management systems are such an important aspect of business operation, they are often called "business systems." Other frequently encountered terms that denote the same concept are: "total system," "unified system," "goal-directed system," "integrated system," and "information system." We use these terms interchangeably.

If we consider these ideas from a general point of view, the definition of man-

3

agement system may cover other kinds of systems. In precomputer days, it was customary to think of systems as "accounting systems," with the elements dollar figures, the relations based on the double-entry bookkeeping method, and the control exercised through budgets. Now, however, we think of management systems in their broad sense, and include accounting systems as one part of the total picture. In the larger view, the invoicing operation, payroll, billing, inventory control, budget allocation, advertising, and similar operations oriented directly to administrative functions, are in the same category as operational systems involving production control, design methods, product development, design engineering, marketing research, and any other area in which the computer is used for the orderly and systematic control of relations among elements, however they may be defined.

There is a growing awareness among computer people that those earlier barriers which separated administration from operations are disappearing under the impact of the computer, which processes a growing mixture of data arising from all parts of the organization. Thoughtful management and systems personnel realize that the heart of their organization is operations and that no system, no matter how sophisticated, can overcome inferior products and services. In fact, the goals and objectives of the typical organization always emphasize that the reason the organization exists is to provide goods, services, and utilities.

1.2   THE LIFE CYCLE OF A MANAGEMENT SYSTEM

As we pointed out in the Preface, we envision three stages in the life cycle of a management system:

1.   Study and design of the system
2.   Implementation as a new system
3.   Operation of the system within the organization

The key words associated with each of the stages are shown in Figure 1-1. In this section we shall cover each of the stages by expanding briefly on the key words in the figure.

The overall purpose of Stage 1 is to *design a new system* for the organization, or for a defined part of the organization. To accomplish this, it is necessary to

STAGE 1	STAGE 2	STAGE 3
STUDY AND DESIGN	IMPLEMENT AND INSTALL	OPERATE, EVALUATE, AND MODIFY
Problem Recognition Determination of Objectives Study Present System Determine System Requirements Design New System Propose Solution	Detail System Design File Design Develop Programs Develop Test Criteria and Data System Test Conversion	Operation Efficiency Analysis System Modification and Maintenance

Figure 1-1   The three stages in the life cycle of a system.

recognize and define the specific problems that must be solved. Generally, one defines the problems of the organization by determining the objectives, both of the organization and of the system. Consequently, it is imperative that the present system be studied. Of course, if there is no present system, as in the case of an organization or subsystem just being formed, the study is typically of identical or similar operations in one or more other organizations.

From the study emerges an understanding of what the system is required to do, not only in a broad sense but in a fair amount of detail. This understanding, coupled with information concerning the future direction of the enterprise, leads to the definition and specification of the proper system requirements: "What must the system do?" and "How well must the system perform?" The answers to these two questions will provide the design objectives of the new system. Only then can the new system be designed. Although this idea seems self-evident, it is almost universally ignored or given only token consideration. We therefore emphasize that the analysts designing a new system and management for whom the system is to be designed must work together in order to insure its proper outcome.

Once the new system is designed, it is necessary to consider the collection of data-processing equipment that can carry out the work imposed by the design. In the typical situation, the team of analysts usually consider several sets of equipment, some of which can be quite different, but all of which may be able to carry out the work of the design, even though there may be varying degrees of effectiveness and cost. It is the responsibility of the study team to search out that particular collection of equipment that is optimum in terms of total cost and efficiency.

The final work of the analysts is to prepare a report on the main features of the system they have designed. The report should include recommendations for equipment to handle the task.

The overall purpose of Stage 2 is to *implement the newly designed system* by converting the plan into reality. The first step is to explain the details of the system design. Input and output files must be designed, flowcharts prepared, programs written for the computer, and test criteria and test data organized. The data flow through the system must then be tested. The real data of the system must be processed, and the outputs of the system must be checked to insure that they conform to the set specifications. Often this verification takes place in parallel operations in which computer operations are compared with the existing system. Finally, there is full conversion to the new system and, after a suitable time to assure accuracy, the new system is ready for independent operation.

The third stage in the life cycle of a management system is its *operation, evaluation,* and *modification*. When the new system is placed in day-to-day operation, many problems, errors, and other difficulties must be met and solved on a realistic basis. The efficiency of the new system must be checked closely to make sure it meets the specifications set for it. Typically, unforeseen difficulties make it necessary to modify the new system. Management personnel, who are usually the recipients of the outputs, are able to spot the deficiencies. The system must consequently be modified. In addition, elements in the external environment can exert great influence. For example, a change in government regulations might have an impact on the system; stockholders, unions, customers, vendors, and foreign exchanges could effect it. Finally, the system must be maintained and serviced to keep it operational. To do this, personnel must be continually trained, equipment must be maintained, and everything that can affect its operation must be considered to make sure it is able to meet the objectives set by management. Understandably, the three stages in the life cycle of a system are not mutually exclusive. In fact, they overlap in various ways and at various points.

1.3 BUSINESS MATURITY AND SYSTEMS

In their continuing effort to be competitive and yet conduct profitable operations, businessmen explore many alternatives. A product or service can be redesigned to make it more attractive in the market place; advertising and sales promotion can be stepped up to reach a wider audience; internal cost reduction programs can be initiated to reduce expenses; and the information system can be redesigned and updated to secure greater efficiencies. Of these alternatives, the search for new products and wider markets usually draws the most attention, while other areas with less direct appeal are secondary in importance. An existing system, for example, despite clear warning signs of inefficiency and obsolescence, often continues to be operated in much the same old way, with only an occasional patchwork repair job to keep it in running condition. As a result, too many enterprises have the outward look of a modern creation, while internally they are operating with an antique power plant.

With growth, a certain maturity evolves. With maturity, sound judgment and intelligent direction can be applied by those in control, whether they carry the title of owner, government bureau head, agency director, professional manager, or any other, to detect and eliminate waste, duplication, and proliferating services. A business system, which should be a sharp instrument of control and a vital generator of dynamic decision-making information, is often outdated in both concept and technology. Many existing business systems were designed around human capabilities and, unfortunately, around human limitations. Furthermore, many are built around outdated and poorly structured organizations. Some systems remind one of the classic figure of a green-visored bookkeeper perched on a high stool, quill in hand, making entries in a ledger carefully and laboriously. Other systems were structured for a number of clerks to busily perform manual calculations or punch keyboards of desk calculators; each clerk usually performing different, but limited, duties. Systems were paced to human skills with their attendant shortcomings in fatigue, limited span of attention, and inaccuracy. Errors were detected by assigning one person to audit another's work, or by the rather expensive method of cross-checking. Nevertheless, these systems worked—because individuals could compensate for many errors. Even with the introduction of punched-card equipment, the system often remained tied to human capacities and machine specializations. Jobs were divided into steps matched to the machines. If the volume grew, if something went wrong, or if bottlenecks occurred, more machines were added, more people were hired, or the work was further subdivided.

Equipment with vastly increased versatility and speed appeared on the market—yet there was no immediate parallel improvement in systems control and methodology. Systems men and managers thought at first that the new machines could be superimposed directly on the existing system. Indeed, this occurred frequently, and often with fairly good results. Work was processed faster and reports did contain more detail. Thoughtful executives, however, began realizing that there were greater advantages to machines than faster speeds. Out of this "rethinking" emerged a completely new idea: redesign each system as a unified entity contributing directly to business goals, and take full advantage of equipment capabilities as well as fast-developing management science techniques. This was the real opportunity to tap the long-unrealized potential of a modern management system.

1.4 DEFINING BUSINESS GOALS

From the organization-wide view, the system is designed to support the primary goals of the business and, consequently, is closely identified with them. This is true whether the goals are formally stated or exist only in the minds of the management personnel. Profit-making, while a common goal for nearly all enterprises (with the exception of special situations like government operations), is too general and vague for useful system consideration. Goals are the special contributions an organization endeavors to make to its environment to fulfill some special purpose.

The primary goal of an appliance company, for example, is to manufacture and sell appliances. Profit-making, though vital in order that the company stay in business, is only part of the governing framework within which it must operate. Starting with the single, specific goal of making appliances, the company from time to time may perform other activities for the purpose of adding to profit or increasing profit margins on appliances. By expanding into such activities as manufacturing other products, mining basic metals, and financing purchases, the company adds other goals. As the company grows, it adds departments, divisions, and other organizational subdivisions to meet the requirements imposed by more complex operations. The final result, if inspected at any moment in time, would of course be a total system of great complexity.

However, it is a total system only in the sense that the whole is equal to the sum of its parts. Over the years, primary business goals may have been forgotten or new goals never formulated, while a number of secondary goals may have emerged to assume unwarranted importance and emphasis. Primary, or true, goals do not include the preparation of reports (unless the business produces reports for profit or legal reasons), or the sending of bills (unless the business is a bill-collection agency). The goal-directed systems approach calls for the reexamination and restatement of true business goals.

1.5 THE ORGANIZATION-WIDE APPROACH

Although they are sometimes poorly designed or even mismanaged, most systems do work. Somehow products are manufactured, records kept, orders filled, and employees paid. The system continues to grow or shrink as new products or services are added or obsolete ones phased out. Reorganizations occur, or perhaps a merger strengthens finances. All the while, the business maintains momentum without being fully conscious of waste, duplication, or illogic.

The key to creating a business system is the organization-wide approach. The business is treated as a unified whole; it is considered initially in broad, generalized terms. True goals are identified in terms of what the business contributes to its environment. From this vantage point, an approach can be defined and expanded into an operating system which fulfills the goals of the enterprise. Items not contributing directly to the satisfaction of a business goal may be considered either secondary in importance or entirely expendable.

The unified systems approach is oriented toward goals and toward activities which attain the goals, rather than toward personnel, equipment, or organization structure. This may be explained more fully by the following example. An aircraft flies passengers and mail between New York and London. This is a primary goal. To achieve it, certain takeoff and landing procedures are used, the aircraft is propelled, navigated, and controlled in space, and it is prepared for the next flight. It is not necessary to mention in the goal statement that a supersonic-type aircraft with an air-supported landing gear was involved, piloted by a man named Eugene Irving, and landing on ramp #23. The goal is stated simply as "fly passengers and freight between designated points," regardless of equipment or personnel. The purpose of a goal statement is to express the results the system must achieve and ignore the specifics of the systems solution.

Under the unified systems approach, the organization is viewed as a whole, as a single entity for which a systematic solution can be proposed, instead of as an organizational structure composed of individual elements. While the latter position has solved problems in the past, it is the unified, organization-wide approach that provides the great promise for the future.

For this reason, our approach is toward the unified system. We present a philosophy and methodology to achieve better systems designs when used by imaginative systems people working in a suitable management and business climate. This first part of our book provides an overview of the methodology and documentation of a system study through three phases:

    (I) studying an existing system
   (II) determining true systems requirements
  (III) designing a new system

As the discussion will reveal, it is a plan for a total systems study. The question might well be asked at this point: Is this the complete usefulness of the plan, or does it have application over a wider range of business situations?

The answer is that the plan is general and flexible and may be adapted to variations in:

    (1) type of business
    (2) size and length of the study
    (3) size of business
    (4) depth of penetration
    (5) level of refinement

Next, we expand upon these five points to clarify the above statement.

1.6   FLEXIBILITY OF APPROACH

Anyone experienced with the design of management systems knows that there is an extremely wide variety of situations for which systems must be designed. Few would disagree with the statement that no two situations are the same. The complexity of the problem is compounded by the fact that there can be a wide variety of designs for each situation. As a consequence, we have tried to insure a presentation that has a wide range of applicability. We shall consider this range for the above five points.

Type of business   Frequently in the past, the framework of systems reference has either been overgeneralized or else held within too rigid limits and centered on a single type of organization or application.

We feel that the philosophy and methodology in this book is flexible enough in design to avoid the twin traps of rigidity and overgeneralization, and in point of fact the approach has been applied to such divergent business fields as wholesale distribution, banking, insurance, electronics manufacture, aircraft manufacture, and public utilities. On the basis of detailed analysis and study, there is no apparent reason why the approach cannot be extended to include organizations in the fields of credit, merchandising, transportation, communications, mining, construction, and government.

Size and length of study   In any type of organization it is possible to use the method for a fast but comprehensive pass at part of the business, determining its goals and operating methods, sketching its structure, and arriving at a significantly improved business application. On the other hand, it can be used for probing a business in considerable depth to portray its detailed structure and operating dynamics for creative redesign. Of course, any level between these extremes may be chosen, depending on time allowed, team size and quality, and study objectives.

Size of business   Experience has demonstrated that the size of a business has no effect on the applicability of the plan of study. Both a small retailer and a giant multidivision corporation can be studied within this framework. In one case, a selectively compressed version would be used; in the other, the full plan may be required.

Depth of penetration   The plan can be applied in varying depths of penetration. Certain activities within a company may require more detailed study than others, depending on the cost of data gathering and the potential for improvement; various forms permit everything from an overview treatment to fine detail. Chapters 8, 14, and 19 discuss these recording forms and describe how data is introduced and displayed.

Level of refinement   The method is further useful over a range of levels in study refinement. Where an enterprise is interested in moderate systems improvement or direct mechanization of an existing system, the plan provides a ready-made structure by which these objectives can be quickly accomplished. In the other direction, it can be employed to its full extent to support the creative study which will set in place an entirely new system design to carry a business many years into the future.

The philosophy and methodology can be viewed as a total plan of action, a set of guidelines for many types of system studies, in companies large and small, for almost any type of endeavor, for simple studies or complex ones; it can be applied in a fully expanded version or in an abridged form.

SUMMARY

Organization, management, and system—these three words are important in the objective of this book: the study of systems from the management viewpoint. A system may be considered as passing through three stages—study and design, implementation, and operation. Our book focuses on the first stage.

As a business grows and expands, so does its need for more refined and sophisticated systems. The design of these new systems requires a definition of business goals and an overall approach. Systems study and design can be accomplished in three phases: studying an existing system, determining true systems requirements, and designing a new system. A flexible approach to these three phases permits the same basic methodology to be used independent of type and size of organization, size and length of study, depth of penetration, and level of refinement.

CHAPTER

Overview: The Study and Design of a System

2.1 THREE PHASES

In Section 1.2 we covered the three stages in the life cycle of a system. The relation between these three stages and the three phases that constitute the subject of this book is shown in Figure 2-1.

The implementation and operation stages are covered in numerous articles and books. As yet, however, there has been little effective material describing the vital first stage of study and design. Many authors and analysts have assumed that the major task of system design is to fit new equipment to an existing system. They seem to have overlooked the fact that these systems grew up around the characteristics and limitations of human beings; that they reflected typical patterns of organization and the division of labor into special classes; that information was handled sequentially, with all inputs recorded before any processing was initiated; that the systems were often dedicated to after-the-fact recording of historical information.

With this attitude toward study and design, existing systems were often just mechanized versions of manual systems; only infrequently were solutions developed from a true grasp of the present requirements of the organization and an understanding of its future requirements. Yet only with a complete recognition of the task during the stage of study and design can a strikingly advanced system be

11

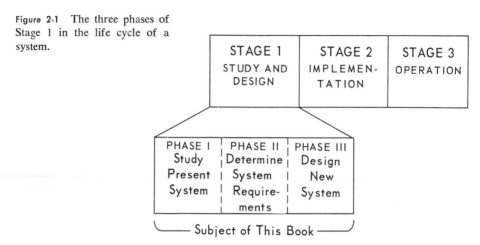

Figure 2-1   The three phases of Stage 1 in the life cycle of a system.

devised. The approach and methodology of the three phases is directed toward changing the pattern and toward providing advanced, substantially-more profitable systems.

A good example of advanced systems is an airline reservation system which ties all locations together to satisfy the goal of providing customers with quick, efficient services. The airlines have built their entire customer operation around these sophisticated systems.

As shown in Figure 2-1, the study and design stage is separated into three phases:

Phase I   The existing system is studied to gain an insight into the organization and its key relationships.

Phase II   Results of the Phase I study are blended with forecasts of foreseeable needs to develop an accurate specification of true system requirements.

Phase III   The new system is designed from specifications of its basic requirements, and then communicated to management in the form of a new system plan.

2.2   UNDERSTANDING THE PRESENT SYSTEM

In order to understand the present system, analysts try to determine what is done in the organization using what inputs, with what resources, to achieve what results. This would hold true in a mechanization study where a manual system is being converted directly to machines, in a study aimed at partial improvement or modification of an existing system, or in a completely creative study leading to a new design. Information is collected and organized into a meaningful pattern to permit an accurate understanding of the organization as it presently operates and reacts to its environment.

A document entitled the *Present Business Description* is the formal output from Phase I. It contains three major sections—General, Structural, and Operational.

The *General* section includes a history of the enterprise, industry background, goals and objectives, major policies and practices, and government regulations.

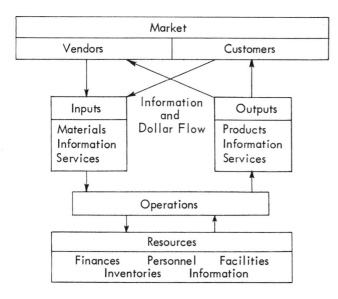

Figure 2-2 A model of a business system.

The *Structural* section contains a model of the business, describing it in terms of products and markets, materials and suppliers, finances, personnel, facilities, inventories, and information. A simplified example of a business model is shown in Figure 2-2.

The *Operational* section employs flow diagrams and a distribution of total resources to present the operating dynamics of the business. These charts demonstrate how the resources of a business respond to inputs, perform operations, and produce outputs.

An appendix is usually added to cover the more detailed working documents needed to explain operations, identify documents, and define the files in which the organization's information is stored.

Mechanization studies frequently change only the physical method of performing a job. On the other hand, improvement studies usually seek to make at least some improvements in the systems being investigated. In both studies, the general and structural sections can be compiled quite rapidly, with more time allocated to the compilation of data for the operational section. We should point out, however, that the application of our philosophy and methodology often leads to extending the scope and the potential benefit of mechanization and improvement studies beyond management's initial objectives. In the creative study, where the objective is to be consciously and deliberately free from past limitations, understanding of the present system is still necessary before present and future system requirements can be defined and established, but emphasis will shift more to the general and structural and away from the operational details.

2.3   DETERMINING SYSTEMS REQUIREMENTS

In determining the requirements of a system, two main questions arise: (1) What is the system required to do, now and in the future? (2) How well must it perform to fulfill these requirements? To find out, known facts about the existing system are blended with information concerning the future. Advanced information is generated through forecasts and predictions on future markets, new services, product volumes, design changes, business trends, advanced processes, regulatory law, and revisions in product mix. Any changes in policy or in objectives contemplated by management along lines of increased specialization or diversification must be considered in future requirements. A proposed system would have to take into account seasonal patterns in labor and costs, as well as market penetration by competitors. Phase II is a mixture of analysis, synthesis, forecasting, construction of models, and even operations research.

Collection and review of information constitute the first steps in determining the requirements of the system. Then the study team must combine creative ideas with precise scientific techniques to generate true requirements. The techniques and methodology of management science have become more available to systems engineers in the last few years. Operations research, for instance, started when known statistical and mathematical techniques were applied to operational problems. For example, during World War II, the use of a long-known sampling technique revealed that aircraft aiming bombs in a pattern obtained much better results than aircraft aiming individually at a target. This technique was referred to as dispersion bombing. The application of operations research and other powerful, generally mathematical and statistical, techniques to business problems (management science) is producing worthwhile and sometimes startling solutions.

The approach used in Phase II is much like that of an architect in designing a new home. First, the architect has his client describe the family's plans and ideas, and learns the income, sizes, and ages within the family group. He observes their present dwelling in terms of taste and preference, and notes the arrangement and sizes of play and study areas and kitchen. Next, he has to bring the family's plans into line with their pocketbook. Will they give up a screened porch and an extra bathroom to have a fourth bedroom? Will they postpone some landscaping and keep the air-conditioning system? With this background information, the architect now is able to formulate requirements within the boundaries of available funds, and draw up definitive specifications for a design satisfactory to the whole family.

Specifications are of prime importance; their precision and accuracy control the eventual effectiveness of solution design. The analysts who study a system to determine its requirements should report their conclusions to the management of the organization.

2.4 REPORT OF THE SYSTEMS REQUIREMENTS

The report prepared by the analysts may be termed the *Systems Requirements Specification*. This document contains a series of information packets, each giving the requirements for a separate activity within the organization. (An activity, which will be explained more fully below, is a combination of operations leading to one or more business goals.) The content of the report for an organization with three activities is shown in Figure 2-3.

The activity specification packets are introduced by a *Summary* section stating

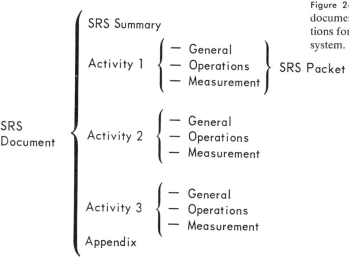

Figure 2-3 Structure of the document containing specifications for the requirements of the system.

the overall goals and objectives of the business, defining the scope of the study, and summarizing the reports to follow.

Each SRS packet has three main sections: General, Operations, and Measurement.

The *General* section describes the goals and objectives of the activity, its scope and boundaries, and lists general considerations such as policies and costs not mentioned in more specialized sections. An activity requirements model shows the relationships among logically required and imposed inputs, operations, resources, and outputs. Figure 2-4 shows an activity requirements model for one activity of an organization.

The *Operations* section specifies what the system designed for the activity must do, what operations it must perform, what inputs it must accept, what outputs it must produce, and what resources—people, equipment, facilities, and inventories —will be required. This section specifies the minimum requirements for input, output, and resources imposed by management or logically required to achieve a goal. The more resources imposed, the less freedom the study team has in designing the new system. Thus, the analysts should do everything possible in Phase II to include only those specific inputs, outputs, and resources logically required or mandated by management.

The *Measurement* section states in what terms the design of the system is to be evaluated in performing the stated tasks of the activity. Measurements are identified, and acceptable limits and present performance levels determined in terms of time, cost, accuracy, and volume.

An appendix contains material which supports and amplifies statements of essential operations. This material is composed of the various sheets and other documents that the analysts prepare during the course of their study. Included are message and file sheets, resource lists, flowcharts, decision tables for operations logic, and definitions of measurement factors. These new terms are defined in detail later; they are listed here only for continuity.

Mechanization and improvement studies have been carried out without extensive

Figure 2-4 An activity requirements model showing the required relationships within an
activity.

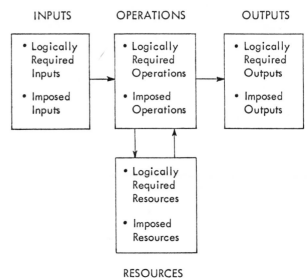

investigation into present and future requirements. One danger in this course of
action is that existing operations are often merely made more automatic, whether
or not they are necessary or even useful. Another danger is that future change may
make the newly designed system inefficient.

2.5   DESIGNING THE NEW SYSTEM

Once the requirements for the new system have been specified, it is
designed and described. Throughout this period, a high level of creative contribution is desirable from the design team if the system is to successfully support the
enterprise over a span of years.

First, reports from the first two phases are reviewed and the design objectives
specified. Then, design alternatives are formulated and described to see how effectively they meet requirements. When more than one activity is included, input,
output, file, operation, and equipment characteristics must be examined, and activities should be integrated wherever desirable.

Activity description is then expanded, and specific equipment is selected for
each alternative solution. Through careful evaluation, the best system is chosen. An
implementation plan is then devised to show the cost and schedule for detailed
systems design, programming, installation, conversion, testing, and personnel training. Finally, the expected performance of the new system is evaluated for its impact
on revenue, investment, and expense.

2.6   THE NEW SYSTEM PLAN

The main effort of the analysts toward the latter part of their study is
the preparation of a report containing their design, or alternative designs, for the

new system. We call this document the *New System Plan,* for that is exactly what it is.

It has been found useful to management personnel, who have to review the recommendations, to have the report divided into five main parts: (1) a summary for management, (2) a section describing the new system in operation, (3) a section telling how the plan will be implemented, (4) a section appraising the economic value of the proposed design, and (5) an appendix containing the key supporting data and information on which the report was based. These major divisions are preceded customarily by a preface containing a letter of transmittal, an introduction, and a table of contents. Each of the five main parts is described below.

The Management Abstract section reviews the work of the first two phases, outlines the proposed system as it will operate, surveys the implementation plan, and emphasizes the system's values for profit improvement, reduction of costs, and associated benefits. Since it is a synopsis of the entire study for management evaluation, it describes the main points of the system concisely but completely.

The New System in Operation section relates how the system will work, what equipment will be needed, what the responsibilities will be for operating personnel, and what the expected operating costs will be.

The Implementation Plans section describes the various steps of installing the new system, showing costs and time schedules.

The Appraisal of System Value section accentuates the benefits to be derived from the new system, relates why alternative designs were rejected, and projects the advantages over the lifespan of the system.

The Appendix includes a selection of key supporting data not shown in other sections. It supplies the technical reinforcement of the system, making it more comprehensible.

The New System Plan is the culmination of the entire systems study and provides a well-documented, thoroughly analyzed framework from which the implementation and operation of the system may be inaugurated.

2.7 ADDITIONAL INTRODUCTORY CONCEPTS

Up to this point we have defined some words and used others without specific definitions. This procedure was necessary in order to convey the general scope of our subject without becoming enmeshed in technical terms without a context to which to relate them. Now that we have established a communication link with the subject, we shall consider a few key definitions.

Of the many phrases used in business vocabularies, some convey definite and meaningful images, while others have become vague and inexpressive. Each key word used in the remainder of this book has a precise definition; these terms will recur throughout the several divisions but will, as far as possible, carry the same meaning. Many have already been used, but a discussion of their exact meaning will fix them for what follows.

We shall use the terms *management system* and *business system* interchangeably. The *business system* is made up of a number of individual systems. Whenever the *enterprise, organization,* or *business* is referred to in this text, it means the entire business system. A business is an assembly of persons and resources organized into a complex whole, for the purpose of fulfilling specific objectives or goals. Thus, a business may comprise all or only part of a company, an agency, a field office, or a government bureau, depending on how the business is defined by its management.

Goals are the contributions a business wishes to make to its environment. In their usage here, goals are precisely spelled out to represent concrete objectives of the business, and they state definitely what the business system must accomplish.

The *environment* of a business is everything outside the scope of the study that influences the business. If a company is considered the business under study, then everything not in the company is in the environment. If one division of a company is selected as the business, then the other divisions of the same company become part of the environment. The environment also includes the external factors influencing the system, such as competitors and competitive products or services, geographical considerations, market status, customer goodwill, and so forth.

A business may be described in terms of organization, goals, or activities. We define an *activity* as a related set of operations. It has few ties with its surrounding environment. It is usually self-contained, and directed toward satisfying one or more of the goals fundamental to the business. An activity generally starts with an input from the environment external to the business, and ends with an output to that environment. However, some activities are concerned with the maintenance of resources and have no significant ties with the environment.

Each activity or combination of activities is performed by means of a system. The *system* includes combinations of personnel, equipment, and facilities working to produce outputs. By extension, the system includes its methods and procedures.

Activities are made up of operations. An *operation* is defined as something which, when initiated by a trigger, converts inputs to outputs, and uses resources to effect this transformation. The relationships of an operation are frequently internal; its inputs may come from another operation within the activity, and its outputs may be delivered to another such operation. A general model of the structure of an operation is shown in Figure 2-5.

A *trigger* is defined as something that starts an operation. A trigger can be the first working day in the month, the eight o'clock whistle, or the arrival of a batch of one hundred invoices. Only one trigger is specified for each operation.

A *process* (or processing step) is one of the actions taking place within an operation, and can usually be described by a single verb whose object is the input, output, or resource acted upon, and whose modifiers (as needed) specify the conditions under which the process takes place. Examples of processes are:

1. Compute monthly withholding tax.
2. Locate information in personnel file.
3. Compile manufacturing report on scrap losses.

Each step in a business mechanism is a process. Related sets of these processes, started by some trigger, accepting some input, and ending with some definable output, form operations. Related groups of operations, preferably reaching to the

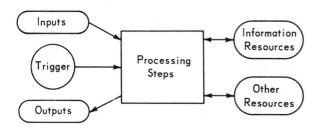

Figure 2-5 The general structure of an operation model.

external environment, comprise activities. Each activity or combination of activities is performed by a system.

Resources are the means for performing an operation. They may be imposed by the user or made necessary by the nature of the inputs or outputs. Resources include personnel, equipment and facilities, inventories, and finances. Inventories may include either information (files) or materials (stock). Inventories serve several purposes: stocks of parts or materials provide a buffer between operations; files keep historical information for later use, or store operation rules for transforming inputs into outputs.

The *customer, management,* or *user* is the person (or persons) for whom a study is undertaken. If a systems planner is studying some phase of the business that employs him, the customer is all or part of his own company management. If he studies another business, the customer is the management of that business. In the former case, working as an advisor for another part of his own business, a systems planner should practice the finesse of the customer-consultant relationship, since many times he will be required to educate himself in the specific operations of the business just as if he were an outsider.

The terms *system planner, analyst, systems engineer,* and *study team* are used variously, and in their generally accepted meanings. Whether working alone or as part of a team, the responsibilities of a systems planner remain the same in regard to searching out facts, organizing them into coherent descriptions, analyzing requirements, and synthesizing new systems.

Other terms, such as activity requirements model, business model, overview, and synthesis are explained when they are first mentioned or are illustrated by example. Those not specifically defined here will be understood in the context of their common usage.

2.8 ACTIVITY FORMULATION

Two major concepts in the philosophy for designing systems have already been introduced: (1) the orientation of a systems study toward business goals, and (2) the consideration of the business system as a unified entity. A third concept, *activity formulation,* is another important central idea of the entire plan.

An activity has been defined as a logically related group of operations. Performance of these operations directly results in the achievement of one or more business goals. Some typical activities are:

1. Provide the demand for a company's product.
2. Provide the checking account service in a bank.
3. Estimate the cost of performing services.
4. Distribute power in a public utility.

Operations, as the principal elements of an activity, transform inputs to outputs. Examples of operations are:

1. Prepare market analysis from estimates and forecasts.
2. Compile master production schedule from orders and propositions.

As a logically related group of tasks or operations cutting across functional lines, an activity can often be self-contained; that is, it can often be made to stand alone, with few informational ties or little interaction with other activities in the business, and directed toward satisfying one or more business goals. Note that there is no implied requirement that business organization follow activity lines or that departments be changed. Nonetheless, such may well be the result.

2.9 APPROACHES TO ACTIVITY FORMULATION

During Phase I in which there is a study of the existing business, the analyst obtains information concerning business operations from many internal and external information sources. In doing so, several approaches may be used to arrive at goal-directed activities.

One approach is *deductive* in emphasis. From a statement of business goals supplied by management, activities are defined more or less intuitively. Depth interviews are then conducted in the several departments or functions of the business to verify the accuracy of the activity that has been defined. Once there is verification (to the degree validity can be established this early), activities are documented in detail.

A second way to define activities is the *inductive* approach, which works almost in reverse. Initially, the team looks at the total resources (dollars) of the business to secure a broad overview of costs and allocations. Then a detailed documentation is performed on operations. After the recording is finished, operations are sorted into logical groups of implied activities. Frequently, this requires a number of successive sorts to achieve more precise arrangements among operations.

Finally, there is the *composite* approach. A goal statement is obtained from management. Then a major activity is identified and selected for documentation. Implied goals are formulated from the documentation and matched against the stated goals of management to see if they agree.

Since identification of activities and assignment of operations to activities presumes a completely new look at a business, an acceptable result may require several approximations on the part of the analyst. This is expected if the business is to be properly divided into areas just large enough to be grasped thoroughly by the study team. The number and scope of the activities is left completely to the judgment of the analyst. In a small business there might be only one activity, but in a large multiplant facility there could be a dozen or more.

Once the activity formulation has been completed and documented, results are presented to management and reviewed as part of the report containing the description of the present business.

2.10   THE MODIFICATION OF ACTIVITIES

When the analysts begin to determine the requirements of the system during the first part of Phase II, they gain further insights into the business which lead to a modification of the activity formulation. The statement of present business goals is revised to conform to the projections of future growth, or to changes in services and products, or other information secured through analysis of future directions. From this combination of present and future goals comes a better statement of goals of the business.

The activities defined in Phase I are then reshaped to agree with the goal statement. As this transition occurs, analysts will begin to leave the position of treating the business system as a whole, and work instead from the viewpoint of activities and activity models. This accent on activities will continue throughout Phase II and into Phase III.

The activity formulation procedure may be explained more effectively in the context of an actual case study selected from a company—Butodale Electronics—that has successfully applied the principles we are presenting. Butodale is a young, fast-developing manufacturer of electronic equipment, and is rapidly outgrowing the model shop business system of its early days. Among the activities developed when Butodale's Phase I study reached the period of initial activity formulation, was one entitled Quotation and Order Acceptance. This activity encompassed the receiving and processing of inquiries, and the returning of a price and delivery quotation to the potential customer. However, the scope of the activity was confined mainly to the sales administration function and showed a usage of only $60,000 out of a total $16,000,000 in expenditures. The study team thereupon modified the goal statements for the quotation and order acceptance activity and reshaped the other activities in Phase II to reflect the situation more appropriately. The outcome was quite different. The Quotation and Order Acceptance was incorporated in an activity called Provide Product Demand. Instead of being a simple response to inquiries, this activity covered the broader task of forecasting potential demand and handling propositions and orders for the entire company—to the point of master scheduling. This last included design engineering. With this extended range, the activity was no longer confined to sales administration, but cut across functional lines of accounting, sales, engineering, and management. Provide Demand, in its revised definition, used $1,650,000 of the total resources figure, and was a primary activity of the business.

After emerging from the reformulation procedure, activities will generally have an individual identity and well-defined boundaries; they will be of a certain size and will be describable in terms of the goals they satisfy. We realize, of course, that the dynamics of a business enterprise will modify activities as time goes on, but for the purpose of putting the system into operation, this initial firmness is necessary.

2.11 THE IMPORTANCE OF FORMULATING ACTIVITIES

By the time the analysts come to Phase III and begin designing the new system, the activities will have been defined. For Phase III itself, a number of alternative system solutions will be designed for each activity. Each alternative must be successively appraised to find a best-system solution. When there are several activities, they are studied for the possibility of integrating common features of inputs, outputs, files, and operation characteristics. Only after consolidation has been resolved can a detailed procedure be written.

This whole idea of activity formulation has merit, even in mechanization and improvement studies, since it breaks the business into logical segments for more effective study and permits its reunification later. The advantages of this approach are considerable in these studies, even if activity reformulation is not carried out to its fullest degree, since the analyst is able to look at the system in an entirely new way. It further ensures that the activities will fit together as the system grows.

SUMMARY

The study and design of a system can be performed in three phases: understanding the present business, determining systems requirements, and designing the new system. The objective of the first phase is the determination of what is done, using what inputs, with what resources, to achieve what results. This includes the preparation of a model of the business system. In Phase II, known facts about the existing system are blended with information concerning the future. Phase II is a mixture of analysis, synthesis, forecasting, construction of models, and operations research. Phase III may require a high level of creative effort. In this third phase, the reports of the first two are reviewed and design alternatives are formulated and described.

3

Planning and Carrying Out a Systems Study

3.1 PLAN FOR THE STUDY

Before a systems study can be carried out, a careful plan of action must be prepared. The plan should state the purpose and scope of the work to be performed, and indicate how the time and resources of the team are to be employed. It should reflect the desires of management as well as the technical considerations for the study team.

The plan is amplified as extensively as management requires. In a small, uncomplicated business, where a single person could handle all tasks, the plan might evolve from several conversations between manager and analyst. In large companies where the study could continue over many months, this informal arrangement would be unsatisfactory. In the latter case, the study purpose would have to be stated precisely, areas defined for inclusion or exclusion, depth of penetration agreed upon, and a cost budget compiled for the estimated span of work. Out of a general agreement on the scope of the project, detailed schedules would be prepared to include personnel assignments and the sequence in which work will affect each selected area of the business.

Often, the manager will state the systems problem as he sees it and wishes it to be corrected: long delivery cycles, poor credit-risk selection, slow response to customer inquiries, or high employee turnover. These views must be appraised and considered in the structure and direction of the study.

The statement of the scope of the project should be recorded in a formal document after the study purpose and boundaries have been completely examined and agreed upon by management and the study team.

3.2 TIME SCHEDULES

Business size, study purpose, allotted time, and team size are variables affecting study schedules and costs.

Detailed study of a small business by a two-man team might be conducted in one week to a month if all goes well. For a multimillion-dollar concern, the same two-man team could probably not undertake more than an overview-level study in a like time period. Examining the operations of a single department or division of a large company, however, might be a reasonable goal to accomplish in one month.

The level of study refinement has a major influence on time schedules. Improvement and mechanization studies require less background information than do creative, complete-system studies. For example, operational data rather than general or structural data is of consequence in Phase I for improvement and mechanization types of study. If time does not permit close analysis of system requirements in Phase II, then the present system description will have to serve as an indication of areas with high potential for improvement. Otherwise, requirements are accepted as they have already been stated or implied.

At the end of Phase III, a mechanization study will emphasize equipment and procedural changes necessary to accomplish the mechanization, while Phase III for improvement studies means modification of existing systems rather than complete new designs. Time schedules will be considerably shorter for these kinds of studies than for a more creative study.

Even when the plan of this book is applied in its complete version for large-scale studies, certain compressions of time are possible. For example, although the phases of understanding the present system, specifying systems requirements, and designing the new system must be performed in series, there are many opportunities for conducting parts of the study simultaneously, if team size permits. Thus, in Phase I several persons could collect data for the general and structural sections at the same time. Similarly, in Phase II the activities are fairly autonomous after reformulation so that the requirements for each one could be analyzed separately and simultaneously.

Activity formulation is an example of a sequenced task which requires time to define, and also time for review through successive evaluations. Required steps in Phase I for one study included:

1. Organize study.
2. Conduct interviews.
3. Group operations into activities.
4. Prepare activity sheets.
5. Reinterview, if necessary.

6. Regroup operations.
7. Modify activity sheets.
8. Complete resource usage sheet.
9. Review results with management.
10. Start over, if necessary.

Interviews take time, and management may be too busy to review results when the team wants them. Time cannot be compressed easily in this work if results are to be worthwhile. Nevertheless, the ability to foresee possibilities for overlapping work within and between the phases of the study will decide how large a team can work effectively at one time, and how long the total study will take to complete. Although overlapping should be planned wherever practical in the preparation of time schedules, there are limits to the extent that time can be telescoped.

There are two major ways in which the time required for a systems study may be determined. The first may be called the addition method and the second, the subtraction method. In the addition method, the time for each part of each phase is determined. Where possible, operations that can be overlapped are scheduled to run simultaneously. Then the separate times are added together to arrive at the target date for the completion of the design of the new system.

In the subtraction method, management usually sets the target date at which the new system must be in operation. Then the analysts must predict the time necessary for Stage 2. This time is subtracted from the target date and this determines the time remaining for the completion of Stage 1 work.

Normally, the addition method is used but circumstances often require the subtraction method. Management's attitude in such situations is that they need an operating system, say in ten months, even though it may not be very efficient, rather than a highly efficient system which will not be ready for two years.

In determining the time requirement, analysts may want to use techniques such as (1) Gantt charts, (2) program evaluation and review techniques (commonly called PERT), or (3) the critical path method (known as CPM.)

3.3   TEAM SIZE AND COMPOSITION

Purpose, scope, time, and depth of study will determine, in large measure, the size and composition of the team of analysts making the study. Under normal conditions, there should be at least two members on the team, even if the business is very small and the study quite limited. Two people working together can furnish enough stimulus to each other to make their efforts far more productive than one person working alone. Whatever size the team, individual talents should offset one another. For example, one member should have a knowledge of methods and procedures, while his counterpart should be knowledgeable about the business system as it presently functions. Large-scale studies might require the skills of a mathematician, an operations researcher, or an economist if a thorough investigation using management science techniques is contemplated.

Requirements for specialized knowledge and skills will vary considerably. Knowledge of functional subjects such as accounting, manufacturing, engineering, and production control will be needed; knowledge of special techniques such as simulation and linear programming may also be necessary. More specialized, but still a requirement in most studies, are the skills of systems synthesis—for example, familiarity with computer characteristics and with communications networks.

The individual assigned to lead the team should have demonstrated abilities in planning, organization, and administration. He has the problem of coordinating the entire project; laying out time, cost, and personnel schedules; reporting progress to management; perhaps selecting additional members for the team. Beyond this, he must understand the scope and purpose of the study to the degree that he can speed up work in some areas, while expanding coverage to others. It is solely his judgment that decides the matter. The team leader is the one person who can never lose sight of end objectives, total costs, and management attitudes.

The leader's attitude influences the team's approach to its work. While functioning in this position as a technical specialist or as an administrator, he must be able to motivate people to work more effectively, and develop a climate in which conflict is directed toward better ways to accomplish a task, rather than on the interplay of personalities.

3.4 PROGRESS REPORTS

Among the personal relationships the team will develop in the course of a study, none will be more critical than building mutual understanding with management. Once a good working relationship has been established through the resolution of study goals and scope, the team must keep management informed periodically of progress. During these review sessions, progress is summarized and measured against scheduled completion dates, current problems are discussed and resolved, and projected schedules are reviewed for the period ahead.

Progress meetings usually are brief and informal. When a major checkpoint is reached, however, such as the end of a phase, longer and more formal presentations will be necessary. Other members of the business are invited for evaluation of critical areas. Some aspects of these reports will require considerable salesmanship (for example, activity formulation), if recommendations depart measurably from past practice. In all these contacts among the team, management, and operating personnel, the finesse of consultant-client relationships is practiced, even if the team is part of the organization itself.

After the study purpose, scope, and objectives have been defined, time and cost schedules drawn up, and communications channels established, the team is ready to perform the study.

3.5 ANNOUNCING THE STUDY

After a statement announcing plans has been prepared, it is communicated to those individuals within the business who will be affected by the study, or who will be contributing time and effort to it. This announcement is particularly important for individuals who come in direct contact with the study team or who will be interviewed during the course of the study. The communication of study plans to employees is a management responsibility, but one which is often not given sufficient attention. Experienced systems analysts know that an effective study requires employee cooperation, particularly at the supervisory level. As far as practical, employees should be included among those who should be told the details of the plans for the study.

3.6   INTERVIEWING

Every organization has a management system, and the main objective of the first phase in a systems study is to learn its existing structure. The information sought exists in two forms, both of which must be used. The first form is made up of published material and organization records and documents. The second form is in the minds of the supervisory and operating employees of the organization and in the informal channels cutting across organizations. There is little doubt that the more valuable information sought is of this second form. The only way this information can be obtained is by interviewing the operating personnel and their supervisors, and possibly by interviewing people in the informal channels. Interviews should be scheduled well in advance, and the person to be interviewed should be given some idea of the subjects to be covered, and how long the interview may take.

In the first interview (more than one is often needed), the analyst is interested in establishing an atmosphere of trust and confidence; consequently, he will usually take few notes and will attempt mainly to understand the individual and his working background. Deep-seated resentments can be readily developed against outsiders who imply they are quite knowledgeable, or who convey an attitude of being out to "really clean up this mess." In one case, a team was working in an organization where the employees felt they were already overburdened with work. The team made a basic mistake: they tried to show management their capability by eliminating two positions in a certain department after one week's study. When news of this got around, everyone's job security seemed to be threatened. The team was never able to establish confidence with these people or even secure accurate answers during subsequent interviews.

A good interviewer takes command of the situation without seeming to, and encourages conversation without asking too many direct questions. Among other considerations, he is prompt for the interview, adheres to his time schedule and subject matter, and makes further appointments when they are convenient to the person being interviewed. Where possible, interviews are conducted in surroundings free from distractions.

3.7   STUDY TECHNIQUES

An analyst employs many different techniques for analyzing an existing management system and for creating a new one. Techniques of documentation,

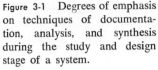

Figure 3-1 Degrees of emphasis on techniques of documentation, analysis, and synthesis during the study and design stage of a system.

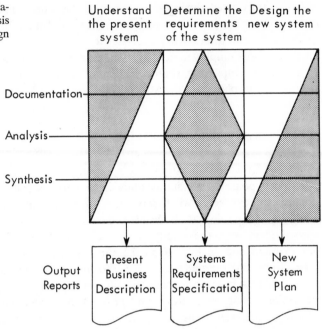

analysis, and synthesis are used with varying degrees of emphasis throughout the three phases in the study and design of a new system. Figure 3-1 presents a rough guide to the amount of effort devoted to these three techniques. The shaded area represents the amount of effort. Thus, in the first phase the main emphasis is on documentation, with little analysis, and minor synthesis. In the second phase, analysis dominates with little documentation and synthesis. In the final phase, the effort is mainly that of synthesis, with less analysis and minor documentation. The outputs from each phase are also shown in Figure 3-1.

Documentation is accumulating and recording information with a clear objective in mind. Only significant data is selected, and just enough is collected to be useful in the study. The questions "What is significant?" and "How much is enough?" are discussed in subsequent chapters.

Analysis is the breaking up of study subjects into manageable elements for individual evaluation.

Synthesis, as opposed to analysis, is the combining of parts or elements into a complex whole; it is the reasoning involved in advancing from principles and propositions to conclusions. An example of synthesis in Phase II is the formulation of true business goals. From sources such as the present system description, statement of present system goals, analyses of demand for current and future products and services, and interviews with management, information is organized and integrated by weighing values, dropping out extraneous considerations, and extracting meaningful facts to produce a set of true goals and objectives that are representative of the business.

Among management science techniques, simulation is particularly useful in systems studies. A *simulation* is an experiment in which real-world conditions are imitated in a model to duplicate or replicate, as closely as possible, the manner in which alternative systems designs would perform, if implemented. Decision rules can be tested for validity over a range of situations, or an entire business system can be evaluated for effectiveness of operation. For example, one simulation, performed on a computer, examined in a matter of minutes the operations of a small factory over a whole year.

Other kinds of models are also useful in systems work. *Queuing models* investigate problems surrounding waiting lines; *Monte Carlo models* introduce variable values into simulations for problems such as production scheduling. Some models are simply descriptive; others must be manipulated on a cut-and-try basis to arrive at an acceptable solution. Some models accept relatively fixed information only; others permit substantial data variation. *Optimizing models* employ the techniques of calculus, game theory, and linear programming. Almost any operational system can be described by one or more models, although design and construction of the complex models generally require the skills of a mathematician and may take months to complete.

3.8   DEPTH OF PENETRATION

Three levels of language can be recognized in the study and design of systems, each one reflecting a different depth of penetration into the detail of the system.

A general-purpose description is at the broadest level. Only major decision points, important events, and key volumes are investigated and reported at this level. The general and structural sections of the Phase I report, Present Business Description, are examples of language at this level.

There is often a requirement for more thorough description and analysis of certain activities and operations. Language at a moderate depth of penetration can be thought of as a middle level. Phrases such as "update file" or "prepare invoice," typically found in the operations section of the Present Business Description, are examples of this level of language.

The most extensive level of penetration is one containing the fine details of a system. A computer program or a detailed set of clerical instructions are two examples from the language at this deepest level.

All three language levels are usually used in system studies—whether the studies are aimed at a completely new system, improvement of an existing system, or straightforward mechanization. An analyst recording information at the highest or overview level, for example, might occasionally be required to look more intensively at certain critical areas, thus requiring an intermediate or detailed view depth of penetration.

3.9   REPORTING TECHNIQUES

When organizing study material, the team is faced with presenting the information to more than one kind of audience. The management group must read, understand, and approve the output reports from each of the three phases, while specialists must check and use the data to write detail systems procedures and computer programs in the implementation stage. Therefore, the display of the results has to be carefully planned to use effective reporting techniques. Visual devices such as graphs, charts, and schematics, as well as a good narrative form, are effective in meeting management's requirements for clear but brief summaries. Flowcharts, decision tables, and procedure statements are effective in meeting the more detailed requirements of analysts and programming specialists.

A *flowchart* is useful for demonstrating a sequence of events and decisions. Through a series of symbols connected by lines, it provides a framework for relating the logical requirements of the operating system. *Narrative form* is valuable when background information is to be presented (as in the Present Business Description), and for listing requirements. *Decision tables* are especially useful for displaying the cause-and-effect relationships in complicated systems logic. *Procedure statements* can be employed to describe special problem areas requiring precise computer-level definition. Study teams presenting the results of their findings frequently use all of these techniques, depending on circumstances.

3.10 DESIGN PROBLEMS AND OPPORTUNITIES

The study team, in approaching its work, may perform in a routine, workmanlike manner and produce acceptable solutions. Or it may find itself in a situation that provides opportunity for the creation of quite original systems. In fact, an unusual design may be required if the new system is to contribute significantly to the profitability and efficiency of future operations. However, straightforward, albeit simple, improvements may be very effective. A combination of both methods frequently is needed to design a truly improved system. It must be remembered that design problems and opportunities are shaped by the two factors that affect all other aspects of organizational life—time and money. These are in limited supply in all organizations. When it comes to design, practical executives usually prefer a routine system that works to a highly creative system that does not, or that requires too much time to develop.

There are various techniques for resolving the many problems encountered by the study team. Two of these are trial and error, and application of scientific analysis and synthesis. Each is helpful in a way, but techniques merely set up the problem for the analyst to solve. Once these techniques have been applied, then logic, hard work, and insight are necessary to achieve the desired results.

Success does not come only by gradually inching forward or by making changes in small increments. It can also be achieved suddenly after extended periods of hard work and application. Consider the following illustrations.

For many years, the accepted way for an engineer to describe a product's structure has been through a bill of materials. This document has become a critical input for manufacturing, and much effort is expended on its form and arrangement. The use of collation charts and single- and multiple-level parts explosions are two examples of interior improvements in form and arrangement. With the advent of the computer, the manual bills were simply converted to magnetic tape or punched cards or stored in memory. Then somebody had a creative idea: bills of materials would not have to be stored at all, if the design logic stored in the mind of the engineer could be reconstructed and stored in a computer program. Product characteristics could then be generated directly from customer specifications, if the design logic were stated in such a way as to make the transformation possible.

As another example, consider a company that maintained a 50,000-ledger card standard cost file. The average record for a part contained ten to twelve lines. Because of its size and complexity, the file was updated just once every two years; consequently, material and labor variances ran as high as 50 percent. One key cause of these high variances was that the price of copper sometimes changed every few weeks. Since copper was used for a large number of parts, making the changes posed such a massive clerical problem that master records were not modified. The company decided to keep the equipment and system it had and to wait until it could afford a computer with a large enough memory to store the entire file on a random-access basis. However, the systems team discovered that the amount of copper used on each part was fixed. If this amount were stored for each part, then by calculation the correct current standard cost could be determined and the entire standard cost system could easily be processed on existing equipment.

The analyst who can find the true nature of business problems and detect the fine interrelationships which exist among operations is usually able to extend the profitability of the system considerably. To a systems engineer operating from the unified systems approach, the general statement of business goals is more important than the particular: it incorporates functions, rather than the means by which functions are performed. From this viewpoint a railroad does not run trains from one terminal to another; it provides a transportation service for passengers and freight between designated points. A door is not a rectangular construction of wood or metal with hinges; it is a control of entry and exit. Through generalized concepts an analyst lifts his thinking out of conventional molds. He should try to view each design study as an opportunity, not a problem.

3.11   SETTING THE SCOPE AND OBJECTIVES OF THE STUDY

In a systems study a team faces many decision points. At the outset there may be differences of opinion with management over the scope and objectives of the study. How far does the team press its views on issues of substance? When the work for each phase is completed and the report is written, how can the effort be measured as to completeness and competence? What pitfalls must be avoided in conducting a study? What level of accomplishment should be set for a team? These questions and others will be asked time and again, often without satisfactory answers.

The recommended basic approach is direct and straightforward. But all through their work, study teams will be called upon to make decisions concerning the quality and depth of their own efforts, decisions which require mature and objective judgment. While each team will be guided ultimately by its own evaluation of these situations, some of the more common areas are mentioned in the next four sections.

3.12   MANAGEMENT CONSTRAINTS

Although the team leader should attempt to adopt a management viewpoint in his thinking, it may be difficult at times to reconcile desires of the team and practical judgments of management. A team that has developed enthusiasm for its work may suddenly be confronted with constraints such as restrictions on the project scope, or by limitations on modifying inputs, outputs, and resources.

Usually, these constraints result from management decisions on what is necessary and proper for the well-being of the organization. For example, study objectives in the beginning may have been stated as the nominal improvement of an existing system, or as the direct mechanization of a manual system without any change at all in the present procedure. The study team may accept this at first, but after delving into the business, it may find opportunities for making considerable improvement, if given more time and people. Management may wish to stay with the initial scope and objectives, or it may request the continuation of a certain document within the system because it is well recognized in the trade, or it may decide that the present equipment is satisfactory and should be incorporated into the new system design.

When these constraints materially interfere with or severely hamper system design, the team leader should make a strong case for their relaxation. His position, however, must be supported with a well-thought-out and documented analysis of costs and results. Should management persist in its position, the team has no alternative but to proceed and accept the restrictions. Most of the time this will not be a difficult problem, and a suitable compromise can usually be worked out.

It is safe to say that all systems studies are carried on within a set of constraints of various kinds. Such constraints normally are not sufficient to serve as excuses for not designing a profitable, working system.

3.13   SOME CAUTIONS FOR ANALYSTS

In some studies there are many chances for analysts to depart from good practices. Even the best-intentioned and most farsighted team leader may fall prey to certain common pitfalls.

One common error, and a most serious one, is *improper problem formulation*. Problem areas are often specified or pointed out by management. The study team should take time to evaluate whether the problem has been correctly stated and is actually the one to be resolved. For example, the problem of devising a better method for handling customer complaints may actually be a problem of product quality. The really basic problem is not always obvious, and much time can be wasted tracking down one which does not exist or has been improperly formulated.

Another danger lies in a team's tendency to concentrate on the techniques of problem solution and thus lose sight of the problem itself. In mathematical modeling techniques, for example, it is fascinating to investigate all the possible combinations of solutions which are generated when resources and inputs are altered slightly. A team may become so engrossed in operating the model that it loses sight of the original problem.

There is also the problem of deciding *how much documentation is needed* to support recommendations and future phases of study. It is easy to say of documentation, "Don't collect too much or too little," but this does not resolve the dilemma. This problem is related closely to two others: *What are the significant areas* to investigate? and *How deeply should they be probed?* Analysts working from the overview level in Phase I, for example, will occasionally have to work at deeper levels of penetration when the situation demands, then return to the overview level as soon as possible. The key to knowing when to probe deeply and amass a greater quantity of data is closely tied to understandings reached at the beginning of a study.

Experienced study teams typically view the organization objectively to maintain proper balance among events. Whenever a period of deep penetration occurs, the analyst should stop for a while to consider where he is, where he has been, and where he is going. In addition, there should be a clear indication of which areas are important (and which not so important) soon after the study begins. Priority should be assigned to the significant areas of opportunity on which major effort will be expended. If the parts of a study are always related to the whole, and major opportunities identified, this knowledge usually leads to a correct decision on how much and how deep.

A common shortcoming in study teams is *the consideration of too few alternatives.* There is seldom only one way to define, attack, and solve a particular problem. Successful teams consider commonly known and standard alternatives, and supplement these with others they have developed to satisfy the special requirements of the situation. This is most important when standard alternatives are only partially satisfactory. The invention of a wholly new approach to special conditions can contribute greatly to effective systems design; of course, the team normally should not try to develop new techniques if standard ones work satisfactorily.

The last common failing is *excessive ambition,* or the attempt to cure all ailments with one potion. Only so much can be accomplished in a study, once the constraints of time, cost, and personnel have been defined. If problems have been formulated correctly, a careful study plan worked out and followed, and a reasonable number of alternatives evaluated, this is all that can be expected of a team in ordinary circumstances.

3.14 QUALITY OF DOCUMENTATION

Data quality is of consequence during all phases of study, but especially so in Phase II, when the validity of the specifications for the requirements of the new system are being tested prior to system design. As data is collected, manipulated, organized, and presented in report form, it must be checked and rechecked for objectivity, reliability, accuracy, validity, relevance, completeness, and usefulness. Each of these quality requirements is explained briefly below.

Objectivity is the absence of potential for bias in information. For example, "Henry Anderson is one of our sharpest, most productive salesmen" is prone to personal bias, while "Last month Fred Miller sold thirteen endowment-at-65 policies worth a total of $175,000" is objective.

Reliability indicates confidence. The same measurement repeated several times on the same object will not produce markedly different results if the measurement process is reliable. Should the results differ substantially, the process would be considered unreliable to the extent of the spread in measurement.

Measurements are subject to constant and variable error: a speedometer may be 5 percent high on all readings (constant); a cutting tool may register -0.005 in one cut and $+0.005$ on the next (variable). *Accuracy* is the absence of constant error.

Validity means that a measurement really measures what it is supposed to measure and nothing else. For example, the number of hours an instructor spends attaining proficiency to teach a subject is not a valid measure of the number of hours a student will require to effectively learn the same subject.

Relevance is concerned with the applicability of information to the subject under consideration. An individual's grades in a logic course may be related to his potential success as a computer programmer; the number of training sessions required to teach repair of engines may be related to the number of sessions required to teach repair of transmissions.

Completeness is the presence of all relevant factors of information. A decision on reordering stock, for example, could not be made if information on stock usage were not available.

Usefulness is the relationship between the significance of a result and the cost of obtaining that result. This is a very rough and relative measure, which says that if the value of a result is considerable, and its cost is low, then it probably is a good buy. Conversely, if the value is not substantial, but the cost is high, it may not be a good buy. For instance, if the cost of a real-time feedback system to record parts completions every ten minutes is high, and the significance of this timeliness is not important, the usefulness of the feedback system is low. At times, a particular result may be absolutely necessary, and therefore the cost is accepted.

3.15 REPORT STANDARDS

Although the study team keeps management informed periodically concerning progress and plans, the reports at the end of the three phases have a special importance and therefore require extra effort, whether presented orally or in written form, or both. These reports are the basis for management's decision on whether the systems implementation and operation stages are to be undertaken.

A written report is desirable; an oral presentation is also advisable. The team must examine the written report for adequacy, conformity, unity, consistency, proportion, clarity, completeness, simplicity, and accuracy. There should be a logical flow and structure of information from introduction to conclusion; form should be the same from one section to another, with events leading from one to another in systematic fashion. The language should be understandable, events explained with commonly-used terms, and sentence structure free from awkward, stilted phraseology. Further, report content should be complete, without being excessively wordy. There should be adequate supporting material included for each topic, with no gaps in coverage. Lengthy narrative can be avoided with visual displays: graphs, diagrams, tables, and so on.

Oral reports are more effective when visual aids are used and the presentation is fairly informal. Instead of covering the same ground as the written report, the oral presentation concentrates on important features and leaves incidental matters for subsequent discussion. Where practical, the written report should be distributed to the management personnel concerned prior to the oral presentation. The management personnel can review it in detail and thus be in a far better position to benefit from the team's efforts.

SUMMARY

A systems study requires a plan of action. A time schedule is necessary, and the estimated time will vary depending upon the purposes of the study. Before the study begins, meetings should be held to define the scope of the study and to determine the size of the study team. Announcement of the study should be made to the personnel whose functions will be reviewed, in order to obtain maximum cooperation.

Much of the information sought during the study can be secured through interviews with personnel in the areas being studied. These interviews are critical to the success of the study, and care should be exercised in scheduling and performing them. Documentation, analysis, and synthesis are used in different degrees in each of the three phases of the study. Documentation is important, particularly in Phase I. The depth of penetration of the study will vary depending upon its objectives.

More than one method of reporting may be necessary, because the information gathered by the team will be presented to more than one audience. Flowcharts, narratives, decision tables, and procedure statements are reporting techniques which can be used. The design of the new system provides an opportunity for creative solutions to the problem. New approaches should be considered. Although the scope and objectives of the study may be well defined and agreed to, management may exert certain constraints and the team must use caution so as to perform within those constraints and yet achieve desirable results.

PART

UNDERSTANDING THE PRESENT SYSTEM

The purpose of Part 2 is to present the detailed aspects of the philosophy and methodology involved in understanding the present business and its management system. As we mentioned earlier, if a study is being made for one part of an enterprise, we still use the same words—business, organization, and system—to refer to that part of the enterprise being studied. The environment will then be all elements outside the area under investigation.

In Part 2, we cover the methodology involved in gathering data and organizing it into a report which is used by management in directing the further efforts of the study team. We shall explain how the existing business applications are reclassified into goal-directed activities for study and analysis. We also examine the potential for including flexibility in alternative approaches. To clarify the meaning and usefulness of the many new concepts and terms, we include examples taken from actual system studies.

4

Understanding
the Present
System

4.1 LIFE CYCLE OF A SYSTEM

As we mentioned in Section 1.2, the life cycle of a system is divided into three *stages*: study and design, implementation, and operation. In the first stage, a new system is designed after studying the present system; in the second stage, the new system is installed; and in the final stage, the new system is placed in routine operation. Since the technology of business management is continually being improved and updated, this cycle is repeated periodically.

In the study and design stage, three *phases* are recognized: understanding the present system, determining systems requirements, and designing and communicating a new system. This part of our text discusses the steps recommended for understanding the present system. We explain why the present system should be understood even though it will be changed by the new design, and we stress the importance of including a study of the business (the organization) as an integral part of the study of the system itself.

4.2 OBJECTIVES IN UNDERSTANDING THE BUSINESS

The main reason why the design of a new system should begin with an understanding of the present business is to compile data that may be used to support the analysis of the requirements of the system. Subsequently, the same data will serve a useful purpose during the formulation of the new design. This data is best presented to management in an organized form. We call this report either the *Present System Description* or the *Present Business Description*. Initially, the business is described in broad, general terms; then it is described by activity classifications assigned by the study team. Under this latter approach, a business is viewed according to the activities or groups of operations which are necessary to achieve one or more of its specific goals. The idea of looking at a business from more than one angle is much like the perspective an engineer employs in preparing a drawing for a complex casting. Side and end views are not sufficient; various cross sections are also required.

The report provides valuable insights into current operations, and establishes a firm base for further analysis. It is more than a description of an enterprise. As a study team becomes acquainted with the customs, practices, personnel, and operations of a business, it will discover areas of strength and weakness and will develop an awareness of trouble spots and problems. Among other tasks, specific business goals are defined, and a suitable group of activities is formulated; operations and functions are recorded; and evidence is acquired on areas with high costs that are sensitive to reduction by introducing system changes.

All these points affect the design of the new system, and the objective of the analysts is to obtain the necessary understanding. The output report formally documents their findings so the information is recorded and available for further use.

We realize, of course, that a large proportion of systems studies are undertaken without the analysts making a formal report of their findings. It takes time, effort, and ability to reduce such information to written form. Usually there is great pressure to get the new system into operation. Shortcuts taken to telescope time usually involve the elimination of formal documentation. Nonetheless, such an understanding is fundamental to design efforts and must be obtained, formally or otherwise.

Reports, such as the one outlined here, can also serve purposes not directly related to the design of new systems. Among the other purposes, reasons, and advantages of this kind of report are:

1. It is directly valuable for management as a description of their company. Usually there is none as comprehensive in existence.

2. It can serve as a valuable tool to gain management's respect for the team's competence. In this way the report can open many doors for further work.

3. It can identify other problems usually not considered within the prime scope of the study, and thus can provide material for future study.

One can readily see that the size, content, arrangement, and style of the report can have many forms. We will consider the report variability next.

4.3 VARIABILITY OF THE PRESENT BUSINESS DESCRIPTION REPORT

The output report which we call the Present Business Description can be written in a variety of ways.

Within its overall framework, it is possible to look briefly at a business, determine general goals and operating methods, sketch structure, and arrive at a picture of operations. On the other hand, it is possible to probe in great depth to produce an extremely detailed report of the structure and its operating dynamics. Which of these extremes, or which of the various in-between levels a study requires, can be determined only in terms of the study purpose, team size, time allowed, and size and complexity of the business.

In performing a systems study, time is usually critical. Most studies are intended to proceed through the full three-phase cycle. The latter two phases are particularly difficult to compress in time, so the study of the present system should be completed quickly, but adequately.

The study can be undertaken at several levels, to support various purposes. Management's aim may be to create an entirely new system, to substantially improve the function of an existing system, or to mechanize all or part of a system (mechanization changes the physical means for doing a job, but may not basically alter the procedure for performing it). The approach and methodology generally vary for each of these purposes. For example, detailed operational data is important for a mechanization study, since this is the information which will be used directly in writing procedures for the conversion. In a major systems design, however, general and structural data are of equal significance, because considerably more insight into the business is required to perform the subsequent phases of analysis and design.

As previously discussed in Section 3.8, various levels of language can be used to describe a business system. All of them are applicable at various times in studies for complete reconstruction, for improvement, or for mechanization. The language level is determined by the particular requirements of the study.

An overview provides a broad understanding for the complete reconstruction of a business. This broad view of a large business discloses critical areas where the most dollars are being spent, or where the most profit is being made. In an advertising agency, for example, a preliminary overview might disclose that of four activities—films, technical literature, space advertising, industrial promotions —space advertising alone may be responsible for 80 percent of agency income. If profit figures for the other three are not out of line with capital investment and costs, space advertising becomes the important area for further study.

In addition, a preliminary overview may disclose parallel operations which have much in common, and therefore a study of one operation would be representative of the whole. In one distribution business, for example, there were 31 warehousing sites; three of these had limited assembly functions, while the other 28 simply stocked products. Twenty of the 28 carried a single product line; the other eight were multiple-line warehouses supplying major population centers. The systems analysts studied two single-line warehouses, one multiple-line warehouse, and one warehouse with limited assembly functions. From these they produced a satisfactorily representative picture of the entire business.

Successively more depth of detail is represented by intermediate and detail views. Most studies require some investigation at these detailed levels for operations that must be described more fully. A computer program in a mechanization study would be an example of description at the most detailed level.

4.4 STRUCTURE OF THE REPORT DESCRIBING THE PRESENT BUSINESS

The method of preparing individual sections of the report describing the present business is discussed below. The general structure of the report is shown graphically in Figure 4-1. This is primarily a recommended structure. In real situations the layout and content of individual sections can vary considerably from business to business. Overall, we recommend that the report be divided into three major sections: general, structural, and operational. The body of the report should be preceded by an introduction; an appendix customarily is added for important support documents.

The general section should contain a history of the enterprise, a statement of goals and policies, and an assessment of its position in relation to the competition. The structural section normally describes the inputs, outputs, and resources of the business. The operational section contains the details of the operating dynamics of an enterprise with emphasis on the flow of events, time cycles, and costs. It is in this final section that the business is first considered in terms of activities. Now let us consider the time schedule in producing the report.

4.5 TIME SCHEDULE AND PLANNING

To conduct a study efficiently and in a minimum of time, a careful plan of action is required. The scope of the study, team composition, time schedules, and task assignments should be planned in some detail. This is an obvious requirement for any well-administered study. No plan can envisage all the problems to be encountered, however, or the precise length of time each task will take. For example, in one recent study several product lines were to be examined as separate units. Although this seemed to be a relatively straightforward assignment, an examination of the files revealed that the records were maintained by functional responsibility (engineering, manufacturing, and accounting) and that there was no continuity or classification for different product lines as they were processed through the business. Much additional time had to be spent analyzing the files in each function to produce a complete product line analysis.

Even though a valid plan has been prepared prior to starting the study, experience has shown that it should be reviewed frequently, and modified to include recent events and changes in thinking. The initial plan, while subject to periodic

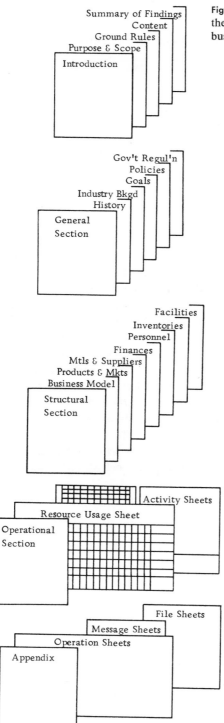

Figure 4-1 General structure of the report describing the present business.

adjustment, should be good enough so that the total planned times and due dates are not severely affected by later events.

A major part of the time schedule is required for gathering data and we shall consider this problem now.

4.6 INFORMATION SOURCES

When one considers the problem of gathering data and information, it is well to divide sources into three main categories:

1. Internal and external records
2. Supervisory and operating personnel
3. Sampling and estimating

All three categories may be used at various points in the study. Record searches predominate in enterprises with well-organized record and file systems, while interviews are emphasized where the record system is less satisfactory. In addition, interviews are valuable to verify and refine derived data and observations.

To develop a data-gathering plan, an analyst must first organize his own file system. A binder, with dividers for each major subject is one way of collecting general and structural information in an orderly fashion. This has the advantage of visually demonstrating the degree of documentation for each topic as data is collected. Later, when the report is written, the analyst reorganizes the compiled data from his binder (and from others, if the study is a large, decentralized one), and prepares a coherent narrative or series of exhibits to summarize findings.

Business information exists in many places, some external to the enterprise, others internal. In most cases, the analyst seeks out data from a wide variety of sources, then verifies his results with personnel who are closely acquainted with the subject matter.

We turn next to an examination of sources of general and structural data.

4.7 SOURCES FOR GENERAL AND STRUCTURAL DATA

During early planning sessions with management, a study team should develop a list of sources for material relating to the general and structural sections of the report it is to prepare. If a large number of references are available, the problem is usually one of condensing pertinent facts.

Where the data has not been published or organized, a number of problems arise. To reconstruct information from manual files such as those maintained in ordinary filing cabinets is time-consuming; such files may be constantly in use, possibly in poor condition, and perhaps maintained in classifications not useful to the study. The operating personnel in the marketing department may file their records according to the customer order number; the engineering department may use drawing numbers; and the manufacturing department may keep its records according to shop order numbers. Files may be dispersed and decentralized in large companies with some non-current information stored at a remote location and thus not easily accessible. When this happens, the analyst should make a preliminary list of requirements and should request clarification on how the data can best be obtained. A complete knowledge of files and records will be necessary in an extensive study; the sooner an analyst becomes acquainted with them, the easier his task will be.

External data can be formal or informal. Trade publications, government statistics, and credit associations are formal sources, and their information is fairly standardized and objective. Brokerage reports are often quite revealing in their appraisals of a company. Informal sources, such as customers of a bank, or policy-holders of an insurance company, or the audience of a TV network, may be somewhat less objective while still offering critical and useful evaluations. Vendors and suppliers to manufacturing concerns may also be considered in this category.

Frequently, information for understanding the general and structural aspects of an organization can be obtained by asking the personnel involved. This possibility should be kept in mind during interviewing, a subject which we now explore.

4.8 INTERVIEWING

The interview is perhaps the most fruitful, and yet the most unpredictable, form of securing information available to an analyst. It is valuable when he has the person's trust and confidence; it is unproductive when he has anything less. Usually, more data is gathered by interview than by any other single method.

Interviews customarily start with the top levels of management. Middle- and first-line management then become the main sources of information during the study, along with professional specialists. Later, individual clerical and factory workers may have to be interviewed concerning their particular job assignments.

The confidence of persons being interviewed must be earned, not presumed. People become suspicious and distrustful if there is even a vague threat (imagined or otherwise) to their job security. With this in mind, the analyst should make the initial interviews informal and concentrate on establishing a mutual working relationship. In the process of gathering data, an analyst conscientiously avoids any connotation of making a stop-watch study, or of appearing to be an efficiency expert. He must encourage the feeling that he has become a part of the business, and at the same time not get involved in day-to-day problems. This advice would apply whether the analyst is making the study for his own company, or for an outside firm.

A thoroughly planned schedule will help to reduce the need to repeat interviews, although analysts often find a few individuals who are quite knowledgeable about the organization and will tend to return to them for additional information. However, a balance among the personnel contacted prevents bias from creeping into the information and spreads the interview load more evenly. As interviews are carried out, careful consideration is given to the length of time for each session, frequency of repeats, and individual productivity of each interview. There is no fixed rule for this—the person being interviewed is the best lead to what is appropriate for length and frequency of interview.

Interviews may be used at any point in a systems study. Data gathering for the general and structural sections of the report is mainly a problem of collecting information, with a nominal number of interviews injected to identify specific goals of the business, potential problem areas, and areas of operations where there are good prospects for reducing costs and improving efficiency.

When operational data is being gathered, however, the analyst has to be much more introspective and interpretive, since he is now formulating activities (as strictly defined in Section 2.7) to agree with what he has learned about the business. Much of the time he has no precedent to rely on, and replies to his questions reflect assumptions, estimates, and judgments. This requires resourcefulness on the part of the analyst to ensure that activity costs, time cycles, and the flow of events are reasonable. One of his most important tasks, therefore, is to separate fact from opinion early in the study.

A serious problem that arises frequently during the accumulation of data, both from records and from interviews, is the fact that the analyst can only examine a portion of it. Then the analyst must turn to estimating and sampling methods.

4.9   ESTIMATING AND SAMPLING

On occasion, file searches and interviews are less than adequate data-gathering methods. This is particularly true in a business which is new and growing, where little management time or effort has yet been spent on such things as time standards, long-range budgets, planning records, or material costs. The above assertion also holds for the established business where more attention is paid to gross dollar budgets than to cost breakdowns of individual operations. In a recent case, a communications system was being considered by a company, but there were no records of volume and frequency data upon which to base analysis of requirements. In cases such as this some kind of estimate must be made.

Estimating   Estimating is an accepted method of developing data, but, where possible, estimates should be checked to control totals or verified by interview. If, for example, three activities (and no others) cut across a single department, activity costs in that department should roughly equal the overall department budget. However, if only one activity is to be studied, a realistic checkpoint to verify the analyst's and the supervisor's estimate should be developed.

Estimating data is a valid and acceptable procedure in systems work, and will save time as long as recognized checks and balances are applied to verify accuracy of the assumptions. In some situations, estimates made in this manner are accompanied by data obtained from samples.

Sampling   Sampling is a measuring technique which can be applied formally or informally. One form of sampling, known as *work sampling,* can be employed to analyze the actions of people, machines, or events in terms of time. Sampling is particularly useful on nonrecurring or irregularly occurring events where procedures have not been issued or data is not available.

A major advantage of sampling lies in the low cost of obtaining data without disrupting or intruding on normal work routines. A second advantage is that there may be a substantial reduction in the time needed to obtain the necessary information. From a relatively few observations, inferences can be drawn concerning the total work under study. The analyst actually uses some form of sampling, however informal, throughout a study. Analysis of last month's incoming orders, random selection of one file drawer for review, and observation of clerks working in a tool crib at 10:00 A.M. are examples of informal sampling.

When tracing a single activity through a business or working in an area where data is not available or not classified, sampling becomes a near necessity. In a tabulating area, for example, the analyst may want to find the amount of machine and operator time consumed by customer billing in relation to the amount of time spent performing all operations.

If the actual sampling is done by someone else, the analyst should determine the sample size and the specific times that observations are to be made. For example, a customer billing sample on the 30th of the month probably would not be representative of the effect this job has on the facility over a month. Rigorous sampling plans are very complex. When the inferences based on samples are of critical importance, it is well to employ the services of a qualified statistician.

SUMMARY

The first stage in a business system is study and design. There are three phases in the study and design stage, the first of which is understanding the present business. The purpose of this first phase is to compile data that may be used to support the analysis of the requirements of the system. This phase produces a report, the Present Business Description, which can be written in a variety of ways. The report usually consists of an Introduction, a General Section, a Structural Section, an Operational Section, and an Appendix. Sources of information for this phase can be grouped as internal and external records, supervisory and operating personnel, and estimating and sampling. Internal records include company files and procedure manuals; external records include trade publications, government statistics, and so on. The information obtained from supervisory and operating personnel is acquired during interviews which should be carefully planned. When estimating and sampling techniques are employed, care must be taken to assure that the results are cross-checked for reasonableness.

5

General Section of the Present Business Description Report

5.1 PARTS IN THE GENERAL SECTION

The general section of the report describing the present business system should clearly and concisely convey the major features of a business in narrative form. It is usually composed of five parts:

1. History and framework
2. Industry background
3. Goals and objectives
4. Policies and practices
5. Government regulations

In this chapter, these topics will be discussed for each part of the general section:

1. Type of data required
2. Examples of what they show
3. Sources of information

Chapter 8 will explain how analysts can organize this data into report form.

5.2 HISTORY AND FRAMEWORK

The present goals and practices of an organization are often shaped by the important events in its history. The part of the report dealing with the organization's history and framework is an identification of major milestones of progress from the past which have influenced the present direction of a business.

Important historical information includes: ideas, attitudes, and opinions of key management and research personnel; excerpts from the original charter; reasons for starting the company; mergers and spinoffs; expansion or curtailment of product lines and services; and reasons for changes in name or products. In addition, the growth of the physical plant and numbers of employees over the years should be mentioned, along with a very general identification of products and services.

The following selected statement of the history and framework of Butodale Electronics is an example of how this kind of information can be displayed:

The Butodale Electronics Company was established in 1946, incorporated in the State of Massachusetts. It was founded by four engineers and scientists who had worked together for a number of years in a large corporation on advanced government project work. Their main objective was to aid research laboratories and manufacturers in design and production of the latest radar, radio, and other electronic equipment.

It is significant that the corporation sales have increased from $170 thousand to $15.9 million since its founding. Some of the major milestones in the last five years were:

1. Establishment of the Worcester Computation Center to develop new fields of application for the analog computer (for example, heat transfer, nuclear engineering, process control engineering).
2. Establishment of the Long Beach and Rio de Janeiro Computation Centers to extend what was started at Worcester and to educate prospective customers in the use of analog computer techniques.
3. Opening of additional sales offices in Chicago and Fort Worth.
4. Expansion and modernization of the original plant in Danvers.
5. The starting of a major drive to secure overseas business, particularly in South America.

Butodale's major product lines have expanded during this period to include small general-purpose analog computers, instruments, and data plotters. (None of these new lines have developed to more than 10 percent of the total annual sales volume.)

The above material implies certain objectives (for example, expansion of overseas operations), and even provides reasons for starting the company. The remainder of this statement goes on to describe recently added product lines.

Butodale history runs to one and one-half pages in the actual report prepared by the analysts, while the history of National Bank of Commerce requires three and one-half pages. Length is not critical, as long as the narrative reveals useful facts. In their initial meetings with management, the analysts customarily request certain general information: annual reports, current and back issues; a prospectus; copies of speeches by management personnel concerning the business; employee orientation handbooks; and published texts on company history. From such material, a history of key events about a company can be put together. In addition, large commercial banks such as New York's Chase Manhattan, First National City, Manufacturers Hanover Trust, and Marine Midland; California's Bank of America; or Philadelphia's First Pennsylvania, often publish reviews of important industries which are available as source data. These summaries are oriented chiefly toward the investing public, but they are handy references for history and background as well as other subjects.

Sources of financial and operating data such as *Standard & Poor's, Dun & Bradstreet,* and other industrial and commercial registers, can be scanned for general information. Biographical registers such as *Who's Who in Commerce and Industry* are valuable when the personality of one man strongly affects the enterprise.

Where a study is directed toward one element of an enterprise, the company's historical data will be of less importance and can be substantially reduced.

This history and framework section naturally leads to the industry background section.

5.3   INDUSTRY BACKGROUND

The industry background part of the report describing the present business, places it in perspective within its industry. Comparative data that indicates why one company is successful and another is not, along with facts on the entire industry, should be included if available. Areas of concentration, strengths and weaknesses, and market potential of the major companies should be assessed. Here, the word "industry" is being used in a generic sense, and is meant to include organizations of all kinds.

The nature of the industry should briefly be summarized, showing demand for its products and services, technological developments leading to progress, growth characteristics, and growth trends. Among individual companies, comparable statistics can be prepared on sales volume, product and service likenesses and differences, territories served, profit margins, and other factors. This is sometimes difficult to do, since many multiproduct-line companies do not release statistics by divisions. However, there often are historical data available that will permit some kind of comparison.

The following example is taken from a study to illustrate the kind of material one finds in industrial background sections:

Butodale finds itself in the electronics industry and specifically in the analog computer area. Analog computers are widely used industrial tools which fall into two categories, general-purpose and special-purpose computers. There is considerable competition in this industry; some of the biggest competitors are ABC Instrument, Jones Instrument, and National Systems, Inc. Many investment analysts feel there will be continued growth for the general-purpose computer but this growth may not be at the same rate as in the past. The company agrees with these conclusions and, therefore, there is considerable stress put on finding new markets and new products. In order to uncover these areas and products the company has set up a New Products Committee and a Market Analysis Section. It is the specific purpose of these groups to plan future growth and to direct engineering effort towards this growth in order that the company may maintain a planned growth pattern of 20% per annum, or greater.

Some of the product areas under scrutiny are instruments, special-purpose computers, and process control equipment. Likewise, industry statistical analyses by marketing areas are developed in order to concentrate effort in the proper industries. There has been no designed plan to integrate this company through component manufacture; however, it is not opposed to this type of growth if necessary to insure a reliable source of supply, and if excess capacity can be sold profitably. Recently the company absorbed the Premium Capacitors Company and is now building high-quality capacitors.

This statement can be read quickly and does not look as if it would take much time or effort to prepare. But it represents considerable research effort on the part of the analysts who must search for the information in various sources. Let us cover some of the potential sources of information for the industrial background section of the report describing the present business.

A useful source of background information is the industry's technical paper or magazine. Almost every industry is served by at least one such publication; some are quite objective and informative. Editorial and research staffs of these publications frequently have files of industry statistics; a few publications issue an annual statistical review which summarizes the state of the industry or field of operations. "Electrical Merchandising" and "Aviation Week" each publish a special issue every year which gives statistics on the retail electrical appliance trade and the aviation industry, respectively. "Electronics" publishes, in the first issue of the year, a special report on the state of the electronics business, with projections for the year to come.

The Department of Commerce publishes a wealth of material on U.S. industry and trade. Government data as a rule is more objective, and at the same time less current than information found in business publications. The Census of Business and Manufacture, for example, maintains diversified statistics on industry which can be used to verify other data. The Department of Agriculture publishes data on the food processing industry; information on the alcoholic beverage trade can be secured from the Treasury Department; data on the drug business may be requested from the Department of Health, Education and Welfare.

Data banks being developed by the government are invaluable sources of information which should be used whenever the material is suitable for this purpose.

In addition, there are now statistical information organizations from which data can be purchased, often in computer readable form if desired.

5.4 BUSINESS GOALS AND OBJECTIVES

Goals and objectives, as used in this book, denote the same general concept. A clear understanding of business goals is necessary before activities can be properly formulated. We wish to point out that in this section of the report the requirement is for specific rather than general statements. We must emphasize that goal definition, good or bad, may predetermine the final system design since activities are keyed to it.

The definition of these goals is normally a relatively brief list of a half dozen or more specific statements. As an actual example, in the report prepared for the Butodale company, the preliminary goal statement reads:

A major objective of this corporation is to expand sales and profits which will guarantee a proper return to stockholders and offer continued opportunity to employees. The present sales goal is to increase gross by at least 20%; a net profit goal of 7% of sales and 15% of net worth has been established.

However, statements like "expand sales" and "guarantee a proper return to stockholders" were considered much too vague and general. In subsequent discussions the goal statement was revised to read:

1. Manufacture and sell standard computer equipment and accessories.
2. Design and manufacture special computer models and accessories to satisfy individual specifications and requirements.
3. Offer computation services and engineering consultation on a fee basis to industry, commerce, and schools, among others.
4. Manufacture spare parts and components for sale to the trade.
5. Repair and maintain installed equipment.
6. Conduct research on new products and services to support present lines and initiate new ones within Butodale's area of knowledge and proficiency.
7. Compensate employees and suppliers for services, and provide a satisfactory return for investors.
8. Demonstrate competence and quality in every product to clearly show advantage over competitive equipment.

This second statement was far more definitive, and reveals the goal structure of the business. These eight points were subsequently incorporated into the report of the second phase of the study. For comparison, let us examine the goal statements for another type of industry.

In the present business report for Custodian Life, the analysts found it appropriate to identify most of the organization's goals with a standard of attainment. Following is the statement from the section containing the goals and objectives for Custodian.

Competition is the dominant factor in the insurance industry and reaches into many different areas of a life insurance company. In the past decade, ordinary life insurance in force in the U.S. has tripled, while group and credit insurance have shown even greater increases. Custodian Life confronts this highly competitive, rapidly expanding market place with these goals and objectives:

New business production each year to equal 16% of the insurance in force at the beginning of the year.

A net gain in insurance in force of 10% each year.

A termination rate not greater than 6% per year of the insurance in force at the beginning of the year.

Development of the accident and health insurance business by an increase in the annualized premium of 49% over the previous year.

Expansion of operations into seven additional states during the next twelve months.

A well-balanced operation with proper consideration given to all groups within the company.

This statement could have been more specifically directed toward the individual services the company offers and the markets it serves. However, management felt the goals so expressed were adequate as they stand, so they were not altered.

These two sets of statements reveal the philosophy and methodology of stating the goals of organizations. It should be clear that a wide variation of statements is possible, depending on the analysts, the industry, management personnel, and on the sources available. While directives, management statements, and other internal publications offer clues to business goals and objectives, the ultimate sources of information are the personal interviews with owners or top-level management. As the Butodale example pointed out, managers often express goals quite generally and not in the specific terms required for the study. A rather searching self-examination may therefore be necessary to produce adequate goal statements.

5.5 POLICIES AND PRACTICES

The goals and objectives of a business are implemented by its policies and practices. Some are common to the industry or field of concentration; others will depart from industry practice as suits the requirements of a specific business.

Policies or courses of corporate action would include a code of ethics, a plan for expanding into new territories, an approach to advertising and publicity, attitudes toward employees, viewpoints on promotion, and the like. Policies are ideas, attitudes, and philosophies, as distinguished from procedures or methods, and the analyst must keep these differences in mind as he compiles the policy statement.

Butodale's policies are heavily employee-oriented as can be determined from the following excerpt from the report for that organization.

> Some of the major policies instituted by Butodale have unquestionably helped the company attain its position of eminence in the analog computer industry. One of these policies is the corporation's attitude toward its employees. Butodale has developed a labor philosophy in which it endeavors not to infringe on the private lives of its people, while offering liberal employee fringe benefits, including educational opportunities. The company makes a strenuous effort to keep layoffs to an absolute minimum. This policy has resulted in a fine labor-management atmosphere. It has made itself felt in pride of workmanship and company loyalty hard to equal in modern industry.

On the other hand, the policies and practices for the National Bank of Commerce are more detailed, as revealed by the following statements in the report for that organization.

> For individual and commercial customers and prospects
>   1. Accessible, flexible facilities for deposit and receipt of cash, checks, bonds, drafts, and other negotiable documents.
>   2. Interest-paying system to encourage time deposits.
>   3. Safekeeping facilities for valuable records.
>   4. Personal, confidential, knowledgeable consultation on all financial matters.
> For correspondent banks
>   1. Direct sending service and fast collection of cash items.
>   2. Full draft collection service.
>   3. Fast currency and coin shipment service.
>   4. Valuable document safekeeping facilities.
>   5. Assistance on large loans and advice on trust matters.
> For loan customers and prospects

1. Facilities and experienced personnel available for consultation and financial advice on all loan matters.
2. Readily accessible facilities for the closing of (and payment on) personal, commercial, or mortgage loans.
3. Extensive advertising program to attract loan prospects to the bank for consultation.
4. Specialists available with a broad knowledge of income-producing investments.
5. Specialists available having detailed financial status information on local individuals and businesses.
6. Analysts available who are well informed on relative valuations of all types of property.
7. Flexible interest-charging structure to encourage large loans and rewards for those who pay when due.

Planned practices to meet goals are:

1. Expand advertising program to reach more potential customers.
2. Enlarge drive-up banking facilities.
3. Increase emphasis on "Installment" type loans.
4. Modernize and reorganize physical and manpower facilities as necessary for most efficient operation.
5. Establish an electronic data center using the latest data processing equipment for processing paperwork; offer such services to local industry at a minimum cost.

Where do the analysts find the information with which to prepare statements such as these? Following is a guide to the answer.

Most companies prepare and publish standard operating procedures, operating and policy instructions, directives, and other internal declarations stating corporate goals, standards, and attitudes. Published information of this type should, where practical, be supplemented with statements from top management verifying whether the items listed are still valid and whether the analyst's interpretations are correct. Company advertisements and publicity releases also reflect the corporate personality, indicating areas in which the company currently operates or seeks to become established. House publications, too, frequently discuss policies, practices, and attitudes, but they cannot be considered totally objective in their viewpoints.

In virtually any enterprise in today's world, government regulations have some impact on the policies of the organization. For this reason, analysts of management systems should not overlook the points made in the next section.

5.6 GOVERNMENT REGULATIONS

Government regulations at all levels—federal, state, and local—can often influence the way a business is conducted.

The discussion of regulations in the report on the present business should answer three basic questions:

1. Which government regulations help the company do business (for example, charters, tariffs, franchises, enabling acts, subsidies)?
2. Which restrict its business activities (for example, consent decrees, utility regulations, regulations on financial enterprises)?
3. Which affect its record-keeping practices?

For example, rulings of the Federal Aviation Agency determine form and content of some airline reports; rules of the Federal Communications Commission require certain reports from communications facilities in specific form; rulings of the Securities & Exchange Commission affect the record-keeping of brokerage houses. However, the general requirements of the SEC affecting stock issue for publicly held corporations would not be spelled out in the report, nor would laws regarding monopolistic practices and restraint of trade. There may be informal government regulation as well as that formalized in laws, such as the attitude of the local government regarding industrial waste. This kind of informal regulation should also be noted in the report.

Now that we have established the philosophical setting for the section on government regulations, let us examine a specific statement taken from an actual report. In the following quotation from the National Bank of Commerce report, we should note that both permissive and restrictive regulations are mentioned.

National Bank of Commerce, organized in 1891, was chartered for business under the National Bank Act of 1864. The National Bank Act created a Bureau of Controller of Currency in the Treasury Department. The Controller, who is Director of the Bureau, has the power to charter national banks and is responsible for the examination, supervision, and rules relating to the operation and powers of such banks. Where state banking regulations are in conflict with national regulations, the national bank is normally required to comply with the state regulation.

National Bank of Commerce, like all member banks, must operate within the limits of the regulations of the Federal Reserve System. Responsibility for Federal Reserve policy and decisions rests on the Board of Governors, who are appointed by the President and approved by the Senate for a term of 14 years; the twelve Federal Reserve banks; and the Federal Reserve Open Market Committee. All national banks must be members of the Federal Reserve System, hold Federal Reserve stock, and must maintain legal reserves on deposit in their district Federal Reserve Bank. National banks must furnish a financial report when requested by Federal Reserve, and are members of the Federal Deposit Insurance Corporation, which guarantees each depositor against loss up to a maximum set by FDIC.

National Bank of Commerce must constantly adjust policies and operational procedures to meet the requirements of new Federal Reserve regulation interpretations.

The statement then lists the areas covered by the regulations of the Federal Reserve System.

To be sure, regulations may not always have a direct effect on an enterprise, but still may influence business policies. A brief statement in the Butodale report illustrates this point:

Government regulations do not play a major role in company plans. However, a very high percentage of sales, perhaps 60%, is subject to renegotiation. Since the government sets profit objectives as a percent of sales, this has an effect on company plans and strategy.

The reader might think that management will know all about the information in the above statements. However, management personnel may change, regulations may vary both in content and interpretation, and the organization itself may have changed since the last time management took a serious look at such information. For these reasons, the section on government regulations can serve a useful purpose.

In general, monopoly and antitrust laws, labor laws, fair-employment laws, and income tax regulations should be noted if they uniquely affect business operations.

As sources for general information on government regulations, analysts usually look in books and journals related to the industry. Annual reports and other company publications sometimes disclose the effect of government regulations on a business.

Commerce and financial laws enacted by the various states, for example, are specifically restrictive on banking and insurance operations; and utilities are closely regulated by state utility commissions. Consent decrees entered into by a business are another example of restrictive regulation. Franchises are examples of permissive regulations, as are federal laws which grant subsidies to industries. Summaries of this legislation, or perhaps the laws themselves, should be read to gain an accurate appraisal of their impact on business. The company's legal department may also be solicited in making this appraisal.

The discussion of government regulations normally terminates the general section of the analysts' report presenting the description of the present business organization. This general section is then followed by the structural section which describes the inputs of the business, its resources, and the outputs it produces. The philosophy is that the general section presents the setting for the goals and environment of the organization, whereas the structural section presents the physical actualities—what it receives from the environment, what resources it has to operate upon the inputs it receives, and what it gives back to the environment. The structural part of the report is the subject of Chapter 6.

SUMMARY

The general section of the report of the present business system is composed of history and framework, industry background, goals and objectives, policies and practices, and government regulations. Historical information includes opinions of key management personnel, original charter, reasons for starting the company, mergers and spinoffs, expansion or curtailment of product lines, and reasons for changes in name. The industry background part of the report places the business in perspective within the industry and useful sources of information are the industry's technical papers and magazines. Information on the goals and objectives is of prime importance in the formulation of activities. Directives, management statements, and other internal publications offer clues to business goals and objectives, but the ultimate sources of information are the personal views of owners or top-level management. The goals and objectives of a business are implemented by its policies and practices. Published procedures, policies, and directives supplemented with statements from top management supply the information for the policies and practices part of the report. Government regulations can often influence the way a business is conducted. The report should include information about which government regulations help the company, which restrict the company, and which affect its record-keeping practices.

6

Structural Aspects
of a System

6.1 STRUCTURAL ELEMENTS

The structural aspects of a presently operating management system involve three major elements: *inputs, resources,* and *outputs.*

Inputs for an organization or system are normally the materials that are received from the environment. For example, a company manufacturing a whip topping would have coconut oil, corn syrup, and water as three major inputs. These inputs might be supplied from three separate sources—an oil company, a corn products company, and the city water authority. A milk company would receive milk from dairy farms and cartons from a paper-container manufacturer as two major inputs. Of course, each company would have several other inputs.

Outputs are normally the products that an organization sends to its customers. Customers, like vendors, are part of the environment. For examples of outputs, let us return to the above two companies. The whip-topping company could transform the oil, syrup, and water into a whip topping to sell to bakeries, hospitals, and housewives. The milk company could put the milk into cartons and sell it to retail stores, restaurants, hospitals, and housewives. Now, we have said that the two companies "could transform" and "could put," but they have to have some means of carrying out these two operations. These means we call resources. Resources are made up of financial support, people, an inventory of material, and production facilities. Thus, the whip-topping company has to have money; managers, chemists, salesmen, and machine operators; storage space for input materials and the finished product; and physical facilities such as a plant, blending equipment, freezer, and sales office.

These three elements—inputs, resources, and outputs—constitute the structure which the study team must understand in order to design a new system. Of fundamental importance is the understanding of the operations by which inputs are transformed into outputs. We shall save the subject of operations for separate treatment in Part 3.

As in the case of the general section, the analysts must search for data and other information. However, the same sources used as a foundation for the general data can again be used for the structural aspects of the system. Consequently, we need not discuss the sources in detail but merely mention that they are the same as described above.

It would be of little value for the analysts to collect a large quantity of data if they had no idea what they were looking for, or what they were going to do with the information once it was obtained. For this reason, a business model is used to exhibit the elements and the relations among them. We showed the general outline of such a model in Figure 2-2. Now we present one in fuller detail.

6.2   BUSINESS MODEL OF THE STRUCTURE

A model of the business sets up the framework for exhibiting the relationships among the inputs, outputs, resources, and operations. The model serves a useful purpose by establishing a classification system for displaying data.

Elements of the business model will vary in emphasis for different industries and enterprises. Physical inputs and outputs are stressed in most models for a manufacturing enterprise, while resources predominate in analyzing an employment agency. Deposits and loans are input and output classifications for a financial institution, but money in general belongs in resources for other enterprises.

Figure 6-0 is an actual model prepared for the Butodale company. Note that the environment here is called the market. It contains both vendors and customers. We see that Butodale deals with 850 vendors. The analysts have classified the vendors according to the dollar volume of their purchases. This has revealed, for example, that there are 15 vendors supplying over $100,000 worth of materials each per year.

The model shows that the combined 850 vendors supply Butodale with 15 classes of items ranging from transistors to converters, and that the total cost of these materials amounts to 45 percent of sales. Probably, the analysts based their summaries on individual dollar figures obtained for each of the materials. This additional information is of interest to management and to the analysts later when they design the new system.

The inputs become involved in company operations, which for Butodale were organized as marketing, engineering, production, accounting, and purchasing. Remember, this is the way the analysts found the present system. The new design may

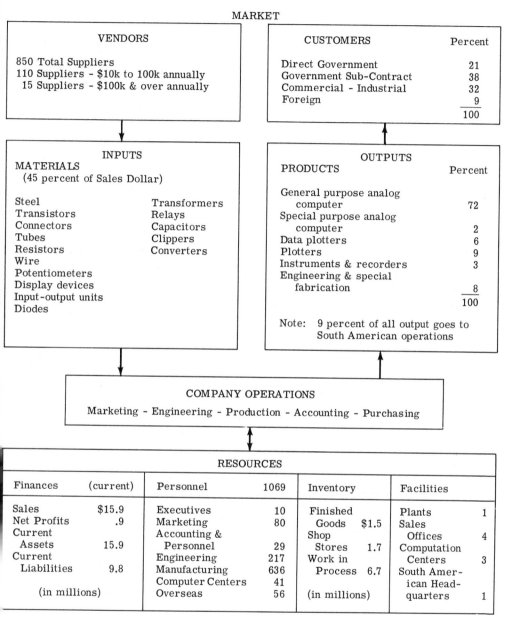

MARKET

VENDORS

850 Total Suppliers
110 Suppliers - $10k to 100k annually
 15 Suppliers - $100k & over annually

CUSTOMERS	Percent
Direct Government	21
Government Sub-Contract	38
Commercial - Industrial	32
Foreign	9
	100

INPUTS

MATERIALS
(45 percent of Sales Dollar)

Steel	Transformers
Transistors	Relays
Connectors	Capacitors
Tubes	Clippers
Resistors	Converters
Wire	
Potentiometers	
Display devices	
Input-output units	
Diodes	

OUTPUTS

PRODUCTS	Percent
General purpose analog computer	72
Special purpose analog computer	2
Data plotters	6
Plotters	9
Instruments & recorders	3
Engineering & special fabrication	8
	100

Note: 9 percent of all output goes to South American operations

COMPANY OPERATIONS

Marketing - Engineering - Production - Accounting - Purchasing

RESOURCES

Finances	(current)	Personnel	1069	Inventory		Facilities	
Sales	$15.9	Executives	10	Finished		Plants	1
Net Profits	.9	Marketing	80	Goods	$1.5	Sales	
Current		Accounting &		Shop		Offices	4
Assets	15.9	Personnel	29	Stores	1.7	Computation	
Current		Engineering	217	Work in		Centers	3
Liabilities	9.8	Manufacturing	636	Process	6.7	South Amer-	
		Computer Centers	41			ican Head-	
(in millions)		Overseas	56	(in millions)		quarters	1

Figure 6-0   A business model for Butodale.

change it considerably, but before there *is* a new design, the present situation must be defined.

The operations of an organization are carried out by resources. In Figure 6-0 we see that the analysts have classified the resources into four main categories: finances, personnel, inventory, and facilities. For each category, they have set up subclassifications which they list in the model, accompanied by figures to indicate dollar and physical amounts.

The model then shows that the inputs are converted into outputs, which for Butodale are called products. We see that the major product is the general-purpose analog computer which makes up 72 percent of sales. The other products sold to customers are listed, together with their relative importance as reflected by the percent of sales figures. The analysts also note here that 9 percent of all output is sold in South America.

Outputs are delivered to the environment which, for the Butodale model, is composed of customers. The customers are divided into four groups. We can see immediately that Butodale depends heavily on government contracts, with direct and indirect government sales being 59 percent of total sales. Only about one third of sales go to domestic business organizations. Another point revealed is that Butodale does not have a significant retail business.

The reader is advised to examine the business model in Figure 6-0 for whatever time is needed to visualize the concepts involved. Such a model is not simple to prepare, even for analysts who examine a well-run organization with good records. This model is always of great interest to management for it puts the elements and relations among them in perspective as an integrated whole so the system can be seen as a total entity.

The model can be fashioned into many different patterns to conform to the type of company, industry, product, or similar variation. Yet in its overall pattern the model remains much as is shown in the example. One can include greater detail if needed, but too much detail in the figure itself can make it unwieldy, and what should be emphasized might be obscured. The general model of the overall structure is probably best portrayed in general terms. Nonetheless, details are of prime importance in getting the information needed for building the new system; for this reason, the remaining sections of the report are devoted to these details. The first area is the firm's products and the market in which it sells them.

6.3 PRODUCTS AND MARKETS

The marketing aspects of an organization are of critical importance for practically all organizations, regardless of other considerations. This area is fundamental in the study of an existing system. Of the many possible ways of viewing the marketing function, we emphasize the products of the business, since they are the outputs, and analyze them in conjunction with the customers who purchase them. Even ultimate consumers who use them, who may or may not be customers of the company itself, may be included in the study. However, the time and cost of going to this level of effort usually prohibit much exploration of ultimate customers for manufacturing or wholesale organizations.

The analysts should begin their study of the existing products and markets by describing the market for the enterprise's products and services, with emphasis on sales and distribution characteristics of existing and planned products as well as information on past and future trends of product demand. Where possible, marketing methods are analyzed. Some of the questions the analysts might try to answer are: Does the enterprise sell directly to the public, or through agents, wholesalers, retailers, and franchised dealers? What specific promotion or advertising strategies are used? What part of the sales dollar does advertising represent? How do products compare with those of the competition?

Discussions of sales or distribution methods also provide insight into the marketing aggressiveness of an enterprise. A map can be plotted to show locations of sales offices and warehouses, sales representatives, and sales wholesalers or retailers. If products or services are sold on long-term contracts, this fact should be included in the report.

Information on trends in product mix, shifts in the composition of income, and breakdown of income by major product lines customarily are noted where they contribute to a total picture of the market.

Now that we understand the philosophy of the method, let us reinforce the concepts with some actual quotations. In the report for the Worthington Hardware Company, the description of products starts by breaking Worthington's sales into nine departments.

The Worthington Hardware Company maintains an inventory of approximately 35,000 items. These items are shown in a general catalog (the index to this catalog is attached in order to identify the products).
The 35,000 items are classified into departments as follows:

Department	Estimated Percentage of Total Items
Athletics	8
Guns & Ammunition	4
Fishing Tackle	7
Electrical	7
Housewares	22
Stoves	2
General	17
Tools	24
Builders' Hardware	9

The list discloses the range of products, and to some extent defines the market area. Builders' hardware, for instance, is purchased mainly by the building trade. The Worthington organization is predominantly sales-oriented, as could be expected of a wholesale distributor, and the analysis in Figure 6-1 compares income, profits, and expenses for the nine departments. The following note which was part of the report explains the way some of the data in Figure 6-1 were adjusted by the analysts:

Overall, hardware departments contribute approximately 70 percent of sales and sporting goods departments 30 percent. Promotion department's sales were included in all department sales prior to the current year. The promotion department plans to publish a promotion booklet four times a year for hardware (spring, summer, fall, and Christmas), and once a year for sporting goods (Christmas).

It is important for analysts to support their tables and graphs with a solid set of statements that reveal the highlights of the evidence.

For Worthington, the market can be explained satisfactorily in terms of departmental output and profit margins. However, the same type of display would not be suitable for the National Bank of Commerce. Instead (and just as effectively), the

Departmental Profit Picture — Previous Year				
Department	Thousand $ Gross Margin	% Gross Margin	% Expenses	Net P/L %	P/L % to Total Sales
Athletics	121	18.9	19.5	- .6	- .04
Guns and Ammunition	188	18.1	16.6	1.5	.25
Fishing Tackle	67	10.8	18.9	-8.1	- .73
Electrical	83	16.2	14.8	1.4	.12
Housewares	176	16.3	19.4	-3.1	- .58
Stoves	13	24.9	24.1	.8	.08
General	160	22.7	22.9	- .2	- .19
Tools	155	20.6	19.6	1.0	.20
Builders' Hardware	167	21.9	21.8	.1	.03
Total	1130	Avg. 18.3	Avg. 19.2	Avg. - .9	Avg. - .86

Comparison of Departmental Sales			
	Previous Year (9 mos.)	Current Year (9 mos.)	% + or -
Athletics	9.4	9.1	- .3
Guns and Ammunition	14.7	14.9	+ .2
Fishing Tackle	11.6	7.9	- 3.7
Electrical	6.3	7.1	+ .8
Housewares	18.2	16.3	- 1.9
Stoves	.3	.4	+ .1
General	12.5	10.8	- 1.7
Tools	12.5	12.8	+ .3
Builders' Hardware	14.6	14.4	- .2
Promotions	--	6.3	--

Figure 6-1 Two types of product analysis taken from the structural section of the report of present business for the Worthington Hardware Company.

market for services was described in its report by showing how the level of available loan funds is determined, and by itemizing the types of output services which use these funds. The following statements for the report illustrate this point.

Output Products

The National Bank of Commerce furnishes loan money and banking services primarily in Shawnee and Wabaunsee Counties.

Amount of loan money available for output to customers is determined as follows:
Total Deposit money
Less outstanding Regular Loan money
Less Long-term outstanding Investment Loan money
Less Cash and Reserve
Equals Available loanable funds.

Output Services

1. *Demand Deposit* Check collection and payment service is offered in order to increase the percentage of demand deposits that can be loaned (or invested) to create interest and fee income. A small fee is charged to cover a portion of the handling costs.

2. Time Deposits   Interest dividends are paid to savings depositors to encourage larger deposits and therefore increase loanable funds.

3. Loan   Secured or unsecured loans for long or short terms are offered. Men experienced in all types of loan financing are available to the bank's customers and prospects.

4. Trust   Trust service is offered to encourage new and retain existing trust deposit funds. A fee charged for administration of estate and pension trusts creates income for the bank.

5. Correspondent Check Clearing and Collection   This service primarily benefits local industry and surrounding banks. Rapid clearing and collection service encourages large deposits, which creates more loanable funds.

6. Safe Deposit   Document safekeeping service is offered to provide a maximum security area for a customer's valuable documents. Fees for use of the Safe Deposit area create incomes for the bank.

Borrowing Customers (Receiving output money)

> Individuals
> Commercial Businesses
> Government
> > Local, state, national (includes bonds and securities)

Types of Loans	Percent of Outstanding Total
Real Estate	20
Financial institution	4
Purchase or carrying securities	3
Farm loans	5
Commercial and industrial	48
Automobile installment	6
Retail consumer installment	5
Single-payment household and personal expenditures	9

A general policy of the bank is to have outstanding loans equal about 40 percent of total deposits.

Depositing Customers (Receiving output services)

Individuals   At the present time the bank has 24,000 individual deposit customers. Records show a total of 36,500 accounts. However, studies show a 50% account duplication between savings and checking.

Commercial   2200 community business establishments are customers of the National Bank of Commerce. The records actually show 2500 accounts, but some customers have multiple accounts. Both large and small businesses use the service offered.

Banks   Out of 609 banks in the state, 277 have active correspondent agreements with The National Bank of Commerce. The records show 365 accounts; however, 88 are considered inactive. The primary market appears to be the area within an 80-mile radius of the bank due to one-day check clearing desired by most banks. About eight banks in the primary market area offer correspondent bank service and are considered competitors.

Government   Local, state, and federal government units are customers. The federal government is the largest single depositor.

The above statements refer primarily to a *short period* or given instant of time. However, a significant time span should be used when illustrating product trends.

The dollar volumes of business can be broken out geographically or regionally, by distribution channel, and by customer or customer type if this method of analysis contributes to a balanced explanation.

In Figure 6-2, which shows four graphs from the report of products and markets for the Custodian Life Company, the information does not fall under exact product classifications but does illustrate sources, trends, and profile-expense relationships, many of which are important output factors. These graphs again illustrate the point made earlier that the contents of the report should vary with the circumstances.

For sources of information, the analyst will find it fruitful to consult sales catalogs and other promotional literature. These contain data on products or services.

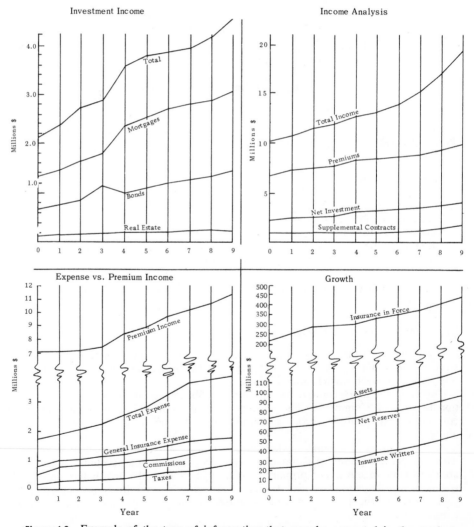

Figure 6-2 Example of the type of information that may be presented in the products and materials section of a report on the present condition of a business taken from the Custodian Life Insurance Company report.

Furthermore, the company's marketing executives will be able to provide extensive analyses of the markets. More often than not they will have available a number of reports showing sales figures by special categories. Following are some examples of data they may be able to furnish:

1. Sales tabulations by customer order, store, warehouse, industry, region, territory, and salesman
2. Industry and company sales forecasts
3. Shipments reports
4. Advertising outlays
5. Product line profit margins
6. Budget sales output
7. Financial operations statements
8. Sales quota reports
9. Warehouse turnover
10. Sales expense reports

Thus far we have looked at the environment as a place to which the ouputs of the organization are sent. Now we turn to the environment as a place that furnishes inputs for the organization.

6.4 MATERIALS AND SUPPLIERS

In order to produce outputs, the organization must have access to its environment to acquire materials from suppliers. As with products and markets, analysts usually gather information on materials and suppliers from various sources. Let us examine some of the sources of data and some of the methods of presentation. Input materials and services can be classified by source, type, total and unit cost, availability, cyclic need, or other features. Major suppliers (sources) are customarily ranked according to annual dollar volume. Procurement practices and competitive conditions in the market should also be appraised because they affect many segments of the business.

In the structural section of the report, an analyst is concerned primarily with input materials, services, and resources which are essential to fulfilling goals of the business. Therefore, office supplies of a manufacturing enterprise or water used to cool grinding equipment in a job shop usually are excluded, while raw materials used in the manufacturing enterprise to produce goods ultimately sold on the market should be included.

In some types of vertically integrated enterprises and some service organizations, relatively few products are procured from outside companies. Several large U.S. manufacturing enterprises, for instance, are so organized that subsidiaries supply everything from raw materials to subsystems of the finished product. Under these conditions, if only one division of the company is being analyzed, the others are treated as part of the outside environment and therefore become potential customers or vendors (outputs or inputs) for the business.

Let us clarify the above general concepts with concrete examples from three different kinds of business—manufacturing, wholesaling, and life insurance.

In the first illustration note the coverage of the procurement and inventory practices in this statement from Butodale on the problems of delivery and quality control:

Approximately 45 percent of the sales dollar at Butodale is the cost of material. Some of the major purchased materials include steel, transistors, tubes, potentiometers, display devices, transformers, capacitors, connectors, relays, wire, and resistors. At present Butodale controls this material by a procedure based on relative annual parts cost. It is important to note that the time lag for material purchased varies from two weeks to four months. An order record card is sent to the buyer, who originates the purchase authorization. Different buyers handle different classes of items. Fifty percent of the time the buyer inspects the order record card; selection is automatic the rest of the time. Ninety percent of the items handled through the inventory control section have Butodale part numbers, which makes processing very fast. When part numbers are missing or not assigned, it is difficult to determine if there is such an item, or if it is ordered directly by name and charged to a project. The company has about 850 suppliers, 125 of whom could be considered major suppliers; of these major suppliers, 110 receive $10,000 to $100,000 of business annually, and the remaining 15 receive $100,000 and over annually. The company endeavors to have multiple sources, but because of the high quality of Butodale equipment, this is not always possible. A limited number of very expensive attachments for systems input and output are required; the purchase of these units is forecast and an agreement negotiated with the supplier, giving an annual requirement with quantities to be delivered at specified dates. This arrangement seems to work satisfactorily. In view of the high quality standards set by Butodale, all incoming material must go through a stringent quality-control check. This, on occasion, causes material shortage if inferior material is received. Records are maintained to reflect these conditions, and to eliminate recurrence of such conditions.

For our second example, we present a table of data concerning the materials and suppliers of a wholesale company—Worthington Hardware. As the reader can well imagine, a wholesaler is not likely to have much raw material or many problems with inventory in the process of being manufactured. Thus, the materials and suppliers will vary somewhat from that of a manufacturing concern. Consequently, in the report for Worthington the analysts prepared the information shown in Figure 6-3. Here we see a straightforward listing of purchases and turnovers for each product line ranging from athletics to promotions. These types of data give management a ready reference to the two major variables that interest them, the status of shelf goods and the movement of shelf goods. We can see that not only are the primary figures given in dollar amounts, but also as ratios for greater understanding.

An organization that does not have products or materials in the usual physical sense, but in the sense of customer service and financial credit, presents a different picture. It is an example of those types of businesses, such as public utilities, in which the availability of supplies must be projected over long periods. For these cases, reserve and emergency sources can be described. In lending institutions, the nature of input fundings, types of investors providing funds, and data on the amount of funds secured in the various categories would normally be included.

	Purchases	Percent of Total	Average Inventory	Percent of Total	Turnover
Athletics	$ 331,850	10	$ 157,905	11	2.4
Guns & Ammunition	561,362	17	256,297	18	2.6
Fishing Tackle	287,549	8	172,309	12	1.9
Electrical	242,294	7	110,865	8	2.9
Housewares	512,356	16	137,474	10	4.3
Stoves	26,091	1	36,969	3	1.0
General	302,370	9	115,530	8	3.3
Tools	395,163	12	118,287	9	4.6
Builders' Hardware	401,165	12	213,704	15	2.5
Promotions	261,125	8	88,337	6	3.8
Total	$3,321,325	100	$1,407,677	100	3.0

Figure 6-3 Example of a table of data concerning the materials and suppliers of the Worthington Hardware Company.

The following material and suppliers narrative taken from the report for Custodian Life is a case in point:

Insurance companies must look to the field of investments to put their premium dollars to effective use. These investments provide a return which is an important factor in the successful operation of the business. Custodian Life looks to three major classes of suppliers to provide these materials (better referred to as investments) which bring a steady income to the company.

The first class, and most important, is the mortgage market, in which $69 million, or 54 percent of the ledger assets, were invested as of July 31. The mortgage investment policy is directed towards single residential loans and two-family residential buildings. However, multifamily and commercial buildings are approved, with the maximum loan on such properties being $300,000. The general terms and limitations applicable to each class of mortgage are determined by the investment committee based upon recommendations made by the mortgage loan department. During the past fiscal year, the net income from mortgages was $2,973,000.

The second class of supplier is the bond market, in which $48 million, or 38 percent of the ledger assets, were invested as of July 31. U.S. Treasury issues are by far the greatest single market, followed by public utility securities in strong second place. The remainder of the market is diversified with balanced holdings in industrials, municipals, Canadian governments, and railroads. The net interest earned from bonds amounted to $1,457,000 during the past fiscal year.

The third class is real estate. This is a very minor item, representing less than 1 percent of the ledger assets. The real estate holdings consist primarily of the home office buildings and several properties adjoining the home office. Operating in the three markets listed above, the Custodian Life has a net investment income of $4,602,000 for the past fiscal year. This amount was second only to the premium income, and provided resources with which to operate the company successfully.

The reader should turn back to Figure 6-2 which reveals trends and relationships for several of these input factors.

When seeking information on materials and suppliers, the analyst should first consult the purchasing department or accounts payable unit in the accounting organization. These departments often compile summaries of dollar expenditures by individual suppliers for a number of different reasons; for example, the Small

Business Administration requires periodic reports from government contractors on purchases placed with small business concerns. For internal control reasons, accounts payable units usually maintain records by vendor to prevent duplicate invoicing; cost accounting may keep records on unit costs; and quality control and inspection sections may have data on vendor performance. Any or all of these functions should be checked for vendor information.

In addition, current operating reports possibly contain information on such variables as commodity lead time, material cost variance, vendor evaluation, and analysis of cash payments reports.

Although inventories were mentioned as part of our discussion above, the coverage of raw, in-process, and finished stock inventories should be saved for the resource section in the report, which includes inventories.

From this examination of the organization's inputs and outputs, we turn our attention to the resources which permit the transformation of inputs into outputs.

6.5   RESOURCES

Resources are those means by which an organization is able to change inputs into outputs. A convenient classification of resources is: finances, personnel, inventory, and facilities. There can also be nonphysical resources, such as patents, "secret processes," unique experience, and skills. This is composed primarily of human knowledge, files, and records. Because it is difficult to record human knowledge, we customarily include only the records and files portion of this resource. In the next four sections, we cover the four classes of resources: finance, personnel, inventory, and facilities.

6.6   FINANCIAL RESOURCES

Financial resources are relatively easy to document if the company is publicly held and government regulations require disclosure, though divisional and departmental data may be restricted. Where a company is a partnership or a closed corporation, financial data are usually confidential; in such situations the analyst must guard against disclosure of such information to unauthorized persons.

For the typical organization, the main exhibits in the financial resources section are a balance sheet of financial operations, a statement of income and retained earnings, and an overhead or expense statement. The form of the balance sheet and earnings report as prepared for an annual report is usually found to be satisfactory for displaying this data. The emphasis on detail varies with the type of enterprise; for example, the statement of a bank's status usually lists the outstanding loans separately under assets, and lists deposits, capital, and reserves under liabilities. Reserves held by an insurance company, or receivable and debt-retirement items of a finance company, may be similarly featured. A consolidated overhead or expense report should be prepared as the principal means for exhibiting the cost and expense allocations for the organization. The consolidated overhead statement for Butodale presented in Figures 10-7 and 10-8 are good illustrations.

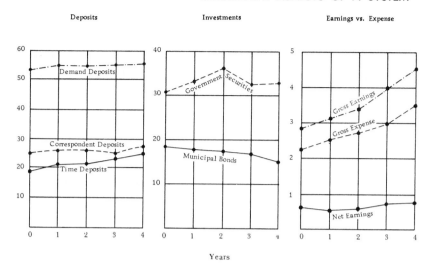

Years

Figure 6-4 Three exhibits taken from the financial resources section of the structural part of the report on present business conditions for the National Bank of Commerce. All figures in millions of dollars.

Financial statements generally should be appended with notes to explain or amplify important transactions.

Company balance sheets and statements of earnings are not illustrated in this chapter, since they are published widely in annual and other reports. However, the financial summary and the balance sheet for Butodale shown in Figures 10-5 and 10-6 may be used as examples. In presenting this information for management purposes it is a good technique to show relations among the data by plotting the data on graphs; for example, financial progress of the enterprise could be compared to its industry, or to major competitors, or to industry leaders. Exhibits taken from the report prepared for the National Bank of Commerce illustrate this type of display as shown in Figure 6-4.

Before preparing the financial resources section of the report describing the present business, the analysts should arrange interviews with the financial officers to find out what information is available, and what is classified as confidential. In a partnership or closed corporation, such records are normally acquired from the accountant; if a division or department of a large company is under study, budgets and cost-distribution records are usually easy to obtain from the financial manager. Outside analysts may have to study the profit statements privately. Occasionally, the officers of an organization will not permit the analysts to have access to certain financial data. This situation occurred in a recent study of a major manufacturing concern. The study team compensated for the tight security on financial data by using ratios that were customary in the industry for companies of this size, and by searching for supporting information in published articles and other appropriate external sources including *Moody's Manuals of Investment* and *Dun and Bradstreet Ratings*. From these sources they were able to prepare a financial resources section that was astonishingly accurate.

Based on primary data in dollar terms, analysts can prepare a large number of derived relationships in the form of ratios, correlations, and trends. There is a limit, however, because it takes time and effort to prepare this information and to present the results graphically. Consequently, a study team must settle for the techniques that are most informative for the circumstances under which they are working. Their attention must then be diverted from financial resources to the human resources. These we consider in the following section.

6.7   PERSONNEL RESOURCES

Human resources are of major importance in a study of any organization. Information on personnel is needed in both the structural descriptions of the business and in the operational aspects considered in the following chapter.

An organization chart is customarily the first exhibit in the personnel resources section of the report prepared by the analysts. If such a chart does not exist, the analysts should draft one from data provided by the personnel (or equivalent) department of the company.

Reports which classify employees by organizational component, skill, location, salary, and other categories often indicate important facts about the business not readily apparent from an inspection of its organization chart.

Other valuable facts concerning personnel are union membership and union relations, local labor markets, turnover statistics, fringe benefits, stock options, and profit-sharing plans. Management attitudes on personnel subjects, and comparisons with other businesses drawing on the same labor pools, are often pertinent and should be included.

In searching for information permitting the analysis of personnel costs by organization component, product or project, and other cost-distribution categories the analysts should first turn to the accounting or cost departments. This preliminary information can be supplemented by interviews with personnel administration and accounting supervisors. From these sources one can obtain such additional factors as the classifications of the employees.

It is true that some companies have organized excellent records on employees and include personal statistics such as formal education, degrees, special courses of training taken, and skills other than those used on their current job. The trend toward more complete records has been accelerated with the wider use of computers. A careful search in several sources, supplemented by interviews, is still the general method for obtaining data on the organization's personnel resources. In the next section on inventory resources, we shall find this same problem repeated since one of the inventories is the inventory of human knowledge.

6.8   INVENTORY RESOURCES

For convenient reference in the following discussion, we will divide an organization's inventory resources into two general classes: physical inventories and information inventories. *Physical inventories* include parts, assemblies, finished products, and money (in the case of financial enterprises), and so on. These physical items, preferably kept in larger supply than is needed for current operations, serve as buffers between the peaks of demand from the environment and the capacity to produce within the business. *Information inventories* include operational experience, decision rules and logic, and historical data concerning operations. A file of account records, a sales catalog, and a library of programs for a computer are examples of information inventories.

In the inventory resources part of the report, the physical inventories should be classified by type (raw materials, components or parts, in-process or semifinished assemblies, and completed products), inventory level, location, value of stock, and cost of maintenance. In some cases, it is difficult to separate facilities from physical inventories. A distinction must be made, however, between stocks consumed in the operation of the business, and permanent facilities. Thus, in the case of a water distillation plant, the tank is a facility, while water is an inventory.

Characteristics of inventories (information as well as physical) found useful for management include: level, flow (both inputs and outputs), turnover, age, cycle, demand, access, and reaction capability to changes in demand. Obsolescence factors are also important—both information and stock usually become less valuable with the passage of time. In the case of physical stocks, the value of raw materials is more accurately predictable than the value of some kinds of finished products which are subject to obsolescence and deterioration.

Besides files of records, there are other kinds of information inventories which cannot be overlooked: standard procedures and instructions, and human experience and information retained in the minds of people. This is "edited" information which has been refined by years of application and practice. Although this resource may be less accessible than files, it is generally more valuable.

One of the benefits of computers has been the ability of systems designers to convert the store of information from the human mind into computer programs. Management personnel have not yet generally recognized this potential of computers, but the situation is changing and greater consideration is being given to this aspect of systems development and application.

Now let us consider some of the possible sources of data which the analysts should consult in their search for inventory resources. Generally, physical-inventory records are located in the accounting and manufacturing departments. Accounting records typically show inventory changes through shipments to customers and receipts from vendors. There may also be classifications by type of material (raw or in-process), consignment and warehouse balances, and material budgets. The manufacturing department customarily maintains files in stockrooms, accumulation areas, and inventory-control sections, and reports inventory status by units, age, manufacturing losses, amount of surplus and obsolete, and special budgets. For inventory policies and practices the study team should consult the inventory-control supervisor or cost accountant.

There may be other considerations in this area of inventory resources that the analysts may observe in the particular organization for which they are designing a new system. However, the ideas presented here should be sufficient for most purposes. It is recognized that the organization must have facilities to house its personnel and inventory resources, convert inputs to outputs, and carry on its other work.

6.9   FACILITIES RESOURCES

The facilities of an organization generally include items such as the amount and kind of land the company occupies, and the size, value, and arrangement of buildings, equipment, and communications networks.

The types of data presented in the section of the report covering an organization's inventory of facilities are usually itemized according to manufacturing plants, sales offices, research facilities, warehouses, and distribution facilities. Information concernng the area of buildings, whether the facilities are leased or owned, and plans for new construction are useful types of data in support of this list. Major items of machinery or other equipment involved in the activities under study should also be classified and listed, with capacity figures added, if meaningful. Equipment listings are often supplemented by layout diagrams of plants and offices. Data-processing equipment is also noted.

In certain types of businesses, the communication network (for example, the communications terminal for a brokerage house with multilocations) is a most essential facility, and its performance should be covered in some depth. A map is a good visual aid to show the different locations (also to show the dispersion of sales offices and manufacturing plants) with connecting lines to point out inter-office connections and switching centers. Costs (operating and original), current and projected volumes and capacities, and response speeds are important. The time and length of queues, periodic fluctuations (rather than cyclic), and volume trends need not be recorded here but they will be useful to management later when operations are presented. At that time data is shown in visual form, such as graphs. When it comes to obtaining data, analysts usually find that facilities are generally well documented. Information may be extracted from plant accounting records or from details maintained in the manufacturing or engineering departments. Communications network data is obtained from equipment vendors or from user personnel.

With all this information collected over a period of days or weeks, the study team is ready to develop the structural section of the report of the present business. At the same time the team must be planning the collection of data relating to the operations that are carried on within the organization. In essence, the organization carries on certain activities utilizing its resources in order to achieve its goals.

In the next chapter we turn to the operations performed by these resources.

SUMMARY

Inputs, resources, and outputs are three major elements in the structural aspect of a management system. Operations are the means by which inputs are transformed into outputs. Resources are used to execute the operations. A business model exhibits the relationships among the inputs, outputs, resources, and operations. The pattern of all business models is much the same, but variations of content are required to conform to the type of company, type of industry, and type of products.

The marketing area of an organization sells outputs to the environment, and this component should be included in the study of an existing business system. Materials from suppliers are the inputs to the organization from the environment. Resources, which are the means for changing inputs into outputs, can be classified as finance, personnel, inventory, and facilities. Information and knowledge are important resources. Analysts should review files and reports, and interview the associated personnel to obtain information about the resources of the organization.

CHAPTER

Company
Operations

7.1 THE SETTING

Before the reader begins this chapter, we suggest that he turn to Section 6.2 and reexamine Figure 6-0 to note its major concepts. These concepts form the overall business model defined for our presentation of management systems. We have already covered *vendors, inputs, customers, outputs,* and *resources.* In this chapter we discuss *company operations* and examine methods of formulating activities, assigning costs to activities, and determining time and frequency data about each activity. Although we refer to forms that are useful for recording the information about an activity, a complete discussion of suggested forms and their use is reserved for Chapter 8.

7.2 THE MEANING OF ACTIVITY FORMULATION

The determination of business goals and the formulation of activities is probably the most important task that analysts must perform during a study of the present organization. In our plan, analysis and new systems design are based primarily on activities. Activity formulation goes far beyond conventional data organization; it requires considerable thought concerning the business in terms of goals, objectives, and purpose, as contrasted to the existing organizational structure. This analysis calls for sound judgment and insight on the part of the analyst as he listens to and interprets established views. These he must analyze and reformulate as basic activities.

The initial definition of activities may be modified later as the analyst becomes more familiar with the business, but early definitions and boundaries usually do not significantly change. Activities are not structured out of a few interviews or from selected data concerning the enterprise. They evolve from intensive examination of the nature and practical requirements of the business. Consequently, we shall discuss several ways to arrive at activity definitions through a series of approximations and successive refinements.

7.3   ACTIVITY FORMULATION METHODS

No one best method exists for defining business goals and for formulating activities to carry out these goals. However, the study team may select from three general approaches to arrive at a definition: deductive, inductive, and composite. All three presume that the team has completed investigations for the general and structural information, prepared a functional organization chart, and broken down the total business costs to show the cost of carrying out departmentalized functions for one year. Within each department the costs are further subdivided into the costs for personnel, machinery and equipment, materials, and miscellaneous items. The reader who does not understand this statement completely may turn to Figure 10-13. There he will see the main departments (management, accounting, personnel, and so on). The cost figures in the first main row under the departments are the subdivided costs of carrying out the departmentalized functions. For example, it cost Butodale $1,000 during the year for machinery and equipment in the personnel department.

In the *deductive* method of activity formulation, management is asked for opinions or direct statements on goals of the business. Then the study team defines activities as it interprets these statements, and confirms or revises them by reinterviewing management. In reaching a final goal statement and the resulting statement of goal-directed activities, lively discussions with management are usually generated. Once an agreement has been reached on the definition of goals, then individual activities can be investigated and documented.

The *inductive* method works almost in reverse. After an allocation of total business costs has been recorded to show the cost of carrying out departmentalized functions, the team starts to document individual operations as they are encountered and identified. These individual operations are then sorted into logically related groups based on interdependency and without regard to the department performing them. Next, a rough flowchart is drawn for each group of related operations. These flowcharts are then studied for content and completeness. It requires considerable insight and many regroupings of operations in order to formulate an activity; and, of course, interviews or reinterviews at this point are usually necessary to verify results.

The *composite* method contains features of the first two. Using the goals stated by management as a guide, the team formulates what they consider to be the activities of the organization. Then one or two major activities are selected for examination. At the conclusion of the investigation, the team prepares a goal statement and compares results to the original definition supplied by management. If the comparison reveals that the goals obtained in both ways are consistent, then it is assumed that the activities have been correctly defined.

The choice of the method used by the analysts is determined largely by how well the true goals are understood and can be stated early in the study, how much freedom the team has, and how far activity definition and scope departs from existing organization patterns. The *deductive* method is normally followed when restraints have been placed on the study team by management, or when goals and activities are well defined in the beginning; the *inductive* method is used where relatively few constraints are placed on the team, and there is considerable freedom of action, or where substantial data gathering is desirable before arriving at a definition. As a result, the deductive method is closely associated with studies leading to the mechanization of an existing system, while the inductive method is more appropriate when an original solution is required. The *composite* method is probably best applied when one or two activities of the business predominate.

7.4 ACTIVITY BOUNDARIES

In a discussion of activities, the question might be asked: "Why is an activity defined, and what is its usefulness in systems studies?" An activity is a set of related operations, usually self-contained and with few ties to the surrounding environment, and directed toward the fulfillment of one or more goals of the business. In most companies, there is often a duplication of effort and hence a duplication of activities. In addition, organizations are frequently structured along the lines of primary and secondary responsibilities with respect to activities. Therefore the above statements may appear too theoretical to the practical businessman. However, the principal reason for so defining activities is to be able to separate a business into manageable and relatively independent elements that can be easily understood, analyzed, and evaluated. A small business may be treated as an entity, but in larger concerns, size works against the analyst. In a very large company, he can quickly lose sight of the objectives he has set up for the study unless he constantly guards against this possibility. The recognition of functional patterns (for example, marketing, engineering, manufacturing, administration) does not always resolve the problem because organizational structuring sometimes conceals the true goals of a business.

The unified systems approach, based on goal-directed activities, focuses the attention of management and the study team on the true goals of a business. By this we mean that we can study a business through its activities, but we do not necessarily have to realign the organization into new or permanent patterns. However, the activity structure must be logical and understandable to management, who ultimately will have to make judgments and decisions in terms of activity alignments. Also, activities should not depart so far from conventional practice that management cannot easily relate activity costs back to established accounting practices.

In some cases, the business may already be organized into functions which closely parallel suitable activity groupings, and the team needs to make only minor realignments to produce a workable activity formulation. This situation occurred in a bank study where management had previously recognized the need for better controls, and was planning cost centers for functions such as commercial checking, special checking, installment loans, commercial loans, mortgage loans, savings, and personal trusts. Since the cost centers were already related to functions which serviced individual markets, and could be identified with particular goals of the business, they provided a basic activity definition for the study team. Furthermore, the bank's management had become accustomed to thinking in terms of the cost centers, and it required little reorientation for them to consider and appraise costs in terms of activities. Even though the cost center plan had not yet been fully implemented, the personnel of the bank were able to compile much of the activity cost data for the study team. As a result, the report of the present organization of the bank was completed well ahead of schedule.

Although activity formulation is performed during the study of the present business, the study team will have an opportunity to modify the preliminary results while determining the requirements of the new system. For example, in the Butodale Electronics case study, the first attempt to define activities produced the following results:

1. Prepare quotations and accept orders
2. Procure material
3. Manufacture general purpose analog computers
4. Provide other end items
5. Sell spare parts
6. Develop engineered products

Later, the team made some adjustments in this list and arrived at this set of activities:

1. Provide product demand
2. Provide material
3. Provide components
4. Provide end products
5. Provide engineered products and spare parts
6. Provide management, personnel, and facilities

The scope of the first activity, prepare quotations and accept orders, was increased to cover all demand up through communicating demand to the shop, rather than just the acceptance or orders and preparation of quotations. In others, a distinction was made between products which are essentially custom designed and ones which are considered "standard." The revised definition also resulted in a better balance in size among the various activities.

There will always be an element of trial and error in achieving activity balance, identity, and boundary. Experience has shown that several approximations are usually required before satisfactory results are obtained.

7.5   EXAMPLE OF ACTIVITY FORMULATION

Let us view some of the above points concerning activities within an organization by looking at a real organization. Because of the company's large size, the example we present is not representative of all situations encountered by systems analysts, but the various steps taken in formulating its activities are indicative of the kind of thinking and interpretation involved in this process.

The purpose of the study was to resolve duplications in function and organization, and to provide more effective overall control of operations. Briefly, the company's structure is shown in Figure 7-1, and in the following discussion we shall use the names in the bottom six boxes for simplicity of reference.

Initially, the analysts studied the parent and subsidiary organizations to see what could be set apart as self-contained activities, not closely interrelated with other activities. They soon found that Exploration and Production could be set apart because its responsibility ended when crude oil was supplied to Pipeline. However, its operation was interrelated with both Pipeline and Crude Oil Purchase and Sale. Pipeline exerted too great an influence on the company information system, since it served as the linkage between Exploration, Crude Oil, and Refining. In contrast to these interrelations, Petrochemical was found to be a highly independent business. Its only interrelationship with other organizations was the "purchase" of material from Refining (which it supplemented through its own purchasing department), so Petrochemical, with its own manufacturing and distribution departments, was set aside as a preliminary activity.

Formulation of activities from the standpoint of organization, therefore, yielded only one—Petrochemical. The next step was to consider other points of view:

1. Did any of the subsidiaries have self-contained functions?
2. Was the key to the definition of activities in product lines, markets, or services?

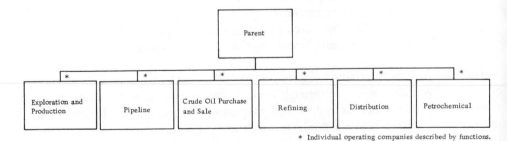

Figure 7-1   Structure of a large petroleum company used as an example of the formulation of activities.

3. How about activities defined by types of raw materials, or kinds of resources?
4. Was there a clue in corporate goals?

A study according to function and product seemed to be a reasonable approach for this company, since every concern that manufactures products uses materials and then processes them through a facility to manufacture the products.

The analysts discovered that Exploration, Pipeline, and Crude Oil were all concerned with providing material to the company; Refining was basically the manufacturing function that used the materials. Consequently, two more preliminary activities were established: (1) provide materials and (2) manufacture products.

Next, Distribution was studied and found to serve three different types of markets:

1. Internal combustion engine fuels (gasoline)
2. Accessories (mainly tires)
3. Heating fuels

Each market had decidedly different characteristics and required different marketing practices and organization. For this reason the analysts decided to establish three activities for Distribution to parallel these markets.

Finally, management and control functions of the parent company were assigned to an activity called "provide management."

Because this company represented a very large organization, the initial activity definition served primarily to identify each separate business unit. As a final step, activities were formulated for each newly defined business.

The outcome was the activity formulation shown in Figure 7-2. At the top of

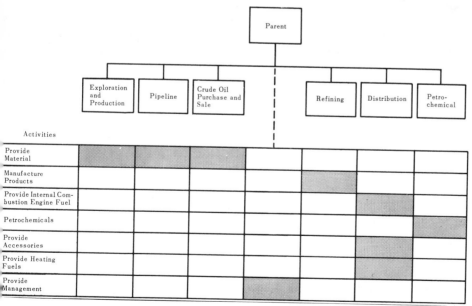

Figure 7-2   An example of activity formulation for a large petroleum company. The shaded areas show the activities carried on by the various parts of the total organization.

the diagram is the parent company with the six previously defined functional subsidiaries directly below. On the left are shown the seven activities defined by the analysts. The shaded areas under each function indicate the activities carried on by the functional unit. Thus, we see that the three left functional units all are engaged in the activity of providing materials. The parent unit provides the overall management activity. The activity of the refining unit is to manufacture products. The distribution unit is engaged in three activities: providing internal combustion engine fuel, providing accessories, and providing heating fuels. Finally, the petrochemical unit provides petrochemicals.

Activity charts, such as the one just discussed, form one of the foundations for understanding the present business structure and we shall say more about them and their use in exhibiting cost relationships.

7.6   ACTIVITY DATA

Even after activities are defined, the study team faces certain problems in gathering data about the activities. Although an analyst still must rely on interviews, file searches, and sampling or estimating to secure data, he may no longer have benchmarks to test against.

Consider, for example, the team assigned to study one or two activities with costs that can be greatly affected by the way one defines the operations. Suppose they have been directed to concentrate on these areas to the exclusion of any others. Further suppose that a single analyst has been assigned a single activity. As he moves through a department, he will find that some department costs apply to the activity he is investigating but others do not. He must, therefore, exercise great caution to insure the accuracy of his results.

The problem is further compounded by the fact that elapsed times are more significant to the study than process times; the flow and sequence of events is more meaningful than the occurrence of events; and operating costs are more revealing than costs usually found in general ledger accounts.

The special problems involved in gathering such operational data are explored in the following sections.

7.7   THE FORMS OF OPERATIONAL DATA

The framework of activities, as exemplified in Figure 7-2, describes the operating dynamics of an organization. Now we shall begin to explore the problem of obtaining and presenting data, including cost data, that will reveal the requirements of the system from an activities point of view.

One fact has emerged from the past twenty years, during which systems analysts have had their first major opportunities to design management systems in a computer age. This fact is that a true understanding of a system must be based on past, present, and future data about the organization. They have also discovered that this involves two related problems. The first problem is to identify and collect data. The second is to organize a reporting method that permits the collected data to be used effectively. We have already identified some of the problems and have indicated that we would go into greater detail. We shall do so in the following sections. We proceed by first presenting mainly abstract ideas to provide a theoretical background for the principles we wish to establish. These abstract ideas are followed by two chapters covering practical applications and case illustrations.

In their search the analysts have to obtain two kinds of data. First, they need to obtain the kind of data that reveals the activities carried on by the organization. Second, they must determine the cost of carrying on these activities. One might expect that there is a close relationship between the activities and their costs. Unfortunately, the relationship is not always simple to establish, and in the typical situation one must seek data in several ways.

The objective of the activity data is to show management what operations are being performed for each activity, whereas the objective of the cost data is to inform management on the cost of performing each activity. The overall forms of operational data therefore must include both kinds of information. Their combined purpose is to show the cost, time, flow, and sequence of the events that take place in an organization.

7.8 ALTERNATIVES IN DATA GATHERING

The study team has two principal alternatives in gathering data for the purpose of showing the cost, time, flow, and sequence of events. These alternatives relate closely to previous methods followed in activity formulation.

Under either alternative, a chart showing the organization divided into functional departments is first prepared and entered on a form similar to that shown in Figure 10-13. We call this form the resource usage sheet. Costs are then compiled by department in categories of personnel, machines and equipment, material, and miscellaneous, and recorded on the top band of this form.

Where few study restrictions have been specified, the team will probably begin with an examination of operations throughout the business (or in one or two major-impact activities, as the case may be) before activity definitions and boundaries are made final. After activities have been formulated, they are flowcharted, and the operational documentation is completed by estimating the costs of the activities (the inductive method of data collection).

On the other hand, in studies with more restrained objectives, such as in improvement or mechanization studies, or where management has stipulated the areas to be investigated and the steps to be followed, the costs of the separate activities can be estimated first. Then the activities can be flowcharted for sequence. Finally, operations can be documented as necessary to support study objectives. This second method just outlined would be the deductive method of data gathering.

The problems which arise in relation to analyzing costs, time, and sequence of events are much the same for both methods, and therefore are treated together over the remainder of the chapter.

7.9   COST SYSTEMS

In addition to the kinds of data we have already discussed as being important for the study of an organization, there are several types of useful cost summaries. These include:

1. Department or product line costs by personnel, equipment, and other categories.
2. Activity costs by these same categories.
3. Resource costs by operational usage.

Inasmuch as activity costs generally cut across conventional accounting classifications, a study team often runs into difficulties preparing cost estimates.

Each industry or field of endeavor (manufacturing, education, insurance, banking, government) has evolved its own accounting practices. Furthermore, there is considerable variation among businesses even within an industry. Before conducting cost studies, an analyst can save time and effort by consulting qualified financial personnel and learning about the special characteristics of the accounting system of the organization under consideration.

Figure 7-3 illustrates a typical manufacturing cost classification scheme. Such a classification is suitable for making departmental cost distributions, but data normally must be reclassified to produce costs by activities or product lines. Unit costs (the cost of a unit of production within a department) are relatively easy to compile under a direct costing system where all expenses are separated between fixed and variable costs. With the more prevalent allocation or burden cost systems, however, an analyst is faced with the problem of allocating expenses and overhead (or burden) to arrive at unit costs.

7.10   COMPILING ACTIVITY COSTS

Activity costs usually have to be compiled by indirect methods. During interviews, the analysts may find that some department heads and supervisors will respond to a direct question such as: "How much of your budget (or your effort, as the case may be) is involved in this specific activity?" If this question cannot be answered with a fairly precise estimate, the question can be rephrased to furnish further guidance in making an estimate: "How much effort or money would you save by eliminating this activity from your department?" Still another approach is to ask: "How much money or effort would it take for you to set up this activity as an independent operation?" Sometimes none of these approaches works, and the analyst and management must make the best estimates they can based on their knowledge of the business.

In a complete business study, estimates can be checked by comparing the total costs allocated to the defined activities with the total costs of the functional departments. In partial studies where only one or two activities are being investigated,

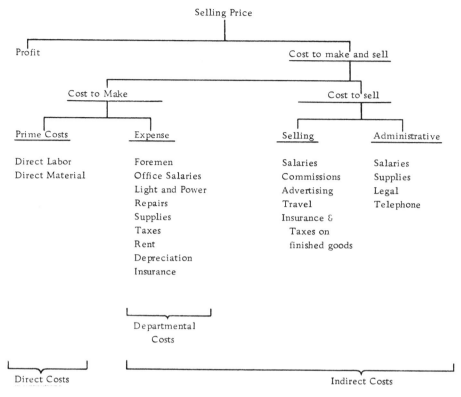

Figure 7-3 A typical cost system for a manufacturing organization, showing how costs may be classsified for accounting purposes.

the estimated costs allocated to activities should always be checked with the cost supervisor, or with other managers.

In one of our case studies, Butodale, the team initiated the activity cost allocation from a consolidated overhead statement. After they had obtained the labor and expense totals for each account (supplies, freight, taxes, wages) within each department, they successively interviewed department heads to determine what share of these accounts applied to each of the several activities. When the interviews were completed, they had sufficient information to show how the costs of the company could be presented both by 19 departmentalized functions and by six defined activities. The total distribution was then reconciled to the consolidated overhead statement. After some adjustments and further consultation with management, the two sets of figures were brought into agreement. This kind of adjustment is normally required at this point in the study.

7.11 PRODUCT OR UNIT COSTS

In some situations, the analysts may find it useful to determine the cost of producing a given product, either as a whole or per unit. However, many companies do not establish product cost accounts and do not publish reports by product lines. Such information is usually confidential, and in any case it requires increased accounting expense to prepare and maintain such information.

The experience of one study team illustrates how product costs may be developed where records by this category do not exist. Working in a manufacturing business ($56 million annual sales), a four-man team was investigating marketing and engineering functions for several selected product lines representing roughly 15 percent of the total sales volume. Since management was very specific in stating the objectives and scope of the study, the team employed the deductive method for estimating costs. The company had little reliable information on costs by product lines. Instead of just guessing at the costs, a method that compelling circumstances sometimes force on the analysts, the team carefully selected a representative month and studied the flow of all orders and inquiries from the time they were received in sales offices until they reached a manufacturing schedule. This method entailed searches of order files in the engineering, marketing, and cost departments. Average unit costs were supplied by the accountants. Then the team assigned overhead costs to these direct engineering and labor costs. After extending the sample to an annual basis, they compared the totals based on the sample with the total sales figures obtained from the marketing department. Some adjustments were needed but they were minor, and both the analysts and management agreed that the cost estimates for the products were sound.

7.12   RESOURCE COSTS

As indicated earlier, resources are defined as physical elements used in performing various operations. They include items such as files, machine tools, data processing and communications equipment, and personnel. Dividing the costs of these resources among operations and activities is made difficult by the characteristics of most cost accounting systems. However, as a guide, data processing facilities can be allocated to each activity according to the amount or percent of time the facilities are used for the activity. Personnel expense can be distributed by multiplying the number of people in a department by the proportion of time they work on the activity and, then, by an average wage for the labor class. Files expense can be apportioned roughly by assigning first-cost and upkeep charges to the section requiring their maintenance. In general, the method must be tempered by weighing the costs of obtaining data by alternative methods against the desired levels of accuracy. Results should always be checked for reasonableness.

7.13   ESTIMATING ELAPSED TIME

An important feature of any management system is the time it takes to perform any given operation and the time that items stand in a line or queue waiting to be serviced. These two kinds of time data provide a measure of the dynamics of the system. Moreover, analysts often must use estimates of time to obtain estimates of cost. Consequently, we shall discuss the problem of estimating time data.

Time data should normally be collected by sampling and analysis rather than by interviews. The main reason is that people are not as accurate with time estimates as they are with costs. When recalling time in relation to events, most people remember the difficult, time-consuming situations or the exceptionally easy and fast ones, but rarely can they identify the average. For this reason, analysts usually find it necessary to personally estimate the time required to perform each operation and the time that elapses between operations. Let us first consider elapsed time.

The time that items wait to be operated upon should be recorded within operations and also summarized for the entire activity. Within operations, this elapsed time is defined as the time between the occurrence of successive inputs, or the time between the arrival of the first input and the availability of an output. Elapsed time is influenced by many factors: volume of transactions, day of the month (banking), month of the year (retailing), and the like. Therefore, data should always be gathered for the peak as well as for the average situation.

Where good time data is not available, sampling methods should be considered. For example, a batch of papers can be time-stamped at successive processing stations as they are being sent out. Stamping documents *after* people have worked on them avoids the implication that the person is being studied by time-and-motion methods. This is important in sampling; people must not feel *they* are being studied rather than their work. Time relationships can also be reconstructed from file data, correspondence, memos, and other information which fixes time directly or indirectly. Mailroom personnel can also be used to record time. In sampling, peaks can be determined by conducting tests during periods when the peak is most likely to occur.

An example of recording elapsed time on a documentation form is demonstrated in Figure 7-4. The forms in the figure are only parts of larger forms that we have found convenient for recording the data and revealing its main features.

In conjunction with his study of Figure 7-4, the reader may turn also to Figures 10-14 and 10-15, which are actual forms completed for the Butodale case study.

In Figure 7-4 we begin with T_1 (the code for "trigger 1"), in the lower left corner of the figure. This trigger is the receipt of I_1 (the code for "input 1"), which is a quote folder. We can thus see that the operation begins when a "quote folder" arrives at someone's desk, which we shall assume is the desk of the supervisor of the operation. (A quote folder is an ordinary manila file folder containing a request from a customer for a bid on some product he wishes to purchase from some company, possibly Butodale.) Here the operation is indicated by the shaded part of the arrow and is called "Assign to Design Group." When the quote folder arrives at his desk, the supervisor may not have the time to look it over immediately. Therefore time begins to pass as the folder waits for service. Eventually, the supervisor examines the folder. To the left of lower center of the figure containing the operations, we see two codes, P_2 and P_3. P_2 is the code for "process 2" and P_3 is the code for "process 3." There is, of course, a first process, and also there may be several other processes, but these are of no particular interest to us here.

It is clear from the entries after P_2 and P_3 that the supervisor must determine which group or groups in the design part of the engineering services department should be given the folder in order to complete the bid. We also see that the third

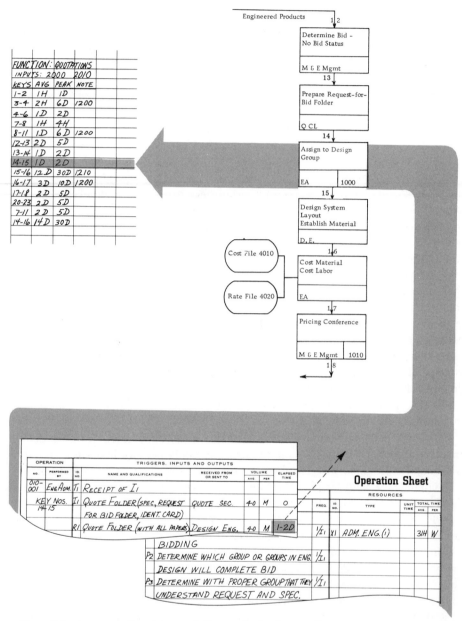

Figure 7-4 A composite picture of the method of recording an operation, showing its place within an activity and then recording its elapsed time on a summary grid of all the elapsed times of an activity.

process the supervisor performs is to determine that the group to whom he gives the folder understands the request and the specifications in the customer request. Now, for all of the waiting and actual work done by the supervisor, we see in the elapsed time box of the form that one or two days have elapsed from the time the quote folder is received from the quotation section until the time the supervisor gives it to the design engineering group.

This elapsed-time figure is shown as applying to the "Assign to Design Group" operation. In this part of the figure it is assumed that the input is received at point 14 (in the vertical flow) and that the output is delivered at point 15. If we follow the arrow to the left, we see the same data in the grid. There the keys, 14-15, refer to the corresponding points on the flowchart on the right. We also see that the analysts have recorded that it usually takes one day for the supervisor to complete the assignment operation, but that during peak periods the normal time is two days.

There are a few other points of interest in Figure 7-4 which we can examine. First, we can see in the operation sheet that the average volume of customer quotation requests is 40 per month. This figure will be useful to the analysts both for estimating the cost of operations for this activity (which is the "provide product demand" activity of Butodale) and also for the second and third phases of the study when the requirements of the system are determined and the new system designed.

A second point of interest is that the resource used (X_1 is a code we use for the first resource) is engineering administration, also called engineering services. The total time required by this resource is shown as 31 hours per week.

A final point of interest is not directly related to this operation but to the "cost material and cost labor" operation at point 16 in the flow. What we wish to point out here is that this operation draws upon two information resources—the cost file and the rate file.

Now that we have reviewed the concept of elapsed time and its recording, let us consider the recording of the amount of time that resources are used.

As we have already stated, analysts frequently have to use unit and total resource usage time as a basis for determining resource costs. To estimate the amount of time it takes each person in the organization to do one particular operation in transforming inputs into an output, the analysts often can use preliminary data from supervisory interviews. Such data can be verified by comparing them to the total man-hours available for the selected period. When it comes to estimating the usage of nonhuman resources (such as machines, equipment, and information records), the amount of time they are used for each operation in an activity is probably best calculated by sampling or estimating. One method is to find the length of time a resource is actually used in the operation, then extend it by operation volume and frequency over a time period. For example, in the process of selecting a vendor from a stock record file, an average look-up and selection may require ten minutes. At 100 orders a week, the resource usage time of the file becomes 1000 minutes per week, which may be recorded as 17 hours per week.

After the analysts have obtained the resource usage data, they should have some convenient form on which to record the information. We have found that a simple table is best. An example is found in Figure 7-5. The reader's attention is directed to the headings: Inputs, Outputs, and File Usage. We shall explain one entry under each heading to clarify the meaning of the information.

Consider the first item under Inputs. The key, 2000, is the analyst's code to refer to the input called "quote request." We see that this input is received from customers at the rate of about 50 per week during 46 weeks per year and at the rate of 70 per week for four weeks during the year. Under Outputs we see that about

Activity Name

FUNCTION : QUOTATIONS

INPUTS : 2000, 2010

KEYS	AVG	PEAK	NOTE
1-2	1H	1D	
3-4	2H	6D	1200
4-6	1D	2D	
7-8	1H	4H	
8-11	1D	6D	1200
12-13	2D	5D	
13-14	1D	2D	
14-15	1D	2D	
15-16	12D	30D	1210
16-17	3D	10D	1200
17-18	2D	5D	
20-23	2D	5D	
7-11	2D	5D	
14-16	14D	30D	
23-25	14-D	90-D	-MAX
		20-D	-MIN

FUNCTION : ORDERS

INPUTS : 2020

KEYS	AVG	PEAK	NOTE
25-28	4D	10D	
28-29	2D	4D	
29-31	1D	3D	
25-31	7D	20D	1220

INPUTS

KEY	NAME	SOURCE	AVG VOLUME	PEAK VOLUME	NOTE
2000	QUOTE REQUEST	CUST	50/W	70/W	1020
	FREQUENCY		46 W/YR	4 W/YR	1030
2010	BID REQUEST	CUST	10/W	12/W	
	FREQUENCY		42 W/YR	10 W/YR	1040
2020	ORDER	CUST	16/W	20/W	1030
	FREQUENCY		44 W/YR	6 W/YR	

OUTPUTS

KEY	NAME	DEST	AVG VOLUME	PEAK VOLUME	NOTE
3000	QUOTATN	CUST	15/W	20/W	1030
	FREQUENCY		40 W/YR	10 W/YR	
3050	ACKNOW	CUST	16/W	—	1050

FILE USAGE

KEY	NAME	MSGS AVG	MSGS PEAK	ACCESS	USAGE TIME	NOTE
4000	PRICING	240K	300K	RANDM	8H/D	1100
4010	COST	1,000K	—	RANDM	—	1110
4020	RATE	2500	2800	RANDM	8H/D	
4030	INSTALLED SYSTEMS	400K	—	RANDM	4H/D	1120
4050	CONTRACT REGISTER	1500	2100	SEQ	8H/D	1130
4060	CUSTOMER INDEX	4000	5500	SEQ	2H/D	
4070	PROJECT INDEX	1500	2100	SEQ	1H/D	
4080	ASSIGN'T SHEET	20	80	RANDM	10H/D	1140

NOTES
1100 – PRICING FILE IS USED IN BOTH END ITEM AND SYSTEMS QUOTATIONS.
1110 – COST FILE IS PRESENTLY MAINTAINED IN 3 DIFFERENT AREAS. NO CARDS HAVE YET BEEN DISCARDED.
1120 – INSTALLED SYSTEMS FILE HAS NOT YET BEEN PURGED.
1130 – CONTRACT REGISTER IS MASTER OPEN CUSTOMER ORDER FILE. WHEN ORDERS ARE COMPLETED, THE RECORDS ARE MOVED TO THE INSTALLED SYSTEMS FILE.
1140 – MUST BE AVAILABLE FOR SECOND SHIFT.
1200 – WIDE VARIATION DUE TO SYSTEM VARIATION. THERE IS NO SUCH THING, STRICTLY, AS "STD SYSTEM"
1210 – MULTIPLE DESIGN "PASSES" (SEE NOTE 1000)
1220 – TIME ALLOWED BY CUSTOMERS TO ACKNOWLEDGE ORDER VARIES FROM 1D TO MAX. OF 30D.

NOTES
1020 – BREAKDOWN OF REQUESTS FOR QUOTATION:

	STD SYSTEMS	207-217	OTHER	STD END ITM	PLOTTER	OTHER
AVG	36/W	32/W	4/W	14/W	10/W	4/W
PEAK	51/W	40/W	11/W	19/W	14/W	5/W

1030 – PLANT CLOSES DOWN FOR 2 WEEKS EACH YEAR, SO THERE ARE 50 WEEKS/YR FOR THIS INPUT. PEAKS OCCUR JUST BEFORE AND JUST AFTER THE 2-WEEK CLOSED PERIOD.
1040 – ENGINEERING DOES NOT CLOSE DOWN ALONG WITH THE PLANT, SO THIS INPUT OCCURS 52 WEEKS PER YEAR. PEAKS OCCUR AT BEGINNING OF EACH FISCAL QUARTER.
1050 – ESSENTIALLY NO PEAKS IN THIS OUTPUT.

Figure 7-5 Operation times and resource volumes and times for the "provide product demand" activity.

15 quotations a week are sent to customers for 40 weeks per year and 20 are sent for 10 weeks during the year. The last item concerns the information resource—files and records. The first entry under File Usage reveals that there are 240,000 pricing records in the file during normal periods, but that this rises to 300,000 records in peak periods. We see that the user can arrive at the particular price record he wants by using a random access method (that is, his search is much like finding a word in a dictionary.) Finally we see that the personnel use this resource for eight hours per day.

These summary data are combined with the time required for operations and the elapsed time between operations to aid the analyst in arriving at the cost figures for the activity. There is such a variety of methods for making these final estimates that no single form can be prescribed. The main necessity is that the analysts indicate clearly the method they used in making the estimates.

In this discussion of time data, we mentioned data volumes and frequencies. Let us next consider these ideas a little more fully.

7.14   VOLUME AND FREQUENCY DATA

Most management systems are characterized by an uneven combination of events and operations. For example, we just mentioned the activity that was triggered by the arrival of a customer's request for a quotation. We noted that the trigger was operated 50 times a week during a normal week and 70 times a week during a peak week.

To obtain such input and output volumes and fluctuations above and below averages, an analyst must search the organization's records for these events over representative periods. But this historical approach has a disadvantage: it produces flat distributions when representative time periods are extended over the entire year (for example, average vouchers per week, shipments for August, orders received for one year), although this defect can be compensated for by pinpointing peaks and studying them individually (in a bank, for example, check-processing peaks occur on the day that factory and office payrolls are distributed). Another disadvantage to the historical approach is that the kinds of records the analyst would like to use often do not exist, or are unsatisfactory. Consequently, when historical records are not productive, the analyst must conduct running tests of inputs and the outputs created by the inputs.

Volume information, of course, is not meaningful unless related to frequency of occurrence. Noting that the average volume is 300 orders per day and peak volume 400 per day gives no idea of how significant the order peak is; if it occurs twice a week or lasts for three months, the peak obviously has greater impact than if it occurs only two days a year.

Clues on peaking times of cyclical and seasonal data are best obtained from people who are familiar with the business. In various parts of a study, an analyst should ask supervisors questions such as: What are customer invoicing days in a billing routine? Are most withdrawals from stock or inventory made during certain hours of the day? In accounting, what is the cutoff day for monthly inter-department transfers?

Now that we have discussed cost, time, and volume data, we next consider the flow of operations within an activity.

7.15   THE FLOW OF OPERATIONS

A powerful tool that analysts should use in presenting management with a clear idea of the operations that are part of an activity, and the sequence in which the operations are performed, is the flowchart. The typical flowchart begins with an indication of a trigger that starts the activity, traces the operations that the trigger activates, incorporates references to important information resources used in particular operations, and ends with an indication of the output from the activity.

In practice, analysts have found it particularly useful to affix the flowchart to the tables showing elapsed times and volumes. This arrangement permits management to have a composite picture of each operation, the time required for it, and the volume of documents involved in the operation.

Examples of flowcharts are included in the following chapter; we also explain the set of documents which are convenient for recording the information related to each activity in the study. Flowcharts are also discussed in Chapter 12 where narrative, decision table, and flowchart methods are compared.

SUMMARY

Formulation of activities is important and requires consideration of business goals, objectives, and purpose. Three types of activity formulation methods are deductive, inductive, and composite. An activity is a set of related operations. The degree of difficulty in determining activity boundaries is related to the functional structure of the organization being studied. An activity sheet is a useful tool for expressing activity relationships to the organization. Gathering cost data about each activity can be difficult, and care must be exercised so that costs are correctly allocated to each activity. A resource usage sheet shows the organization divided into its functional departments. The cost of each of the functions is determined as a step in grouping costs by activity. Useful cost data includes department or product line cost, other activity costs, and resource costs by operation. In studying a system, it is important to determine the time required to perform an operation, and the time that the items stand in line waiting to be serviced. Peak periods must be recognized and volumes recorded for such periods. A flowchart is a powerful tool for presenting the relationship among the operations of an activity.

CHAPTER

Documentation for the Study of an Existing System

8.1 INTRODUCTION

As already mentioned, we envision three phases in designing a system (1) understanding the existing system, (2) determining the true requirements of the system, and (3) designing and describing a new system to fulfill these requirements.

In the first phase, the aim of the methods man, systems engineer—whoever is observing and analyzing the system—is to understand what the business or system does, and to a degree *how* it is done, in terms of activities that thread through the business. In the second phase, the observer analyzes what is logically necessary (or, alternatively, what is specified as necessary by the controlling management) to accomplish the goals of the specific activity under study. In the third phase, a system which can meet those requirements is designed and then described.

The specific aim of this present chapter is to demonstrate a set of recording forms that can be used for documenting the first phase—understanding the existing system. Other forms will be discussed in conjunction with the phase in which they are used.

The documents and forms, together with the rules for filling them out, are in effect a language for describing systems. They are useful for full-scale systems studies in depth, and it is for this purpose that they were developed. But they are equally useful for quick short-term surveys of existing systems, for system analyses, for describing new systems, or for case studies of advanced applications.

The recording forms and the techniques for using them work together. They provide a clear, formal description of what is involved in a system or an application. The fields in the various descriptive forms guide the observer in making a logical review of existing practices and procedures.

These documents substantially ease the problem of communicating the characteristics of a system or installation. If the forms are completed as prescribed, anyone familiar with this book can read them and quickly determine what the system does, as a preliminary step to further study, whether his purpose is to make improvements or modifications. Moreover, the use of these documentation techniques prepares the analyst for their further use in making system studies in depth.

The level of detail to which a system—existing or planned—is studied is a major variable at the discretion of the user of these techniques. This book covers the full use of all forms, but this level of detail is often not necessary nor indeed desirable. The observer should go only as deep as is required to do the job at hand.

The techniques and forms discussed in this text have been tested by use in systems studies of a number of diverse businesses. These techniques are of course not a final answer to the problem of describing the characteristics of a business system. However, they have proved valuable and workable, and they do guide the analyst to a logical study of system characteristics. They are perforce general in approach, and in specific instances there may be tailored-to-order techniques that are more powerful or more descriptive for a particular problem or solution. For example, certain computer-room procedures may be more efficiently described by a symbolic flowchart (with narrative description giving volumes and flow rates), and supported by record and report layouts. In the event that a specific technique has proved successful in a particular area, it should be used. The reader may design any forms he desires. It is the content that is relevant, and with the amount of data collected during a study, the typical systems analyst must use some kind of systematic collection and recording mechanism. The forms are like a road map for the analyst. They are the framework and structure for the study of a business in a *disciplined* manner.

8.2 FIVE BASIC DOCUMENTS

The desire to examine an existing business, activity, or system usually arises from some other requirement. Generally, the basic purpose of a survey is to determine quickly what is done, from what source, with what resources, to achieve what results.

More specific purposes include the need to understand how a system or activity fits into a larger organization, that is, into its environment. A coherent description of present operations is needed as a basis for further analysis of how an existing system meets present or projected demands. Quick surveys can also determine exact costs of personnel, machines and equipment, material, and facilities; they can provide a clear picture of overall efficiency in terms of elapsed times in a sequence of operations, unit operations times, and operating volumes.

A system survey seeks only the information needed to provide understanding of the system or activity for its particular purpose. Its aim is to show how men and equipment, using such resources as buildings, inventories, materials, information, and files, respond to inputs to produce outputs and results.

Documentation forms for describing a system must be easy to use if they are to be valuable for surveys. They should also be logically organized, and clearly segregate and identify the key information needed for understanding an existing system in operation.

Let us consider the five main purposes that the documentation of an existing organization must serve: (1) to find the cost of using resources for activities, (2) the description of activities, (3) the description of operations, (4) the description of input and output documents, and (5) the description of records and files. The five documents we shall describe in this chapter were developed in an effort to satisfy these purposes. For convenient reference we identify them to correspond to the above five purposes: (1) resource usage sheet, (2) activity sheet, (3) operation sheet, (4) message sheet, and (5) file sheet.

The relationship among these forms is illustrated in Figure 8-1. The organizational structure comprising an activity, and a cost analysis of the activity, appears on the resource usage sheet. The flow of the activity itself is displayed on the activity sheet.

The arrow in Figure 8-1 connecting the activity sheet and the resource usage sheet represents two kinds of relationships, one direct and one indirect. The direct relationship is that the activity sheet shows the pattern of operations for a given activity, and the arrow points to the major row of the resource usage sheet showing

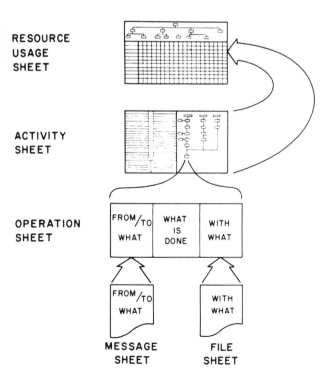

RESOURCE USAGE SHEET

ACTIVITY SHEET

OPERATION SHEET

| FROM/TO WHAT | WHAT IS DONE | WITH WHAT |

| FROM/TO WHAT | | WITH WHAT |

MESSAGE SHEET   **FILE SHEET**

Figure 8-1   Relationship among the five basic documents used in studying an existing organization.

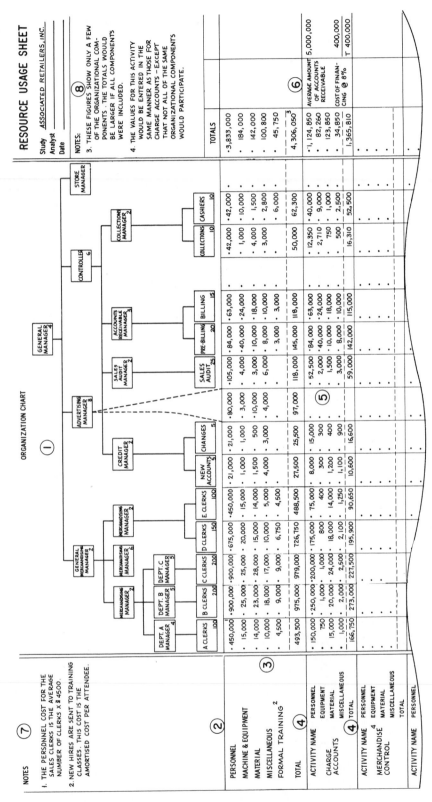

Figure 8-2 A portion of the resource usage sheet from the Associated Retailers company used as an example. The key notes from 1 to 8 are explained in Section 8.3.

the overall cost structure for the activity as a whole. The indirect relationship is that the analysts may have used some of the volume and time data from the activity sheet to assist in estimating costs shown on the resource usage sheet.

Operations within each activity are further described on the operation sheets, with details on information inputs and outputs (from or toward which the operation works) and information resources (with what the operation works) provided on message and file sheets. These forms permit the analyst to describe the activity in motion; they reveal the flow of incoming materials or information through the internal workings of the system to output products, services, or information.

The resource usage sheet fits each system under study into its larger context. It shows the organization and structure of the business environment. It also provides a rapid analysis of costs for the organizational components being surveyed and shows the cost impact for each activity or system.

The activity sheet traces the flow of a single activity, breaking it down into its major operations. Each activity sheet presents as large a group of related operations as can be handled conveniently. It includes a flow diagram of the activity with individual blocks representing various operations (each of which can be more minutely described on operation sheets). Key characteristics such as volume and time can be recorded in tabular form.

The resource usage sheet and the activity sheet work together to provide a quick look at a business system. In order to obtain a closer look at the operation of a system, the observer may use forms that permit a more detailed documentation. These are the operation sheet and the message and file sheets.

There can be an operation sheet for each block on the activity sheet. It is used for recording the related processing steps that form a logical operation. It describes what is done, with what resources, under what conditions, and how often, to produce what specific results. Its primary purpose is to show the relationships between inputs, processes, resources, and outputs.

The message sheet is one of two forms that support the operation sheet. It describes the inputs and outputs—in effect, to whatever level of detail the management and the analysts desire, from what source or toward what result an operation is working.

The file sheet describes a collection of records, an information file; it is the second of the two forms supporting the operation sheet, and shows with what information the operation works.

These five forms are useful for providing a coherent description of a system. Moreover, they can be used at several levels of detail. The resource usage and activity sheets together display the dynamic mechanism of an activity; together with the operation sheet they provide a fairly detailed operational view. The operation sheet by itself permits a look at critical operations and, when it is supported by the message and file sheets, provides a closeup of information used in or produced by such operations. Message and file sheets by themselves permit observation and analysis of information inputs, outputs and resources, with again a variable level of detail as desired by the analyst.

When describing what is done (on the operation sheet, in the field reserved for process description and qualifications), the observer can choose from several levels of detail by exercising a choice of descriptive verbs. Such verbs as *prepare, re-*

produce, update are descriptive of processes at one level of detail. The language of a computer compiler, such as Cobol, PL/I, or Fortran is an example of a far more detailed language.

The amount of detail to be entered on these forms is somewhat discretionary, and depends on what level of understanding is needed as well as on the time allotted for the survey. Information can be omitted; the observer can single out critical operations from the activity sheet and avoid making up operation sheets for every operation. Short-cut methods can be used for entering information. Many of the fields on the message sheet can be left blank, since a sample of the completed message form is customarily attached. Qualification of content may not be needed on the file sheet, nor even the description of content. However, analysts should avoid the trap of assuming they can remember all details. Systems built on memory often collapse with disastrous results.

Now we shall present the technical details of each of the five documents, and show two examples of their use—one in a nonmechanized system and the other in a mechanized system.

8.3   RESOURCE USAGE SHEET

The purpose of the resource usage sheet is to present, on a single page, the organizational framework and cost analysis of that segment of the business into which the activity under study fits. It is filled in at two points in the first phase: the organization chart and overall costs are prepared at the beginning of the study, and the activity cost figures, which emerge only during the study, are recorded in the latter part of the study.

For specific reference, we have taken a partially filled-in sheet from an actual study, Associated Retailers, Inc. It is shown in Figure 8-2. On this form we have written encircled key numbers ranging from 1 to 8. For each of the keys we have an explanation of the concept or feature the reader should know in order to understand the form and its contents.

Notes for the key numbers on the resource usage sheet in Figure 8-2

1. The structural organization is shown in an organization chart. This chart can be constructed from a company organization table or chart, or it can be developed from interviews. The area allotted dictates a 3- to 5-level chart. Organizational components of the bottom level are aligned over the vertical cost columns. Hierarchic equivalence of the bottom-tier boxes is valuable but not necessary; if a group of units have little effect on the activity, they can be lumped together on the next higher management level shown. Where it is necessary but topologically difficult to associate higher tier units with a cost column, we draw two dotted lines from the box to the sidelines of the column. Where possible, the command lines of the organization structure should be traced back until they join in a single management box. In Figure 8-2 the organization chart is not complete.

2. The first horizontal band under the organization chart is used to enter inclusive resource costs, summing the costs for each department that affects the

activity or activities being studied. There should be a cost tabulation for every box in the bottom tier of this part of the chart. The figures can be historical costs, budgeted cost for the current year, or management estimates. Personnel costs should represent all salaries (including that of the head of the department) and direct fringe benefits. Machine and equipment costs include total annual machine rentals except where machines or equipment are purchased; in this case an annual cost is computed by amortizing or using approved write-off procedures. If machines are both purchased and rented, the sum of both costs must be developed. Material costs include annual expenditures for office supplies such as forms, paper, and punched cards.

3. The miscellaneous classification allows for unusual and significant costs not otherwise classified. These include personnel training, money costs in a financial enterprise, warehousing costs in a wholesaling organization, and overhead costs if significant and available. Totals in each box are the sum of these inclusive resource costs.

4. In the other horizontal bands, below the inclusive summaries, are entered activity resource costs for each activity under scrutiny, which are developed during the study. The definitions of the entries are the same. The values reflect only that portion which applies to the activity named in the identifying box at the left. For example, in Figure 8-2, all the equipment and material costs of the billing and prebilling departments result from the charge account activity, and are so entered; 38 percent of the total costs of the new accounts department are ascribable to charge accounts, resulting in an entry of $10,600 in that column. The $10,600 is increased from $10,450 for adjustment purposes.

5. Costs are not entered for organizational components that have nothing to do with the activity, as is the case for the advertising manager.

6. Two unlabeled columns at the far right are used for miscellaneous items, and for costs which are difficult to classify or not assignable to organizational units. The first of these columns identifies the item and the second displays the best cost figure available. These entries may fall into the top cost band (for inclusive or departmental summary figures) or into activity bands. Costs of inventories, including raw materials, in-process goods, or finished goods; costs of money, including collection costs and bad debts; costs of accounts receivable —these are among the items to be listed in these columns.

   Totals are developed horizontally for the inclusive departmental costs and the various activity costs. Miscellaneous items in the special columns on the right are summed into the grand totals. If all activities involving the departments in the bottom tier of the organization chart are presented on the activity cost breakdowns, the sum of the activity totals should be the inclusive departmental total.

7,8. Notes may be written in either the upper left or upper right corners of the resource usage sheet.

8.4 MESSAGE SHEET

A message may be defined as any communication of information—a formal document, informal letter, or oral statement. A message sheet is a form that has been designed as a convenient document on which analysts can record the key information of a message, whether it is an input or an output. Thus, entries in the various fields of a message sheet describe and define the characteristics of the input

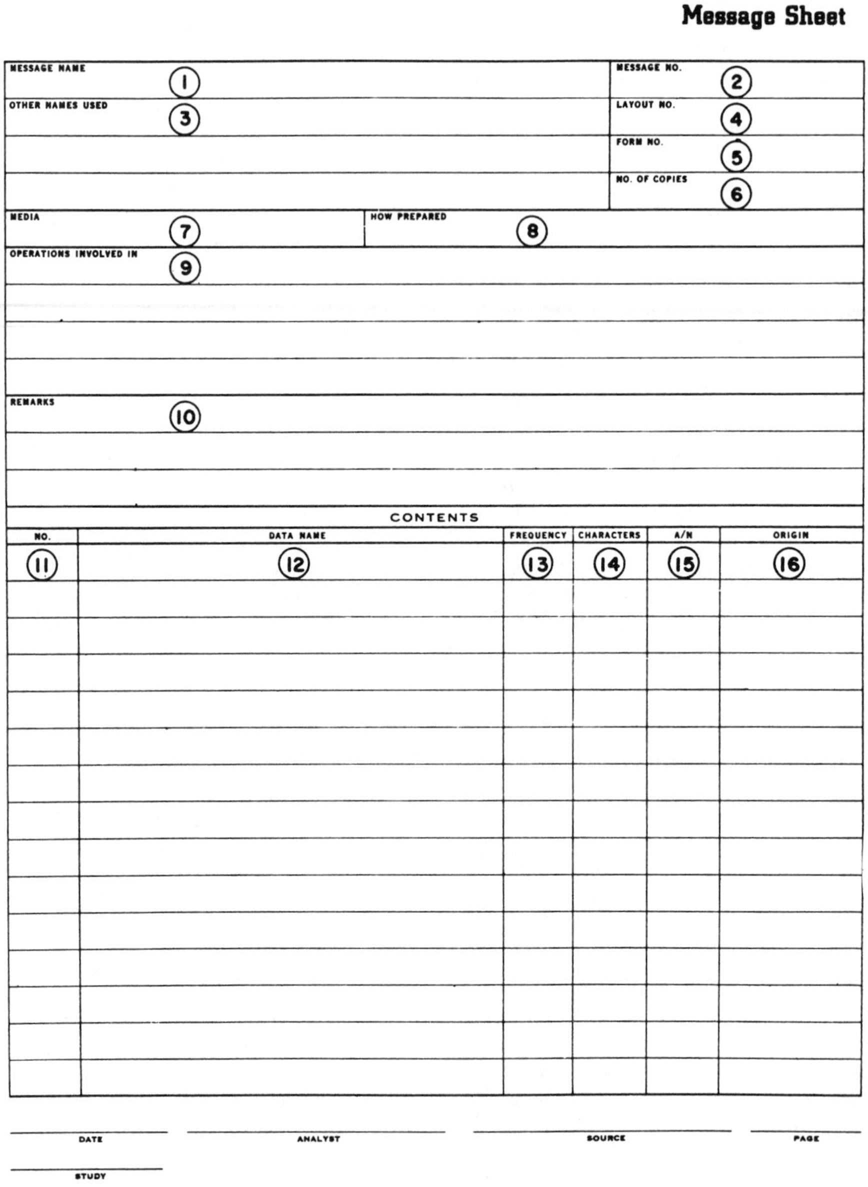

Message Sheet

MESSAGE NAME ①		MESSAGE NO. ②
OTHER NAMES USED ③		LAYOUT NO. ④
		FORM NO. ⑤
		NO. OF COPIES ⑥
MEDIA ⑦	HOW PREPARED ⑧	
OPERATIONS INVOLVED IN ⑨		
REMARKS ⑩		

CONTENTS

NO. ⑪	DATA NAME ⑫	FREQUENCY ⑬	CHARACTERS ⑭	A/N ⑮	ORIGIN ⑯

DATE _____   ANALYST _____   SOURCE _____   PAGE _____

STUDY _____

Figure 8-3   A blank message sheet. The 16 key numbers are explained in Section 8.4.

or the output conveyed by the message. There usually are a large number of message sheets for a study. Also, as indicated in Figure 8-1, the analysts use the message sheets in the preparation of operation sheets.

Figure 8-3 is a general example of a blank message sheet developed for the above purposes. In it are 16 key numbers that have been encircled for ease in studying the form. Immediately following are the explanations of these key points.

It is usually advantageous to attach a sample copy of the business form described in the message, preferably filled in with sample data.

Notes for the key numbers on the message sheet in Figure 8-3

1. MESSAGE NAME   This is a unique name for the message.

2. MESSAGE NO.   This is the unique identifying number for the message, with prefix indicating message type (R for report and S for signal) and suffix numerals indicating copies. Thus, the designation R 131.3 identifies the third copy of message 131.

3. OTHER NAMES USED   Frequently used alternate names and synonyms are listed.

4. LAYOUT NO.   Layout is the physical format of a message: each format is identified by a layout number. The layout is independent of both the messages using the format and the data within the format. Several message types may use the same layout number, with the fields differently interpreted on each. Layout defines physical locations of fields and field characteristics, permitting relatively flexible form design for a series of messages having the same layout number.

5. FORM NO.   This number is assigned to identify the message form; it is usually printed on the form.

6. NO. OF COPIES   This figure includes both the number of copies prepared with the original and the number of copies later reproduced.

7. MEDIA   This entry displays the media employed in original and later reproduction.

8. HOW PREPARED   This pertains to reports, and describes the means by which basic fields are entered on the original message (by hand, typewritten, card-punched, and so on).

9. OPERATIONS INVOLVED IN   This is the identifying number of each operation using the message as input or output.

10. REMARKS   Enter here all supplemental data on message definition or handling (security, access, and so forth).

11. NO.   The identifying number of the data element can be any number; usually 01 to 99 are used. The message number and this number uniquely identify the data element for later reference.

12. DATA NAME   This is the title for the data element.

13. FREQUENCY   Three types of entries appear here. If the data does not appear on every message carrying this message number, the frequency of appearance is entered as a decimal fraction. If the data appear once on each message, the entry is 1; if more than once, the number of appearances, or the possible range and average, is entered. Whenever a range is entered, the average should also be noted.

14. CHARACTERS   This field shows the maximum number of characters in the data element.

15. A/N   Enter A for alphabetic, N for numeric, and AN for alphameric (including special symbols).

16.   ORIGIN   Enter the operation number for the operation that either initially accepts the data element into the system, or originates the data. Operations that merely post the data to the message are not entered.

8.5   FILE SHEET

The file sheet is used to display the detail concerning information resources, such as cost records, price records, and rate records. Normally, there are many file sheets for each study. It is generally helpful to management and to the analysts themselves if examples of actual records from each file are attached to the file sheets. The analysts use the collection of file sheets (together with the message sheets) to complete the operation sheets.

Figure 8-4 contains an example of a blank file sheet. In the figure are 18 key numbers which refer to the notes immediately following.

Notes for the key numbers on the file sheet in Figure 8-4

1.   FILE NAME   There is a unique name for each file.

2.   FILE NO.   There is also a unique number for the file, with prefix F and suffixes indicating copies. The designations F 131.2 and F 131.4.2 identify copies 2 and 4 of file 131; copy 4 is located at a site "2" remote from the main file.

3.   LOCATION   The name or number is given for the organization housing the file (or portion of the file) and the physical location if pertinent.

4.   STORAGE MEDIUM   This is the type of housing for the file, such as tub file, tape storage cabinet, three-ring binder, etc. This entry is indirectly related to the medium of the information itself.

5.   ACCESS REQUIREMENTS   Several types of information appear here: who is or is not permitted access to the file, classified by job titles or by such entries as "Military—Top Secret" or "Company Confidential"; the availability of the file, in terms of what hours and how long the file is open daily; and access characteristics, including how often and how quickly reference must be made.

6.   SEQUENCED BY   File sequence keys are described in this field. File sequence is described by minor key *within* intermediate keys *within* major key. A file of open purchase orders might, for example, be sequenced by transaction date within purchase order number within part number. Sequence keys are sometimes not contained in the messages themselves, yet must be described in this field. In the case of the purchase orders, transaction date might be missing from the messages; new transactions would be filed in back of existing transactions within the purchase order number and part number sequences.

7.   CONTENT QUALIFICATIONS   Details are displayed on file contents if file name is not sufficiently descriptive. A file named "Purchase Order File" might, for example, be qualified as "purchase orders for vendors within 25 miles."

8.   HOW CURRENT   This gives the age of transactions when entered in the file.

9.   RETENTION CHARACTERISTICS   Removal rules for each type of message in the file are entered here.

10.   LABELS   These identify the file, carrying a code or phrase, such as "Master Payroll" to uniquely establish the file identity. Other information, such as date,

File Sheet

FILE NAME ①				FILE NO. ②		
LOCATION ③		STORAGE MEDIUM ④				
ACCESS REQUIREMENTS ⑤						
SEQUENCED BY ⑥						
CONTENT QUALIFICATIONS ⑦						
HOW CURRENT ⑧						
RETENTION CHARACTERISTICS ⑨						
LABELS ⑩						
REMARKS ⑪						

CONTENTS

SEQUENCE NO.	MESSAGE NAME	VOLUME		CHARACTERS PER MESSAGE	CHARACTERS PER FILE	
		AVG	PEAK		AVG.	PEAK
⑫	⑬	⑭	⑮	⑯	⑰	⑱

DATE _____   ANALYST _____   SOURCE _____   PAGE _____

STUDY _____

Figure 8-4   A blank file sheet. The 18 key numbers are explained in Section 8.5.

number of records, is often carried as well. This field is particularly useful for tape or disk files.

11.   REMARKS   Noted here are miscellaneous data and problems such as rapidly expanding size, excessive or inadequate retention cycles, or need for duplicate files differently sequenced.

12.   SEQUENCE NO.   This gives the relative sequence number for order of messages within the sequence keys of the file (for files in which multiple records

are filed together). If report A and report B are to be processed for a common master report C, and report A must be filed in front of report B, then it is given sequence number 1 and report B is given sequence number 2.

13. MESSAGE NAME   This shows name and number of messages appearing in the file. The name should correspond to the name on a related Message Sheet.

14. (VOLUME) AVG.   The average number of this type of message in the file is shown.

15. (VOLUME) PEAK   The peak number of this type of message in the file is shown.

16. CHARACTERS PER MESSAGE   This field displays the size of an average message. The number entered here is the total of each data element's character count multiplied by frequency; if a range and average appear, the average is used.

17. (CHARACTERS PER FILE) AVG.   The average file size for this message is given. Multiply the character count per message by the volume average to arrive at this figure.

18. (CHARACTERS PER FILE) PEAK   The peak file size for this message is given. Multiply character count per message by volume peak to arrive at this figure.

8.6   OPERATION SHEET

The operation sheet is used by the analysts to describe the processing steps that make up a series of operations, together with the triggers, inputs, outputs, and the resources used in each operation.

In preparing this form the analyst draws heavily from the information in the message and file sheets and combines the information thereon with information about the process which he obtains by observing, interviewing, and sampling.

Figure 8-5 contains the top portion of a blank operation sheet. In it are 20 encircled key numbers which refer to the notes given immediately below.

Notes for the key numbers on the operation sheet in Figure 8-5

1. OPERATION   This field consist of two subfields.

2. NO.   This is a six-digit operation number. The first three digits refer either to the department which performs the operation, or to the activity which includes the operation. The last three digits form the unique operation number. Operation numbers need not be consecutive.

3. PERFORMED BY   The name or number of the organizational component responsible for performing the operation is entered here.

4. TRIGGERS, INPUTS, AND OUTPUTS   This field consists of five subfields.

5. ID. NO.   This differentiates among triggers, inputs, and outputs. T1 identifies the trigger for each operation. Inputs are identified by a series starting with I1. Outputs are identified by a series starting with R1.

6. NAME AND QUALIFICATION   The name of an input or output must correspond to that appearing on a related message sheet. Copies or parts of copies involved

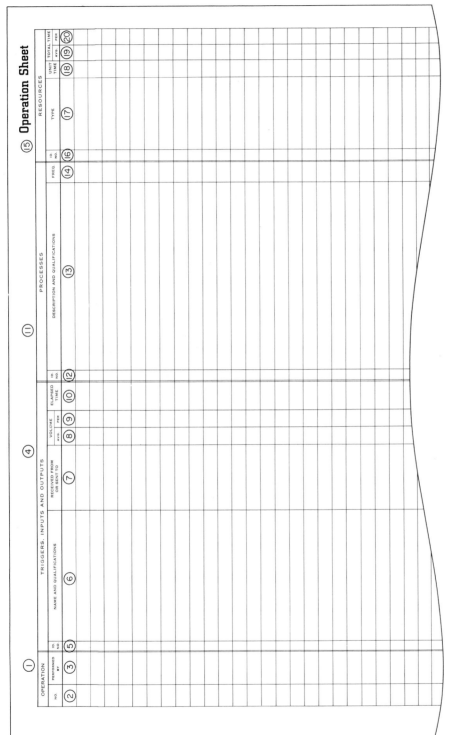

Figure 8-5   The top portion of a blank operation sheet. The key notes in the circles are explained in Section 8.6.

are indicated in parentheses after the name. If only a selected group of a named input or output is involved, the group qualifications are entered; the qualifying statement specifies constraining values. Normally only one trigger will be defined for each operation. Triggers may fall into many categories: receipt of an input, a time of day, week, or month, or a frequency per unit time; receipt of multiple inputs; or a combination of inputs and times.

7.   RECEIVED FROM OR SENT TO   Enter here the name or the number (or both) of the organizational component from which the input is received or to which the output is sent. If outside the activity under scrutiny, indicate the sender or receiver in general terms; customer, vendor, salesman, government, etc.; if inside, use the lowest-level component involved. If an output is sent solely for filing, indicate destination file by name.

8,9. VOLUME   Indicate the average quantity for each input, output, and multiple-input trigger, during any given time period.

8.   AVG.   Use the arithmetic mean of the volume figures.

9.   PER.   In defining time periods, choose a meaningful length of time. Since this data may help determine costs, the time period should be consistent, if possible, across the operations and with costing and accounting policies. Consider cyclic concepts in making entries for such cases as file processing.

10.   ELAPSED TIME   This is determined as follows: A zero is entered for the input which normally arrives first; if more than one type of input is needed to start the process, average elapsed time between availability of the first input and availability of subsequent inputs is shown for each subsequent input. For each output, list the average elapsed time between time zero (the availability of the first input) and the arrival of the output at its destination. Where practical, elapsed time should be given in working days or fractions of a working day.

11.   PROCESSES   This field includes three subfields.

12.   ID. NO.   The identification number segregates the processes that make up the operation. Processes are identified by a number series starting with P1.

13.   DESCRIPTION AND QUALIFICATIONS   This subfield consists of a verb and its object, plus occasional qualifying phrases. Verbs should be broad enough to obviate the need for details, clear enough to avoid ambiguity. Such verbs as *determine, prepare, reproduce, insert, attach, select, post, arrange, edit, adjust, reject, destroy* have been adequately defined and exemplify the type of verb to use. The object of the verb should refer to inputs, outputs or resources, and should tell what information is affected or transformed by the action implicit in the verb. Additional phrases (*to . . . , for . . . , into . . . , using . . . , etc.*) are entered as needed to explain the process. Conditional clauses (*if . . . , when . . . ,*) are also employed.

14.   FREQ.   This field gives the frequency of performance in terms of the number of executions per input, output, or operation. Frequency may also be expressed as unit operating time, or as a statement of the cycle: MC could indicate an operation performed on a monthly cycle.

15.   RESOURCES   This field includes four subfields.

16.   ID. NO.   This segregates the various resources used in the operation. Resources for each operation are identified by a separate number series starting with X1.

17.   TYPE   Here are shown the classifications of operating personnel and machines or equipment, with the numbers of each in parentheses. Names and

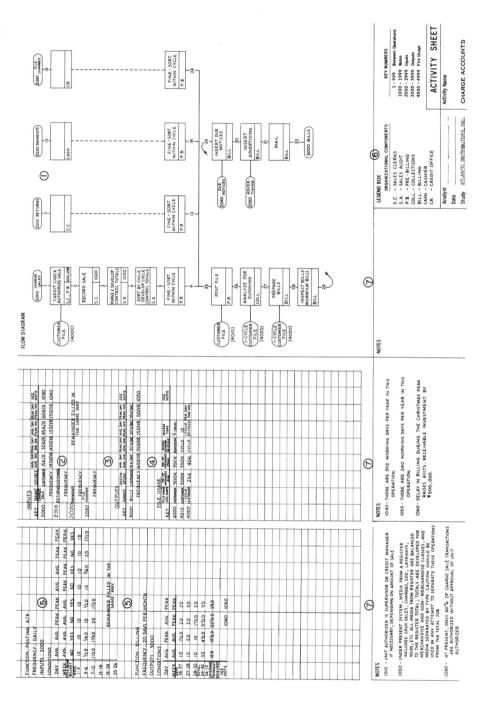

Figure 8-6 An example of an activity sheet taken from an actual case study. The encircled seven key numbers are explained in the notes in Section 8.7.

classifications of materials are entered, with appropriate volumes; raw materials, work in process, forms, finished goods, all are listed. Resource data includes files; these are identified by name and type of message, using names and numbers corresponding to entries on message and file sheets.

18. UNIT TIME   Resource usage per operation is defined here. For a given resource, unit time may be separately defined for each process and again for the whole operation. The figure should represent average time for the total resource named. Thus, ten minutes from each of three clerks would demand an entry 1/2 H/OP under UNIT TIME opposite the entry CLERKS (3) in the TYPE subfield. Unit time is not given for materials, nor, in most instances, for files.

19,20. TOTAL TIME   This defines the total resource usage per process or operation over a selected time period. The entry represents the average time that the total resource is employed; unit of time selected should be compatible across operations and with the accounting policies.

19. AVG.   The quantity and time unit are shown.

20. PER   List the selected time period.

8.7   ACTIVITY SHEET

The activity sheet is used by both management and the analysts to provide an insight into the dynamics of an activity, and a measurement of the magnitude of the processing problems in the activity. It is developed in part at the same time that the operation sheets are prepared, and in part from the data on the operation sheets. The activity sheet covers five major topics: a flowchart on the right shows the operational flow of the activity; a tabular section on the left covers the characteristics of inputs, the characteristics of outputs, the characteristics of file usage, and the elapsed times involved in the activity.

As we mentioned above, the activity sheet shows the operations within an activity, whereas its corresponding major band on the resource usage sheet shows the cost of carrying on the activity.

Figure 8-6 is an example of an activity sheet taken from an actual case, Atlantic Distributors, Inc. The seven encircled key numbers relate to the notes below.

Notes for the key numbers on the activity sheet in Figure 8-6

1. The flow diagram charts the mechanism of the activity in action. Operation boxes identify each related set of processing steps which can be defined as an operation. Local jargon or more formal operative verb phrases may be used to describe the operations. Space at the bottom of the operation box is used for indicating, in abbreviated form, the organizational component which performs the operation, and for footnote reference numbers. Inputs are flagged in small oval balloons in which are entered the key number and name of the input; outputs are similarly treated. All files referenced during, or used in, the various operations are flagged in the larger oval balloons. Key numbers are assigned to inputs, outputs, and files for cross reference to the tabular grid that takes up the left half of the activity sheet. Between-operations key numbers are also assigned for cross reference. The number series used for cross referencing is printed in the LEGEND box (6) on the activity sheet.
   The four other major areas covered by the activity sheet—characteristics of

inputs, outputs and file usage, and definitions of elapsed time—all are entered on the tabular grid. Since the space requirements for the four uses vary from one activity to another, no subdivisions or headings are preprinted; the analyst subdivides the grid in the manner most suitable to his purposes. Detail level of any and all entries in the grid can vary; only those details which point up significant operating conditions should be entered.

2,3. Entries describing input and output characteristics should define the inputs and outputs; the two classes of entries are grouped separately. Key number series for inputs is from 2000 to 2999; for outputs, 3000 to 3999. Name of input or output should correspond to the name on a message sheet. Sources of inputs and destinations of outputs shown on the activity sheet are always in the environment external to the activity sheet. Volume of each input or output is expressed as quantity per unit time; if there are significant variations in the volume over the course of a year, these are spelled out. Causes of volume variation (calendar cycles or seasonal fluctuations) are shown. Frequency per year is shown for each volume level given. If batching is an input or output characteristic, batch size and batch-size variations are shown. If any of these items require additional explanation not easily entered in the grid, footnotes are added.

4. File usage is defined in terms of the size of the file and its access characteristics. The key number references the specific usage in the activity flow diagram; the same physical file may be used in several ways. File name may also change from use to use. Quantity of messages in the file is given for average and peak conditions if the difference is significant; quantity shown may be for all messages in the file or for just the type of message involved in the operation. Type of access (random or cyclic) is shown for each operation which is keyed to the file. Access time may be given as a maximum allowable figure, as a minimum attainable figure, or as a mean operating figure.

5. A tabular format is used to display elapsed time; in the table, combinations of the several controlling conditions are laid out, and the elapsed time for each set of conditions is then entered for every critical operation. Conditions include average and peak days during both average and peak weeks or seasons under various operating conditions. Where elapsed time is not appropriate, the fact that another event takes place may be entered; under certain volume conditions, for example, subcontracted assistance may be sought. Function name for the elapsed-time tabulation describes a sequence of operations. Frequency is given for the operations within this subset. Key-number designations for inputs or outputs cross-reference the definitions of the inputs and outputs. A table for the various operations is set up and the elapsed times entered; these may be totaled for long operating sequences.

6. The LEGEND box on the activity sheet provides space to define the organizational components abbreviated in the operation boxes, and to give the physical locations if pertinent. Key number series specifications are preprinted in this box. Here, too, the analyst enters his name, the date the activity sheet was completed, and the identifying name of the activity.

7. Footnotes are entered in the three NOTES boxes. Numbers are assigned to footnote references from the series 1000 to 1999 as the necessity to use footnotes arises.

8.8 DOCUMENTATION IN A NONMECHANIZED SYSTEM

The charge account system of a department store is typical of activities that are almost independent of other parts of the related business. The sale of goods is the department store's chief activity, with stock buying, advertising, inventory management, and personnel as other typical activities. Within the sales activity, charge accounts may be considered a major subdivision, with cash sales and time purchases as other subdivisions.

The charge account activity in some department stores remains a nonmechanized clerical system; our first example of documenting a study will deal with such an activity. For our illustration we use a case study which we call Associated Retailers, Inc.

The section of the business which includes the charge account system is displayed on the resource usage sheet shown earlier in Figure 8-2. This basic form shows the economics both of the system and of its immediate environment.

In the resource usage sheet in Figure 8-2, the organizational structure of a major section of the department store is graphically illustrated in the organization chart. In each box on the chart is shown the total number of people directly employed in the organizational component represented by the box. Employees in any lower-level components not shown on the chart are totaled into the proper lowest-level box on the chart. Upper-level boxes show only their own immediate employee totals not including components subordinate to them.

The lower section of the resource usage sheet is a cost tabulation. Costs of personnel, machines and equipment, materials, and so forth are summarized for each organizational component in the bottom tier of boxes in the chart. Higher-level components may also be summarized in this tabulation, as is the advertising manager's component in Figure 8-2. Costs for the higher-level organization components are usually prorated among the departments under the jurisdiction of the higher-level manager. Thus, the personnel costs tabulated on the resource usage sheet are comprehensive for the entire organization table as drawn. Unusual items of significant cost—such as an insurance policy carried on the president's life—would not be prorated, but would be separated out in the unlabeled columns at the right side of the sheet.

Costs used in this tabulation may be budget figures for the current year, actual figures from the previous year, or estimates. Note that in Figure 8-2 the formal training of personnel was considered important enough to be separated as a cost factor in the summary tabulation. Total costs for each organizational component are tabulated immediately below the related box on the organization chart, and grand totals for the section of the business covered by the resource usage sheet are developed in the TOTALS column at the right.

The costs are then allocated to activities. In Figure 8-2 the specific activity that this study is considering, the charge account system, is broken out in a separate tabulation. The costs shown for each activity are part of the summary costs listed in the top section of the cost tabulation. Thus the total cost budgeted for Department A and its 100 clerks is $493,500; of this, $166,750 is the cost included in the charge account activity.

Merchandise control and cash sales are other activities that might be examined in the same manner as charge accounts; the same organizational components would not necessarily participate. Conversely, note that the advertising department does not directly participate in the charge account system, and so no costs are entered in this block.

Two unmarked columns at the right of the tabular section can display various data such as the average amount of money invested in inventories or accounts receivable. Where possible, the cost of having the money invested would also be shown. In this case, the first of the two unheaded columns describes the item, and the second shows the amount. The average investment in accounts receivable and the cost of maintaining this investment are tabulated in Figure 8-2.

By summing horizontally, the analyst can develop the total costs for each activity. In Figure 8-2, the totals indicate that charge accounts involve $1.37 million in annual costs, about 31 percent of the total cost of $4.3 million.

The resource usage sheet permits a rapid analysis of the structure into which the system fits, and of the costs of the activities that make up the system. Its principal function is to document the organizational and economic information from a study. In the example of the charge account system of a department store, it provides a quick look at the way in which the charge account activity fits into the department store organization.

The activity sheet, shown in Figure 8-6, includes a flow diagram which shows the sequence of operations performed by the various departments to provide the charge account service, and a tabular section in which amplifying information is listed. The flow diagram starts with an action from the external environment—the customer's purchase of merchandise on his charge account—and carries through the mailing of bills.

To keep the flow path narrow, Figure 8-6 shows only operations on charge sales. Returns, payments, and file changes are parallel paths in the charge account activity, feeding into the posting and billing sequence. Details are omitted from this example; in a full study, these three sequences would be entered in the same detail as charge sales.

The tabular section at the left of the activity sheet displays amplifying information about the operations that make up the activity. This grid is unlabeled, without reserved spaces for specific information. Use of the grid is therefore at the discretion of the analyst. In Figure 8-6, the far left section displays elapsed times, volumes, and frequencies for critical operations. Elapsed time is shown for each of eight sets of conditions. The other section is used to show detail information on volumes and frequencies of the inputs and outputs.

Special attention is given to information resources, the files that are referenced or changed during the various operations. The flow diagram shows which operations use which files; specifics of file usage are then detailed in the grid section. In Figure 8-6, the details on file usage include pertinent statistical information on the average and peak activity of the file and its access time.

The file name (usage name) describes the file in its specific usage. Thus, in Figure 8-6, the same physical file is referenced in keys 4000, 4010 and 4020. In the first case it is subject to random reference in less than a minute for checking credit limit and authorizing the sale. It is next referenced sequentially every day for posting the day's business. In key 4020, one-twentieth of the file is pulled out each day for the monthly billing cycle.

In the legend box at the lower right-hand corner of the activity sheet, the observer enters the names (and locations, if important) of the departments involved in the activity; the full-name entries explain the abbreviations used in the flow

OPERATION			TRIGGERS, INPUTS AND OUTPUTS						PROCESSES				RESOURCES			
NO.	PERFORMED BY	IO NO	NAME AND QUALIFICATIONS	RECEIVED FROM OR SENT TO	VOLUME AVG	PER	ELAPSED TIME	IO NO	DESCRIPTION AND QUALIFICATIONS	FREQ	IO NO	TYPE	UNIT TIME	TOTAL TIME AVG	PER		
04 010 BILLING	T1	RECEIPT OF IO I1					P1	COUNT TRANSACTION SLIPS	1/I1	X1	CLERKS (5)	20 MIN OP				
(KEY NOS.	I1	CUSTOMER RECORD	COLLECTIONS	20K	D	O	P2	COMPARE COUNT TO NUMBER OF TRANS-	1/I1	X2	XEROX COPIER (2)		13H	D		
27-28)	I2	TRANSACTION SLIP		160K	D	O		ACTIONS ON CUSTOMER RECORD								
	R1	CUSTOMER RECORD	ANALYSIS SECTION OF BILLING	20K	D	7MIN	P3	RETURN CUSTOMER RECORD AND TRANS-	1/150I1							
	R2	BILL		20K	D	7MIN		ACTION SLIPS TO COLLECTIONS								
	R3	TRANSACTION SLIP		160K	D	7MIN		DEPT. FOR ERROR TRACING AND								
	R4	ERROR SHEET	COLLECTIONS SUPVR	5	D	8H		CORRECTION.								
							P4	ENTER ACCOUNT NUMBER AND NATURE	1/150I1							
								OF ERROR ON ERROR SHEET.								
							P5	COPY BILL FROM CUSTOMER RECORD	1/I1							
							P6	ATTACH TRANSACTION SLIPS TO BILL	1/I1							
							P7	ENTER INITIALS ON CUSTOMER RECORD	1/I1							
							P8	SEND CUSTOMER RECORD, BILL, AND	1/10I1							
								TRANSACTIONS SLIPS TO ANALYSIS SECTION								
							P9	SEND ERROR SHEET TO ANALYSIS SUPVR.	1/D							
04 020 BILLING	T1	RECEIPT OF IO I1					P1	INSPECT BILLS FOR LEGIBILITY AND	1/I1	X1	CLERKS (2)	2MIN OP				
(KEY NOS.	I1	CUSTOMER RECORD	FILE SECTION OF BILLING	20K	D	O		ATTACHED TRANSACTION SLIPS		X2	MICROFILM CAMERA		4H	D		
28-29)	I2	BILL		20K	D	O	P2	RETURN CUSTOMER RECORD, BILL, AND	1/700I1							
	I3	TRANSACTION SLIP		160K	D	O		TRANSACTION SLIPS TO FILE SECTION.								
	R1	CUSTOMER RECORD	COLLECTIONS			1H	P3	ENTER FILE CLERK INITIALS AND NATURE	1/700I1							
	R2	BILL	MAILING SECTION OF BILLING	NOTE 1		5MIN		OF ERROR ON ERROR SHEET.								
	R3	TRANSACTION SLIP				5MIN	P4	MICROFILM BILL	1/I1							
	R4	ERROR SHEET	FILE SECTION SUPVR	2	D	8H	P5	SEND BILL AND TRANSACTION SLIPS	1/10I1							
		① VOLUME HAS CYCLIC FLUCTUATION:							TO MAILING SECTION.								
		FREQ	165D/YR	55D/YR	15D/YR	5D/YR		P6	SEND CUSTOMER RECORD TO COLLECTIONS.	1/250I1						
		VOLUME	15K/D	30K/D	20K/D	35K/D		P7	SEND ERROR SHEET TO FILE SECTION SUPVR.	1/D						

DATE   ANALYST   BILLING DEPT. — SCHULTZ   ASSOCIATED RETAILERS INC.   CHARGE ACCOUNTS   6
    SOURCE   STUDY   ACTIVITY   PAGE

Figure 8-7   The operation sheet for the charge account activity of the Associated Retailers company.

diagram. A numbering system is specified in this box which is useful for cross-referencing the flow diagram to the tabular grid section and to footnotes. Boxes marked NOTES (below the grid) provide space for footnotes to amplify and explain peculiarities of the activity being described. In Figure 8-6, for example, the analyst has noted the various media emerging from the RECORD SALE operation (note 1020) and the number of working days for sales (note 1040) and preparing bills (note 1050).

Now let us consider one of the operation sheets for the charge account activity of Associated Retailers, Inc. The completed form is shown in Figure 8-7.

The operation sheet is the principal means for collecting and displaying operational data. It explodes the operation boxes on the activity sheet to describe in more detail what is done, from or to what, with what.

Included in the information entered on the operation sheet are triggers, inputs, and outputs; the description and qualifications of the processing steps; and the resources used in the various steps. When a single sheet is used for more than one operation, as is frequently the case, all the material for each operation is segregated from the one following by a horizontal line drawn across the page.

The operation sheet in Figure 8-7 is thus subdivided. Note, too, in this illustration that there need not be any connection between a trigger, input, or output on the one hand and a process or resource entered on the same line; the three major sections of the sheet are tabulated without horizontal reference to each other except within heavy lines separating operations.

Inputs and outputs are identified by sequences of numbers starting respectively with I1 and R1 (for *result*). Inputs to an operation are items entering from the external environment or transferred from a previous operation. Outputs are items that are produced by the operation to go into the external environment or to a subsequent operation. The name of an information input or output must correspond to an identifying name on a corresponding message sheet which further describes the item.

Triggers are identified by the letter T. Each operation is started by one and only one trigger. A trigger may be the arrival of an input item or items; it may be a time of the day or day of the month; it may be a combination of a time plus the availability of input items. In the operation sheet in Figure 8-7, it is the accumulation of ten customer sales records that triggers the file-posting operations; although ten documents are required, this is still considered one trigger.

The organization component from which an input is received, or to which an output is sent, is also listed. The volume figures on inputs and outputs are listed, together with the time elapsing from the arrival of the first input to the arrival of each output at its destination. In the example in Figure 8-7, the outputs go to the next department, and so arrive all at the same time. In some cases, one output may be required locally while another may be used in a remote location; elapsed times for the various outputs include transfer periods embodying the average time required for delivery by messenger, mail, and so forth.

The DESCRIPTION AND QUALIFICATIONS field lists the processing steps that make up each operation. The process description consists of a verb and its objects plus necessary modifiers. Verbs should be selected which are broad enough to make details unnecessary but clear enough to avoid ambiguity. The object of the verb should answer the question "What?" in reference to inputs, outputs, and resources. Each process is assigned a number prefixed by P.

The frequency with which the process is performed is also displayed; where possible, it should be expressed in terms of the number of executions per input, output, or operation. Where this means of expression is not feasible, the frequency per unit of time is valid for processes occurring cyclically; but in these cases the cycle period should be shown (monthly cycle, weekly cycle, and so on).

The resources section of the operation sheet is concerned with people, equipment, information, and facilities which are used in the various process steps that make up the operation. Resources are identified by a sequence of numbers starting with X1. Classifications of operating personnel and the number of each class are entered; names or classifications, or both, of raw materials, blank forms, and so forth, are listed with the approximate volume of each.

Entries under UNIT TIME show how much of a particular resource is used per operation, or per input or output. Unit time is not specified for materials, nor generally for files; it is commonly shown for equipment and personnel. When it is specified, it should cover the total resource named even if a multiple-unit resource; thus, five clerks who each contribute four minutes make a total contribution of 20 minutes of unit time. This figure is clarified by an entry CLERKS (5) that appears in the TYPE column of the resources section.

Entries under TOTAL TIME show the average usage of the resource per process or per operation. Unit of time selected should be consistent with cost information.

This column should be left blank for material resources, and generally for files as well.

Now let us consider an example of a message sheet from the charge account activity of the Associated Retailers company. The details of information inputs and outputs are recorded on message sheets. A message is considered to be any notice or communication entering or leaving an activity, regardless of the medium of transmission. It may be recorded or unrecorded. Signals, for instance, are unrecorded messages of a transitory nature such as a telephone call. The contents of a formal message, on the other hand, are fixed in nature, order and relative length, and the message is recorded on some more or less permanent medium.

The message sheet displays the name or names by which the message is identified. In Figure 8-8, the message sheet for the customer record indicates that this form is also called a customer master or a billing master. The message medium is shown and the method by which it is prepared. The message sheet displays both the operations which originate data in the message and the operations that merely use the message. The form in Figure 8-8 supports the two operations—prepare bills, and inspect and Microfilm bills—displayed in Figure 8-7, in both of which the customer

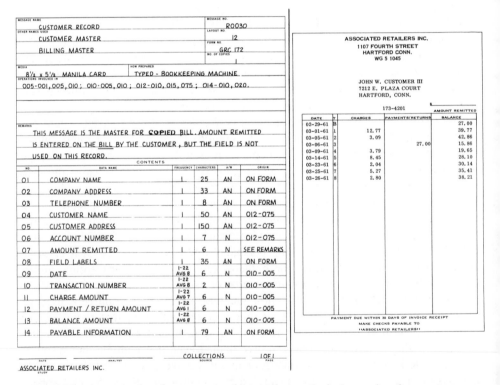

Figure 8-8   An example of a message sheet and an attached sample of a customer record to which the message sheet refers. The activity concerns charge customers in the Associated Retailers company.

record is involved, but neither of which originates data on the record. Consequently the numbers of these operations appear in the field OPERATIONS INVOLVED IN but not in the field ORIGIN.

Data elements and arrangement of fields are tabulated in the CONTENTS section of the message sheet.

To further illustrate this display, a copy of the actual customer record in Figure 8-8 is associated with the message. In many cases, the attachment of the source forms eliminates the need for filling in the CONTENTS section of the message sheet; the analyst can satisfy the survey requirements by identifying the message, describing the medium and preparation method, listing the operations which supply information for the message, and attaching a sample copy.

Signals are displayed on message sheets when they are critical inputs to an operation. For a customer-service or telephone-order department, incoming telephone calls are typical input signals that would require description on a message sheet.

The last document we shall consider in this example is a file sheet. An example from the charge account activity of the Associated Retailers Company is shown in Figure 8-9. A file sheet is used to identify, locate, and describe each ordered collection of messages that is needed as an information resource in an operation.

The upper sections of the file sheet identify the file by name, number, location, and storage medium; display access requirements; describe the type of material in the file; and outline the retention characteristics. If pertinent, they show who is and who is not allowed access to the file; tell how long the file is open and how often, or how quickly it must be referenced, and similar operating characteristics.

The file sheet in Figure 8-9 describes the customer file of the charge account activity. This file serves three purposes in the charge account operation: (1) it must be quickly referenced for credit authorization when the customer is in the store to buy, (2) it must be posted daily with new charges (and also with credits from payments and returns), and (3) one-twentieth of the total file must be billed daily for a monthly billing cycle. These details are entered in the ACCESS REQUIREMENTS field. In other fields are entered content qualifications (further explained by the entry in RETENTION CHARACTERISTICS), and information on the immediacy of the file data and the method of sequencing the records in the file. Entries regarding file growth or peculiarities of usage appear under REMARKS.

The lower section, under CONTENTS, provides space for identifying and characterizing the documents stored in the file. Data is entered both for average and peak volumes of documents and for average and peak volumes of characters. The latter is of only incidental importance in a manually maintained file (as in the charge account activity), but becomes critically important in mechanized filing systems.

The five descriptive forms work together to enable an analyst to document the critical characteristics of an existing system. In the charge account activity which has been discussed, the resource usage sheet provides a graphic illustration of the way in which the activity fits into a section of the department store, and of the cost of that activity. The activity sheet then displays the flow of operations that make up the servicing of charge accounts. The operation sheet permits closer analysis of two operations selected for their critical effect on the activity. The message and file sheets permit a closeup of inputs to and outputs from the activity and the information resources used by it.

Now let us examine the documentation that was developed during a study of a mechanized system.

FILE NAME				FILE NO.		
CUSTOMER FILE				F 0400		

LOCATION		STORAGE MEDIUM	
COLLECTIONS DEPT.		TUB FILE	

ACCESS REQUIREMENTS

① ≤ 1 MIN (CREDIT CHECK); ② ≤ 1 DAY (POSTING); ③ CYCLE :

1 CYCLE / DAY , 20 CYCLES / MO. (BILLING)

SEQUENCED BY

ACCOUNT NUMBER

CONTENT QUALIFICATIONS

CUSTOMER RECORDS HAVING ACTIVITY WITHIN LAST 6 MONTHS.

HOW CURRENT

DATA UP TO 1 DAY OLD WHEN ENTERED.

RETENTION CHARACTERISTICS

CUSTOMER RECORDS NOT HAVING ACTIVITY WITHIN LAST 6

MONTHS ARE MOVED TO INACTIVE FILE.

LABELS   ——

REMARKS

FILE USED FOR 3 PURPOSES : CREDIT CHECK , POSTING , BILLING .

CONTENTS

SEQUENCE NO.	MESSAGE NAME	VOLUME		CHARACTERS PER MESSAGE	CHARACTERS PER FILE	
		AVG	PEAK		AVG	PEAK
01	CUSTOMER RECORD	500K	550K	553	276,500K	304,150K

DATE	ANALYST	COLLECTIONS - ALDRICH	1 OF 1
		SOURCE	PAGE

ASSOCIATED RETAILERS INC.
STUDY

Figure 8-9 An example of a file sheet from the charge account activity from the Associated Retailers company.

8.9 DOCUMENTATION IN A MECHANIZED SYSTEM

The purpose of this section is to give the reader an opportunity to see some of the basic forms that were used to document the information for the study of a mechanized system. The forms shown here were taken from a case study of the system of a wholesale distributor, Atlantic Distributors, Inc. The particular activity under investigation was defined as "order-processing."

The order-processing activity of a wholesale distributor provides a good example of a mechanized business system. The fact that machinery is used to perform many operations in the activity does not alter the requirements of the study in any substantial way, although it does place greater restrictions on certain types of information—records contained on punched cards for instance, may need to be more rigorously described. But the main purpose of the study is to gain a coherent understanding of the system. The same basic five data collection forms are used.

The use of these forms to describe a mechanized system makes it easy to arrive at a clear understanding of the dynamics of system operation. The mass of detail data which conventionally emerges from a study of a mechanized system is considered only as supporting documentation. The structure and dynamic flow of the activity are clearly exposed in the five recording forms.

The information entered in the resource usage sheet is the same in both the mechanized and nonmechanized cases. The top part contains an organization chart of the business structure (in this case, the wholesale distributor) which contains all components affecting the activity of interest. The bottom part contains a summary tabulation of costs for each organizational component, with costs broken out and itemized for each activity, and summed for an activity total. The resource usage sheet for Atlantic Distributors is not shown because the material is so similar to that already given in the nonmechanized system example. Let us turn directly to the activity sheet.

The activity sheet in Figure 8-10 traces the mechanism of the order-processing activity. Note that there are three main sequences: the preparation of orders for shipment; the preparation of will-call orders; and the preparation of invoices, into which sequence both of the others feed. The orders-for-shipment sequence can be started by a salesman's order received by mail or telephone, or by customer purchase orders however received. In the case of a telephoned salesman's order or customer purchase order, a preliminary step is needed to prepare the sales order before the main sequence is begun with a credit check. Note that the straight line flow of the main sequence is not interrupted by what, in some documenting or programming systems, would be considered an exception loop: the preparation of a back order. The operation is included in the main path; if a back order is necessary, it is prepared as a normal tabulating room operation. If it is not needed, the step is skipped. Volume for the "short list" indicates frequency of execution.

In such an activity as order processing, the condition and frequency of inputs, and the elapsed times for various processes under average and peak loads, are critical parameters. These are listed in detail in the grid section on the activity sheet. Peculiarities of the system and amplifying data are displayed under NOTES.

Two outputs from the activity are the invoice to the customer and the "short

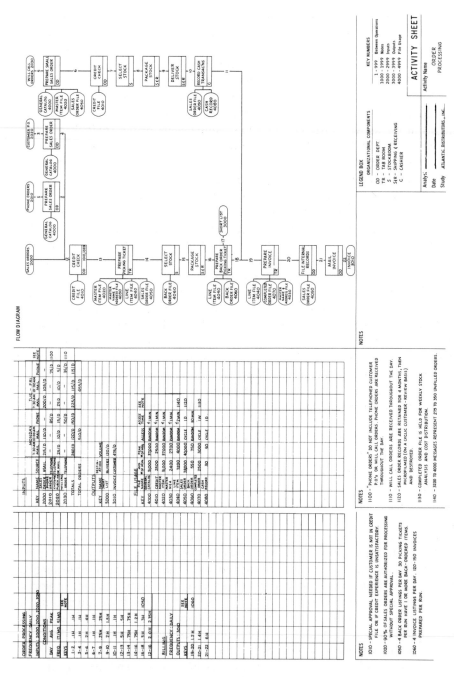

Figure 8-10   An example of an activity sheet for a mechanized system. In particular, it is for the order processing activity of Atlantic Distributors.

OPERATION PERFORMED BY	ID	TRIGGERS, INPUTS AND OUTPUTS — NAME AND QUALIFICATIONS	RECEIVED FROM OR SENT TO	VOLUME AVG	PER	ELAPSED TIME	ID	PROCESSES — DESCRIPTION AND QUALIFICATIONS	FREQ	ID	RESOURCES — TYPE	UNIT TIME	TOTAL TIME
TAB ROOM KEY NOS. (8-14)	TI	RECEIPT OF SALES ORDER					P1	SELECT MASTER ITEM CARD FOR EACH LINE ITEM ON SALES ORDER	15/TI	X1	KEYPUNCH OPR. (3)	24H	OP
	II	SALES ORDER	ORDER DEPT.	475	D	0				X2	TAB MACHINE OPR.	4½H	OP
	RI	PICKING TICKET	STOCKROOM	475	D	1/10 D	P2	PREPARE LINE ITEM CARD	15/TI	X3	KEYPUNCH WITH CARD INSERTION DEV.(3)	24H	OP
	R2	LINE ITEM CARDS	FILE	7125	D	1/12 D	P3	REFILE MASTER ITEM CARD	15/TI	X4	SORTER	1H	OP
	R3	NAME AND ADDRESS CARDS	FILE	1425	D	1/12 D	P4	SORT LINE ITEM CARDS TO STOCKROOM LOC'N WITHIN CUSTOMER NO.	1/10TI	X5	ACCTG. MACH.	1H	OP
	R4	CONTROL SHEET	ORDER DEPT.	48	D	1/10 D	P5	SELECT NAME AND ADDRESS CARDS	1/TI	X6	PANEL	1H	OP
	R5	SALES ORDER	ORDER DEPT.	475	D	1/10 D	P6	INSERT NAME AND ADDRESS CARDS IN FRONT OF LINE ITEM CARDS FOR EACH CUSTOMER.	1/TI	X7	MASTER ITEM CARD FILE (3)	24H	D
							P7	PREPARE PICKING TICKET AND CONTROL SHEET	1/TI	X8	MASTER N&A FILE	2½H	D
							P8	FILE NAME AND ADDRESS CARDS AND LINE ITEM CARDS	1/TI	X9	LINE ITEM FILE	4H	D
TAB ROOM KEY NOS. (19-20)	TI	RECEIPT OF PICKING TICKET					P1	SELECT NAME AND ADDRESS CARDS AND LINE ITEM CARDS	1/TI	X1	TAB MACHINE OPR.	4½H	OP
	II	PICKING TICKET	STOCKROOM	475	D	0	P2	COMPUTE INVOICE AMOUNT AND COST AMOUNT AND GROSS PROFIT	1/TI	X2	CALCULATOR	1H	OP
	RI	INVOICE	ORDER DEPT.	475	D	½ H				X3	PANEL	1H	OP
	R2	PICKING TICKET	ORDER DEPT.	475	D	1 H	P3	PREPARE INVOICE	1/TI	X4	PUNCH	1H	OP
							P4	SELECT NAME AND ADDRESS CARDS	1/TI	X5	PANEL	1H	OP
							P5	FILE NAME AND ADDRESS CARDS	1/TI	X6	ACCTG. MACH.	1H	OP
							P6	FILE LINE ITEM CARDS	1/TI	X7	PANEL	1H	OP
										X8	LINE ITEM FILE	4H	D
										X9	MASTER N&A FILE	2½H	D
										X10	COMPLETED ORDERS FILE	2½H	D

TAB ROOM – PANELLI   ATLANTIC DISTRIBUTORS INC.   ORDER PROCESSING   3

Figure 8-11 An example of an operation sheet for two operations in a mechanized activity. The form was taken from the Atlantic Distributors case study.

list" which guides the buyers. The merchandise can reasonably be considered an output, but for the purpose of this information-system example, it has not been covered.

Files are of paramount importance in the order-processing activity. File usage data is displayed in great detail. Five of the files must be randomly accessible in less than two minutes. A comparison of input volumes with these file access requirements quickly discloses whether or not the file arrangement is creating a bottleneck in the activity. This comparison also permits an estimate of when danger may arise.

Earlier we mentioned the connection between activity sheets and operation sheets. For a demonstration we present an operation sheet that supports two operations: (1) the "prepare picking ticket" operation occurs between points 13 and 14 of the flowchart, and (2) the "prepare invoice" operation between points 19 and 20. This operation sheet is shown in Figure 8-11.

The picking ticket is used in the stockroom to select the merchandise for packing and shipment. The invoice is one of the two outputs to the activity's external environment. Both operations are mechanized sequences using tab room facilities which are listed in the RESOURCES field on the Operation Sheet.

Note that, although the whole order-processing activity is considered as having two outputs (the customer invoice and the "short list"), each processing step has its own inputs and outputs. There are five outputs, for example, from the operation PREPARE PICKING TICKET: (1) the picking ticket itself, sent to the order department, (2) line item cards and (3) name and address cards, to be filed for

MESSAGE NAME				MESSAGE NO.	
LINE ITEM CARD				R 3008	
OTHER NAMES USED				LAYOUT NO.	
PARTS CARD				02	
				FORM NO.	
				D 17130	
				NO. OF COPIES	
				1	

MEDIA		HOW PREPARED	
PUNCHED CARD		KEYPUNCHED – FROM MASTER ITEM CARD [1]	

OPERATIONS INVOLVED IN
030-001, 030-007, 030-010, 030-017, 030-020, 030-021,
AND ACCOUNTING DISTRIBUTION
AND STOCK ANALYSIS

REMARKS
[1] ORIGINALLY PREPARED FROM MASTER ITEM CARD (OPERATION 030-001).
LATER ENTRIES ARE KEYPUNCHED OR CALCULATED.

CONTENTS

NO.	DATA NAME	FREQUENCY	CHARACTERS	A/N	ORIGIN
01	ITEM NUMBER	1	6	N	030 - 001
02	ITEM NAME	1	10	AN	030 - 001
03	DEPARTMENT CODE	1	1	AN	030 - 001
04	COMMODITY CODE	1	1	AN	030 - 001
05	UNIT OF MEASURE	1	2	A	030 - 001
06	QUANTITY ORDERED	1	5	N	030 - 001
07	QUANTITY FILLED	.20	5	N	030 - 007
08	QUANTITY BACK ORDERED	.20	5	N	030 - 007
09	UNIT COST	1	5	N	030 - 001
10	TOTAL COST	1	6	N	030 - 010
11	UNIT GROSS MARGIN	1	4	N	030 - 001
12	TOTAL GROSS MARGIN	1	5	N	030 - 010
13	UNIT SELLING PRICE	1	5	N	030 - 001
14	TOTAL SELLING PRICE	1	6	N	030 - 010
15	CUSTOMER NO.	1	4	N	030 - 001

DATE	ANALYST	TAB ROOM	1 OF 2
		SOURCE	PAGE

ATLANTIC DISTRIBUTORS INC.
STUDY

Figure 8-12 An example of a two-page message sheet describing the layout of a punched card for a mechanized system. (The second page is shown in the second part of this figure.)

use in the invoice-preparation sequence, (4) a control sheet used by the order department for picking ticket control, and (5) the sales order—not prepared in this operation, but rather the input to it—which is sent back to the order department.

The sales order is the only input to this operation, and its arrival is the trigger. This is an example of a single-input trigger; it indicates that the operation is performed for each input. The analyst should be alert for such a trigger, since possible

MESSAGE NAME			MESSAGE NO.			
–CONTINUED–			R 3008			
OTHER NAMES USED			LAYOUT NO. 02			
			FORM NO. D 17130			
			NO. OF COPIES			
MEDIA		HOW PREPARED				
OPERATIONS INVOLVED IN						
REMARKS						

CONTENTS

NO.	DATA NAME	FREQUENCY	CHARACTERS	A/N	ORIGIN
16	SALESMAN NO.	1	2	N	030 – 001
17	STOCKROOM LOCATION	1	4	AN	030 – 001
18	TRANSACTION CODE	1	1	AN	030 – 010
19	DATE PICKED	1	3	N	030 – 010

DATE   ANALYST   SOURCE TAB ROOM   PAGE 2 OF 2

ATLANTIC DISTRIBUTORS INC.
STUDY

Figure 8-12 (continued)   The second page of the message sheet for the line item card.

increases in efficiency may be obtained by batching input items and using a multiple-input trigger of six or ten orders or more. Noticing these conditions during the preliminary survey sometimes eases subsequent design problems.

In the invoice-preparation operation, again a single input—the picking ticket, received after use in the stockroom—triggers the sequence. The sole output besides the picking ticket is the invoice itself; both are sent to the order department.

The process descriptions include the individual steps which the machines perform, and also the multiple references to files. These process steps, incidentally, are described by verbs which are very like the verbal language of a computer programming language: *sort, prepare, compute.* The steps of a tabulating room procedure are similar to computer subroutines of the type used during the execution of a program.

Frequency data listed as a process qualification should be fairly precise estimates, as should the times required of the various mechanical, material, and informational resources.

The supporting documentation illustrated for this mechanized example consists of the line item card described in the message sheet in Figure 8-12, and the file in which these messages are stored, described in the file sheet in Figure 8-13.

In Figure 8-12, the fields of the line item card (R2 from the first operation in the operation sheet) are precisely delineated in the CONTENTS section of the message sheet; a second page is required to list the information. The descriptive data in the upper half of the sheet displays the operations with which the unit record is involved; typically, a punched card will be used in multiple operations.

In Figure 8-13, the reader should review every item, and note the retention characteristics of the file. During the order-processing activity, the line item card and its associated customer name and address cards constitute a transient record, needed only until the picking ticket is returned to the tab room after the stockroom has filled the order. This information is shown on the file sheet, plus the added information that the file is purged in a special machine run every two weeks to make sure that no order or back order has been overlooked.

Message characteristics are taken off the message sheet, multiplied by average and peak character volumes per file. In the case of a multiple-record file (as in the present example) the total volumes and character counts should be recorded in order to display the overall characteristics of a mechanized file.

The reader should not forget that there will normally be a separate operation sheet for each operation in the activity and as many message and file sheets as needed to provide the information required on significant reports or signals.

As in the preceding example of a nonmechanized system, the basic reporting forms permit a clear picture to be developed of the workings of a business system. They answer the question: What is being done? To a great extent, they also permit the analyst to find out how it is done, in terms of the activities and operations that thread through the business system. This topic is explored next in more detail.

8.10 DEVELOPING AN UNDERSTANDING OF A BUSINESS ACTIVITY

Having demonstrated the use of the five reporting forms in displaying characteristics of both a nonmechanized and a mechanized business activity, it now becomes advisable to discuss briefly the procedure by which an analyst can arrive at an understanding of a business with the help of the forms. This procedural discussion may illuminate the way in which these forms guide the study team and management to an understanding of an existing system. We have earlier discussed these points as abstract ideas. Now that we have covered two applications, a restatement of some of the ideas should help clarify any questions that the reader may still have.

In using the five basic forms, the analyst should think in terms of activities

FILE NAME				FILE NO.		
LINE ITEM FILE				F 3404.1		

LOCATION   TAB ROOM

STORAGE MEDIUM   IBM CARD TUB FILE

ACCESS REQUIREMENTS
DATA FOR ORDER MUST BE AVAILABLE WITHIN 2 MINUTES.

SEQUENCED BY
STOCKROOM LOCATION WITHIN CUSTOMER NUMBER

CONTENT QUALIFICATIONS
NAME AND ADDRESS CARDS AND LINE ITEM CARDS FOR PICKING
TICKETS IN PROCESS OR BACK-ORDERED.

HOW CURRENT
1 TO 5 HOURS OLD WHEN ENTERED. REMAIN IN FILE UNTIL
STOCKROOM HAS ATTEMPTED TO FILL PICKING TICKET.

RETENTION CHARACTERISTICS
DATA NORMALLY REMOVED UPON RECEIPT OF PICKING TICKET,
SPECIAL PURGE RUN ONCE EVERY 2 WEEKS.

LABELS   —

REMARKS   —

CONTENTS

SEQUENCE NO.	MESSAGE NAME	VOLUME		CHARACTERS PER MESSAGE	CHARACTERS PER FILE	
		AVG.	PEAK		AVG.	PEAK
01	CUSTOMER NAME CARD	320	400	61	19,520	24,400
02	CUSTOMER ADDRESS CARDS	640	800	65	41,600	52,000
03	LINE ITEM CARDS	2250	2800	52	117,000	145,600
	TOTALS	3210	4000	178	178,120	222,000

DATE   ANALYST   SOURCE   TAB ROOM   PAGE   1 OF 1

ATLANTIC DISTRIBUTORS INC.
STUDY

Figure 8-13   An example of a file sheet from a mechanized system.

rather than in terms of sets of machinery or blocks on an organization chart. The
characteristics of an activity that are implicit in the use of the term throughout
this text are that it is self-contained and goal-directed. In other words, an activity
is a set of operations aimed at a single goal or small number of related goals, with
only a few connections to any other activity. Three or four paths all aimed at a
single goal may be grouped into a single activity, but branching paths with multiple
goals are seldom single activities.

Activities may vary widely in size and complexity depending on the approach of the study and the level at which understanding is sought. Thus the sales system in a department store, or the materials system in a manufacturing enterprise, may each be considered as an activity. In the latter case, the system includes everything from the procurement of raw materials to the disposal of the finished article. On the other hand, invoicing—a small subsystem which is logically a part of both department store sales and the manufacturing enterprise—may also be considered an activity.

The procedure for developing a survey of an activity starts and ends with the preparation of a resource usage sheet, representing the structure of the business into which the activity fits. The first step is to lay out, on the resource usage sheet, the organization chart for the whole business, or for that part of the business which includes the system or activity under study.

The second step is to acquire the summary cost figures for each organizational component on the bottom tier of the chart. Cost figures for the preceding fiscal period are often available in the accounting department of the company. In many companies, fairly precise budget figures for the current fiscal period may be available; these may be more valid than historical cost figures if one section of the business is growing at a different rate than others.

If neither accurate budget figures nor historical cost figures are readily available, reasonable estimates by department managers are used. Interviews with department managers may be necessary in any case to apportion departmental budgets among personnel, machines and equipment, materials, training, and other costs called for in the tabulation on the resource usage sheet.

The next step—actually a series of steps—is critical to a successful study. The analyst must trace the activity through the organization to find all the departments affecting it and to determine exactly what each department contributes to the end result. Here again, interviews with operating personnel and managers in each department will be necessary. The analyst must be particularly alert to unravel from the rest of the business those operations and processes connected with the activity of interest to him. For example, the department store sales audit department purges charge-sale records and develops control totals, but it also may handle time sales and other transactions. It is necessary to determine fairly precisely how much time and effort this department expends on charge sales, and exactly what the department does for the charge account activity.

The processing steps in each operation are recorded on operation sheets. The associated inputs, outputs, and triggers are recorded, and the effort expended by the department is apportioned as accurately as available information will allow. Messages and files are given special attention on the message and file sheets that support each operation sheet. Fields on these three working documents guide the observer in his search for and collection of data.

The operations are next assembled in logical sequence. A flow diagram prepared from these operations in sequence is then laid out on the activity sheet; the process of preparing the flow diagram will disclose any skips in the operation sequence. Information on volumes, times, elapsed times, operation cycles, characteristics of inputs and outputs, and file usage is then entered in the grid section of the activity sheet from the data on the various operation sheets. The information on the operation sheets regarding the apportionment of departmental resources, equipment, materials, and manpower is next used to fill in the blocks on the resource usage sheet where the costs of the activity are summarized. The refinement and summing of these figures, and the addition of notes to explain peculiarities of the system, are the final steps in the procedure.

As operations are being grouped into activities, the analyst may find that some are too large and need to be subdivided, or he may find that several operations are actually a series of processes, and could be efficiently combined. It is not unusual for initial documentation plans to be modified in the light of subsequent appraisals and evaluation. It is also a temptation at this stage to consider questions of whether to merge processes or operations for reasons of economy, or to mechanize them, or to eliminate them because of their redundancy. The purpose of studying an existing system though, is to understand, not to solve; the report should be a descriptive document, not a proposal. Merging operations, eliminating them, or otherwise reorganizing the system may take the form of notes for subsequent phases of study and design, or as incidental recommendations to management in the report introduction. As the team sees opportunities for improvement, it must avoid getting involved in their implementation at this point, since this can only cause delay.

Experience has shown that if a team is diverted from its main objectives and tries to carry out short-range improvements, it rarely returns to complete the original study; if one analyst leaves for the same reason, he probably will not rejoin the team. Thus, opportunities to improve the system should be brought to management's attention, but suggestions advanced on how they may be implemented require use of persons other than those on the team. Possibly, these conditions may be corrected with the introduction of the new system at a later date, or the condition may not even exist once the new system is in full operation. Since the impact of the new system cannot be predicted by the end of the study of an existing system, the effort spent on implementation of short-range improvements may be totally wasted.

The end product of the study should be a coherent description of the system as it exists. Its basic dynamics are displayed on the resource usage and activity sheets, and the details of the processing steps are described on the operation sheets; message and file sheets provide closeups of information inputs, outputs, and resources.

With this description completed and refined, it becomes possible to proceed with analysis of the true requirements for a new system. This is the second phase of stage one in the life of a business system, and is the subject of Part Three of our book. Before considering requirements for the new system, however, we will discuss the preparation of the report on the existing system and present such a report for our continuing case study, Butodale.

SUMMARY

A system study requires documentation so that the information is recorded and available for later use. Forms can facilitate documentation but must be used in various ways as needed. Five basic documents for recording information during the analysis of an existing system are: resource usage sheet, activity sheet, operation sheet, message sheet, and file sheet. The resource usage sheet fits each system under study into its larger organizational context. The activity sheet traces the flow of a single activity and breaks it down into its major operations. The operation sheet records the related processing steps that form a logical operation. The message sheet and the file sheet support the operation sheet. The message sheet describes the inputs and outputs of an operation. The file sheet shows with what stored information an operation works.

Preparing and Presenting the Report of the Existing System

9.1 PURPOSE OF THE REPORT

The final task for the analysts studying an existing system is to organize and present results to management in a written report that we call the Present Business Description.

The report includes a letter of transmittal, an introduction, general, structural, and operational sections, and an appendix where necessary. In evaluating what should be included, and how much, a study team should ask themselves: Why do we have a report? What useful purposes does it serve? Among other objectives, the report must:

1. Demonstrate an understanding of the existing business.
2. Develop a new view of the business in terms of activities.
3. Establish benchmarks in time, cost, and accuracy.
4. Serve as an adequate base for conducting later phases of the study.
5. Present in one place a complete description of the business (many people know certain parts well, but few have the total picture in mind).
6. Provide a dictionary of terminology and language, which is unique to the business.

7. Communicate the description for proper interpretation by a diverse audience.

In the following sections we present various ideas that we have found useful both to the analysts who prepare the report and to the management personnel who read it.

9.2 INTRODUCTION TO THE REPORT

The Introduction sets the climate for the report, and gives the ground rules for performing the study as they were agreed to initially by management and the team.

The purpose of the study is stated, and the study scope defined. Was the study undertaken to create a wholly new system, or to improve the existing system? Was the objective to obtain dollar savings by improving operating efficiency, or was it to raise the quality of performance of the business? Whatever the purpose of the study, it should be explained in the Introduction to the report, even if it is already widely known. The principal points covered in stating the scope are:

1. Area of the business included (and excluded) in the study.
2. Level of detail to be applied, and to what activities and departments.
3. Modifications of the original agreement or study plan.

Closely related to a discussion of scope are those special extensions of authority (or restrictions on authority) which apply to the conduct of a study. This statement includes rules on access to confidential information, restrictions on the release of operating data, contacts with employees and managers for interviews, permission to investigate special situations, use of processing facilities, and other matters which pertain to sound business practice and the maintenance of good relations.

Then the purpose of each major report section is briefly discussed. The purposes may be stated as:

Section	*Purpose*
General	Describe the environment in which the business operates, and the position of that business in the environment.
Structural	Amplify the description of the business in terms of inputs, outputs, and resources.
Operational	Define activities and relate them to the established framework of the business.
Appendix	Present more detailed documentation on the activities of the business.

The final part of the Introduction is a summary of the team's overall results and recommendations. What are the key facts on each of the activities in regard to size, volume, cost, and time? What suggestions does the team have on possible immediate improvements? What other insights of value to management were gained in the study? This last part of the introduction is vital, and gives management some idea of the value of the study, even though it is devoted mainly to a description of the present system.

9.3   REPORT MECHANICS

At the conclusion of data gathering, the study team usually has a large collection of notes, exhibits, flowcharts, and miscellaneous documents representing the sum of their efforts over the time of the study. Now the problem is to sort the wheat from the chaff—combine, condense, and edit the material, and convert it into a report that has subject-by-subject balance, continuity, and flow. Examples presented in earlier chapters can be used as guides for preparing individual parts of the three major report sections. Once the preparation of these sections has been accomplished, the total report is evaluated once more for completeness, sequence, and relationships among the several parts.

The general section, with its emphasis on narrative, is directed mainly to the top management audience, as is the structural section. However, the presentation of structural information shifts from a concentration on narrative to a more extensive use of visual aids employed to achieve maximum data coverage within a minimum of reading time. Wherever possible, data is displayed in the form of line charts, bar graphs, pictures, layouts, floor plans, lists, and summaries. Some narrative is still required for transition, explanation, and interpretation, as well as for the maintenance of pace and flow of ideas.

The operational section is aimed principally at the systems engineer or analyst audience, and resource usage and activity sheets may be included here without annotation. However, a number of study teams have found that considerable interest has been shown in these forms by managers (particularly the resource usage sheets and summaries of volumes and elapsed times), and a nominal amount of explanation may be helpful to point up significant data and results.

When they are part of a study, operation, message and file sheets, and special detail exhibits are located in the appendix without further notation.

The length of the report depends largely on the size and complexity of the business to be described. In Butodale, for example, the general section runs six pages, and the structural section contains 27 pages. Worthington Hardware has 12 and 23 pages, respectively; National Bank of Commerce contains 16 and 25 pages to cover these two sections. The inclusion of a great deal of data on manufacturing equipment lengthened Butodale's facilities section, and added little to an understanding of the business. The same can be said for four pages of notes appended to the financial statements in the Worthington report.

9.4   AUDITING THE REPORT

As the study team assembles data into a final report, individual sections are tested against accepted standards for good business reports. Considering the importance of time and economy, the information content should be adequate for its immediate purpose, without being too detailed. Various parts of the report should demonstrate coherence and unity, so that each part evolves sequentially from the preceding parts. Consistency implies that events of the same importance will be treated generally in the same way, or to the same level of detail, so that the report audience need not switch their frames of reference from subject to subject.

There are a few specific questions the study team can ask which help to appraise the report.

Are there any gaps? Are operations missing from the documentation of any activity? Do the activities traced out in the operational section adequately represent the business or business sector which is in the scope of the study? If activities have been omitted, they should be noted to show the impact they have on the activities described in the study.

Do the descriptions at each of the various levels give roughly the same kinds of information, in the same detail, and in the same form? Coherence and consistency within each of the three sections is important for easy comprehension. Detailed descriptions of products and markets in the structural section, for example, should be matched in tone, form, and detail by the descriptions of materials and suppliers—if both are equally important. Two equally important activities traced out in the operational section should be documented to the same depth; if message sheets are prepared for one activity, they should be prepared for the other; if input and output operations are omitted from one, they should be omitted from the other. An audience is affected by the proportion and balance of a report, and if an unimportant process is omitted from the documentation of one activity and not from that of another, it will assume unwarranted importance in the second case.

Is the environment consistent across the entire present business description? Environment, according to our earlier definition, includes the surroundings which are directly outside the scope of the study. In the study of a complete business, consistent environment is no problem: it is everything not in the organization studied. But if one part of a company has been set off as the business (the subject of the study), then other departments of the company which influence the study become part of the environment.

Is the level of detail adequate for the phases to follow? A subsequent phase of requirements analysis follows, as does the phase in which a new system is designed and communicated. Before the study of the present system can be considered finished, the analyst should determine whether or not the information serves as a *foundation* for determining requirements of the system and for designing the new system. If not, the team should seek further operational data.

9.5 DYNAMIC ASPECTS OF THE REPORT

So far the study has been referred to as describing and understanding the present business, but in a sense it has other important purposes. The general and structural sections portray static elements of the business, but in the operational section the business is described by activities which contribute to goals and objectives, a recasting which slices through the enterprise from an entirely new angle. Starting from the broad base of organization and costs on a resource usage sheet, the description moves into a display of individual activities on activity sheets, supplemented where necessary by operation, message, and file sheets. Thorough understanding of the business must be demonstrated in two directions: as the documentation descends progressively to more detail, and as it builds upwards from file, message, and operation sheets to activity and resource usage sheets. Each of the documentation forms contributes data to other forms. If operation sheets are weak in time and cost information and strong on the sequence of events, then flowcharts of activities can be drawn up accurately but there will not be sufficient factual data for a cost allocation on the resource usage sheets, or for the tabular section of the activity sheet. The team must be sensitive to the total data requirements and be continually thinking about the impact of the particular file they are studying in relationship to broad data requirements. Description of a communications network from the complete system to its elemental parts and back to its whole again is a typical example of how description interacts from section to section. The capacity is set for the network in the structural section, while utilization and operations variability are covered in the operational section. Failure to inject flow and relationship among the several sections will produce a total description of the business, but a highly static, rather than a dynamic one.

9.6   PRESENTATION OF THE REPORT

When the report is finished, a letter of transmittal is prepared as a cover document (even though the recipient may be the analyst's own management). The principal function of this letter is to transmit the report formally; it need not be long or detailed. Since this is a well-recognized document, it need not be expanded on here, except to mention that key officials are thanked for their interest and cooperation, and a request is made for an audience to review the findings in the near future.

The report should be presented to management far enough in advance of a formal review session to permit knowledgeable discussion when the analyst makes his oral summary.

An oral presentation can be made more effective with the use of enlarged exhibits to illustrate general and structural data and the resource usage sheet. Narrative from the general section can be converted to flipchart sheets. Under no circumstances should the report be read nor should the presentation cover the data exactly as it is contained therein. The presentation will be far more effective if it is extemporaneous and well prepared charts are used for emphasis.

9.7   A TYPICAL PROCEDURE

Figure 9-1 contains a diagram illustrating a typical procedure for collecting data and for preparing a report of an existing organization.

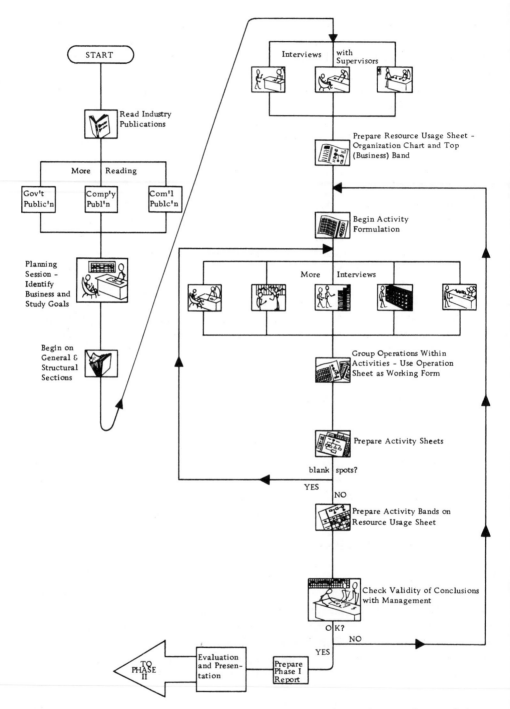

START

Read Industry
Publications

More   Reading

Gov't
Public'n

Comp'y
Publ'n

Com'l
Publc'n

Planning
Session -
Identify
Business and
Study Goals

Begin on
General &
Structural
Sections

Interviews   with   Supervisors

Prepare Resource Usage Sheet -
Organization Chart and Top
(Business) Band

Begin Activity
Formulation

More   Interviews

Group Operations Within
Activities - Use Operation
Sheet as Working Form

Prepare Activity Sheets

blank spots?

YES

NO

Prepare Activity Bands on
Resource Usage Sheet

Check Validity of Conclusions
with Management

O K?

NO

YES

TO
PHASE
II

Evaluation
and Presen-
tation

Prepare
Phase I
Report

Figure 9-1 A procedure for collecting data and preparing a report of an existing organization.

In studying the flow shown therein, the reader should put himself in the place of an analyst, or the leader of the study team. As a matter of fact, a modification of this diagram could be useful in the preliminary part of the study in which the analysts explain to management what they propose to do during their work in studying the business. Another use of this diagram could be in estimating times for the study. As the analysts go through a study, they can keep a record of their time for each aspect shown in the diagram. After a few studies they will have an idea of the time required for each kind of search and preparation. Then, when entering a new study, they will have some data for making time estimates from start to completion.

9.8   LOOKING AHEAD

After the report describing the existing system has been prepared, audited, presented, and accepted by management, Phase I is complete. In actual practice, though, there is no abrupt demarcation among the three phases, since the transition is progressive and some of the work overlaps. While studying the present business, an analyst is always looking ahead to the requirements of system specifications and design, and in later phases he looks back to recall earlier results and conclusions.

Concurrently with Phase I report preparation, some team members will be refining goal and activity definitions, and analyzing system requirements. In this work, many different analytical techniques will be applied to devise a system specification. The analysis surrounding a determination of system requirements is the subject of Part 3 of this book.

SUMMARY

The report of the existing system consists of a letter of transmittal, an introduction, general, structural, and operational sections, and an appendix when necessary. The introduction includes definitions of the purpose and scope of the study and a summary of the team's overall results and recommendations. The general section describes the environment in which the business operates. The structural section amplifies the description of the business in terms of input, output, and resources. The operational section defines activities and relates them to the established framework of the business. The appendix presents more detailed documentation of the activities of the business. Before it is presented to management the report should be carefully audited for correctness and completeness. The report is reviewed with management and an oral presentation made using visual aids to supplement the report. The information in the report of the existing system is used in the next phase of the study: System Requirements Specification.

10

The Existing System for Butodale

10.1 INTRODUCTION

Chapter 10 presents extracts from a report for a real organization. The purpose is to provide some tangible results of the methodology we have covered thus far. This way, the ideas and principles given earlier, and illustrated briefly with two applications in Chapter 8, can be considered in the broader context of a fuller report. We shall present those parts that we feel will optimize the contribution to the reader's knowledge and understanding of management systems. The Butodale Electronics Company is the fictitious name given to a real company. In some instances, additional examples have been created to assist in the understanding of certain important concepts.

We recommend careful examination of the material in order to acquire a general impression of the total content. To aid the reader, there is a guide to the report in the next section. It will serve to emphasize certain main points within the report.

For convenient reference and for consistency with the numbering system we have employed, we have renumbered the figures that appear in the case study. Consequently, they bear the numbers 10-1, 10-2, and so on, rather than the designations, I, II, and so on that appeared in the original report. Another point we wish to make is that the actual years for the company's data have been coded as 0, 1, . . . , 8, 9, 10.

10.2 GUIDE TO STUDYING THE BUTODALE CASE

First, we recommend that the reader merely examine the main sections of the report in order to compare its contents with the general outline proposed in Section 4.4. This overall perusal will give him a chance to see the report as a totality in much the same way that management personnel normally examine a report when they first receive it.

As far as the technical aspects of report writing are concerned, we realize that style and arrangement vary with the organization and the circumstances in which the report is prepared. Consequently, what the reader sees in the following section could be arranged in various formats. Here we are not concerned with style and arrangement but only with content. The principal requirement is that it be convenient to use and suitable for the purpose of conveying information.

The main topic in the Introduction to the report is the scope. A brief statement is needed because management should see immediately what the study has covered.

The general section contains many things that one would ordinarily expect management to know very well. However, in a dynamic business most members of management are busy with their functional specialties and seldom get to see the overall picture. Also, remember that the analysts have talked to many people in the company and have examined many records. Even in a large company, such a study may never have been done before and this composite picture usually surprises most people in management.

From the history, background, and policies sections of the Butodale report, notice the impression one gets of a young, dynamic company. One can almost see the early beginning with a small group of energetic men succeeding in starting a company and then working hard to expand it. The statistical summaries were included primarily to give management an idea of growth, and a quick idea of the distribution of sales among their products.

The structural section opens with Figure 10-1, which contains Butodale's business model. Notice that the environment is called the "market" and that it comprises both vendors and customers. Notice also the number and type of items Butodale purchases, and their outputs. The analysts listed four types of resources —two of them given with dollar amounts, one with numbers of people, and one with the number of facilities. Here, it might also be well to include dollar figures. This model usually attracts management's attention and in most organizations it is the first diagram to be discussed at some length during the oral presentation. It helps to focus management's attention on the "nature of their business."

The next significant exhibit is Figure 10-3, which shows the growth of sales for each major product. At a glance, management can get a quick, accurate picture of the performance for the last five years. The other financial statements may be of less interest as they are routine financial documents, yet they are important inclusions for completeness of the report. Figure 10-9 is of greater interest for it shows dynamic growth in sales and net worth. Note that the profit picture is not so strong. If these exhibits are frequently used by management, they form an important input to the study team in beginning the synthesizing of a requirements statement covered later.

The organization chart in Figure 10-12 is often of interest because in many organizations this kind of chart may not exist, or may be out of date.

Perhaps, the main single exhibit of interest to management would be Figure 10-13. In addition to the routine presentation of functional departments and their costs are the six activities that the study team discovered, defined, and described. This method of viewing the company is unusual for most organizations and draws considerable attention. At a glance we find that it costs Butodale about $1.5 million to carry on the activity of providing the demand for the company's products. The other activity of providing end products excited management very much. In fact, their evaluation of these two activities in conjunction with their study of the corresponding activity sheets shown in Figures 10-14 to 10-17, brought them to the conclusion that the study team should concentrate their efforts on these two activities during the second phase of the study.

This type of exhibit is particularly important in decentralized companies functionally organized (marketing, manufacturing, engineering, and the like) under a general manager. Each functional element optimizes its own function with respect to data handling. But this usually creates problems in managing the interfaces among functions. Identification of these interfaces through "horizontal" activity formulation and accumulating total activity costs can often lead to the identification of fundamental problems of concern to a "general manager." It further leads to key requirements for "data processing."

Ordinarily, top management does not spend much time on the appendix. Some members of the junior levels of management and supervision, however, should be more concerned with this information. In reviewing the material, the reader may wish to examine R-2000. This message sheet contains the description of the typical customer request for a quotation from Butodale. In Figure 10-15 it can be seen that this message serves to trigger the activity. This single trigger starts the whole left side of the activity of providing product demand.

Next, note message R-3000. This is the output of the left side of the activity shown in Figure 10-15. It is the physical document that Butodale sends to the customer in response to the request for a quotation. The document shown immediately after message R-3000 is a photograph of a blank quotation sheet that Butodale uses.

Next, let us consider a file sheet and an operation sheet. Turn to the file sheet number F-4050.1 shown in Figure 10-41. Note that it is the description of a quote folder—an ordinary manila folder—into which the customer's request for a quotation has been placed. Now turn to the operation sheet for operation number 001-540 shown in Figure 10-18. Here we see that the arrival of the quote folder triggers the start of this operation. In the flow diagram in Figure 10-15 we see that operation 540 is to "prepare bid sheet." Returning to the sheet for operation 001-540, we see that there are four processes in the operation, P1 to P4, and that there are four resources X1 to X4. From this sheet, one can easily envision the quote specialist (X1) performing the four processes by using the operational reference manuals, the cost file (F-4010), and the price catalog. Thus, one personnel resource uses three information resources to perform four processes in accomplishing the "prepare bid sheet" operation of the "provide product demand" activity.

We just mentioned that the quote specialist used the cost file. It is described in the file sheet numbered F-4010 shown in Figure 10-36. An actual example of the kind of record in the file is shown on the next page after F-4010. In the flow diagram in Figure 10-15 we notice that the cost file is attached to the 630 operation, "cost material and cost labor," and to the 570 operation, "prepare bid summary." However, it could also have been attached to operation 540 because it also uses the file.

We regret that lack of space prevents us from including all the operation, message, and file sheets, but we feel that the ones we have just discussed will provide a start for an examination of the remaining exhibits and will provide the reader with an understanding of the documentation needed for studying an existing organization from an activities point of view. We now present the case study itself.

10.3   BUTODALE'S PRESENT BUSINESS DESCRIPTION

INTRODUCTION

Purpose and Scope

PURPOSE

The management of Butodale Electronics Company requested that a study be made of the complete organization and its procedures. It was anticipated that the study would be conducted in three phases, namely:

1. Review the existing company.
2. Establish requirements for a new system.
3. Design and propose a new system employing automated procedures as much as possible.

The first phase has been completed and the purpose of this report is to present the results of that phase. Similar reports will be prepared as each of the two remaining phases are completed.

PROJECT SCOPE

The complete company has been studied in accordance with the original understanding. It was expected that during the study the team would search out those areas which could be automated with cost reduction. We believe that we have determined which areas meet those requirements and we explain them in this report.

Ground Rules

It was agreed that Butodale Electronics would authorize access to whatever data the team deemed necessary for the study.

The study team agreed to treat all information as confidential, and to obtain approval prior to removing documents, forms, and other company records from the normal storage locations.

Butodale management agreed to the request for interview facilities and time. Furthermore, the team was provided two offices, a conference room, and a supply room for use throughout the study. In addition, a secretary was to be assigned to the team full time and a clerk-assistant part time.

Thus far the study team has had excellent cooperation from all employees and we should like to express our appreciation. Further, to the best of our knowledge, the study team has acted within the initial requirements agreed to.

Content

The report consists of four sections: general, structural, operational, and appendix. The content of each section is:

General   The general section describes Butodale's history, its industry background, its policies and practices, its objectives and goals, and the government regulations that affect it.

Structural   The structural section provides a business model view of Butodale in terms of its vendors, inputs, outputs, customers, company operations, and its resources.

Operational   The operational section presents the structure of Butodale both from the point of view of nineteen departmental functions and six operational activities.

Appendix   The appendix contains the main documents that support the data presented in the operational section. Also, the methods and formulas the team used in arriving at the cost estimates are shown.

Summary and Findings

The study team was able to define six major activities for Butodale. These are:

1. Provide product demand
2. Provide material
3. Provide components
4. Provide end products
5. Provide engineered products and spare parts
6. Provide management, personnel and facilities

Now that the first phase of the study has been completed, it appears that the balance of the study should place emphasis on two activities: provide product demand and provide end products. We should like to review this report with Butodale management and explain why we recommend that our efforts be concentrated on these two activities.

GENERAL SECTION

History and Framework

The Butodale Electronics Company was established in 1946, incorporated in the State of Massachusetts. It was founded by four engineers and scientists who had worked together for a number of years in a large corporation on advanced government project work. Their main objective was to aid research laboratories and manufacturers in design and production of the latest radar, radio, and other elecrtonic equipment.

It is significant that the corporation sales have increased from $170,000 to $15.9 million since its founding. Some of the major mile-stones in the last five years were:

1. Established the Worcester Computation Center to develop new fields of application for the analog computer (for example, heat transfer, nuclear engineering, process control engineering).

2. Established the Long Beach and Rio de Janeiro Computation Centers to extend what was started at Worcester and to educate prospective customers in the use of analog computer techniques.

3. Opened additional sales offices in Chicago and Fort Worth.

4. Greatly expanded and modernized the original plant in Danvers.

5. Instituted a major drive to secure overseas business, particularly in South America.

Industry Background

Butodale is in the electronics industry and specifically in the analog computer area. Analog computers are widely used industrial tools which fall into two categories, general-purpose and special-purpose computers. There is considerable competition in this industry; some of the biggest competitors are ABC Instrument, Jones Instrument, and National Systems, Inc. Many investment analysts feel there will be continued growth for the general-purpose computer, but this growth may not be at the same rate as in the past. The company agrees with the conclusions and, therefore, there is considerable stress put on finding new markets and new products. In order to uncover these areas and products the company has set up a New Products Committee and a Market Analysis Section. It is the specific purpose of these groups to plan future growth and to direct engineering efforts towards this growth in order that the company may maintain a planned growth pattern of 20% per annum, or greater.

Some of the product areas under scrutiny are instruments, special-purpose computers, and process control equipment. Likewise, industry statistical analyses by marketing areas are developed in order to concentrate effort in the proper industries. There has been no designed plan to integrate this company through component manufacture; however, it is not opposed to this type of growth if necessary to insure a reliable source of supply, and if excess capacity can be sold profitably. Recently, the company absorbed the Premium Capacitors Company and is now building high-quality capacitors.

Policies and Practices

Some of the major policies instituted by Butodale have unquestionably helped the company attain its position of eminence in the analog computer industry. One of these policies is the corporation's attitude towards its employees. Butodale has developed a labor philosophy in which it endeavors not to infringe on the private lives of its people, while offering liberal employee fringe benefits, including educational opportunities. The company makes a strenuous effort to keep layoffs to an absolute minimum. This policy has resulted in a fine labor-management atmosphere. It has made itself felt in pride of workmanship and company loyalty which are hard to equal in modern industry.

Another policy is building a superior product. Rigid quality control is a key to manufacturing ascendency and, together with the labor policy, has produced an outstanding product with significant stature in the industry.

A third policy bears on market penetration. Butodale does not attempt to compete directly with giants in the industry, but rather to supplement them and their products and not engage in direct competition with their long-established lines.

Objectives and Goals

A major objective of this corporation is to expand sales and profits which will guarantee a proper return to stockholders and offer continued opportunity to employees.

The present sales goal is to increase gross by at least 20%; a net profit goal of 7% of sales and 15% of net worth has been established.

Government Regulations

Government regulations do not play a major role in company plans. However, a very high percentage of sales, perhaps 60%, is subject to renegotiation. Since the government sets profit objectives as a percent of sales, this has an effect on company plans and strategy.

Statistical Summary

PERSONNEL AND SPACE

Past 10 Years	Number of Individuals	Factory and General Office Square Footage
0	116	37,500
1	203	37,500
2	341	61,500
3	426	61,500
4	565	61,500
5	717	113,000
6	789	113,000
7	844	126,000
8	856	126,000
9	1069	130,000 (expandable to 250,000)

PRODUCT SALES FOR THE CURRENT YEAR

	Dollars (000)
General purpose analog computers	10,480
Large plotters	910
Data plotters	870
Computer Centers	725
Engineering and special fabrication	1,062
Small plotters	515
Multichannel recorders	347
Special purpose analog computers	320
Repair and service	180
Small general purpose analog computers	333
Instruments	173
	15,915

STRUCTURAL SECTION

Markets and Products

The domestic sales organization breakdown is as follows:

	Personnel
A. *General Office*	
Sales administration and clerical	8
Advertising and sales promotion	6
Development Engineering sales	4
Service Engineering	25
Standard Parts sales	10
B. *Branch Office*	
Eastern Region	11
Central Region	3
Southwestern Region	4
Western Region	7
Manufacturers' Representatives	1

Standard Products Market

The market for the General Purpose Analog Computer, which makes up almost three fourths of Butodale's sales dollar, is quite difficult to identify. Applications, to date, have been in the research departments of large corporations; the customer list includes a generous portion of top American industry. Note, however, that although the term "General Purpose" implies a catalog or standard product, each computer is engineered to precise customer specifications.

The company merchandises the large computers through its own sales force, having four branch offices in the United States and one in South America. It also uses its computer centers to good advantage in the selling effort. Prospective customers can solve sample problems at these centers to gain a better appreciation of the equipment. The centers are also used for demonstrations and presentations.

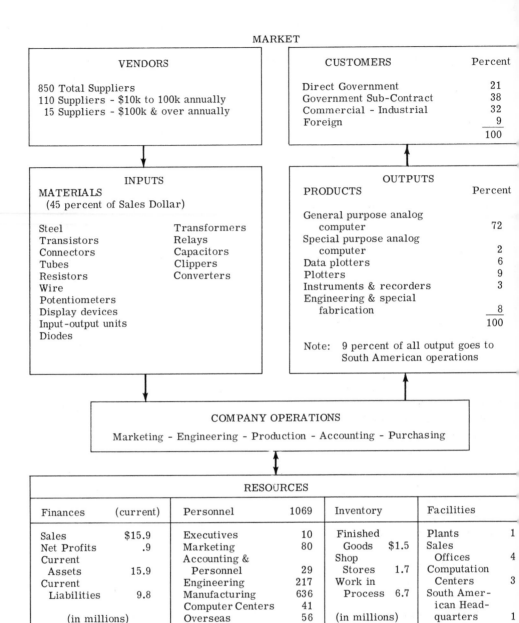

MARKET

VENDORS	CUSTOMERS	Percent
850 Total Suppliers 110 Suppliers - $10k to 100k annually 15 Suppliers - $100k & over annually	Direct Government Government Sub-Contract Commercial - Industrial Foreign	21 38 32 9 100

INPUTS

MATERIALS
(45 percent of Sales Dollar)

Steel	Transformers
Transistors	Relays
Connectors	Capacitors
Tubes	Clippers
Resistors	Converters
Wire	
Potentiometers	
Display devices	
Input-output units	
Diodes	

OUTPUTS

PRODUCTS	Percent
General purpose analog computer	72
Special purpose analog computer	2
Data plotters	6
Plotters	9
Instruments & recorders	3
Engineering & special fabrication	8
	100

Note: 9 percent of all output goes to South American operations

COMPANY OPERATIONS

Marketing - Engineering - Production - Accounting - Purchasing

RESOURCES

Finances	(current)	Personnel	1069	Inventory		Facilities	
Sales	$15.9	Executives	10	Finished		Plants	1
Net Profits	.9	Marketing	80	Goods	$1.5	Sales	
Current		Accounting &		Shop		Offices	4
Assets	15.9	Personnel	29	Stores	1.7	Computation	
Current		Engineering	217	Work in		Centers	3
Liabilities	9.8	Manufacturing	636	Process	6.7	South Amer-	
		Computer Centers	41			ican Head-	
(in millions)		Overseas	56	(in millions)		quarters	1

Figure 10-1   A business model for Butodale.

Because the general purpose analog market is difficult to ascertain, the company has diversified its line to include a smaller computer and several sizes of plotting boards, as well as instruments. This diversification of products has presented additional distribution problems. Butodale has resolved these problems by having manufacturers' representatives handle the smaller, diversified lines. These new products and the method of merchandising them have only been in operation for a year, so it is difficult to forecast their full impact on sales.

SPARE PARTS MARKETING

Another source of revenue is the sale of spare parts to existing customers. These parts may be used as replacements, as spares, or to increase the capacity of the system. The market is approximately $1.5 million annually and it is handled primarily on a telephone or correspondence basis. It certainly will continue to grow in direct proportion to the sales of major equipment.

ENGINEERED PRODUCTS MARKETING

The third major source of revenue is design and manufacture of specially engineered products in response to bids accepted. The present market is slightly more than $1 million and has been rising at a rate of approximately 20% per year since the company's founding. Profit is substantially lower than on standard products and spare parts, so Butodale does not actively market engineered products. It is significant that almost all basic engineering for standard products has been done when designing engineered products, thus, Butodale bidding depends on interest in the engineering design work required.

MATERIALS AND SUPPLIERS

Approximately 45% of the sales dollar at Butodale is the cost of material. Some of the major purchased materials include:

Steel	Capacitors
Transistors	Connectors
Tubes	Relays
Potentiometers	Wire
Display Devices	Resistors
Transformers	

	Year				
	5	6	7	8	9
Gen'l pur. analog comp.	4.0	6.6	8.1	7.9	10.5
Spec. pur. analog comp.	.3	.5	.9	.6	.4
Large & small plotters	.5	.8	1.7	1.4	1.4
Data plotter	.1	.2	.3	.3	.9
Engineering	.4	.6	.8	.5	1.1
Recorders	.2	.3	.3	.3	.4
Computer Centers	.3	.4	.5	.4	.7
Small gen'l pur. comp.	.2	.2	.2	.2	.3
Repair Service	-	.1	.1	.1	.2
	6.0	9.7	12.9	11.7	15.9

Figure 10-2 Comparative sales by product for Butodale for the last five years (years 5-9 of the past decade). All figures are in millions of dollars.

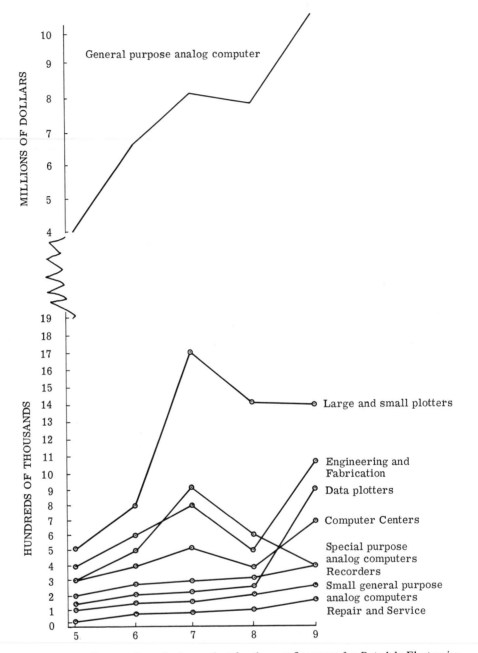

Figure 10-3 Comparative sales by product for the past five years for Butodale Electronics.

At present Butodale controls this material by a procedure based on relative annual parts cost. It is important to note that time lag for material purchased varies from two weeks to four months. An Order Record Card is sent to the buyer, who originates the purchase authorization. Different buyers handle different classes of items. Fifty percent of the time the buyer inspects the Order Record Card; selection is automatic the rest of the time. Ninety percent (90%) of the items handled through the inventory control section have Butodale part numbers which makes processing very fast. When part numbers are missing or not assigned, it is difficult to determine if there is such an item, or if it is ordered directly by name and charged to a project.

Forms Flow	Annual Volume
Purchase Orders	13,500
Debit Memo or Shipping Notices	3,250
Individual Receipts of Material	34,000
Stores Requisitions	23,000
Material Requisitions	3,500
Work Orders Packaged	1,500

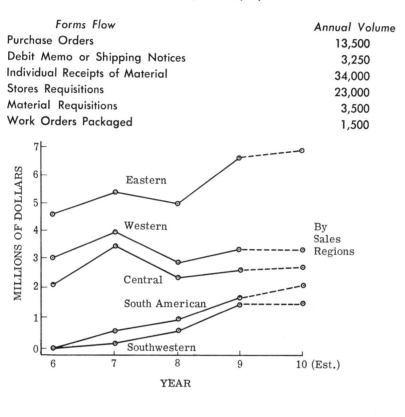

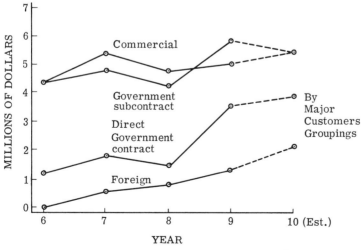

Figure 10-4 Sales by customer group and region for Butodale Electronics.

The company has about 850 suppliers, 125 of whom could be considered major suppliers. Of these, 110 receive $10,000 to $100,000 of business annually and the remaining 15 receive $100,000 or over. The company endeavors to have multiple sources, but because of the high quality of Butodale equipment, this is not always possible. A limited number of very expensive attachments for systems input and output are required; the purchase of these units is forecast and an agreement negotiated with the supplier giving an annual requirement with quantities to be delivered at

		9	8	7	6	5	4	3	2	1	0
Thousands $	Net Sales	15,915	11,670	12,944	9,745	6,037	4,570	4,261	2,174	1,265	753
	Net Earnings before Taxes	1,763	709	2,226	2,184	1,138	547	258	268	175	49
	Net Earnings after Taxes	887	355	1,075	1,070	561	258	129	138	89	27
	Working Capital	6,154	5,691	4,938	3,612	1,733	1,030	726	568	284	150
	Long Term Debt	610	1,658	1,276	975	25	25	65	40	40	40
	Net Worth	7,548	5,277	4,206	3,046	2,057	1,452	909	685	427	261
	Stockholders (number)	3,143	2,170	1,485	921	717	527	418	314	151	77
	Earnings per share	.98	.80	2.48	2. 61	3.00	1.58	.79	.83	.42	.11
	Dividends - Common Stock	100% stock	3% stock	3% stock .50	100% stock .50	.25	.25	.10	--	--	--

Figure 10-5   Financial summary for Butodale Electronics for the past ten years.

ASSETS	9	8	7	6	5
Current Assets					
Cash and Receivables	1,436,711	781,346	834,790	185,488	133,847
Billings Receivable	4,916,245	4,139,861	2,946,381	2,573,222	1,862,585
Employee Receivables	10,761	9,278	5,004	3,614	2,005
Subscriptions Receivable	240,843	235,189	391,244	170,285	36,243
	6,604,560	5,165,674	4,177,419	2,932,609	2,034,680
Inventories					
Work-in-process	6,743,617	4,410,855	4,586,238	4,529,811	2,586,715
Less Partial Delivery	607,320	901,438	810,104	585,316	953,764
	6,136,297	3,509,417	3,776,134	3,944,495	1,632,951
Finished Goods	1,526,334	590,007	310,842	151,725	138,749
Shop Stores	1,675,381	1,163,425	1,210,777	1,117,663	553,892
	9,338,012	5,262,849	5,297,753	5,213,883	2,325,592
Total Current Assets	15,942,572	10,428,523	9,475,172	8,146,492	4,360,272
Fixed Assets					
Plant and Equipment	3,371,493	2,355,864	1,874,386	1,576,334	925,747
Depreciation Reserve	1,106,285	881,469	631,491	521,820	376,210
	2,265,208	1,474,395	1,242,895	1,054,514	549,537
Miscellaneous Charges	165,007	142,916	101,247	67,289	61,309
Overseas Investment	137,500	110,000	----	----	----
TOTAL ASSETS	18,510,287	12,155,834	10,819,314	9,268,295	4,971,118
LIABILITIES & SURPLUS					
Current Liabilities					
Notes due banks	7,710,000	3,565,000	3,410,000	2,700,000	1,324,500
Accounts Payable	758,391	421,769	210,479	503,781	327,604
Reserve for Federal tax	659,244	249,653	846,215	1,058,342	558,912
Other	633,871	551,090	493,246	505,038	196,214
TOTAL	9,761,506	4,787,512	4,959,940	4,767,161	2,407,230
Long-term notes & mortgages	567,249	1,658,379	1,276,501	975,500	25,350
TOTAL LIABILITIES	10,328,755	6,445,891	6,236,441	5,742,661	2,432,580
Contingency Reserve	100,000	100,000	100,000	100,000	100,000
Subscriptions on common stock	268,286	263,744	463,808	181,387	46,213
Common stock - $1.00 par value	908,617	447,391	436,755	409,371	187,246
Stock Premiums	2,943,812	1,476,819	1,083,499	808,679	728,439
Earned Surplus	3,960,817	3,421,989	2,498,811	2,026,197	1,476,640
TOTAL CAPITAL & SURPLUS	7,813,246	5,346,199	4,019,065	3,244,247	2,392,325
TOTAL LIABILITIES & CAPITAL	18,510,287	12,155,834	10,819,314	9,268,295	4,971,118

Figure 10-6   Butodale's consolidated balance sheet.

specified dates. This arrangement seems to work satisfactorily. In view of the high-quality standards set by Butodale, all incoming material must go through a stringent quality-control check. This, on occasion, causes material shortages if inferior material is received. Records are maintained to reflect these conditions and to eliminate recurrence of such conditions.

	Labor	Expense	Distribution/Remarks
Salaries	$2,453,800		
Overtime & Fringe Benefits	786,000		
Indirect Materials		$627,500	Purchasing
Shop Supplies		430,300	Note 1
Freight - Inbound		68,300	Purchasing
General Engineering	450,400	95,600	Expense to Prod. Eng'g.
Field Engineering	52,500	342,000	Expense to Sales & Serv.
Engineering Administration	68,400	21,000	Expense to Prod. Eng'g.
Drafting & Photo Supplies		72,600	Engineering Service
Plant Eng'g. Supplies		162,900	Maintenance
Terminated Contracts	26,000	9,100	Expense to Management
Rent		21,000	Management
Utilities (Power, Heat, Water, Sewer)		101,200	Management
Taxes - Real Property		39,200	Management
Taxes - Miscellaneous		13,000	Management
Depreciation - Buildings		83,200	Management
Depreciation - Equipment		201,800	Note 2
Repairs - Equipment (Mat'l)	13,700	34,500	Note 1 (Exp. only)
Vehicles (Rent, Operation, Depreciation)		20,200	50% Sales & Serv: 50% Supply
Insurance		67,000	Management
Travel & Entertaining		251,600	Sales & Service
Advertising		167,300	Sales Admin. & Adv.
Foreign Operations & Taxes		101,400	- Excluded -
Office Supplies		96,000	Note 3
Office Equipment (Rental & Depre.)		60,300	Note 4
Telephone & Telegraph		101,600	Management
Professional Fees		19,100	Management
Interest		303,700	Management
Miscellaneous Expense		13,000	Management
Totals	$ 3,850,800	$ 3,524,500	
Add Direct Labor	2,601,700		
Exclude Computer Center & Overseas	-562,600	-205,200	
Total Salaries & Wages	$ 5,889,900	$ 3,319,300	Net Indirect Expense

Figure 10-7   Butodale's consolidated overhead statement. *See* Figure 10-8 for notes.

NOTE #1 - Distribution of Shop Supplies & Equipment Repair

- Shop Supplies
  Shop Supplies $253,900
  Material Writeoff $176,400 to purchasing
- Equip. Repair Mat'l.   34,500
              288,400

Distribution Base: Number employees in user departments

Allocation

Supply Rec'g. & Shipping	$ 21,000
Manufacturing Process	46,000
Components Assembly	75,000
Final Assembly	46,000
Special Components	32,000
Production Tooling	10,000
Quality Control	58,400
	$288,400

NOTE #2 - Depreciation of Mfg. Equipment

TOTAL CHARGES $201,800

Distribution Base: By acquiring department or current usage as determined by maintenance manager.

Allocation

Management	$ 22,000 (Air Cond.)
Mfg. Process	18,000
Components Assembly	6,000
Quality Control	31,000
Maintenance	15,000
Eng'g. Services	6,000
Computer Centers	103,800 (Excluded)
	$201,800

Figure 10-8   Supplement to Butodale's consolidated overhead statement.

NOTE #3 - Office Supplies

TOTAL CHARGES $ 96,000

Distribution Base: Number employees in user departments.

Allocation:

Management (postage & misc.)	$ 26,000
Accounting	14,000
Personnel	6,000
Spare Parts	7,000
Sales Admin. & Adv.	11,000
Purchasing	12,000
Mfg. Admin. & Subcontr.	20,000
	$ 96,000

NOTE #4 - Office Equipment Rent & Depr.

TOTAL CHARGES $ 60,300

Distribution Base:
   Rentals - As used
   Depreciation - Number employees in user depts.

Schedule:

Accounting	$ 22,000
Personnel	1,000
Spare Parts	2,000
Sales Admin. & Adv.	3,000
Purchasing	3,000
Mat'l. Control	24,300
Mfg. Admin. & Subcontr.	5,000
	$ 60,300

Figure 10-8   (continued)

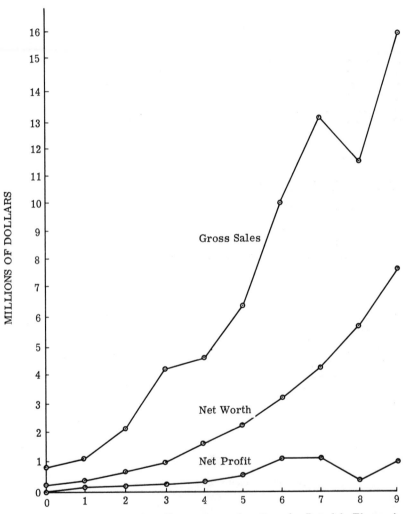

Figure 10-9 Ten-year growth pattern for Butodale Electronics.

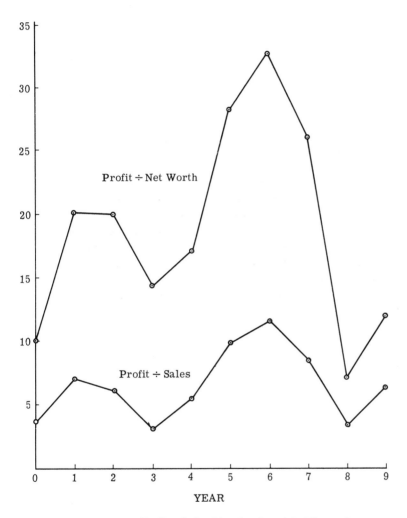

Figure 10-10   Profit relationships for Butodale Electronics.

Figure 10-11 Profit as a percent of net worth and as a percent of sales for the past ten years.

Year	Profit Net Worth %	Profit Sales %
0	10	3.5
1	20	7.0
2	20	6.0
3	14	3.0
4	17	5.6
5	28	9.3
6	33	11.0
7	26	8.3
8	7	3.0
9	12	5.5

Personnel

Butodale employs skilled personnel in the electronic, mechanical, and clerical fields. The wage rate is competitive with its neighbors. Butodal hires its service and development engineers on a national basis and moves them to the required area. While little difficulty is encountered in hiring clerical and mechanical personnel, there is stiff competition among other companies in the surrounding area for those with electronics skills; Butodale has gained a slight edge on the market with its past record of treating employees fairly and equitably.

The company has a broad (mostly company-paid) employee benefit program including:

Life Insurance
Hospitalization
Retirement
Tuition Reimbursement
Stock Option
Annual Bonus (dependent on profit results)
Professional society dues (75%), plus initiation fee.

The manufacturing and clerical people are on an hourly basis with time and one-half for over eight hours per day or 40 hours per week. The company-employee realtionship is carefully cultivated and, as a result, turnover, even in the clerical group, is quite low.

The personnel breakdown of the company's 1069 employees and managers is as follows:

President and Top Management		9
Public Relations		1
Personnel and Accounting		29
Personnel and Industrial Relations	8	
Accounting	21	
Marketing		80

Engineering		217
Product Engineering	73	
Services	97	
All Other	47	
Manufacturing		636
Materials	71	
Quality Control	109	
Operations	394	
Subcontracting	3	
Maintenance	28	
Administration	31	
Other Operations (but excluded from this study)		97
Computer Centers	41	
Overseas Operations	56	
	Total:	1069

CLASSIFIED BY FUNCTION

Department		Total	Super-visor	Clerical	Other	Skilled	Semi-skilled	Un-skilled
Administration	39							
Exec. Off. & P.R.		10	10	0	0	0	0	0
Personnel		8	2	6	0	0	0	0
Accounting		21	3	18	0	0	0	0
Marketing	80							
Sales & Ser.		56	8	8	40	0	0	0
Parts Sales		10	2	8	0	0	0	0
Sales Admin.		14	4	4	6	0	0	0
Engineering	217							
Product Eng.		73	5	12	56	0	0	0
Eng. Ser.		97	6	11	80	0	0	0
Other Eng.		47	5	2	40	0	0	0
Manufacturing	636							
Purchasing		22	1	14	7	0	0	0
Material Control		15	1	10	4	0	0	0
Supply-R&S		34	4	7	0	0	13	10
Qual. Control		109	11	7	6	21	53	11
Production Tool'g		19	1	1	17	0	0	0
Comp. Ass'y		152	8	0	0	2	14	128
Final Ass'y		81	4	1	0	0	39	37
Special Components		61	3	0	0	1	10	47
Mfg. Process		81	5	7	0	9	23	37
Sub-contracting		3	1	2	0	0	0	0
Maintenance		28	3	0	0	6	8	11
Mfg. Admin.		31	11	11	9	0	0	0
		972	98	129	265	39	160	281
Excludable Sections								
Computer Centers		41						
Overseas		56						
		1069						

INVENTORY

Since a major portion of the end product is customized, it is not desirable to manufacture to inventory. However, because there are a large number of standard components used, Butodale endeavors to forecast sales, and stock a number of them for immediate support to production schedules. This means that work-in-process inventory is made up of both this pre-planned stock and project stock where a system is being assembled and tested for a specific customer's order. It should be noted that general and administrative expense is applied to this work-in-process inventory.

The inventory is divided into the following major categores:

Shop Stores. Purchased parts and some fabricated mechanical parts used to support preplanned and project stock.

Work-in-process Inventory. Material and labor already expended against preplanned and project stock (including components completed except for final quality control).

Finished Goods Inventory. End products and components ready for sale or on customers' orders. NOTE—*Indirect Material* includes low-cost purchased parts and fabricated mechanical parts commonly used in components, and end products not carried as inventory.

Direct Material. Includes materials purchased directly for preplanned or project stock but not placed in Shop Stores inventory; it goes directly to work-in-process.

Inventory Breakdown at December 31:

	Number of Parts	Value (in dollars)
Shop Stores	3120	1,675,381
Finished Goods	850	1,526,334
Work-in-process	350	
Preplanned Stock		2,750,000
Project Stock		3,182,894
In-process-stores		810,723
*Indirect Material	5000	410,385

*Not included in inventory; comprises-3000 purchased parts and 2000 fabricated parts.

Shop Stores Inventory Annual Usage—(divided into three classes):

Class A—$10,000 or more annual use

Class B—Less than $10,000 annual use, including items with long lead time and new items that may develop into Class A

Class C—Items of low unit cost with common usage

Total annual use (issues from Shop Stores)—$4,637,000

	Items	Percent of dollar
Class A	90	65
Class B	240	11
Class C	2790	24

Direct Material & Shop Stores—$6,384,000

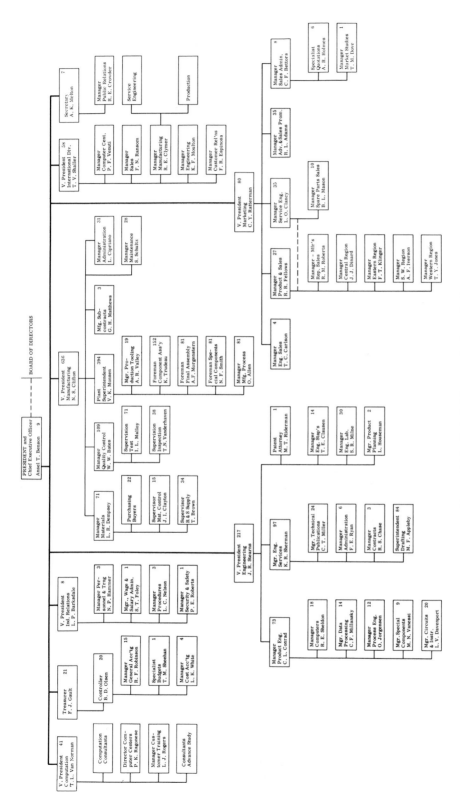

Figure 10-12 Butodale's organization chart.

Analysis of Shop Stores Inventory
December

Number of Items	Price Category (in dollars)	Total (in dollars)
1830	Under 2.00	463,319
717	2.00 to 5.00	285,008
238	5.00 to 10.00	178,916
156	10.00 to 25.00	265,312
97	25.00 to 50.00	182,694
33	50.00 to 100.00	64,371
49	100.00 and over	235,761
3120		1,675,381

Facilities

BUILDING

130,000 square feet expandable to 250,000 square feet; Butler type building, partly prefabricated 80' spans north and south, 20' spans east and west.

Roof: Sheet metal with 1-½" Fiberglas insulation.

Light: Provide 65 ft. candles at bench level.

Heat: Combination gas and oil, hot air. Gas operated until outside temperature drops to 32°, then switched to oil.

Fire protection: Overhead sprinkler system with 100,000 gallon underground water tank. Fire hoses throughout the plant. Roof vents fused at 212° to open.

Area of grounds: 40 acres.

Parking: 500 cars, expandable to 1500.

Air Conditioning: Two systems; front office area has a central compressor and chiller. Plant area has 50 individual units, each rated at 7-½ tons. Water is circulated thru a water tower to exchange the heat before it is returned to the individual systems. Each unit is individually thermostatically controlled to maintain a temperature 10° below outside temperature with 50% to 60% relative humidity.

Shipping Area: Wirebound crates to reduce weight for shipping by air.

Finished Goods Stores: Completed units for replacement parts and field expansions of systems.

Receiving Section: All incoming material counted, checked and distributed.

In-process Stores: Material fabricated at plant. Completed components ready for final asembly.

Supply: Purchased material inventory. Packaging area. (Parts packed to work-order quantity.) Printed Circuit assembly area. Automatic insertion equipment, eyelet machine.

Ultrasonic cleaner: Completely cleans, rinses and dries printed circuit boards. Used to remove flux and other contamination after dip-soldering.

Solder dipping operations: Completely solders all connections in one operation.

Harness fabrication: For installation at Butodale or in the field.

Wire preparation area: Automatic wire stripper, automatic taper pin installing machines. 1600 miles of wire used a year.

Finished amplifiers:

Quad amplifiers, printed circuit

Dual amplifiers, printed circuit

Dual amplifiers, wired version to meet high specs

LK-5 printed circuit components

Completed LK-5's:

1100 Plotters

D.A.S. & D.D.F.G.: Display comparing old design (mechanical) to new design (electrical).

PZC: Winding sine cards and mandrels. (Wire size .0017) Cleaning and checking mandrels (microscope). Displays of arms for plotters.

Network Final Wiring: Ovens for temperature cycling resistors networks checked for .002% accuracy. New phase shift checker to insure operation of networks in any oven position.

Plotter Test: Several types of plotters, vertical or horizontal plotters operated on signals from radar or other computing devices. Horizontal data and line plotters operated from information on cards or punched tape.

Plotter Assembly: Display of data plotter drawer wiring sequence including harness boards.

Special Wiring Group: Assembly and wire non-standard items.

Accessory Rack assembly and Wiring: Any combination of single bay racks bolted together and equipped with standard modules to accommodate additional computing elements for the 207 Computing System.

207–217 Assembly and Wiring Group: Computer built as a basic unit with 18 harnesses. Possible maximum expansion equals 58 harnesses.

Systems Test: All elements of the computing system brought together and tested out by a team of test technicians and engineers. Final cleanup and preparation for packing.

Final Test: Computing systems operated on typical customer problems.

OTHER FACILITIES

Office Equipment	Owned	Rented	Total
Typewriters	47	57	104
Adding mach. & calc.	23	10	33
Bookkeeping mach.		3	3
Dictating mach.		5	5
Cars	10	7	17
Trucks	5		5
Keypunch	3	3	6
Verifier	3	2	5
Collator	1	1	2
Sorter	1	1	2
Acct. Machine	2	2	4
Document orig. mach.	1	1	2
Calculating punch	1	1	2
Interpreter	1	1	2

OPERATIONAL SECTION

Resource Usage Sheet

Activity Sheets

Provide product demand

Provide end products

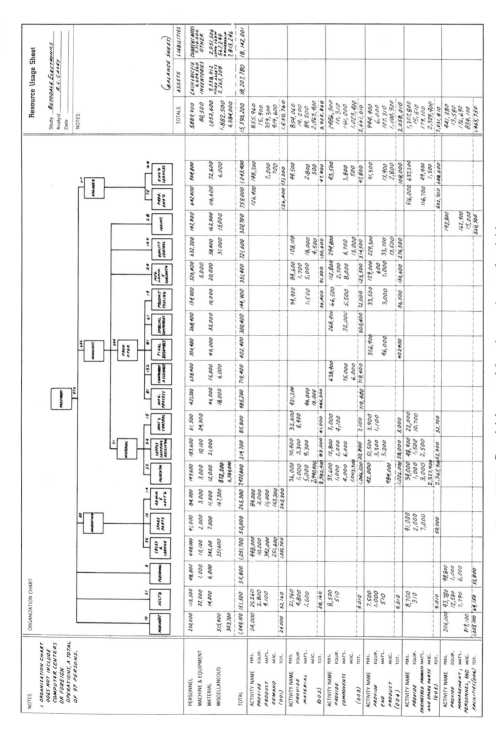

Figure 10-13   Butodale's cost of functions and cost of activities.

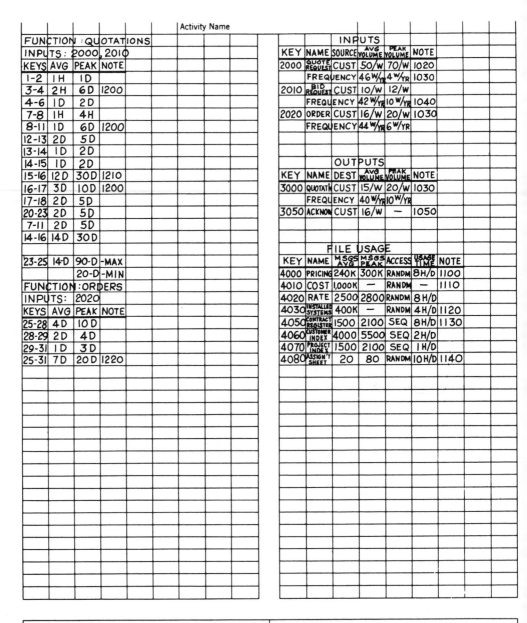

Figure 10-14 Operation times and resource volumes and times for the "provide product demand" activity.

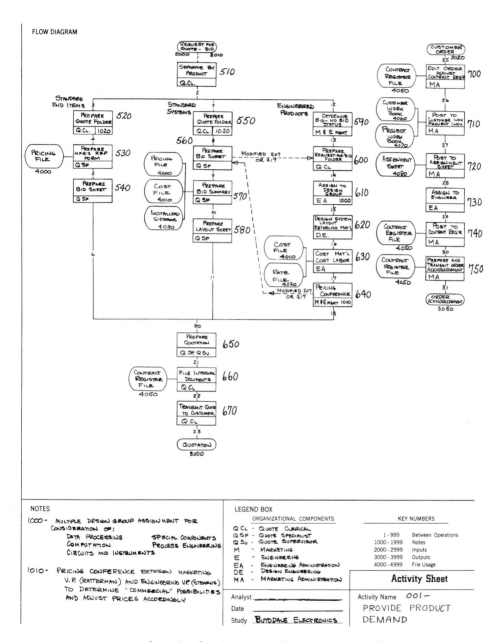

Figure 10-15 Operation flow for the "provide product demand" activity.

FUNCTION: ASSEMBLY AND TEST

INPUTS: 3050

KEY	AVG	PEAK	CYCLE	NOTE
1-2	2 D	5 D	DAILY	
2-3	60 D	90 D	—	1100
3-4	30 D	450 D	—	1100
1-4	90 D	140 D		

FUNCTION: COSTING AND INVOICING

INPUTS: 3010

KEY	AVG	PEAK	CYCLE	NOTE
6-7	1 D	3 D	WEEKLY	
7-8	1 D	3 D	WEEKLY	
9-10	½ D	—	DAILY	
11-12	2 D	5 D	DAILY	1120
12-13	1 D	3 D	WEEKLY	
13-14	2 D	3 D	DAILY	
14-15	½ D	1 D	DAILY	
15-16	1 D	3 D	DAILY	
6-8	2 D	5 D	—	
13-16	3 D	7 D	—	
1-16	100 D	1500 D	—	

INPUTS

KEY	NAME	SOURCE	AVG VOLUME	PEAK VOLUME	NOTE
3010	MAT'L COST	MAT'LS CONT'L	100/D	140/D	1000

FREQUENCY

KEY	NAME	SOURCE	AVG VOLUME	PEAK VOLUME	NOTE
3050	ORDER ACKNOW	MKTG. ADMIN	16/W	—	1010
		NO PEAKS			

OUTPUTS

KEY	NAME	DESTIN	AVG VOL.	PEAK VOL.	FREQ.	NOTE
3020	JOB PROGRESS	Supt.	65 JOBS	110 JOBS	DAILY	
3030	HOT LIST	SEE NOTE	30 PARTS	50 PARTS	DAILY	1020
3040	QUAL. REPORT	Q/C	5 ITEMS	20 ITEMS	DAILY	
3060	PAYROLL REPORT	GEN'L ACCT'G	300 MEN	335 MEN	WKLY	
3070	SHIP'G REPORT	Supt	4 ITEMS	12 ITEMS	DAILY	
3080	PERFCE REPORT	Supt.	200 ITEMS	400 ITEMS	WKLY	
3090	COMPL PROJECT	Supt.	15 ITEMS	45 ITEMS	WKLY	
3100	INVOICE	Cust.	15/W	20/W	DAILY	
3110	PACKING LIST	Cust.	15/W	20/W	DAILY	

FILE USAGE

KEY	NAME	MSGS AVG	MSGS PEAK	ACCESS	USAGE TIME	NOTE
4050	CONTRACT REGISTER	1500	2100	RANDOM	2 H/D	
4070	PROJECT INDEX	1500	2100	RANDOM	2 H/W	
4080	ASSIGN. SHEET	20	80	RANDOM	10 H/D	1030
4090	ROUTING FILE	250	350	RANDOM	8 H/D	
4100	JOB TICKETS	2000	3200	SEQ	3 H/W	
4110	STAND'D FILE	5000	5500	SEQ	12 H/W	
4120	WORK IN PROCESS	400	750	SEQ	8 H/W	
4130	ACC'T'S REC'BLE	4000	5500	SEQ	8 H/W	

Activity Sheet

NOTES

1000 FROM PROVIDE MATERIAL ACTIVITY, OPERATION 002-800

1010 FROM PROVIDE DEMAND ACTIVITY, OPERATION 001-750. NO PEAKS.

1020 HOT LIST DISTRIBUTED TO:
MGR. - COMPONENT ASSEMBLY
MGR. - FINAL ASSEMBLY
MGR. - MANUFACTURING PROCESS

1030 MUST BE AVAILABLE FOR SECOND SHIFT AND OVERTIME WORKERS.

NOTES

1100 - MANUFACTURING CYCLE TIME VARIES FROM 3 MONTHS TO 5 MONTHS

1110 - TESTING CYCLE TIME VARIES FROM 1½ MONTHS TO 2½ MONTHS.

1120 INCLUDES LOOKUP, POSTING, COMPUTING VARIANCE.

Figure 10-16 Operation times and resource volumes and times for the "provide end products" activity.

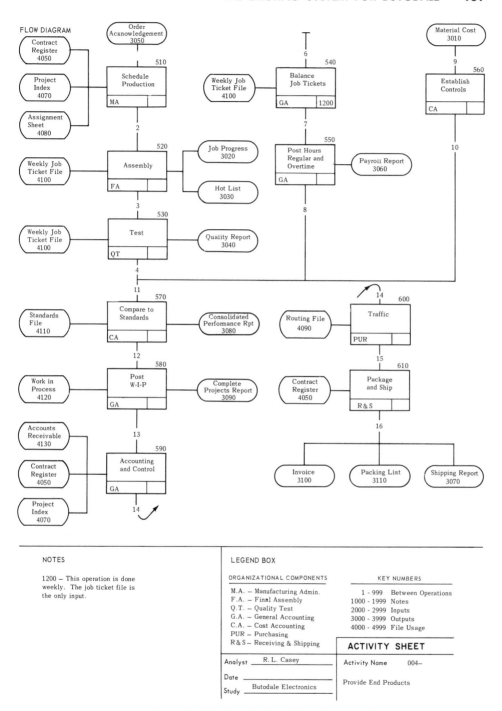

Figure 10-17   Operation flow for the "provide end products" activity.

APPENDIX

SELECTED OPERATION SHEETS

SELECTED MESSAGE SHEETS

SELECTED FILE SHEETS

OPERATION 001-540 — QUOTE SECTION

OPERATION	TRIGGERS, INPUTS AND OUTPUTS				PROCESSES			RESOURCES			
NO / PERFORMED BY / ID NO	NAME AND QUALIFICATIONS	RECEIVED FROM OR SENT TO	VOLUME (AVG / PER)	ELAPSED TIME	ID NO — DESCRIPTION AND QUALIFICATIONS	FREQ		ID NO — TYPE	UNIT TIME	TOTAL TIME (AVG / PER)	
001-540 QUOTE SECTION	T1 RECEIPT OF I1				P1 SELECT PREPRINTED END ITEM AND COMPONENT SHEETS TO ALIGN WITH QUOTE REQUEST IN QUOTE FOLDER.	1/I1		X1 QUOTE SPECIALIST	2H /OP	1/I1	
	I1 QUOTE FOLDER (ALL PAPERS)	QUOTE SEC'N CLERK	1½ / D	0	P2 MODIFY COMPONENT GROUPS AS NECESSARY	1/3I1		X2 OPERATIONAL REFERENCE MANUALS	1H /OP		
	R1 QUOTE FOLDER (F-4050.1)	QUOTATION SUP'VR	1½ / D	1-2 D	TO AGREE WITH QUOTE REQUEST BY ENTERING: • "PARTIAL" TO REDUCE PLUS IN COMPONENTS • "MODIFY" TO SUBSTITUTE COMPONENTS OR PARTS • "SPECIAL" TO CHANGE ENTIRE GROUP • FULL DESCRIPTION AS NECESSARY			X3 COST FILE (F-4010)	1H /OP		
	NOTE: 2 OUT OF 3 QUOTATIONS ARE STANDARD AND TAKE APPROX ½–1 HR. MODIFIED ORDERS TAKE 4–6 HRS. EXCESS TIME (IN ELAPSED TIME COMPARED TO RESOURCE TIME) IS DUE TO QUOTE SPECIALIST PERFORMING OTHER DUTIES AND LETTING END ITEM QUOTES WAIT.				P3 PREPARE COST AND PRICE SHEET	1/I1		X4 PRICE CATALOG (F-4000)	1H /OP	1/3I1	
					P4 ADD ALL ITEMS TO QUOTE FOLDER	1/I1					

R.L. CASEY — ANALYST DATE
A.R. HOLMES — SOURCE
BUTODALE — STUDY
001- PROVIDE DEMAND — ACTIVITY
1 OF 1 — PAGE

Figure 10-18 Operation sheet for operation 001-540.

| OPERATION | | TRIGGERS, INPUTS AND OUTPUTS | | | VOLUME | | ELAPSED TIME | PROCESSES | | | FREQ | RESOURCES | | | UNIT TIME | | TOTAL TIME | |
NO.	PERFORMED BY	ID NO.	NAME AND QUALIFICATIONS	RECEIVED FROM OR SENT TO	AVG	PER		ID NO.	DESCRIPTION AND QUALIFICATIONS			ID NO.	TYPE		AVG	PER	AVG	PER
001-580	Quote Section	T1	Receipt of I1					P1	Select standard rack diagrams for components		1/I1	X1	Quote Specialist(s)		1/4 H	/OP	8H	D
		I1	Quote Folder (F-4050.1)	Quote Specialist	10	D	0	P2	Enter appropriate assembly number in each rack position used		16/I1	X2	Operational Data Reference Manuals					
		I2	Quote Folder (F-4050.1)	Quotation Sup've.	10	D	1 D	P3	Select floor layout sheet (207-217 only. Other std. systems do not require floor layout)		7/8 I1							
								P4	Enter component and/or end item description in floor layout diagram		7/8 I1							
								P5	Place layout sheets in quote folder		1/I1							
001-650	Quote Section	T1	Receipt of I1 or I2					P1	Review of quote or bid by quote section supervisor		1/I1	X1	Quote Section Sup'vr.					
		I1	Quote Folder (completed) (F-4050-1)	Quote Specialist	12	D	0		Quote Section Supervisor			X2	Quote Clerk					
		I2	Bid Folder (completed) (F-4050-2)	Marketing V.P.	2	D	0	P2	Type quotation from bid sheet		1/I1	X3	Typewriter					
		R1	Quotation (5 parts)	Quote Clerk	14	D	1-2 D	P3	Prepare identification cards (3)		1/I1							
		R2	Identification cards (3)	"	14	D	1-2 D	P4	Select advertising literature		1/I1							
		R3	Quote/Bid Folder	"	14	D	1-2 D	P5	Assemble quotation and internal documents.		1/I1							
		R4	Drawings, Prints, etc.	"	10	D	1-2 D											
		R5	Advertising Literature	"	14	D	1-2 D											

ANALYST R. L. CASEY   SOURCE A. R. HOLMES   STUDY ButoDALE   ACTIVITY 001 – PROVIDE DEMAND   PAGE 1 OF 1

Figure 10-19   Operation sheet for operations 001-580 and 001-650.

OPERATION

No. 001-630 Performed by: ENGINEER & ADMIN

TRIGGERS, INPUTS AND OUTPUTS

ID. NO	NAME AND QUALIFICATIONS	RECEIVED FROM OR SENT TO	VOLUME AVG	PER	ELAPSED TIME
T1	RECEIPT OF I1				
I1	BID FOLDER (WITH ALL PAPERS PLUS PRINTS, DRAWINGS LAYOUTS, MATERIAL SPECS, TIME ESTIMATES, ETC.) (F-4050.2)	DESIGN ENG'RG	10	W	0
R1	BID FOLDER (COSTED) (F-4050.2)	ENGINEERING V.P.	10	W	1-8W

PROCESSES

ID. NO	DESCRIPTION AND QUALIFICATIONS	FREQ.
P1	Determine if proper entries of time and material are entered in bid folder by design engineering groups.	1/I1
P2	Modify estimates based on experience with individual engineer.	1/I1
P3	Compute costs for material	1/I1
P4	Compute labor cost	1/I1
P5	Set bid price. Confirm with design engineering group manager.	
P6	Send bid folder to V.P. Eng'g.	1/I1

RESOURCES

ID. NO	TYPE	UNIT TIME	TOTAL TIME AVG	PER
X1	ADMIN. ENGR. (2)		8H	D
X2	COST FILE (4010)		8H	D
X3	RATE FILE (4020)		8H	D
	NOTE: 2 ADMINISTRATIVE ENGINEERS FULL TIME FOR LIAISON BETWEEN DESIGN GROUPS AND QUOTE SECTION.			
	NO TIME ESTIMATES PER BID: USE ELAPSED TIME.			

R.L. CASEY — ANALYST — DATE

F.E. RYAN — SOURCE

BUT0 DALE — STUDY

001- PROVIDE DEMAND — ACTIVITY

1 of 1 — PAGE

Figure 10-20 Operation sheet for operation 001-630.

MESSAGE NAME REQUEST FOR QUOTE				MESSAGE NO. R-2000	

OTHER NAMES USED

LAYOUT NO. NONE

FORM NO. NONE

NO. OF COPIES 1

MEDIA LETTER OR NOTE   HOW PREPARED HAND OR TYPEWRITTEN

OPERATIONS INVOLVED IN
001 – SIX, 001 – 52 X, 001 – 55 X

F - 4050.1

REMARKS
COVERS ONLY CATALOG, STANDARD AND MODIFIED STANDARD PRODUCTS.
SEE ALSO R 2010

CONTENTS

NO.	DATA NAME	FREQUENCY	CHARACTERS	A/N	ORIGIN
1	DATE	1	MAX 6	N	CUST/SALES
2	CUSTOMER NAME	1	MAX 30	A	"
3	CUSTOMER ADDRESS	.9	MAX 40	A/N	"
4	CUSTOMER NUMBER	.1	5	N	"
5	PRODUCT SPECIFICATIONS	1	AVG. 350	A/N	"
6	QUANTITY	1	3	N	"
7	REQUEST QUOTE BY DATE	.5	MAX 6	N	"
8	REQUEST DELIVERY DATE	.3	MAX 6	N	"
9	SPECIAL INSTRUCTIONS	.2	AVG. 150	A/N	"
	ESTIMATED TOTAL		460		

R.L. CASEY   A.R. HOLMES   1 OF 1
DATE   ANALYST   SOURCE   PAGE
BUTODALE
STUDY

Figure 10-21 Message sheet for quotation request.

MESSAGE NAME			MESSAGE NO.	
REQUEST FOR BID			*R-2010*	

OTHER NAMES USED	LAYOUT NO.

	FORM NO.

	NO. OF COPIES
	1

MEDIA	HOW PREPARED
LETTER	*NORMALLY TYPEWRITTEN*

OPERATIONS INVOLVED IN

001-51X, 001-59X, 001-60X

F-4050.2

REMARKS

COVERS ONLY ENGINEERED PRODUCTS

CONTENTS

NO.	DATA NAME	FREQUENCY	CHARACTERS	A/N	ORIGIN
	SAME AS R 2000				
	EXCEPT				
5	*PRODUCT SPECIFICATIONS*	*1*	*AVG. 1000*	*A/N*	
	ESTIMATED TOTAL		*1110*		

R.L. CASEY	*A.R. HOLMES*	*1 OF 1*
DATE / ANALYST	SOURCE	PAGE

BUTODALE
STUDY

Figure 10-22   Message sheet for bid request.

MESSAGE NAME CUSTOMER ORDER				MESSAGE NO. *R- 2020*		
OTHER NAMES USED *PURCHASE ORDER*				LAYOUT NO. ✳ *QO 561*		
				FORM NO. ✳ *QO 561-2 OR -3*		
				NO. OF COPIES *1*		
MEDIA ✳			HOW PREPARED ✳			
OPERATIONS INVOLVED IN *001 — 70 X*						
F - 4050						
REMARKS ✳ *TWO COPIES OF QUOTATION SHEET (R-3000) ARE SENT TO THE CUSTOMER. MORE THAN 95% OF CUSTOMER ORDERS USE ONE OF THESE COPIES TO PLACE A FIRM ORDER AND ACCOMPANY IT WITH A PURCHASE ORDER. THE REMAINING CUSTOMER ORDERS CONSIST OF A PURCHASE ORDER REFERENCING THE QUOTE SHEET.*						
CONTENTS						
NO.	DATA NAME		FREQUENCY	CHARACTERS	A/N	ORIGIN
	✳ *SAME AS R-3000*					
	NOTE:					
	IF R-3000 IS NOT USED AS CUSTOMER ORDER,					
	FILE COPY IS REPRODUCED TO CREATE R 2020.					

R.L. CASEY   *C.F. BETTORS*   *1 OF 1*

DATE   ANALYST   SOURCE   PAGE

BUTODALE

STUDY

Figure 10-23   Message sheet for a customer order.

MESSAGE NAME			MESSAGE NO.	
QUOTATION			R-3000	

OTHER NAMES USED	LAYOUT NO.
QUOTE, QUOTE SHEET, BID	QO-561

FORM NO.
QO-561-1 THRU-5

NO. OF COPIES
5

MEDIA	HOW PREPARED
5-PART FORM	TYPEWRITTEN

OPERATIONS INVOLVED IN
001-65X, 001-66X, 001-67X, 001-70X

F 4050.1 IF QUOTE;
F 4050.2 IF BID

REMARKS

THE MESSAGE ISSUED IS A QUOTATION, WHETHER IN RESPONSE TO A REQUEST FOR QUOTATION (R-2000) OR REQUEST FOR BID (R-2010). TWO COPIES ARE SENT TO CUSTOMER; ONE COPY IS USUALLY RETURNED AS R-2020

CONTENTS

NO.	DATA NAME	FREQUENCY	CHARACTERS	A/N	ORIGIN
1	CUSTOMER ORDER # AND DATE	1/PG	AVG. 12/18 MAX	4-A 12/16-N	001-650
2	OUR ORDER # AND DATE	1/PG	16	N	
3	VIA AND TERMS	1/PG	10/30	A/N	
4	BILL TO (3-5 LINES)	1/PG	100/150	A/N	
5	SHIP TO (1-5 LINES)	1/PG	50/150	A/N	
6	ITEM #	.4/PG	1/2	N	
7	QUANTITY	1.9/PG	4/5	A/N	
8	DESCRIPTION	1/PG	1509/2000	A	
9	UNIT PRICE	2.3/PG	3/6	N	
10	PRICE (TOTAL)	.4/PG	5/7	N	
11	DELIVERY DATE	1/PG	6	N	
12	MISC.	.5/PG	70/100	A/N	
	(TOTAL PER PAGE)		1746/2447		
	PAGES: MIN — 1 AVE — 6				
	MAX — 17	(SEE ATTACHED SAMPLE)			

R.L. CASEY	A.R. HOLMES	1 OF 1
ANALYST	SOURCE	PAGE

BUTODALE
STUDY

Figure 10-24 Message sheet for a quotation.

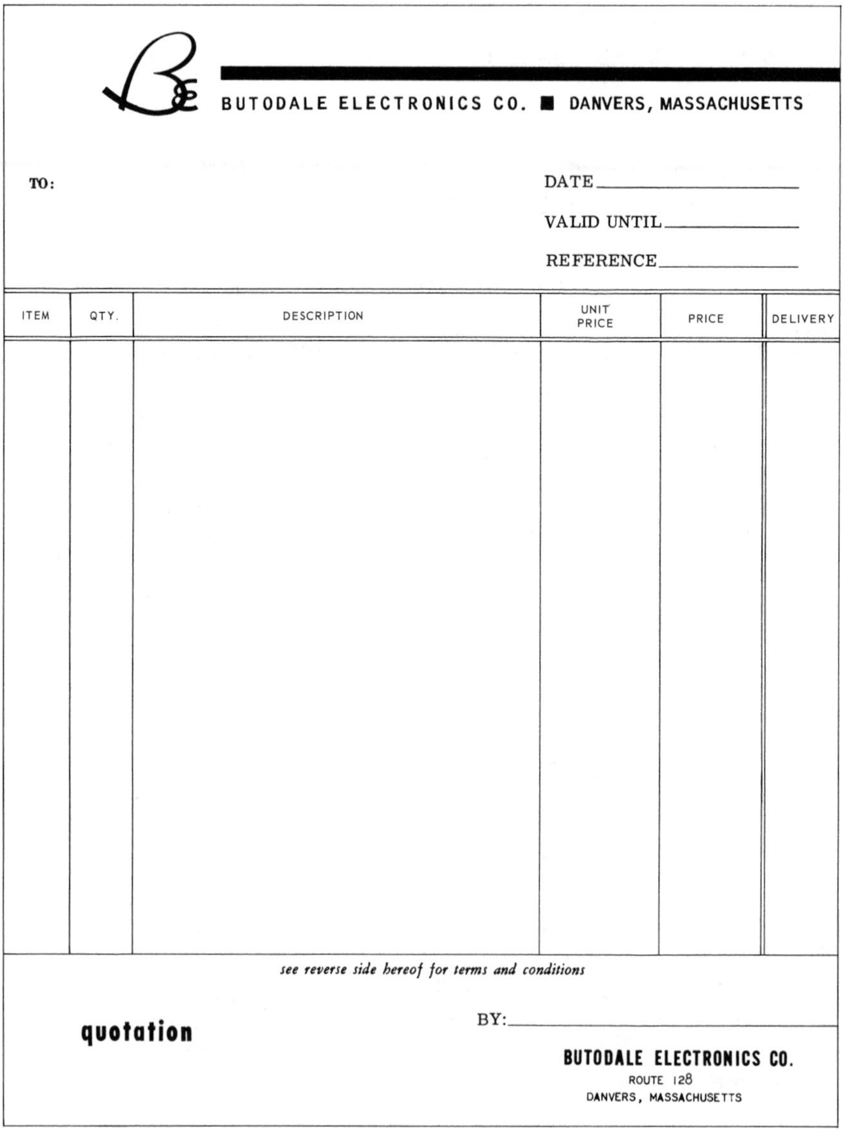

BUTODALE ELECTRONICS CO. ■ DANVERS, MASSACHUSETTS

TO:

DATE ____________

VALID UNTIL ____________

REFERENCE ____________

ITEM	QTY.	DESCRIPTION	UNIT PRICE	PRICE	DELIVERY

see reverse side hereof for terms and conditions

quotation

BY: ____________

BUTODALE ELECTRONICS CO.
ROUTE 128
DANVERS, MASSACHUSETTS

Figure 10-25 Blank quotation form.

MESSAGE NAME MATERIAL COST	MESSAGE NO. R-3010

OTHER NAMES USED COST CARD	LAYOUT NO. _____
	FORM NO. _____
	NO. OF COPIES 1

MEDIA 3 X 5 CARD	HOW PREPARED MANUAL (002-800)

OPERATIONS INVOLVED IN

002 - 800

004 - 56X

004 - 57X

004 - 58X

REMARKS

CONTENTS

NO.	DATA NAME	FREQUENCY	CHARACTERS	A/N	ORIGIN
	SIMILAR FORMAT TO				
	SAMPLE ATTACHED				
	TO F - 4010				

R. L. CASEY   L. K. WHITE   1 OF 1

DATE   ANALYST   SOURCE   PAGE

BUTODALE

STUDY

Figure 10-26 Message sheet for material cost.

MESSAGE NAME		MESSAGE NO.	
JOB PROGRESS REPORT		R- 3020	

OTHER NAMES USED	LAYOUT NO.
	FORM NO.
	NO. OF COPIES 3

MEDIA	HOW PREPARED
PAPER	HAND WRITTEN

OPERATIONS INVOLVED IN

004 - 520, USED AS A PRODUCTION AND SCHEDULING MANAGEMENT AID.

REMARKS

PREPARED DAILY BY PRODUCTION FOREMAN. ONE OR TWO COMMENTS ON EACH JOB HANDLED THAT DAY.

CONTENTS

NO.	DATA NAME	FREQUENCY	CHARACTERS	A/N	ORIGIN
	PERCENT COMPLETE (ESTIMATE)	1	2	N	
	ESTIMATED COMPLETION DATE	1	4	N	
	COMMENTS ON QUALITY, PROBLEMS				
	SCHEDULE ETC.	1	100	A	
	JOB # (ORDER #)	1	6	N	

R.L. CASEY   L. CIPRIANO   / OF /

DATE — ANALYST — SOURCE — PAGE

BUTODALE

STUDY

Figure 10-27   Message sheet for a job progress report.

MESSAGE NAME HOT LIST				MESSAGE NO. R-3030	
OTHER NAMES USED				LAYOUT NO.	
				FORM NO.	
				NO. OF COPIES 3	
MEDIA PAPER		HOW PREPARED MANUALLY			
OPERATIONS INVOLVED IN 004 - 520					
REMARKS USED TO PROMPT PART AND MATERIAL EXPEDITING					

CONTENTS

NO.	DATA NAME	FREQUENCY	CHARACTERS	A/N	ORIGIN
	ESTIMATED DAYS BEHIND SCHEDULE	1	2	N	
	PART #	1	6	N	
	JOB (ORDER #)	1	6	N	

R.L. CASEY   L. CIPRIANO   1 OF 1
DATE   ANALYST   SOURCE   PAGE
BUTODALE
STUDY

Figure 10-28   Message sheet for the hot list.

MESSAGE NAME QUALITY REPORT				MESSAGE NO. R-3040	
OTHER NAMES USED REJECT SHEET				LAYOUT NO.	
				FORM NO.	
				NO. OF COPIES 2	

MEDIA PAPER (TABULAR)	HOW PREPARED MANUALLY

OPERATIONS INVOLVED IN 004 - 530

REMARKS

CONTENTS

NO.	DATA NAME	FREQUENCY	CHARACTERS	A/N	ORIGIN
	LOT SIZE	1	3	N	
	SAMPLE SIZE	1	3	N	
	# REJECTED	1	3	N	
	JOB # (ORDER #)	1	6	N	

R.L. CASEY
DATE ANALYST

BUTODALE
STUDY

I.L. MALLOY
SOURCE

1 OF 1
PAGE

Figure 10-29 Message sheet for the quality report.

MESSAGE NAME ORDER ACKNOWLEDGMENT				MESSAGE NO. R - 3050	
OTHER NAMES USED				LAYOUT NO. _____	
				FORM NO. _____	
				NO. OF COPIES 3	
MEDIA LETTER		HOW PREPARED TYPEWRITTEN			
OPERATIONS INVOLVED IN 001 - 75 X					
004 - 51 X					
F - 4050					
REMARKS ORIGINAL TO CUSTOMER					
FIRST COPY TO F - 4050					
SECOND COPY TO T.R. FELLOWS (SALES MGR.)					
CONTENTS					
NO.	DATA NAME	FREQUENCY	CHARACTERS	A/N	ORIGIN
1.	TODAYS DATE	1	$^{AVE}/6_{MAX}$	N	
2.	CUSTOMER NAME AND ADDRESS	1	$30/70$	A	
3.	REFERENCE #'s	1	$6/18$	A/N	
4	DELIVERY DATE	1	6	N	
5	PRICE	1	$5/7$	N	
6	MISC. COPY	1	$120/400$	A	
7	AUTHORIZED SIGNATURE	1	$12/30$	A	
	ESTIMATED TOTAL		$179/531$		

R.L. CASEY   C.F. BETTORS   1 OF 1
DATE _____   ANALYST   SOURCE   PAGE
BUTODALE
STUDY

Figure 10-30   Message sheet for the order acknowledgment.

MESSAGE NAME					MESSAGE NO.
PAYROLL REPORT					*R- 3060*

OTHER NAMES USED	LAYOUT NO.
HOURS LIST	
	FORM NO.
	NO. OF COPIES
	3

MEDIA	HOW PREPARED	
STOCK TAB PAPER		*ACCOUNTING MACHINE*

OPERATIONS INVOLVED IN
004 - 550   P/R   ACCOUNTING

REMARKS

CONTENTS

NO.	DATA NAME	FREQUENCY	CHARACTERS	A/N	ORIGIN
	DEPARTMENT		3	N	
	MAN		5	N	
	SHIFT		1	N	
	CODE ("X" OVER SHIFT FOR O.T.)				
	REGULAR HOURS (XXO)	✳	3	N	
	OVERTIME HOURS (XXO)	✳	3	N	
	TOTAL HOURS	✳	3	N	
	CARD COUNT	✳	2	N	
	MAN TOTAL COUNTS EXCEPT MINOR	✳	3		
	MINOR TOTALS OF ✳ BY MAN	325	11		
	INTERMED. TOTALS " " " SHIFT	36	21		
	MAJOR " " " " DEPT.	27	21		
	FINAL " " " OVER ALL	1	22		

R.L. CASEY   *R.F. ROBINSON*   *1 OF 1*

DATE   ANALYST   SOURCE   PAGE

BUTODALE
STUDY

Figure 10-31 Message sheet for the payroll report.

MESSAGE NAME SHIPPING REPORT				MESSAGE NO. R-3070		
OTHER NAMES USED				LAYOUT NO.		
				FORM NO.		
				NO. OF COPIES		
MEDIA		HOW PREPARED				
OPERATIONS INVOLVED IN						
REMARKS NOT REVIEWED						

CONTENTS

NO.	DATA NAME	FREQUENCY	CHARACTERS	A/N	ORIGIN

R.L. CASEY   1 OF 1
_____   _____   _____
DATE   ANALYST   SOURCE   PAGE
BUTODALE
STUDY

Figure 10-32   Message sheet for the shipping report.

MESSAGE NAME CONSOLIDATED PERFORMANCE REPORT.				MESSAGE NO. R-3080	
OTHER NAMES USED				LAYOUT NO.	
				FORM NO.	
				NO. OF COPIES 3	
MEDIA STANDARD TAB PAPER		HOW PREPARED TAB EQUIPMENT			
OPERATIONS INVOLVED IN 004 - 570					
COMPLETE PREPARATION PROCEDURE DOCUMENTED IN COST ACCOUNTING D P SECTION					
REMARKS SHOWS % DEVIATION FROM STANDARD BY OPERATION.					

		CONTENTS					
NO.	DATA NAME			FREQUENCY	CHARACTERS	A/N	ORIGIN

R.L. CASEY   L.K. WHITE   1 OF 1
DATE   ANALYST   SOURCE   PAGE

BUTODALE
STUDY

Figure 10-33 Message sheet for the consolidated performance report.

MESSAGE NAME COMPLETED PROJECTS REPORT.				MESSAGE NO. R- 3090		
OTHER NAMES USED				LAYOUT NO.		
				FORM NO.		
				NO. OF COPIES 2		
MEDIA STANDARD TAB PAPER		HOW PREPARED TAB EQUIPMENT				
OPERATIONS INVOLVED IN 004 – 580						
Complete procedure documented in General accounting D.P. section						
REMARKS Lists completed (weekly) projects with scheduled and actual completion dates						
CONTENTS						
NO.	DATA NAME		FREQUENCY	CHARACTERS	A/N	ORIGIN
	R.L. CASEY ANALYST		R.F. ROBINSON SOURCE			1 OF 1 PAGE
BUTODALE STUDY	DATE					

Figure 10-34   Message sheet for the completed projects report.

FILE NAME *PRICING FILE*				FILE NO. *F-4000*		
LOCATION *QUOTATION SECTION*		STORAGE MEDIUM *3 × 5 TRACK-INDEX Roller CaBinets*				
ACCESS REQUIREMENTS *MANUAL, RANDOM — 10 SECOND SEARCH;*						
RECORD STAYS IN FILE						
SEQUENCED BY *END ITEM OR PART #*						
CONTENT QUALIFICATIONS *STANDARD SELLING PRICE IS SHOWN.*						
HOW CURRENT *DAILY*						
RETENTION CHARACTERISTICS *UNTIL ITEM/PART DISCONTINUED*						
OR PRICE CHANGED						
LABELS						
USED IN 001-53X, 001-57X,						
REMARKS *FILE CARD FORMAT IS SHOWN BELOW; THERE IS NO*						
MESSAGE SHEET TO DESCRIBE "PRICING FILE CARD".						

CONTENTS

SEQUENCE NO.	MESSAGE NAME	VOLUME		CHARACTERS PER MESSAGE	CHARACTERS PER FILE	
		AVG.	PEAK		AVG.	PEAK
1	*ITEM OR PART #*	*240K*	*300K*	*7*	*1,680K*	*2,100K*
2	*DESCRIPTION*			*6/30*	*1,440K*	*9,000K*
3	*EFFECTIVE DATE*			*6*	*1,440K*	*1,800K*
4	*PRICE*			*3/7*	*720K*	*2,100K*
5	*UNIT OF MEASURE*			*2*	*480K*	*600K*
	TOTAL			*24/52*	*5,760K*	*15,600K*

R.F. CASEY	*A.R. HOLMES*	*1 OF 1*
DATE ANALYST	SOURCE	PAGE

BUTODALE STUDY

Figure 10-35 File sheet for the pricing file.

FILE NAME COST FILE				FILE NO. F - 4010		
LOCATION QUOTATIONS SECTION			STORAGE MEDIUM 3X5 TRACK-INDEX ROLLER CABINETS			
ACCESS REQUIREMENTS						
SEQUENCED BY DATE WITHIN BUTODALE PART NUMBER.						
CONTENT QUALIFICATIONS						
HOW CURRENT						
RETENTION CHARACTERISTICS NO CARDS HAVE YET BEEN DISCARDED.						
LABELS						
USED IN 001 - 57 X, 001 - 63 X,						
REMARKS FILE CONTINUES TO GROW, AS NO DISCARD RULES EXIST. OLDEST CARDS ARE AGE OF COMPANY'S RECORDING SYSTEM.						

CONTENTS

SEQUENCE NO.	MESSAGE NAME	VOLUME		CHARACTERS PER MESSAGE	CHARACTERS PER FILE	
		AVG.	PEAK		AVG.	PEAK
	HISTORICAL COST DATA CARDS	1,000 K UPWARDS. FILE INCREASES				
		AT RATE OF 4200 CARDS PER				
		MONTH.				
	(SEE ATTACHED SAMPLE CARD)					

R.L. CASEY	QUOTATIONS	1 OF 1
ANALYST	SOURCE	PAGE

BUTODALE
STUDY

Figure 10-36   File sheet for the cost file.

HISTORIAL COST DATA

Type No. — *Sample*

5.001.ANC.3

Item

Pre-Patch Panel

Proj No.	Qty.	Std. Cost	Unit Direct L.	Unit O/H	Unit Material	Actual Cost	Unit Time
6843	253	122.⁷⁸	12.⁹¹	36.⁹²	T/₁ + 24.89 44.86	119.⁵⁸	
6083	150	80.⁰⁰	11.⁶⁰	40.¹⁴	T/₀ + 2.¹³ 72.61	122.²²	
5533	800	66.⁶⁷	9.⁴⁵	12.⁸⁴	T/₁ + 3.⁷⁶ 48.81	74.⁸⁶	*

*Cost Less G. A.

Figure 10-37 Sample of a record from the cost file.

FILE NAME RATE FILE		FILE NO. F-4020	

LOCATION ENGINEERING ADMIN.   STORAGE MEDIUM 3×5 CARDS

ACCESS REQUIREMENTS
MANUAL, RANDOM

SEQUENCED BY
OPERATION TYPE SEQUENCE FOR FIRST SECTION
MATERIAL CODE   "   "   "   SECOND   "   "

CONTENT QUALIFICATIONS

HOW CURRENT

RETENTION CHARACTERISTICS

LABELS

REMARKS
USED IN 001-63X (COSTING SPECIAL PARTS ETC.)

CONTENTS

SEQUENCE NO.	MESSAGE NAME	VOLUME		CHARACTERS PER MESSAGE	CHARACTERS PER FILE	
		AVG.	PEAK		AVG.	PEAK
	FLEXIBLE FORMAT SIMILAR					
	TO F-4010					
	APPROX. 4000 CARDS IN FILE					
	OPERATION OR MATERIAL #					
	RATE/COST FOR: DIRECT LBR					
	O/H					
	MATERIAL					
	MISC. NOTES AND REFERENCES					

R.L. CASEY   F.E. RYAN   1 OF 1
DATE   ANALYST   SOURCE   PAGE

BUTODALE
STUDY

Figure 10-38   File sheet for the rate file.

FILE NAME INSTALLED SYSTEMS				FILE NO. F-4030		
LOCATION MARKETING ADMIN.			STORAGE MEDIUM MANILA FOLDERS			
ACCESS REQUIREMENTS						

SEQUENCED BY
BUTODALE ORDER NUMBER WITHIN SYSTEM TYPE

CONTENT QUALIFICATIONS

HOW CURRENT

RETENTION CHARACTERISTICS
NEVER BEEN PURGED

LABELS
USED IN OOI-57X

REMARKS
INTENT OF FILE SEEMS VAGUE; A DIFFERENT SEQUENCE MAY MAKE INFO READILY USABLE.

CONTENTS

SEQUENCE NO.	MESSAGE NAME	VOLUME		CHARACTERS PER MESSAGE	CHARACTERS PER FILE	
		AVG.	PEAK		AVG.	PEAK
	SAME AS					
	F-4050					
	15 FILE CABINETS (4-DRAWER)					
	ESTIMATED 4,500 FOLDERS					

DATE	R.L. CASEY ANALYST	A.R. HOLMES SOURCE	1 OF 1 PAGE

BUTODALE STUDY

Figure 10-39 File sheet for the installed systems file.

SEE ALSO F-4050.1 AND .2

FILE NAME CONTRACT REGISTER FILE			FILE NO. F-4050		
LOCATION MARKETING ADMINISTRATION		STORAGE MEDIUM MANILA FOLDERS			

ACCESS REQUIREMENTS

SEQUENCED BY

CONTENT QUALIFICATIONS
F-4050.1 AS QUOTE IS PROCESSED; F-4050.2 AS BID IS PROCESSED. DESIGNATION OF .1 AND .2 IS DISCONTINUED AS ORDER IS PROCESSED.

HOW CURRENT

RETENTION CHARACTERISTICS
WHEN DELIVERY TO CUSTOMER IS MADE, FOLDER IS MOVED TO F-4030

LABELS

REMARKS
001-66X, 001-70X, 001-74X, 001-75X, 004-51X, 004-59X, 004-61X

	CONTENTS					
SEQUENCE NO.	MESSAGE NAME	VOLUME		CHARACTERS PER MESSAGE	CHARACTERS PER FILE	
		AVG.	PEAK		AVG.	PEAK
—	F-4050.1 QUOTE FOLDER	50/w	70/w	460	23,000	32,200
—	F-4050.2 BID FOLDER	10/w	12/w	1,110	11,100	13,320
—	OPEN ORDERS					
	TOTAL	1500	2100			

R.L. CASEY   A.R. HOLMES   1 OF 1
DATE ANALYST   SOURCE   PAGE
BUTODALE
STUDY

Figure 10-40   File sheet for the contract register file.

FILE NAME QUOTE FOLDER					FILE NO. F - 4050.1	
LOCATION			STORAGE MEDIUM MANILA FOLDER			
ACCESS REQUIREMENTS						
SEQUENCED BY						
CONTENT QUALIFICATIONS						
HOW CURRENT						
RETENTION CHARACTERISTICS						
LABELS						
REMARKS						

CONTENTS

SEQUENCE NO.	MESSAGE NAME	VOLUME		CHARACTERS PER MESSAGE	CHARACTERS PER FILE	
		AVG.	PEAK		AVG.	PEAK
1	R-2000 REQUEST FOR QUOTE	50/w	70/w	460	23,000	32,200

R.L. CASEY   A.R. HOLMES   1 OF 1

DATE   ANALYST   SOURCE   PAGE

BUTO DALE

STUDY

Figure 10-41   File sheet for the quote folder.

FILE NAME				FILE NO.			
REQUEST - FOR - BID FOLDER				F-4050.2			
LOCATION —			STORAGE MEDIUM MANILA FOLDER				
ACCESS REQUIREMENTS							
SEQUENCED BY							
CONTENT QUALIFICATIONS							
HOW CURRENT							
RETENTION CHARACTERISTICS							
LABELS							
REMARKS							

		CONTENTS					
SEQUENCE NO.	MESSAGE NAME		VOLUME		CHARACTERS PER MESSAGE	CHARACTERS PER FILE	
			AVG.	PEAK		AVG.	PEAK
1	R-2010 REQUEST FOR BID		10/w	12/w	1110	11,100	13,320

R.L. CASEY   A.R. HOLMES   1 OF 1
ANALYST   SOURCE   PAGE

BUTODALE
DATE / STUDY

Figure 10-42   File sheet for the request-for-bid folder.

FILE NAME	CUSTOMER INDEX BOOK			FILE NO. F-4060	

LOCATION	MARKETING ADMIN.		STORAGE MEDIUM POST BINDERS (4 VOLUMES) COLUMNAR PAPER		

ACCESS REQUIREMENTS

SEQUENCED BY

CUSTOMER   NAME

CONTENT QUALIFICATIONS

ACTIVITY   IN   PAST   10   YEARS

HOW CURRENT

DAILY

RETENTION CHARACTERISTICS

LABELS

REMARKS

HAND   ENTRIES   POSTED   ON   ORDER   RECEIPT

001 — 71X

CONTENTS

SEQUENCE NO.	MESSAGE NAME	VOLUME		CHARACTERS PER MESSAGE	CHARACTERS PER FILE	
		AVG.	PEAK		AVG.	PEAK
	CUSTOMER NAME					
	CUSTOMER #					
	REFERENCE #'s AND DATES					
	BUTODALE ORDER #AND DATE					
	APPROXIMATELY 4,000 CUSTOMERS					
	MINIMUM ENTRIES — 1					
	AVERAGE ENTRIES — 4					
	MAXIMUM ENTRIES — 50					

R.L. CASEY   C.F. BETTORS   1 OF 1

DATE   ANALYST   SOURCE   PAGE

BUTODALE

STUDY

Figure 10-43 File sheet for the customer index book.

FILE NAME	PROJECT INDEX BOOK				FILE NO. F-4070			
LOCATION				STORAGE MEDIUM Post Binder, Columnar Paper				
ACCESS REQUIREMENTS								
SEQUENCED BY BUTODALE ORDER #								
CONTENT QUALIFICATIONS ORDER RECEIVED OR PROJECT INITIATED								
HOW CURRENT DAILY								
RETENTION CHARACTERISTICS WHEN BINDER IS FULL, SHEETS BEARING PROJECTS CLOSED 6 MONTHS ARE PUT IN DEAD STORAGE.								
LABELS								
REMARKS HAND ENTRIES ARE POSTED AS PROJECT IS INITIATED (001-71X) AND COMPLETED (004-59X)								

		CONTENTS						
SEQUENCE NO.	MESSAGE NAME		VOLUME		CHARACTERS PER MESSAGE	CHARACTERS PER FILE		
			AVG.	PEAK		AVG.	PEAK	
	PROJECT IN BINDER (30 PROJECTS/PAGE)		1,500	2,100				

R.L. CASEY   C. F. BETTORS   1 OF 1
ANALYST   SOURCE   PAGE

DATE

BUTODALE
STUDY

Figure 10-44 File sheet for the project index book.

FILE NAME ASSIGNMENT SHEET				FILE NO. F-4080		
LOCATION MANUFACTURING ADMIN.		STORAGE MEDIUM "SCHEDUGRAPH" BOARD				
ACCESS REQUIREMENTS DAILY — PHOTO COPIES DISTRIBUTED TO MARKETING AND MANUFACTURING DAILY						
SEQUENCED BY DUE DATE						
CONTENT QUALIFICATIONS ACCEPTED ORDER OR ACTIVE PROJECT						
HOW CURRENT BOARD SHOWS PREVIOUS 2 WEEKS AND FUTURE 28 WEEKS –						
RETENTION CHARACTERISTICS PHOTO COPIES SHOW CLOSING DAILY STATUS BOARD CHANGES CONTINUALLY						
LABELS						
REMARKS 001-72X, 004-51X						

CONTENTS

SEQUENCE NO.	MESSAGE NAME	VOLUME		CHARACTERS PER MESSAGE	CHARACTERS PER FILE	
		AVG.	PEAK		AVG.	PEAK
	PROJECT OR ORDER #					
	PRODUCT TYPE					
	SCHEDULE DATES					
	DUE DATE					

R.L. CASEY — DATE / ANALYST   L. CIPRIANO — SOURCE   1 OF 1 — PAGE

BUTODALE STUDY

Figure 10-45   File sheet for the assignment sheet.

PART

DETERMINING SYSTEM REQUIREMENTS

The purpose of Part 3 is to present the philosophy and methodology involved in determining system requirements. After completion of the study of the present business and before designing the new system, it is necessary to determine what the system is required to do and how the performance of the system will be evaluated.

In Part 3 we cover the methodology involved in determining systems requirements and the preparation of a report which we call the *System Requirements Specification*. We explain how the information gathered during the study of the existing system assists in determining the requirements for the new system. However, in this second phase it is necessary to look beyond present relationships to establish the logical requirements needed to meet future goals and objectives.

Additional documentation methods are explained as they apply to this phase, and Part 3 concludes with the System Requirements Specification for two activities of the Butodale case study.

11

System Goals and Activity Alignment

11.1 INTRODUCTION

In determining the requirements of a system, the analysts must answer three questions:

1. What is the system required to do?
2. How well is it to do it?
3. How is the system's performance to be evaluated?

In understanding an existing organization, the study team concentrates on gaining understanding and insight into a business as it presently operates and reacts to its environment. Now it is necessary to look beyond present relationships to find out what the system is logically required to do to meet future business goals and objectives.

A goal statement is valuable as a definition of purpose and intent; it acquires larger significance when it is related directly to the activities of a business. An activity is a series of logically related operations which support and fulfill a specific business goal. Since an activity is goal-directed in nature, it demonstrates a justification for existence; this characteristic is often absent in contemporary organizational alignments.

Activities are defined by the analysts as they study the existing organization and, along with the statement of present goals, are the basis for requirement definition. The goal statement and activity formulation are vital inputs to this work, because it is possible to analyze what is required of a system only if it is first known what useful purpose the system serves.

System requirements cannot be determined solely from an understanding of present conditions; future plans and growth have an equally important influence. To the present, judgments of the future must be added by forecasting the impact of new products and services, changes in mix, volume trends, design and process innovations, enactment of regulatory laws, and competitive products. In the conduct of this work, a study team hypothesizes, analyzes, synthesizes, and simulates to establish true systems requirements reflecting both the present and the future.

The objective the team works toward is a report on system requirements, activity by activity. The report shows operations that must be performed, inputs that must be accepted, outputs that must be produced, resources that should be employed, and factors for measuring performance of system designs.

The goal statement, the definition of activities, and time, cost, and accuracy data for individual operations within an activity (and in summary) are principal inputs to the requirements specification. The Phase I report describing the present business furnishes a substantial share of the information for requirements specification, but data about the future must still be secured. Often the goal statement and activity formulation are not sufficiently precise, or should be revised in the light of new study findings. Both should be appraised early in Phase II before definitive requirements specifications are established.

11.2 STUDY SCOPE

The study of requirements begins after the report of the existing organization has been accepted by management and approval is given to continue. This second part of the study ends with management approval of the system requirements specifications. Between these two points, the study team engages in the diverse tasks of specifying the requirements for the new system. These tasks include:

1. Analyzing, defining, and modifying present and future objectives to produce a statement of true business goals.
2. Modifying existing activities or creating new ones to align with these redefined business goals; specifying activity scope and boundaries.
3. Analyzing each activity to establish required inputs, operations, outputs, and resources.
4. Refining these requirements through several iterations.
5. Constructing measures of effectiveness for each activity.
6. Documenting system requirements.

Requirement complexity varies from activity to activity. Since activities initially are defined to be relatively self-contained, complexity can be reduced by analyzing each one individually. We must realize that there will normally be some conflict and overlapping among activities. Therefore, later, when designing the new system, the activities can be integrated, and any inconsistencies or incompatibilities can be worked out. Analysis by activity may disclose certain overall constraints (technical or managerial) which may limit the study team's range of possible solutions. Recognition of these constraints is necessary for successful systems design. After requirements have been determined, acceptable and desirable performance levels are identified. This sets up a series of performance targets to be met in systems design.

The development of requirements may be a relatively straightforward process, or it may involve difficult and complex analysis. Interviews and data analysis provide satisfactory information for specifications in many instances; in others, a high level of technical competence in the use of management science techniques is required.

11.3   THE REPORT OF SYSTEMS REQUIREMENTS

The System Requirements Specification is the descriptive name we use for the output report from Phase II. The analysts should begin the report with a summary section describing the present and future business goals, the general considerations of the overall system, and pertinent information on the several activities as they affect the business.

The balance of the report can be a series of packets, one for each activity, each composed of three sections: general, operations, and measurement. Figure 2.3 shows the structure of a report assembled according to this plan.

The general section customarily outlines activity goals and objectives, scope and boundaries, and other information such as policies and costs that are not examined in the more specialized sections.

The operations section should state what is required of an activity (what it must do) in terms of inputs it must accept, operations it must perform, outputs it must produce, and resources (personnel, equipment, facilities, inventories) it must use to support operations. These elements can be summarized at the beginning of the section in a form that we call the activity requirements model. This form is discussed in Section 12.2.

The measurement section specifies factors and rating scales for evaluating a system designed to perform the activity under a variety of conditions.

Taken together, these activity packets communicate a specification of system requirements that will be readily understood by management and useful to the study team in developing a workable and efficient design for the new system.

The work of the analysts outlined in this book is designed for application to many kinds of industries, to enterprises of different size, and to studies with widely divergent objectives: creative design, mechanization of an existing system, or the continuing modification and improvement which all systems periodically undergo. For each of these situations, it is necessary to prepare a specification of system requirements, however brief.

For major, creative systems design, a statement of requirements is necessary in its full meaning and context, since new systems characteristics will significantly differ from the old. In improvement studies, the statement of requirements may only point out areas of opportunity, thereby upgrading what may have started out to be a simple modification study. Even in a straightforward mechanization study, the statement of requirements can be valuable for bridging the gap between two essentially different types of systems, and may establish a base for more effective design. In each case, it is a matter of determining logical requirements rather than just accepting those that are inherited, or convenient.

The report containing the specifications is a definition of requirements at the problem level in contrast to the solution description of the report containing the proposed design for the new system. This definition forms the base that makes the flexibility of a solution possible—and the base upon which new systems can be built as the organization changes.

11.4   GOALS

Goals of the present business were defined in Phase I, and activities were formulated to meet these goals. In Phase II, goal and activity statements should be reviewed and refined to accommodate changes that occur as a business plans for the future. The goals directly considered are those within the scope of the study. After the analysts and management have reached a mutual understanding on the true goals of the present and future business, activity definitions can be reshaped, and activity scope is realigned to conform to the new goal statement.

In an established business, there is a pronounced emphasis on the demands and pressures of daily work, and often insufficient regard for future events. A billing date arrives and statements must go out; sales decline, and a promotional scheme must be devised to boost new orders; productive capacity is exceeded, and work must be subcontracted. Operating personnel usually have little time to consider the goals of a business; this is more properly the responsibility of those who plan for operations in future time periods. Top managers or business owners decide what the goals should be. But product planners and systems analysts must know and understand these goals if systems designed to support the business are to be effective.

No matter how well the goals of an enterprise may have been thought through by management, they are seldom expressed in a form useful to the systems analyst. The problem in goal analysis is to change the usual broad, generalized statements into direct, specific definitions of what a business is attempting to do. Where goals exist only in the minds of management, they have to be extracted and formulated through interview and discussion. The more clearly and precisely goals are expressed, the more valid the specification of systems requirements will be.

Goals reveal purpose in a business; they state what a business is to do. In this respect, goals are ends rather than means. A sound goal statement shows not just present goals, but future goals that account for what a company strives for during the next month, next year, and even the next decade. A business goal is stated in terms of:

1. Products and services to be supplied.
2. Maintenance of resources, both physical and informational.

3. Improvement of relationships and communications with consumers, suppliers, governments, shareowners, and the general public.

Goals have to be defined before activities can be isolated. For a given goal, an activity (or activities) is designed to support the goal.

The degree of attention devoted to goals varies with the study. Precise goal definition, in a study aimed at creating a new system design for a large and complex business, must provide adequate direction for the study team; precision becomes less important in improvement or mechanization studies. We wish to emphasize that the methodology we present is a useful tool for *less* than an entire business, since most studies are of this kind. In most businesses, a considerable amount of time elapses from the inception of an idea to its practical implementation as a finished product or service. To maintain competitive advantage, a business must continually look ahead and plan for new products and services, often years before they are brought to the market. These ideas both determine future goals and support management's plans.

The existence and availability of short- and long-range business plans provides the team with an important input for their study. A typical long range plan contains a wide variety of data about the future business:

1. Types of new products
2. Development of new and present markets
3. Possible changes in product mix
4. Research and development projects
5. Plant expansions and new site selection
6. Projections of cash flow to finance corporate growth
7. Projections on sales and manpower
8. Economic and business environment

In some cases these plans exist partially or even only as ideas in the minds of managers, and the study team must draw them out in interviews.

In a large bank study, for example, the future-planning documents revealed the imminent introduction of new services, such as no-check payroll processing, retail credit servicing, automatic loans, and utility bill payment and collections. Individual interviews with bank officers also revealed that non-return of checks, customer accounts payable processing, and a community credit reference service were under consideration for the future. These services were also incorporated in the future-goal statement.

One study team, faced with poorly defined advance plans, asked each manager to make a list of future goals as he would personally express them on topics of new services and growth for the next ten years. The individual replies were correlated and the most appropriate and most frequently mentioned items were compiled into a composite report.

The study team used this report as a basis for discussion at a management meeting, where an acceptable future-goal statement was finally devised.

11.5 SOURCES OF INFORMATION FOR GOALS

Within a business, analysts can gather information about the future from many different sources. The marketing manager is concerned with future plans on new products, distribution, and market penetration; engineering and research managers are sources for new product and technology data; the manufacturing manager controls plans for the employment of new processes and materials that can affect current and future products.

Throughout Phase II, trend and projection data will be needed to establish numbers for future systems requirements. This information can also be usefully applied to goal definition, especially when long-range plans have not been documented in detail.

An organization's annual report often furnishes clues to future goals. The following excerpts are from the report of a large manufacturer:

On expansion
An aggressive plan of expansion and acquisition has been continued by management while increasing available sales and manufacturing capacity, and, at the same time, allied fields with exceptionally good earning potentials have been entered.

On distribution
Immediate and economical delivery is an especially strong competitive advantage of the company to both its commercial and industrial customers. Recognizing the trend of large industrial companies as well as the newer small technological concerns to locate their research and, in many cases, production facilities away from the traditional population centers, the company began systematically enlarging its market facilities with this in mind. Its branch warehouses from coast to coast are being improved with better inventories, automated billing and invoicing, and efficient stock control.

On capacity
An additional 240,000 square feet of facility will be ready for occupancy this summer, freeing [additional] space presently needed for manufacturing and product development.

Internal projections should be supplemented by forecasts from other sources. Trade associations customarily predict industry trends; government bureaus and brokerage houses develop analyses by industry and commodity; research foundations and centers have information on product and other technological changes. Special studies on a variety of subjects may be of considerable value in determining futures: export markets, consumer attitudes, requirements for presently unsupplied goods and services, and so on.

Figure 11-1 indicates trends of cosmetic sales. The trends projected from this data helped management decide on future compositions of product mix, and on where to concentrate marketing efforts.

Developments and trends in urban renewal, additional legislation on health and welfare, changes in leisure-time habits, and new patterns in income by family groups can be analyzed for their effect on future conditions.

Although an analyst can draw on considerable company, industry, and govern-

SALES GROWTH OF SELECTED COSMETICS ITEMS
(All sales figures expressed in millions of dollars)

	10	9	8	7	6	5	4	3	2	1	0
Rinses, Tints, Dyes	74	67	46	37	32	28	24	14	13	12	11
Spray Hair Fixatives	91	81	76	81	82	75	38	23	16	5	2
Shaving Cream - Aerosol	54	51	44	39	36	30	27	20	-	-	-
After-Shave Lotion	49	47	44	41	38	35	32	30	28	27	26
Liquid Facial Cleansers	29	29	26	26	26	25	21	8	-	-	-
Lipsticks	121	100	91	82	76	71	64	56	54	35	32
Mascara, Eyebrow Pencil, Eye Shadow	21	18	15	12	10	9	8	7	6	6	5
Toilet Water and Cologne	103	93	84	73	65	58	53	51	49	48	46

Figure 11-1   Trends of cosmetic sales for an eleven-year period.

ment material for future goal formulation, this raw data must be related directly to the future operations of the particular business. Until such data is translated into a plan for facilities, manpower, and materials, it is not particularly useful. The systems analyst, in analyzing this type of data, can serve as a catalyst to management thinking. The ultimate decision on what goals are appropriate for the future of a business rests with management.

11.6   AN EXAMPLE OF SETTING GOALS

The modification of a preliminary goals and objectives statement can be shown in the study of a large commercial bank. The study's initial statement emphasized present goals:

GOALS AND OBJECTIVES—PHASE I

1. Maintain and increase time and deposit balances to provide lending and investment ability consistent with customer needs and bank profit planning.
2. Increase speed, accuracy, and control of operations without incurring increased costs.
3. Improve customer service by reducing teller and loan processing time.
4. Pay interest rates and establish interest policies that are competitive with the banking industry, and as prescribed by Federal Reserve regulations.
5. Maintain loans outstanding at a figure consistent with and prescribed by bank policy through the extension of credit to qualified applicants.
6. Strengthen and maintain dealer relationships through continued good service, fair policies and practices, and competitive plans.
7. Serve the financing needs of the community and provide a profitable return to the bank on investments.
8. Make each customer a total bank customer.
9. Protect the quality of the loan portfolio and produce accurate and timely records for the customer.
10. Fulfill the borrowing requirements of present and potential individual and business customers, in order to provide a safe and profitable return to the bank.
11. Portray the bank's image by presenting positive identification factors to the public.

The goal statement, developed while the analysts were studying the existing management system, was inclusive enough, but it contained a mixture of performance, system, and business goals; many were tied to a general-purpose goal—profit. Early in Phase II, the goal statement was reappraised and modified to read:

GOALS AND OBJECTIVES—PHASE II

1. Offer a balanced package of banking services to the community and surrounding areas which recognize customer needs, comply with federal, state and local regulations and laws, and are competitive in cost, accuracy, and timeliness.
2. Maintain and increase time and demand deposit balances to provide lending and investment ability.
3. Maintain outstanding loan balances at a level consistent with established bank policy, and by accepting only qualified applicants.
4. Secure new and total bank account affiliations through promotional programs, and maintain the quality of bank-customer relationships and services.
5. Provide for the extension of bank services into newly developed surburban areas within the bank's established jurisdiction.
6. Explore and develop new banking financing practices and services for individual and business customers.
7. Strengthen and maintain community and employee relationships through continued good service, fair policies and practices, and forward planning.

A study of the two sets of goals reveals that the new set not only brings sharper focus, but also discloses how the bank will develop in the future.

11.7 ACTIVITY REFORMULATION

Activities are the means by which goals are accomplished. Formulated during the study of the existing organization, they undergo modification as future business goals are developed. Individual activities should correspond to individual goals in a fairly close one-to-one relationship, but there will be instances when a number of activities contribute to a single goal, or when a single activity will contribute to two or more goals.

Let us consider an example of an initial statement of activities which were realigned to match a restatement of goals. We use the above goals for the commercial bank. For this bank, the analysts originally defined the activities as:

ACTIVITIES—PHASE I

1. Commercial checking accounts
2. Special checking accounts
3. Commercial loans
4. Mortgage loans
5. Foreign banking
6. Investments and stock transfer
7. Marketing, advertising, and public relations
8. Correspondent banking
9. Legal and real estate
10. Savings accounts
11. Cashier and comptroller
12. Installment loans

Early in Phase II these activities were reviewed with bank management and compared with the new goal statement. It was clear that the early definitions could be realigned. After some time, management and the analysts redefined the bank's activities as:

ACTIVITY FORMULATION—PHASE II

1. Demand deposits
2. Time deposits
3. Installment loans
4. Mortgage loans
5. Commercial loans
6. Marketing

Commercial and special checking accounts, having similar characteristics, were combined into the demand deposits activity. Demand and time deposits were maintained separately for legal reasons. Correspondent banking was absorbed into each of these activities by type of service (demand deposit, time deposit). The three loan activities were, in effect, separate product lines, relatively self-contained, each one starting from and terminating in the outside environment. Advertising, public relations, international banking, legal, and real estate activities were set aside from the immediate study for lack of transaction volume, although some of their operations were picked up in the selected activities. Each of the six activities included certain elements of the bank's functional costs (for example, all activities were entered through teller operations and employed central files).

11.8 ACTIVITY SCOPE

The alignment process yields broad activity definitions. These generalized statements must now be sharpened to provide a scope and boundary for each activity. For the wholly new activity, there is no other way to describe its content.

It is just as important to decide what is excluded from an activity as it is to decide what is included. Precise terminology is necessary to avoid the uncertainty of ambiguous function names. A clear, complete, and understandable reference is needed to prevent confusion between adjacent activities on the part of the study team. The scope and boundary statement describes both what is and what is not included; the format of the description is secondary.

The provide product demand activity statement from Butodale Electronics illustrates these points by treating the activity scope in the following manner:

This activity is concerned with accepting customer orders and preparing bids and quotations for potential customers. Requests and orders are received from company salesmen, manufacturers' representatives, or are placed directly by the customer. They include orders for standard and custom-designed equipments and spare parts, but do not include requests for computation services. Standard equipments are processed routinely and the customer is furnished documents including price quotations, descriptive data, layouts, diagrams, and other information necessary to make the purchase decision.

The statement then goes on to mention special cases:

> Where the equipment is special, this activity includes management and engineering reviews, engineering design and layout, and the compilation of special cost data.
> After receipt of a formal order, the contract is edited and clarified for communication to engineering and manufacturing. Present volume of requests averages 15-20 weekly for standard products, and 3-4 for engineered products. This is expected to rise to a combined total of 25-30 weekly.

While it is not necessary to mention volumes in a scope statement, such information does indicate the activity size. The statement goes on to tell what is not included in this activity:

> Provide product demand does not include market forecasting, determination of plant schedules (this is actually worked out in conference with manufacturing when available capacity does not conform with customer requirements in regard to requested shipping dates), or the calculation of costs and prices.

A final sentence summarizes the statement:

> The principal inputs, then, to this activity are customer orders or requests for quotation, and the principal outputs are quotations and specifications to the customer and communication of accepted orders to manufacturing.

An alternative method to the above type of activity statement is simply to list the operations performed and the operations excluded. The study team for Custodian Life Insurance Company chose the latter technique, which is appropriate when operations are clear-cut and self-explanatory:

> *Operations performed by the New Business activity*
> Review application and related forms
> Request medical and policyholder history
> Prepare processing documents
> Assemble application data
> Underwrite application
> Request additional information
> Prepare declination letter
> Calculate premiums
> Prepare policy
> Prepare internal records
> Prepare external records
> Provide new business statistics on current basis
>
> *Operations not performed by the New Business activity*
> Determine outside underwriting services
> Determine underwriting standards
> Set limits for policy size
> Initiate new plans of insurance
> Determine medical standards
> Determine premium rates or dividend schedules

Recognition of exclusions as well as inclusions avoids making unwarranted assumptions about an activity. An integrated material control activity, for example, usually includes production scheduling and control, inventory control, traffic and transportation, receiving and shipping, purchasing, and other operations related to overall material flow. Sometimes, however, the purchasing activity is under Accounting, or is independent. The inclusion-exclusion coverage should also point out the presence or the absence of functional work. In purchasing, traffic may be an identifiable function—or it may be performed by a buyer.

11.9   ACTIVITY VALIDATION

After the analysts have completed the alignment of activities, their statements should be validated by comparing them with the activity sheets developed earlier, or by having them reviewed by management. We shall discuss both methods of validation.

When finished with the alignment, the analysts should review the activities as a whole to determine if they are complete and meet the established goals; whether they are independent, and whether they are of a size feasible to design and implement. Completeness of coverage can be determined by comparing the aligned statements with the activity sheets. The independence feature is determined by comparing the individual statements as a unit against each of the others within the activity, and to other activities to check for conflicts and overlapping. This audit confirms that each activity is relatively independent and has few interactions with other activities. The review by management of activity formulation serves two purposes:

1. It advises management of the team's approach and progress.
2. It allows management to make known any preferences about the sequence in which activities are to be analyzed.

Management may have several compelling reasons for assigning priority to activities for analysis and implementation, and their decision establishes the sequence of events for the study team. The total dollars expended in an activity frequently help decide which activity is selected for initial study: activities with a high potential for payoff will generally be accorded priority.

In some studies, activities having input from or output to the environment are analyzed first. In other studies, outputs from one activity serve as inputs to the following one. One output from a design engineering activity, for example, can be a bill of materials; the content of the bill of materials establishes the input to the manufacturing-planning activity. Unless there is a strong reason for conducting the manufacturing study first, the engineering analysis takes precedence. Single-activity studies, of course, pose no sequencing problem.

Once management approval has been secured on activity definitions, and priorities have been assigned, schedules can be drawn up for the balance of the work the analysts must do to determine the requirements of the system.

SUMMARY

In determining systems requirements the analysts must ascertain what the system is required to do and how the performance of the system is to be evaluated. Systems requirements cannot be determined solely from an understanding of present conditions; future plans and growth have an equally important influence. The goal statement, the definition of activities, and time, cost, and accuracy data for individual operations within an activity are principal inputs to the requirements specification. Requirement complexity varies from activity to activity. The System Requirements Specification consists of a summary section, and a series of packets, one for each activity. Each activity packet consists of three sections: general, operations, and measurement. Goals have to be defined before activities can be isolated. Information about goals can be obtained from many sources, including the marketing manager, engineering and research manager, and production manager. Activities are reformulated and modified as future goals are developed. The scope and boundary of each activity must be determined, and it is important to specify what is included and what is excluded from each activity. Activity statements prepared by the analysts should be reviewed by management for validation.

12

System
Requirements

12.1 CENTRAL THEME

The central theme in requirements specification is to determine what a system is required to do, activity by activity, in terms of:

1. Outputs it *must* produce
2. Inputs it *must* accept
3. Operations it *must* perform
4. Resources it *must* use

To define system requirements, a study team moves away from present operations as they were described for the existing organization and develops a specification from the position of what is logically necessary (or imposed) to fulfill the goals of an activity.

It is extremely important to specify only those inputs, outputs, operations, and resources which are really required since extraneous specifications will constrain the new system design to be developed in Phase III. The flexibility permitted the system designers is inversely proportional to the tightness of the requirements specification.

The logically required specifications are established first, and are then adjusted to accommodate practical considerations. This produces a more valid specification than one devised by building on present operations directly. Most activities contain many variable and interacting factors and conditions that make it difficult to achieve a requirements specification in a single attempt; frequently several tries are necessary to produce a satisfactory statement.

A study team normally begins by developing descriptive requirements for inputs, operations, outputs, and resources. They then add quantitative data (such as volume and time) to this description. Management Science techniques, such as correlation analysis, sampling, trend projection, forecasting, and simulation, are applied where necessary to increase the precision of the specifications.

12.2 ACTIVITY REQUIREMENTS MODEL

Many analysts have found that the preparation of a preliminary version of an activity requirements model is a useful starting point for the analysis of requirements, even though the model may be subsequently revised. Figure 12-1 shows an abstraction of the relationships in such a model.

Inputs or outputs are stated first since they are usually more closely associated with the goals and objectives of the activity than are operations or resources.

After specifying inputs or outputs, the study team progressively works through an activity to establish a logical sequence of operations required in its performance.

Analysis of required resources results first in the identification of those that are imposed; logically required resources emerge as relationships are developed among inputs, operations, and outputs.

12.3 REQUIRED OUTPUTS AND INPUTS

Activity outputs are often closely related to activity goals. Many activities in an established organization are often subject to constraints. For example, the form of an invoice may be so firmly fixed that management may not permit any change. In somewhat the same way, the method and form of paying employees may be set by a rigid union contract. These and other constraints usually make it easier

Figure 12-1 An abstract model used in specifying the requirements of an activity.

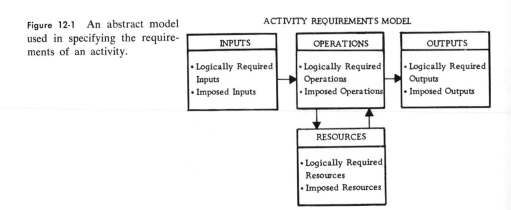

for the analysts to establish an activity's output requirements than its input requirements. Administrative practices often reduce the room for creativity in designing a new system. Because of this, outputs are defined first by most study teams in analyzing an activity. Outputs from one activity that become inputs to another are defined in the form that is acceptable to the second activity. Once outputs are defined, the team can decide what information (inputs) is required to produce the outputs (and, in turn, what operations are required to transform the inputs into outputs) or what operations must be performed to produce the output (and what information is therefore required).

Customer acceptance controls the form and content of many outputs—particularly in a business competing in services, such as banking. Legal and audit stipulations either affect outputs, or are outputs in themselves (insurance and banking reports, small business administration reports, Social Security and income tax reports, and similar forms). Industry practice, as recognized by individual companies or as published by trade associations, also affects output formats. An output may be required by another activity within the business; it may also be required as feedback for repetitive processing or recycling of the activity.

Required inputs have many of the characteristics of required outputs and similarly may be imposed by the environment or other activities. In addition, some inputs are logically required to furnish information for outputs, and provide access to, or maintain, resources.

The determination of logically required inputs and outputs is illustrated in the Butodale study. The goals and objectives of the activity carried on to provide the demand for Butodale's products had been identified as:

1. Sell custom-designed and standard computer equipments and accessories.
2. Communicate individual specifications and requirements for special computer models.

This activity, according to the scope statement shown earlier, was concerned with accepting customer orders and preparing bids and quotations for potential customers. The analysts asked themselves, "What outputs are logically required to meet these objectives?" The second goal suggested one output: equipment specifications. The activity covered both custom-designed and standard units; therefore some customers ordered from a catalog, while others negotiated a specification and quotation through a series of conferences and letters with the engineering department. For the former, the order was acknowledged and a price and delivery schedule confirmed; for the latter, quotations of estimated price and delivery were prepared and supported by drawings and specifications outlining special equipment features and performance characteristics. Besides these outputs to the customer, the manufacturing department required customer order information to plan production schedules and determine shipping dates. A preliminary specification for outputs was developed from the following information:

1. Quotations
2. Acknowledgments
3. Bids

4. Letters of transmittal
5. Prints and drawings
6. Specifications
7. Audited firm orders
8. Communication of firm orders to shop

After examining the eight outputs, the study team had to decide whether to first establish inputs or the operations required to produce these outputs. From their earlier study of the activities, they knew that operations were extremely complex in engineering, sales, and manufacturing planning, so inputs were selected. The analysts then asked themselves, "What inputs are logically required?" Certainly, firm orders were a prime input; where a prospect was inquiring for information, his letter (or telephone call, wire, or any other suitable form) was also an input. The required inputs were described briefly as:

1. Request for quotation
2. Request to bid
3. Formal orders
4. Telephone calls
5. Letters
6. Wires

With inputs and outputs thus defined, operations were then identified—as they were logically required to transform these inputs into outputs, not necessarily as they were presently performed. Now let us consider the operations.

12.4   THE LOGIC OF OPERATIONS

If a team can define the cause-and-effect relationships which govern the transformation of inputs to outputs, they have established a sound basis for specifying required operations.

Actions do not just happen in a business; they are caused by some event or combination of conditions. The logic behind these operations must be identified before an analyst can see the connections among the events. This logic may take many forms:

1. There may be a specific, identifiable cause or condition which determines the action. ("If the credit rating is OK, approve the order; if not, reject it.")
2. It may be imposed as a directive. ("Response time on telephone calls may not exceed 18 seconds." Reason: a survey found that people intending to place an order hang up after this length of time when the ring is unanswered.)
3. It is the only practical alternative to a situation; or it is an industry-wide practice (passbook for savings bank customers).
4. It is the selection of a series of sequential operations, all of which have to be performed but not necessarily in a specific order (auditing an invoice).

Any or all of these are used in the development of requirements. Sometimes there is a direct cause-and-effect relationship among events; at other times there is a process of selecting, or combining practical alternatives.

Narrative form is often used to document simple operations. The following paragraph reveals the basis for determining an insurance premium rate:

> Premium rate for a policy depends on the status of an applicant's health, age, occupation and sex. When these conditions are not covered in the appropriate instructions, rate is established by the underwriting department.

Although narrative form is widely used to inform people about operations, practices, and procedures, it can be supplemented by two alternative methods that have considerable merit for the documentation of operations—flowcharts and decision tables.

12.5 FLOWCHARTS

Where decision logic becomes too complex for successful explanation through narrative form, techniques such as flowcharts or decision tables can be used to demonstrate significant relationships among operations. As an example, let us consider the logical operations required in determining whether a customer's order can be filled or must be refused.

Figure 12-2 contains the narrative form of the steps in the process. Figure 12-3 contains the same process expressed in flowchart form. The symbols in the flowchart have been numbered and the statements in the narrative have been lettered to facilitate the following explanation.

In the example, one of four results must occur. They are:

1. Fill the order from stock
2. Fill the order by making the item
3. Fill the order by purchasing the item
4. Refuse the order

---

a. If the order is for a stock item and the item is in stock, prepare its shipment and send it to the customer.

b. If the order is for a nonstock item and it is feasible to make the item, have it made, prepare its shipment, and send to the customer. Otherwise, examine the feasibility of purchasing the item.

c. If it is feasible to purchase the item, then order it. When it is received, prepare the shipment and send it to the customer. Otherwise, prepare a refusal notice and send to the customer.

d. If the order is for a stock item but the item is not in stock, follow the procedure for a nonstock item.

Figure 12-2 Narrative form stating the logical decisions and operations involved in handling a customer's order.

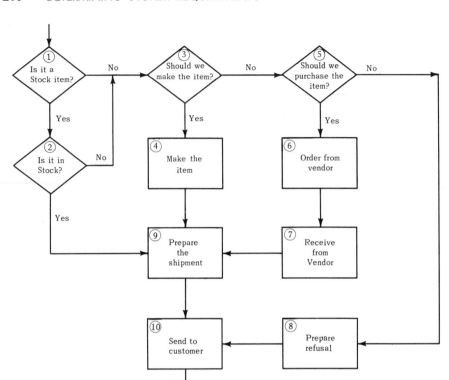

Figure 12-3 Flowchart exhibiting the logical decisions and operations in handling a customer's order.

In the narrative form statement "a" is the procedure for obtaining result 1 above. The same procedure is expressed in the flowchart through symbols numbered 1, 2, 9, 10.

Figure 12-4 is a table showing the statements of the narrative form and the corresponding symbols of the flowchart which are executed to obtain each of the above four possible results. Figure 12-4 also shows the equivalent rules of a decision table expressing the same basic logic as in the narrative and flowchart forms. We discuss decision tables next.

12.6 DECISION TABLES

The basic objective of decision tables is to arrange and present the logic of a set of operations in a form which will facilitate the understanding of the relationship between the conditions and the resultant actions. A decision table expresses logic in tabular form just as a flowchart expresses logic in a diagrammatic form or a Boolean equation uses symbolic representation.

Figure 12-5 is an example of a decision table. It expresses the same logic as the narrative in Figure 12-2 and the flowchart in Figure 12-3.

The decision table in Figure 12-5 consists of: (a) Condition stub (b) Condition entry (c) Action stub (d) Action entry. The equivalent narrative statements and

Result (output)	Type of Item	Narrative Statements	Flowchart Sequence	Decision Table Rule
1. Fill the order from stock	Stock	a	①, ②, ⑨, ⑩	1
2. Fill the order by making the item	Stock	d, b	①, ②, ③, ④, ⑨, ⑩	2
	Nonstock	b	①, ③, ④, ⑨, ⑩	5
3. Fill the order by purchasing the item	Stock	d, b, c	①, ②, ③, ⑤, ⑥, ⑦, ⑨, ⑩	3
	Nonstock	b, c	①, ③, ⑤, ⑥, ⑦, ⑨, ⑩	6
4. Refuse the order	Stock	d, b, c	①, ②, ③, ⑤, ⑧, ⑩	4
	Nonstock	b, c	①, ③, ⑤, ⑧, ⑩	7

Figure 12-4 Table showing the relation among the steps in narrative form (Figure 12-2), in flowchart form (Figure 12-3), and in decision table form (Figure 12-5).

flowchart sequence for each decision table rule are shown in Figure 12-4. In the decision table the decision rules are numbered. Each of these rules can be expressed in statement form. Thus, Rule 1 represents the statement, "Fill the order from stock." The complete equivalent descriptions of the rules are shown next so the reader can see them exactly. The seven rules are:

1. Fill the order from stock
2. Make the item and send it to the customer
3. Order the item and send it to the customer
4. Send the customer a refusal notice
5. Make the item and send it to the customer
6. Order the item and send it to the customer
7. Send the customer a refusal notice

Perhaps the best way for the student to study the decision table is to trace each of the seven possible paths on the flowchart while at the same time following the entries in a single column in the decision table for each path followed in the flowchart.

12.7 COMMENTS ON THE METHODS

Each of the three methods of portraying decisions and operations has advantages and disadvantages. The narrative form is customarily used by management and supervisory personnel who usually find it the most convenient. However,

Rule No.	1	2	3	4	5	6	7
Is it a stock item	Y	Y	Y	Y	N	N	N
Is the item in stock	Y	N	N	N			
Should we make it		Y	N	N	Y	N	N
Should we purchase it			Y	N		Y	N
Make the item		X			X		
Order & receive the item			X			X	
Prepare shipment	X	X	X		X	X	
Prepare refusal				X			X
Send to customer	X	X	X	X	X	X	X

The left of the table is labeled "Condition stub" and "Action stub"; the right is labeled "Condition entry" and "Action entry."

Figure 12-5 Decision table containing the logical decisions and operations in handling a customer's order.

narrative form can easily be misleading because of varying interpretations of the words and the complexity of multiple conditions.

The flowchart form has the advantage of being explicit, but it may be rejected by management, and on occasion by scientific personnel, because of its specialized expression of logic. In fact, analysts should not be too surprised if their flowcharts and decision tables are greeted with lack of interest by some members of management. However, for computer programming purposes the flowchart form is advantageous. Programmers usually write computer programs from flowcharts or mentally picture the logic in flowchart form as they are writing the program. One problem with flowcharts is that they try to picture parallel cases with a serial method of representation.

The decision table form is also explicit. Decision tables generally have the advantage of requiring less space than flowcharts. Decision tables can be used for documenting decision logic at almost any level of complexity. They are particularly valuable as an analytical technique, and are the preferred technique by some analysts, although flowcharts are more widely used. Like flowcharts, decision tables help to insure logical completeness and accuracy.

The method the analyst should use—narrative, flowchart, or decision table—depends upon the complexity of the problem, his audience, his own inclination, and the use that will be made of the logical expression. Since one, two, or all three methods may be required in preparing the information for a study, it is important that members of the study team be capable of using all of them. Space does not permit further discussion of the methods here, and the reader is referred to the bibliography for sources of further information.

12.8 REQUIRED OPERATIONS

We have just discussed three different ways that an analyst can represent the logic of a set of operations. Now let us consider how analysts determine the operations required for the performance of an activity.

Required operations are those that are necessary to produce a required output, accept an input, maintain a resource, or satisfy an activity goal. They may also be present to satisfy audit or legal requirements.

Operations are determined through observation, by hypothesizing operations logic from required inputs or outputs, or by experimentation. Observations of present operations always must be analyzed in terms of future rather than present circumstances.

Several types of relationship are generally evident among operations. There may be *causal dependence*—an operation is required because of the outcome of another operation. In a charge-account activity, the recording of a sale and posting of the file are dependent upon the completion of a sale. *Sequential dependence* occurs when one operation must follow another. In an order-processing activity, the order is received; a picking ticket is prepared; stock is selected, packaged, and shipped; and an invoice is prepared. Stock cannot be shipped until selected and packaged; the selection process must follow the preparation of the picking ticket. This is a sequentially dependent set of operations. When operations are required at periodic or fixed intervals, a *time dependence* relationship is established. For example, a retail store may bill A-F customers on the 10th of the month, G-R customers on the 20th, and S-Z customers on the 30th; operations relating to charges for each group of customers must be performed at these times.

Certain operations in a series of sequential operations may not be carried out in parallel with others, while other operations can be overlapped to reduce total cycle time. Many retail businesses, for example, prepare a multiple-copy order for parallel processing by accounting (setting up the invoice and charge records), stockrooms (stock picking and packaging) and inventory control (reordering). Another example of the overlapping of operations is shown in processing a batch of 100 invoices; calculation of price times quantity is started for the first invoices in the batch, while price lookup and posting is still going on for the bulk of the batch.

An effective approach in analysis of operations is to start with required outputs and attempt to reconstruct the logical sequence back to the required inputs, or vice-versa. In this way, the transformation pattern or logic between inputs and outputs is clearly identified. Systems planners using this approach have found that they tend to identify only processing steps which are really necessary. Another approach is to decide how present system operations (displayed on activity sheets and detailed on operation sheets) need to be modified to accommodate the newly-stated required outputs and inputs. Only occasionally, however, do unusually profitable systems evolve from this approach.

In specifying required operations for the provide product demand activity at Butodale, the study team used the scope and boundary statement as a base for postulating operations.

For standard orders, these operations were designated as logically required:

1. Assemble records relating to an individual order.
2. Determine a delivery schedule.
3. Edit the order in accordance with standard practices.
4. Complete internal and external records.
5. Enter the order on a shop schedule.

For special orders, in addition to the above five, the following three operations were set forth:

1. Establish a design configuration as necessary to meet special customer requirements.
2. Compile special costs and delivery data.
3. Issue quotations and bids.

For the activity requirements model, this statement of operations was documented as follows:

1. Classify incoming requisitions.
2. Prepare quote folder.
3. Prepare bid sheet.
4. Compile cost and price.
5. Establish system configuration on layout sheet.
6. Complete internal and external records.
7. Conduct engineering edit and management review.
8. Issue quotations and bids.
9. Audit and record firm orders.
10. Describe and enter orders to shop schedule.

After the logically required operations of an activity were developed through such an analysis, results were compared with the information on the previously prepared activity and operations sheets. This comparison served as a check on the team's work to insure that requirements were not overlooked.

12.9   REQUIRED RESOURCES

Operations in an information system usually imply the use of resources. Analysts have found that resources are more likely to be subjected to constraints than are operations. When compiling their first list of requirements, they usually make sure to include those resources that will be imposed on the new design. Warehouses, teller windows, and branch offices, for example, are usually imposed even when a business is planning a major expansion or merger. However, to maximize their profitability, linear programming may be used to determine optimal location, size, and number. Likewise, computer simulations of batching operations may be used to determine the effect of changes in location, grouping, and utilization of imposed manufacturing resources such as machine tools and personnel.

The same situation exists for raw, in-process, and finished stock inventories. Inventories, per se, will usually be imposed, but their level (as the result of using different reordering rules) can be established by using computer simulations of inventory management.

The list of personnel requirements is usually confined to skill and job descriptions. The number of individuals employed by a business probably will not change (with the exception of normal hiring to fill vacancies and newly created positions), but the types of positions and their work content may be altered considerably when the new system is installed. Therefore, personnel requirements carrying over to the new system are expressed in terms of what is presently known about position descriptions and costs.

As far as information resources (files) are concerned, they should be described by name—the present name for the resources that already exist, and a name that indicates content for those that do not. Some files are imposed, others are developed by reclassifying logically required information (presently considered as input) as a file.

Generally, resources are left relatively open in the report of requirements (except for those that are imposed), to permit the analysts greater freedom in designing the new system.

As an example, the required resources for the activity needed to provide product demand at Butodale were composed mainly of source files and personnel connected with the performance of the activity. They are:

1. Quotation specialists—engineers
2. Management—typists—clerks
3. Marketing specialists
4. Calculators—typewriters
5. Cost file—assignment sheets
6. Price catalog
7. Rate file
8. Installed systems file
9. Contract register
10. Customer index
11. Project index

This concludes our consideration of the main parts of the model of requirements as separate entities. Now we propose to illustrate the model as a whole, citing our case studies for reference.

12.10   ACTIVITY MODEL EXAMPLE

The activity requirements model for the provide product demand activity at Butodale is shown in Figure 12-6. We want to emphasize that this activity did not exist as an entity except in the minds of the study team. The outputs, for example, were presently produced by many different departments. Quotations, acknowledgments, and letters of transmittal were processed by the sales administration and engineering sales departments; bids were processed by engineering sales and product engineering; prints and drawings were handled by engineering services; and firm orders were taken care of by the sales administration and manufacturing administration departments. Operations were scattered throughout an equally wide variety of departments.

Identification of required inputs, outputs, operations, and resources is not just a simple, straightforward review of the existing system, organization, or activity struc-

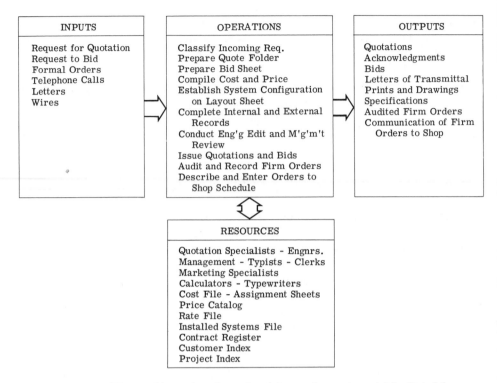

INPUTS	OPERATIONS	OUTPUTS

Request for Quotation
Request to Bid
Formal Orders
Telephone Calls
Letters
Wires
	Classify Incoming Req.
	Prepare Quote Folder
	Prepare Bid Sheet
	Compile Cost and Price
	Establish System Configuration
	  on Layout Sheet
	Complete Internal and External
	  Records
	Conduct Eng'g Edit and M'g'm't
	  Review
	Issue Quotations and Bids
	Audit and Record Firm Orders
	Describe and Enter Orders to
	  Shop Schedule
		Quotations
		Acknowledgments
		Bids
		Letters of Transmittal
		Prints and Drawings
		Specifications
		Audited Firm Orders
		Communication of Firm
		  Orders to Shop

RESOURCES
Quotation Specialists - Engnrs. Management - Typists - Clerks Marketing Specialists Calculators - Typewriters Cost File - Assignment Sheets Price Catalog Rate File Installed Systems File Contract Register Customer Index Project Index

Figure 12-6   The provide product demand activity requirements model for Butodale

ture to isolate extraneous tasks and reports. It requires a careful analysis of logical necessities that are usually scattered throughout the business. Then it requires a creative definition of the systems requirements necessary to meet activity goals. In addition, more than one pass through an activity is usually needed for the team to arrive at a statement of true requirements. After the first pass, subsequent iterations can be made "in reverse" to check requirements accuracy, starting with inputs and proceeding through operations before outputs or resources are established. For example, at the Commercial National Bank, the study team worked from inputs to operations to outputs for the demand deposit activity, since inputs arrived directly from the outside environment (customers). The goal statement and definition of activity scope and boundaries again served as the starting point for analysis. Inputs were specified as they were imposed (utility bill payments), and as they were logically required by the goal statement (deposits from customers). Operations were determined as they became necessary to process each of the inputs, and outputs were identified from the operations. During this analysis, the value of checking out requirements by reversing the analysis was graphically demonstrated. The operation "calculate service charges" was omitted on the first pass, because there was no direct indication that such an operation was logically required from the input statement. However, in working back from outputs, this operation was recognized from the general ledger entries on depositor statements.

The activity model does not show the quantitative aspects of operations. We will explore these now.

12.11   QUANTITATIVE REQUIREMENTS

After the descriptive model of requirements has been completed, rate, frequency, and cost data are developed for inputs, outputs, operations, and resources. Although the subject is treated independently here, in an actual study much of this task is performed concurrently with the building of the rough model of requirements.

Special documentation forms, which are normally included in the report, are used to show certain details for each input and output within an activity. A more detailed explanation of these and other documentation forms for Phase II appears in Chapter 14.

Inputs and outputs should be analyzed for peak and average volumes and rates, cyclic and periodic properties, trends, and patterns to the degree of detail necessary. In classifying requirements, analysts find useful the methods of aggregation (putting like-items together) and segregation (differentiating unlike items). If, for example, customer orders for specials, standards, and spare parts are processed under entirely separate controls and have different cycles, then each parts category should be treated individually.

Much Phase I data on peak and average volumes can be used here, as long as it is expanded to reflect future requirements. Sales forecasts, operating budgets for future time periods, and management plans secured when analyzing goals, are sources for this information. If forecasting data is not available, estimates of potential growth can be made from industry forecasts, or from present averages extended into the future. Sampling techniques are used whenever possible in trend projection to reduce the volume of data.

Figure 12-7 is an input-output sheet as it has been filled out for the provide demand activity in Butodale Electronics. Pertinent information on inputs is located at the top; data on outputs is shown below. The input-output sheet is a summary, not a detailed descriptive form; it shows pertinent characteristics of messages that must be accepted or produced by the system designed for the activity. Amplification of data, when useful, is placed in the Appendix of the report. If, for example, the format or content are fixed (imposed), a message sheet, together with a sample of the message, can be included in the Appendix. Summary data on traffic peaks, appearing in the notes column of the above mentioned input-output sheet may be referenced to Appendix displays of traffic distributions and variations, if significant.

As far as the quantitative requirements for operations are concerned, we have to consider them from the present and for the future. In Phase I, operations were described as they are presently performed; in Phase II, operations are characterized by indicating the kind and number of input factors they must accept, the kind and number of output factors they must produce, and how often they must be performed. In most cases this numerical data is estimated from the same statistical projections used to establish volume and frequency of inputs and outputs.

An operation is further characterized by the nature and estimated number of processes involved in its execution. This data is particularly useful in systems design. For example:

1. How many arithmetical and logical processes must be performed?
2. How many relations (comparison of one factor with another) must be examined?
3. How many times will a resource be consulted for data (retrieval or lookup)?
4. How many edit or audit functions will be necessary in the operation?

A required operations sheet should be included in the report, and it can be applied as a working paper in analysis. When completed, this sheet contains a narrative description of each required operation, along with the number of input

NO.	NAME	RATE	MEDIA	SOURCE DESTINATION	NO. OF FIELDS	NO. OF CHAR.	F O R M	C O N T	NOTES
I1	REQUEST FOR QUOTATION (R-2000)	50/W	WIRES TELEPHONE LETTERS	CUSTOMER					AVG. PEAK STD SYSTEMS 22 30 / 207-217 20 27 / OTHER 8 13
I2	REQUEST FOR BID (R-2010)	10/W	LETTERS	CUSTOMER					PEAK VOLUME 12/W 10 WKS A YEAR
I3	CUSTOMER ORDERS (R-2020)	17/W	8½x11 4 PART	CUSTOMER					PEAK 20/WK 6 WEEKS A YEAR
R1	QUOTATIONS * (R-3000)	15/W	8½x11 4 PART	CUSTOMER				X	PEAK 20/WK 10 WEEKS A YEAR
R2	ACKNOWLEDGMENTS (R-3050)	17/W		CUSTOMER SHOP (PROVIDE END PRODUCTS ACTIVITY)			X	X	NO PEAKS
R3	NEW ORDER SCHEDULE (F-4080)	17/W		SHOP (PROVIDE END PRODUCTS ACTIVITY)				X	COMMUNICATES DATA ON FIRM ORDERS
R4	CUSTOMER ORDER (R-2020)	17/W		SHOP				X	DETAILS OF FIRM ORDER ARE ENTERED ON CONTRACT REGISTER

*INCLUDES LETTERS, DRAWINGS, SPECIFICATIONS, LAYOUTS AS NECESSARY TO SUPPLEMENT QUOTATION

R.L. CASEY   DEMAND   BUTODALE   1
DATE   ANALYST   ACTIVITY   STUDY   PAGE

Figure 12-7 Input-output sheet for the provide product demand activity.

and output data fields used in the operation, the number of times the operation will be executed within a selected time span, and a summary of the types of processes making it up. Flowcharts and decision tables used for special analyses should be placed in the Appendix. A required operations sheet for Butodale's provide product demand activity is shown in Figure 12-8.

Finally, let us look at quantitative requirements for resources. Present and future physical and informational resources may be described on a resource sheet as shown in Figure 12-9.

Personnel, identified by occupational skill, are grouped wherever practical. Costs are projected from payroll registers and from the report of the present business. Equipment should be identified by name and type. Costs should be projected on a consistent base. Wherever practical, equipments are grouped by function to compress the list. Facilities are listed by name, location, size, and utility, with emphasis on those that may be affected by systems design.

File resources are identified, established, and costed from the results of the required-inputs analysis. File sheets can be used to describe the characteristics of each information file. Special attention should be placed on the characteristics of a file that may have been changed in requirements analysis. Considerations should be given to:

1. Size of the file in characters
2. Retention rules
3. Age of data
4. Peak and average message volume
5. Access requirements

Categories such as "sequenced by," "labels," "storage medium," and "location" should be omitted unless imposed, since these characteristics will be developed in new systems design. The resource sheet shows only a descriptive file name, application, and cost, wherever possible; the file sheet provides the definitive information. For studies involving communications facilities, the network diagram should be modified to show planned addition or deletion of trunk lines and terminals. The need for duplexing equipment, if these requirements are imposed or logically needed, should also be noted.

Finances become an important consideration in resource requirements analysis when a major change or expansion in an activity is contemplated, such as those necessitating large outlays in capital equipment. Many companies have standard policies connected with the outlay of funds for new equipment purchases; these policies can be described in the Appendix and referenced by a note on the resource sheet.

An area often requiring special attention is the physical inventory for retail and manufacturing concerns. Inventory may be described either as a dollar inventory value for one or more forecasted sales and production levels, or as a series of decision rules developed from simulation experiments. When the latter is the case, descriptions of the rules are included on a required operations sheet, and are summarized with anticipated results on a resource sheet. Inventory rules include:

NO.	OPERATION NAME	INPUT FACTORS	OUTPUT FACTORS	FREQUENCY OF EXECUTION	PROCESS SUMMARY
01	CLASSIFY INCOMING REQUESTS	5	10	60/W	7 LOOKUP
	ALL REQUESTS FOR BID (R-2010) OR QUOTATION (R-2000)				3 EDIT
	ARE SEPARATED INITIALLY INTO 3 GROUPS: STANDARD				6 RELATIONAL
	END ITEMS, STANDARD SYSTEMS, AND ENGINEERED				
	PRODUCTS.				
02	PREPARE QUOTE FOLDER (F-4050.1)	7	12	15/D	2 LOOKUP
	A FOLDER IS PREPARED FOR EACH REQUEST				4 EDIT
	TO HOLD CUSTOMER PAPERS AND DOCUMENTS				3 RELATIONAL
	GENERATED WITHIN BUTODALE TO FILL THE				
	ORDER.				
03	PREPARE BID SHEET (R-3000)	15	20	45/W	10 ARITHMETIC
	A BID SHEET IS PREPARED FOR EACH REQUEST				50 LOGICAL
	FROM PRICE, COST, AND INSTALLED SYSTEMS FILES				30 LOOKUP
	DEPENDING ON THE TYPE REQUEST, EACH IS PRO-				
	CESSED SOMEWHAT DIFFERENTLY. A GPAC* HAS				
	APPROXIMATELY 13 MAJOR INTERCONNECTED				
	COMPONENTS AVAILABLE IN DIFFERENT GROUPINGS.				
	INPUT-OUTPUT DEVICES ARE OPTIONAL IN 6 MODELS.				
	ALTHOUGH CONSOLE AND GROUPS DESCRIPTIONS				
	ARE STANDARD, THEY MAY BE MODIFIED AT				
	CUSTOMER REQUEST.				
04	DETERMINE SYSTEM LAYOUT	27	38	12/W	60 ARITHMETIC
	A GPAC MAY HAVE ANY ONE OF SEVERAL CON-				32 LOGICAL
	SOLES, AND ANY ONE OF SEVERAL RACK CONFIGURATIONS.				5 EDIT
	*GENERAL PURPOSE ANALOG COMPUTER				15 LOOKUP

R.L. CASEY — DATE / ANALYST   DEMAND — ACTIVITY   BUTODALE — STUDY   1 OF 3 — PAGE

Figure 12-8   Required operations sheet for the provide product demand activity.

1. Frequency of forecast.
2. Frequency of stock level review.
3. Required service level (safety stock requirements).
4. Application of special inventory practices such as item control according to the annual usage value of the item, and the use of economic order quantity.
5. Type of order system (fixed quantity per order or fixed interval of ordering).

NO.	OPERATION NAME	INPUT FACTORS	OUTPUT FACTORS	FREQUENCY OF EXECUTION	PROCESS SUMMARY
05	DECIDE BID STATUS ON ENGINEERED PRODUCTS, A MANAGEMENT CONFERENCE IS HELD TO DETERMINE SPECIAL CONSIDERATIONS, PRICES, AND PROMISED DELIVERY.	40	70	40/M	30 LOOKUP 50 RELATIONAL 80 LOGICAL 10 ARITHMETIC
06	DESIGN SYSTEM LAYOUT ON ENGINEERED PRODUCTS, ENGINEERING DESIGN AND DRAFTING IS REQUIRED TO LAY OUT ALL SPECIAL REQUIREMENTS.	200	600	20/W	700 LOOKUP 200 LOGICAL 50 ARITHMETIC 40 RELATIONAL 300 EDIT
07	COST SPECIAL COMPONENTS FOR EACH SPECIAL ITEM, COSTS AND PRICES ARE ESTABLISHED TO SUPPORT THE FINAL QUOTATION.	10	18	150/W	4 LOOKUP 16 ARITHMETIC 10 RELATIONAL 8 EDIT
08	PREPARE QUOTATION (R-3000) THE CUSTOMER IS SUPPLIED A DOCUMENT DESCRIBING THE PRODUCT, ITS RACKS AND ATTACHMENTS, AND THE TOTAL PRICE, WITH OPTIONS.	75	100	20/W	30 LOOKUP 10 LOGICAL 100 EDIT 200 POSTING
09	ESTABLISH INTERNAL RECORDS DETAILS OF THE PROPOSAL ARE RECORDED ON INTERNAL DOCUMENTS AND IN THE CONTRACT REGISTER FILE. (F-4050)	200	800	20/W	10 LOGICAL 10 LOOKUP 500 POSTING 20 EDIT

R.L. CASEY   DEMAND   BUTODALE   2 OF 3

DATE   ANALYST   ACTIVITY   STUDY   PAGE

Figure 12-8 (continued)

The level of future inventories may also be estimated from an analysis of inventories in relation to sales, if inventories have been adequately controlled in the past.

Other methods of estimating the size and content of a required inventory include:

1. Computing inventory level at various levels of sales by summarizing average inventory level of all parts stocked.
2. Comparing stock/sales ratios with those of others in the industry from analysis of balance sheets or published industry statistics.

NO.	OPERATION NAME	INPUT FACTORS	OUTPUT FACTORS	FREQUENCY OF EXECUTION	PROCESS SUMMARY
10	TRANSMIT QUOTATION (R-3000) THE QUOTATION IS MAILED TO THE CUSTOMER WITH SUPPORTING DATA INCLUDING A LETTER OF TRANSMITTAL, PRINTS, DRAWINGS, LAYOUT, SPECIFICATIONS, ETC.	10	10	20/W	25 LOGICAL 10 LOOKUP 10 EDIT
11	EDIT INCOMING ORDERS (R2020) FIRM CUSTOMER ORDERS ARE EDITED AGAINST THE CONTRACT REGISTER FILE (F-4050) AND POSTED TO THE CUSTOMER (F-4060) AND PROJECT INDEX. (F-4070)	150	30	16/W	10 LOOKUP 150 EDIT 75 POSTING
12	PREPARE & TRANSMIT ACKNOWLEDGMENT (R-3050) THE CUSTOMER IS NOTIFIED OF THE ORDER RECEIPT, AND ACCEPTANCE AND DELIVERY DATES ARE RECONFIRMED.	30	30	16/W	10 LOOKUP 15 ARITHMETIC 30 EDIT
13	COMMUNICATE ORDERS TO SHOP THE CUSTOMER ORDER IS POSTED TO AN ASSIGNMENT SHEET (F-4080) AND PREPARED FOR SHOP RELEASE, OR TO ENGINEERING. SPECIAL CONDITIONS AND TERMS ARE COMMUNICATED TO INTERESTED PARTIES AT THIS TIME.	10	15	20/W	10 LOOKUP 20 POSTING 10 LOGICAL 10 EDIT

DATE **R.L. CASEY** ANALYST **DEMAND** ACTIVITY **BUTODALE** STUDY **3 OF 3** PAGE

Figure 12-8 (continued)

3. Classifying into raw, in-process, and finished stock by value, then computing average level.
4. Analyzing high yearly value parts, models, or services in depth.

12.12 REFINING THE REQUIREMENTS

At this point, the study team has produced system input, operation, output, and resource requirements for each of the activities within the scope of the

NO.	NAME AND DESCRIPTION	AMOUNT	COST	NOTES
P1	MANAGEMENT (PARTIAL)	2	$24,000	REVIEW QUOTATIONS
P2	SALES AND SERVICE MANAGER, SALESMEN, SERVICE ENGINEERS, SECRETARIES, CLERKS	56	$448,000	
P3	ADMINISTRATION & ADVERTISING MANAGER, MEDIA SPECIALISTS, SECRETARIES CLERKS, ANALYSTS, SUPERVISORS	14	84,000	
P4	COST CLERKS	2	9,000	
P5	ACCOUNTS RECEIVABLE CLERKS	4	19,000	
P6	PRODUCT ENGINEERS	3	26,400	
P7	ADMINISTRATIVE ENGINEERS	2	13,400	
P8	PUBLICATIONS SPECIALISTS	3	20,100	
E1	VEHICLES		10,100	DEPRECIATION & RENTAL
E2	TYPEWRITERS	15		
E3	CALCULATORS	2		
E4	DICTATING MACHINES	2		

R.L. CASEY   DEMAND   BUTODALE   1 of 1
DATE   ANALYST   ACTIVITY   STUDY   PAGE

Figure 12-9   Resource sheet for the provide product demand activity.

study. The results may adequately state what the system is required to do, particularly in the case of improvement or mechanization studies. More likely there is a need to reconsider certain of these requirements and to refine them by one or more passes back through each activity, this time applying a slightly different approach (that is, if outputs were determined from inputs, the analysts would now work in reverse). The need to refine requirements, and resolve any apparent conflicts or problems, usually is discovered when the activity is to be validated as an integrated whole.

In certain advanced studies it may be desirable to call upon other sophisticated techniques of management science—especially if the study team is involved in creating a unique new design, or where relatively few constraints have been placed on their actions. For example, a computer program to simulate systems may be used to develop an understanding of true requirements through the simulation of the structure and action of complex, real-life situations. Vital information about the maximum and the average size of queues, response time, and percent use of selected resources may be obtained from each simulation run. The model must accurately reflect real conditions, and its output requires expert interpretation. There may be, however, no other way to secure this information at a reasonable cost.

SUMMARY

To define system requirements, the study team develops specifications for each operation from the position of what is logically necessary to fulfill the goals of an activity. Establishing logical requirements may necessitate several tries because most activities contain many variables and interacting factors. An activity requirements model, showing inputs, operations, outputs, and resources is a useful framework for the analysis of requirements. After the study team has defined the relationships that govern the transformation of inputs to outputs, they have a sound basis for specifying required operations. Operations may be documented by narrative, flowchart, or decision table forms. Each of the three methods has advantages and disadvantages. Flowcharts and decision tables are particularly useful if the operations are to be programmed for a computer. Required operations are those that are necessary to produce an output, to accept an input, to maintain a resource, or to satisfy an activity goal. Types of relationships among operations include causal dependence, sequential dependence, and time dependence. Operations usually imply the use of resources and the resources may be subject to management constraints.

13

Measuring the Performance of Systems

13.1 INTRODUCTION

When analysts design a new system, they should have some method for determining how well alternative system designs perform. In anticipation of this need, the measurement method for making such an evaluation is devised at the time the analysts are determining the requirements of the new system. In fact, the process of measurement development should go on continuously throughout this phase of the study.

Measurement factors are the standards by which the new system will be judged. When peak and average volumes, frequency of execution, rate, elapsed time, and other numerical data are being compiled for inclusion in the working papers, value ranges can be determined and recorded on a scale. Thus, if "record update time" has been identified as a significant measurement factor, and records are presently updated in an average of six days and a maximum of eight, a measurement scale can be plotted from zero to ten days.

The identification of measurement factors and the development of appropriate measurement scales are usually performed simultaneously with the formulation of input, output, operations, and resource requirements.

13.2   MEASUREMENT FACTORS

Some measures are direct and quantitative, and can be shown on numerical scales: the dollar cost of a system, the number of days from the receipt of a customer order to product shipment, the average number of errors in preparing invoices, and similar variables. Measures can also be indirect, or derived from combinations of factors. The measures include items such as budget variance, return on investment, productive efficiency, and inventory turnover. A third group of measures consists of those that are qualitative or subjective: service effectiveness, customer goodwill, or product appearance. This latter class is difficult to measure; performance is usually expressed in abstract terms such as "outstanding," "excellent," and "fair."

Study teams have found that a number of representative measures are needed for a balanced appraisal of system performance. To achieve this coverage, major measurement categories are selected, then more precise factors are defined for each activity. "Time" is a major measurement category in an airlines study; it can be refined to such precise factors as "customer inquiry response time" and "record update time." A total of six to twelve of these specific factors may be sufficient for a comprehensive measurement of a single activity. The factors may be quite different from one activity to another.

Some major measurement categories and possible factors are:

1. Cost—operating, maintenance, unit.
2. Time—response (input, operations), access, elapsed, cycle, process, turnover.
3. Accuracy—frequency and number of errors, significance of errors.
4. Reliability—stability, durability, life.
5. Security—legal, safety, secrecy.
6. Quality—appearance, tolerance.
7. Flexibility—variability, sensitivity.
8. Capacity—average load, low load, peak load.
9. Efficiency—performance ratios.
10. Acceptance—customer, employee, management, stockholder.

This list shows many of the criteria by which a system's performance can be measured. In a study for a brokerage house, measurement criteria were first identified and described for the entire business as follows:

COLLINS, McCABE, AND COMPANY

1. *Execution Response Time*—Customer service must be as good as, or better than, the present system.
2. *Error Rate*—Critical, since money errors are absorbed by the firm. Errors also affect customer and industry relations and must be the same as or lower than the present system.
3. *Reliability*—Affects the entire system, but especially input transactions

and order execution. Includes ability to install new system with no service interruptions, and to conclude posting without fail before business operations of the next day.

4. *Capacity*—Management requires a system to operate at double present daily volume, while at the same time working efficiently under variable loads.

5. *Cost*—Comparable to present system. Value will be determined on a cost/customer service basis.

6. *Security*—Certain procedures must meet industry regulations, audit practices, and account security.

7. *Update Response Time*—An important factor, but dependent on the type of account inquiries.

8. *Inquiry Response Time*—Again, this is a function of the class of inquiry, but it is important since inquiries result in trades.

Each of the descriptions gave an indication of values and importance to the business, but further work was required to segregate them into measurements for each activity and translate the measures into precise rating scales.

The measurement factors developed for Custodian Life show a different pattern:

CUSTODIAN LIFE INSURANCE COMPANY

New Business Activity

1. *Volume Increase Capability*—The new system must be capable of handling double the present volume, without overtime.

2. *Accuracy*—Defined as the degree of conformity and correctness in all documents and records. Measured by the total number of detected errors requiring reprocessing.

3. *Processing Time*—The number of days it takes to process a life insurance application from its receipt at home office to issuance of policy, by policy type.

4. *Appearance*—Prepared documents and reports will be judged for legibility, neatness and arrangement.

5. *Personnel Cost*—Annual salaries and employee benefits allocated to the operation of the activity.

6. *Equipment and Supply Cost*—Includes the costs of machine purchases and rentals, maintenance and parts charges, magnetic tapes and cards, and service fees.

7. *Operational Efficiency and Control*—The degree to which operational efficiency is controlled by management. (Is the status of an application always known? Are schedules maintained on time? Can the system handle anticipated peaks? and so on.)

8. *Conformity to Practices*—The extent to which company policies and practices are complied with, and the degree to which the system provides statistical data for management information and action.

Some factors are defined only in general terms; others state exactly what performance level is required. A number of other factors, such as personnel-training costs and flexibility to change, were considered earlier, but were eliminated because of lack of significance and difficulty of measurement.

13.3 RATING SCALES

A rating scale shows ranges of values for each measurement factor. Three sets of values are shown on the scale:

1. Present operating point
2. Acceptable performance range
3. Desirable performance range

Operating points for the present system are secured from the Phase I analysis and from data gathered during Phase II. For example, in the brokerage house, present operating points for incoming customer orders were designated as shown in Figure 13-1.

An acceptable range covers the points at which activity performance satisfies future conditions. A desirable range is a statement of performance that will be more difficult to achieve through design, yet represents a more satisfactory level of attainment.

With values defined in this fashion, systems designers are able to propose a range of solutions in Phase III, and evaluate and adjust the cost vs. response time trade-off.

Sometimes targets can be approached from a different viewpoint. This is illustrated by the measurement scale for an invoicing operation shown in Figure 13-2.

The present performance of the invoicing operations was not considered acceptable, because much time (nine days, at least) elapses until shipping papers are forwarded to the billing section. However, what happens if a system can be designed to include the invoice with the shipment—without holding up the shipment? This will not be resolved until systems design takes place, but at least the performance targets are extended to evaluate the desirability of such a possibility.

There are other methods of displaying ranges of values for measurement factors. For example, values for elapsed time measurements can be shown in the form of

Figure 13-1 Present operating points for the incoming "orders per day" measurement in a brokerage house.

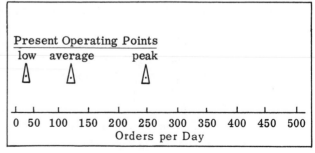

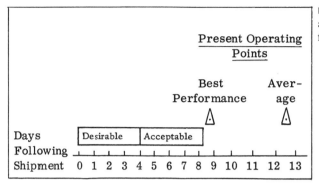

Figure 13-2 Present, acceptable, and desirable operating points for an invoicing operation.

cumulative curves. A specific illustration of this method is shown in Figure 13-3, which shows what percent of the items take how much elapsed time. The point on the present system curve defined by the intersecting dotted lines reads: "Thirty percent of the total number of items processed are handled in under ten hours." The other points are read similarly.

Often, rating scales have significantly different ranges of values for quite similar measurement factors. In these cases, a separate scale should be constructed for each one. Unwarranted complexity would be introduced by attempting to display too many factors simultaneously.

The physical appearance of a printed document is an example of a qualitative factor. However, it can be measured on the same type of scale as for quantitative variables. Figure 13-4 presents such an example. In it the attribute is the "ap-

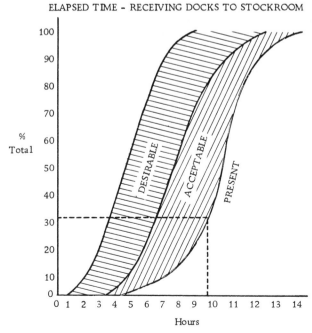

Figure 13-3 "Less than" relation between (1) the number of hours an input received from a vendor sits on the receiving dock waiting to be taken to the inventory stock room and (2) the cumulative proportion of shipments. The bands indicate performance levels.

Figure 13-4 An example of the use of a scale for a qualitative factor. Here the qualitative factor is the "appearance" of an invoice.

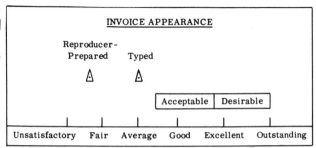

pearance" of an invoice. The scale ranges from unsatisfactory to outstanding. Each point on a qualitative rating scale should be supported by a narrative definition. For example, "Good" means that the invoice is uniform in printing darkness, has no corrections, strikeovers, or smudges, and can be read without difficulty. Line item entries should be in ascending part number sequence for easy reference, and the totals should be quickly identifiable.

If a study team can design a new system that operates within the high range of desirable performance in most factors, it can be assured that the design is at a near-optimum condition. If, however, costs and other special considerations restrain performance of the design to acceptable ranges in a number of categories, the study team can be confident that system performance is still within satisfactory bounds, since acceptable performance levels were reviewed and approved by management.

13.4 SETTING VALUES FOR RATING SCALES

The study team is responsible for selecting measurement factors and constructing a rating scale for each one, but a final determination on acceptable and desirable values and ranges of value for each factor should be accomplished jointly with management. Before measurement data is reviewed with management, however, requirements analysis should be fairly well along, and a substantial amount of information developed to support each rating scale. When a computer is used to simulate the management of inventories, the results of a number of simulations may be gathered to show how several management decision rules influenced inventory investment for various sales forecasts. In this case, of course, management should be interviewed before the simulation to determine the inventory policies to be tested.

In the measurement review with management, a systems analyst is not merely seeking information; he is trying to discern how a manager feels about his business, what factors are important to him, and what he expects the business to gain from a new system. During these reviews, it is useful to develop an insight into the feelings, opinions, biases, and pressures on an individual as well as to form an objective appraisal on a subject. A manager may have strong opinions on certain topics. If the opinions are controversial, or pertain to business policies which are not widely discussed, then it is important to find out how these beliefs affect system requirements.

To diagnose the real reasons behind management decisions and opinions, a systems analyst not only has to be well prepared with factual data, but he must be adept at leading discussion on sensitive subjects and developing insight into the meaning behind statements made by the managers. What factors have a bearing on the subject: labor contracts? employee attitudes? satisfaction of a large and demanding customer? poor industry outlook? attitudes among consumers and suppliers? trade reciprocity? Many times it will be difficult to discover and interpret some of the deep-rooted problems which influence a management position; if they are not expressed openly, the study team has difficulty in deciding just what is desirable and acceptable in a business.

While these conditions have to be faced in most studies, the systems analyst emphasizes first the need for evaluation based on objective data, then adjusts these decisions to accommodate subjective opinions and judgments when they must be recognized. This approach affirms that there must initially be an order, a logic, and a magnitude to events; when this is defined, results can be qualified by the experience, judgment, and even intuition of management.

An important aspect of the analyst's work has to do with interaction among the factors, for example, performance versus cost. The analyst cannot treat these factors as independent but must use appropriate statistical methods for assigning weights to the factors and for measuring the amount of interaction.

SUMMARY

Measurement of acceptable and desirable performance levels is rarely an absolute process. The team must be aware of the need for measurement early in Phase II, and be constantly seeking a series of factors which are particularly appropriate for the study and which adequately measure management objectives. Scales and values on the scales are evolved simultaneously with requirements analysis, but become usable measures only after they have been thoroughly reviewed with, and approved by, management. Once they have been worked into a cohesive framework, the measures form the basis for judging the validity of various systems designs.

14

Documentation
for System
Requirements

14.1 REVIEW

Effective understanding of the existing system is normally not of great interest to the analysts unless it can be used as the basis for improving the system and enlarging its capabilities. But the path from a completed study to a new system is not simply a matter of supplementing the study of the present system by undisciplined or intuitive insight; the end result of this process is frequently just the mechanization of previous mistakes and compounded errors.

As we have stressed in this part of our book, the necessary intermediate step between a system study and the design of a new system is the rigorous determination of what the true requirements of the new system will be. The procedure is not as clear-cut as the procedure for describing an existing system, but certain guideposts can be noted. A related group of forms have been developed to help the observer recognize these guideposts, and to help him increase the effectiveness of his approach. These forms, and the manner in which the previously discussed descriptive forms provide source data for the analysis of system requirements, are the subject of this chapter.

Understanding an existing system is essential to the analysis of system requirements. If such a study has been performed, the five types of descriptive forms on which the system is documented compose a readily accessible and coherently organized body of known facts. Where such a study has not been performed, other conventional survey documents or equivalent information is necessary.

Other important information to guide the analysis of requirements may be found in forecasts and predictions of future markets, new products or services being planned by management, contemplated changes in design or product mix, or other changes in management policies and objectives. Such changes may include increased specialization or diversification, or expansion of the enterprise along either horizontal or vertical patterns. Changes in the pattern of availability of labor or of raw materials may also influence the activity. Government regulations must also be considered; these include the rulings of regulatory agencies, the labor codes, health and welfare rulings, consent decrees governing the permissible operating areas of certain enterprises, and so forth. The rules of regulatory agencies frequently affect the form and content of certain reports, and obviously must be considered in the analysis of information-system requirements.

The outputs from the system are a prime determinant for system requirements. The system functions to produce goods, services, or information, which are the system outputs. Outputs may be logically required or they may be imposed by management; in either case, production of the output is a primary goal toward which the system is directed.

Outputs are not, however, the only factors which influence the requirements of the system. Processing steps leading to these outputs, and even inputs to the processing steps, may be imposed by the environment, as when a government ruling specifies the method of accounting for certain funds. These additional constraints may significantly affect the system requirements.

After all prespecified operations or inputs have been considered, the outputs may be permitted to determine the operation and input requirements. Outputs in many cases imply specific operations. The characteristics of an invoice, for instance, are determined by the environment (it must be capable of being transmitted to the customer and being read and understood by him or his processing equipment) and possibly by management preference (as to size and form). These characteristics may identify many operations, inputs, and resources. Where the output form or the content is not explicitly predetermined, greater flexibility and creativity in system design are permitted. The outputs, once determined, suggest classes or types of operations. They also determine or suggest resources. And working backward one more step, the operations, resources, and outputs often indicate input requirements.

To document the specification of the requirements of a system, three additional forms have been developed. They enable the analyst to summarize the requirements of inputs-outputs, operations, and resources (informational and material). We have named these three forms: (1) input-output sheet, (2) required operations sheet, and (3) resource sheet. We shall first explain each of these in detail and then present examples of their use.

14.2 THE INPUT-OUTPUT SHEET

The input-output sheet is a summary form for recording the characteristics of required inputs and outputs. It is not a detailed descriptive form; detailed

Input–Output Sheet

NO.	NAME	RATE	MEDIA	SOURCE DESTINATION	NO. OF FIELDS	NO. OF CHAR	F O R M	C O N T	NOTES
(1)	(2)	(3)	(4)	(5)	(6)	(7)	(8)	(9)	(10)

Figure 14-1   The top part of a blank input-output sheet. *See* Section 14.2 for the notes referenced by the ten encircled key numbers.

descriptions, where needed, are displayed on supporting message sheets. Fields on the input-output sheet are reserved for the name of the message, medium of transmission, source or destination, number of fields, number of characters, and so forth. If the characteristics of the input or output are imposed by management, or logically required, the fact is noted. Both external and internal messages are reported on the input-output sheet, and this record helps ensure that necessary connecting operations will not subsequently be overlooked. When analyzing a system at the operational level, the analysts should relate all the input and output items of a specific operation together in the same input-output sheet or successive sheets; this is not necessary, of course, when analyzing the input, output, and resource requirements as related to the activity as a whole.

Figure 14-1 contains the headings of a blank input-output sheet. Ten encircled numbers from 1 to 10 serve to reference the ten main fields in the form. How to use each of the keyed fields is explained immediately below.

Notes to explain key numbers on the input-output sheet

1. NO.   The identification number serves the purpose of reference and separates inputs from outputs; inputs are identified by a number series beginning with I1, outputs by a series starting with R1.

2. NAME   This should be descriptive and reflect contents, appearance, or purpose. In the case of messages, the message number should also be included.

3. RATE   This figure should characterize arrival or departure frequency of the item in terms of volume for some unit of time. Typical entries might be 1,200 per day, 1,000 per hour, 20 per month; the figures reflect projected rates determined through analysis.

4. MEDIA   Includes punched cards, teletypewriter, telephone, index cards, cathode-ray tubes, letters, telegrams, and so forth. This field specifies the means by which the input or output is represented. If management has not specified the means for representing or transmitting the items, permissible alternatives may be entered here; if the area is completely unspecified, a note to that effect is entered.

5. SOURCE/DESTINATION   Pertains to sources of inputs and destinations of outputs. Source and destination are generally expressed in terms of an organizational component, an activity, or, in the case of a principal input or output, an organization or entity outside of the activity under scrutiny.

6. NO. OF FIELDS   Represents the average number of data fields on the document being described.

Required Operations Sheet

NO.	OPERATION NAME	INPUT FACTORS	OUTPUT FACTORS	FREQUENCY OF EXECUTION	PROCESS SUMMARY
①	②	③	④	⑤	⑥
		⑦			
①	②	③	④	⑤	⑥
		⑦			

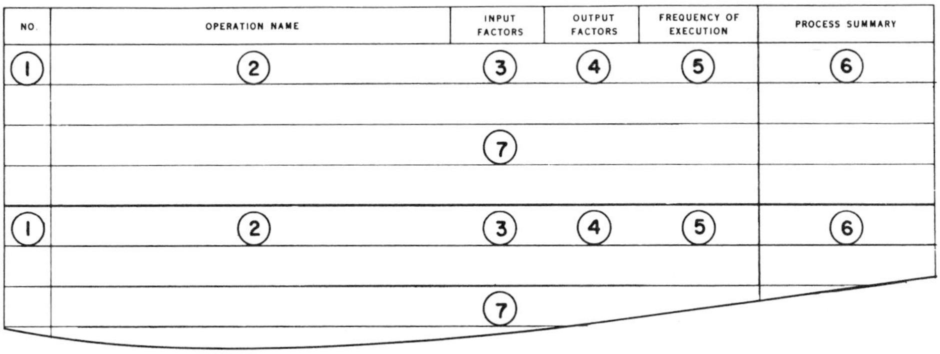

Figure 14-2   The top part of a blank required operations sheet. *See* Section 14.3 for the notes referenced by the seven encircled key numbers.

7. NO. OF CHARACTERS   Represents the average size of the message, measured in characters.

8. FORM   An X in this column indicates that the format has been specified by management. When the format of the message has been specified, a message sheet representing it should be included as supporting material. The column is left blank when the format is not fixed in advance.

9. CONT.   An X in this column indicates that the content has been specified by management, which means that the fields which make up the input or output item have been determined. The entry is left blank when management specifies the function or purpose but not the contents.

10. NOTES   The notes column is used to indicate special situations regarding any of the preceding items, or other information which bears on input-output requirements. Batching characteristics, for instance, are spelled out here if they are significant; acceptable alternatives to management specifications are also noted.

14.3   THE REQUIRED OPERATIONS SHEET

The required operations sheet summarizes the input factors, output factors, and frequency of execution of each logically necessary operation. A narrative description of the operation describing what the operation does and what it logically must do is entered on this form. The analyst also estimates the number and kinds of processes that compose the operation. Processes include logical and arithmetical, table lookup, editing, relational (comparing one factor with another), and so forth.

Figure 14-2 contains the top part of a blank required operations sheet. Seven encircled numbers serve to reference the seven main fields in the form. Each of the seven keyed fields is explained immediately below.

Notes for key numbers on the required operations sheet

1. NO.   An identification number is assigned to each operation for reference.

2. OPERATION NAME   A descriptive name is given to each operation to describe either what the operation does or its end product.

3. INPUT FACTORS   This field displays the total number of data fields in all input items used in, or files referenced by, the operation. The figure is not the total number of fields in the input media, but rather the total number processed in the operation.

4. OUTPUT FACTORS   This field displays information of the same type, and adheres to the same rules as field 3. Only data fields produced by the operation are entered.

5. FREQUENCY OF EXECUTION   This is determined by analysis. A convenient time span is selected and the total number of executions for this time period is displayed. Exceptional considerations, such as unusual workload distributions, are expressed in the narrative description (see field 7).

6. PROCESS SUMMARY   An estimate is made of the total number of process steps. Processes are classified into practical categories (arithmetical, logical, relational, editorial, and so forth) and summarized by these classifications to characterize the size and complexity of the operation.

7. (NARRATIVE DESCRIPTION)   This section of the required operations sheet is used to describe what the operation does (but not how it is done). It is also used to point out special considerations normally covered in the other categories. In characterizing the operation, some indication of the inputs and outputs should be given, as well as an indication of the transformations that must take place in order to change inputs into outputs.

14.4 THE RESOURCE SHEET

The resource sheet summarizes the material and informational resources that are either logically necessary or imposed on the operation. Again, in an analysis at the operational level, all the resources related to a specific operation should be summarized on one resource sheet or successive sheets. All resources are summarized: types of people, present or projected equipment, facilities, and files.

Figure 14-3 contains the top part of a blank resource sheet. Five encircled numbers serve to reference the five main fields in the form. Each of the five keyed fields is explained immediately below.

Notes for the key numbers on the resource sheet

1. NO.   Besides serving as a reference, the identification number specifies which of the four types of resources is being represented. The series starting with P1,

Resource Sheet

NO.	NAME AND DESCRIPTION	AMOUNT	COST	NOTES
①	②	③	④	⑤

Figure 14-3   The top part of a blank resource sheet. *See* Section 14.4 for the notes referenced by the five encircled key numbers.

E1, F1 and V1 respectively are used for personnel, equipment, facilities or inventories. (Identifying numbers of any kind or length may be used, but for convenience they should be kept short.)

2. NAME AND DESCRIPTION   The name of the resource should represent what it is, as well as characteristics such as capacity or capability which help identify it. Personnel are generally described by occupational specialty. Equipment should be described by general type, purpose, or function, unless the make and model are specified by management. Facilities are defined by type and location; contents are not entered in this category. Thus a reservoir might appear, but not the water; or a filing cabinet, but not the file. Both material and informational inventories are listed; the water or the file would be listed in this latter category.

3. AMOUNT   This is usually represented by a quantity: number of people, number of pieces of equipment, and so forth. For facilities, amount is normally specified in terms of capacity, in square or cubic footage. If resources are available only partially or part-time, the actual amount is entered; seven people available half the time would indicate an entry of 3 1/2 people.

4. COST   Either cost-per-unit time or cost per unit is shown. Cost-per-unit time reflects the total cost of an item over a period of time multiplied by the number of items. Some fixed percentage should be added to personnel-salary costs to reflect fringe benefits. Other overhead costs should be included. Similar pieces of equipment are totaled before they are entered on the resource sheet. Yearly rental figures should be entered for equipment unless it is purchased; in this case, write-off or depreciation procedures should be used to amortize the purchase price into an annual figure. Certain materials—blank forms, for instance—are more practically defined by unit costs.

5. NOTES   This column is used to record special considerations, add supplemental information, indicate alternate resources, and so forth. Other uses might be to indicate the capacity of machines, or provide a detailed description of complex equipment.

14.5 SUMMARY CHARACTER OF THE THREE FORMS

The reader should note that the three forms just described implicitly require a systematic approach to determine the system's requirements. Note also that the general and summary character of these three documents guides the analyst to look more closely at *what is to be done* than at *how it is to be accomplished*. The stress in this second phase of study and design is on the results the system must achieve; the third phase of system design considers the procedures by which, and the equipment with which, these results are to be achieved.

The analyst must understand that system requirements can be determined conceptually. A business system is approached as a single entity, existing for the purpose of achieving an imposed goal. The mechanisms required to achieve that goal are then inferred, and the resources, operations, and inputs defined. From this point on, the analyst can concern himself with how, in terms of hardware and equipment, the outputs are generated. Of course, imposed characteristics resulting from capital investment in existing equipment or materials must be considered, but when these limitations are not present, the analyst should free himself from considerations of method and materials until he understands the true requirements of the system.

The use of the three summary forms in deriving the requirements of a system will be demonstrated by extending the nonmechanized and mechanized examples already covered in Sections 8.8 and 8.9. This demonstration assumes that the reporting forms discussed in those sections are serving as information sources, as a body of known facts, to support the determination of system requirements. We begin with the nonmechanized example and recommend that the reader review Section 8.8 briefly before beginning the next section.

14.6   REQUIREMENTS IN A NONMECHANIZED SYSTEM

The final output from the nonmechanized charge account activity, as shown on the activity sheet in Figure 8-6, was the mailed bill which left the activity to go to the customer. The preparation of this bill was one of the operations described on the operation sheet in Figure 8-7. The bill can be considered a logically imposed output from the activity.

The input-output sheet in Figure 14-4 lists the bill as the output of an operation in the charge-account activity. The rate figure shown, 4.6 million a year, flags this as a critical output in a nonmechanized activity. Other pertinent statistics are summarized: the number of fields and number of characters, with explanatory notes, and a breakdown of rate fluctuations over the course of a yearly cycle. The medium of preparation is noted as unspecified, which allows a fair degree of freedom in setting up an operation to produce the bill.

One input logically needed under any circumstances to produce a bill is some kind of customer record, from which the bill is essentially an excerpt. Since customers prefer to see transaction slips supporting the data on the bill, these slips can also be considered as required inputs. Summary data on volumes, fluctuations, and so forth are given for these inputs. Note that the medium and form of all three messages are not specified; however, the X in the CONT column indicates that the contents of all three are fixed.

As a matter of record, the study documentation showed that the bill is presently prepared by duplicating the customer record by a copy process. This does not constitute specification of either the form or the medium, and the analyst should pass this fact over as incidental unless management has stipulated a continuation of the copy process for preparation of bills. Similarly, the transaction slips are presently stapled to the bill prior to mailing; a redesign of format for either or both forms might save staples or paper or both by leading to an equally secure but different procedure (for example, putting the transaction slips in a pocket formed by folding the bill in a certain way).

These are later considerations, of course; they are mentioned here merely to reinforce the point that the analyst at this stage should consider only *what must be done*. He cannot yet allow himself to become entangled in considerations of *how it is done*.

The required operations sheet in Figure 14-5 defines the operations required to produce a bill, and two related operations. The first entry gives the name of the operation, using a verb phrase of the same type as used in the activity and operation sheets in the phase one study. Input and output factors and frequency of execution are also shown in this identifying field.

Input factors are the different fields of data that must be accepted by the operation; this figure is the total of all input elements from all sources used by the operation. The 38 input factors used in preparing bills include customer name

NO.	NAME	RATE	MEDIA	SOURCE DESTINATION	NO OF FIELDS	NO OF CHAR	FORN	CONT	NOTES
									Input-Output Sheet
I 1	CUSTOMER RECORD	20 K/D	①	CUSTOMER FILE	② 49	② 409		X	① NO SPECIFICATION
									② CUSTOMER RECORD HAS: 4 "FIXED" FIELDS – 292 CHAR 5 "TRANSAC'N" FIELDS – 13 CHAR PER TRANSACTION, AVG. 9 TRANSACTION PER RECORD PER MONTH
I 2	TRANSACTION SLIP	— ① 7.8 M/YR	②	SALES FLOOR	③ 18	③ 535		X	① RATE FLUCTUATION :
									FREQ. | RATE
									143 D/YR | 15 K/D
									143 D/YR | 30 K/D
									13 D/YR | 45 K/D
									13 D/YR | 60 K/D
									② NO SPECIFICATION
									③ TRANSACTION SLIP HAS : 12 "FIXED" FIELDS – 485 CHAR 4 "TRANSAC'N" FIELDS – 25 CHAR PER TRANS'N. AVG. 2 TRANS PER SLIP.
R 1	BILL	— ① 4.6 M/YR	②	CUSTOMER	③ 45	③ 481		X	① RATE FLUCTUATION :
									FREQ. | RATE
									165 D/YR | 15 K/D
									55 D/YR | 30 K/D
									15 D/YR | 20 K/D
									5 D/YR | 35 K/D
									② NO SPECIFICATION
									③ BILL HAS : 9 "FIXED" FIELDS – 364 CHAR 4 "TRANSAC'N" FIELDS – 13 CHAR PER TRANS, AVG. 9 TRANS PER BILL.

DATE   ANALYST   CHARGE ACCOUNTS   ASSOCIATED RETAILERS INC.   1
ACTIVITY   STUDY   PAGE

Figure 14-4 Example of a completed input-output sheet for a nonmechanized activity—charge accounts.

and address, merchandise-identifying fields and charges from transactions slips, data on returns and payments, factors for calculating discounts and carrying charges, and so forth. The same rules apply to the entry which shows the number of output factors. In both cases, the entry gives the number of elements used in or produced by the operation, not the number of characters or fields on the input or output documents.

Required Operations Sheet

NO.	OPERATION NAME	INPUT FACTORS	OUTPUT FACTORS	FREQUENCY OF EXECUTION	PROCESS SUMMARY
01	PREPARE BILLS	38	45	19K/D	25 LOGICAL
	DETERMINE BALANCE FROM CHARGES, PAYMENTS,				17 ARITHMETIC
	AND RETURNS; SPECIAL ARITHMETIC IS REQUIRED FOR				4 RELATIONAL
	DISCOUNT CALCULATION AND PAST DUE CARRYING				3 LOOKUPS
	CHARGES. PRINT A BILL AFTER EXTENSIVE EDITING.				25 EDITS
02	MICROFILM BILLS	4	4	19K/D	4 LOGICAL
	PHOTOGRAPH BILLS WITH MICROFILM EQUIPMENT.				3 LOOKUPS
	CODE FILM FOR INFORMATION RETRIEVAL.				
03	INSERT DUE NOTICES	12	17	1800/D	8 LOGICAL
	DETERMINE PAST DUE STATUS ON BILL BALANCE.				3 ARITHMETIC
	SPECIAL HANDLING IS REQUIRED ON 3 OR MORE				4 EDITS
	MONTHS PAST DUE ITEMS. INSERT DUE NOTICE IN				
	BILL ENVELOPES AS REQUIRED.				

DATE ANALYST CHARGE ACCOUNTS ACTIVITY ASSOCIATED RETAILERS INC. STUDY 01 PAGE

Figure 14-5 Example of a completed required operations sheet for a nonmechanized system—charge accounts.

The steps involved in the operation are then described in sequence in a brief narrative. The narrative will implicitly suggest certain of the processing steps and many of the inputs and information resources. Unusual characteristics are noted; thus the analyst who prepared the description in Figure 14-5 noted that "extensive editing" was required before the bill was printed.

The number and kinds of process steps are estimated and entered in the process-summary field. Supporting the previous remark about extensive editing in Figure 14-5 is the estimate of 25 editorial steps required to prepare a bill.

Operation 02, "microfilm bills," is required to maintain records of the bills sent out. The microfilm process would not normally be mentioned specifically; it was, we may assume, made a requirement because of storage-space considerations and the department store's capital investment in microfilm equipment. The "due notice" exception routine is obviously imposed as a requirement by the collection department.

The object of the summary on the required operations sheet is to solve this problem: Given necessary (or imposed) outputs and inferred (or imposed) inputs, what are the steps in between? The narrative description helps define the process steps. The process summary gives an estimate of the magnitude and complexity of the operation.

Working with the description and summary, it is possible for the analysts to make a preliminary approximation of what resources will be needed to achieve the goals. This first approximation includes all required resources—people, facilities, equipment, files—and is summarized on the resource sheet. The resource sheet for the analysis of the bill-preparing operation is shown in Figure 14-6.

Four classes of resources are generally required: personnel, equipment, facilities, and inventories. Files are included as information inventories. Description, amount, and cost are listed for each resource. Personnel resources are usually identified by occupational skill. Equipment resources should, at this stage, be identified by broad purpose or function rather than by name or type. Facilities are identified by name and location; the contents of the facility—equipment, merchandise, and so forth—are described in other categories on the resource sheet. Inventories and files are described in terms of their intrinsic properties, such as name, location, file medium, volume, number of fields, and characters per message.

Resources are apportioned to the task under analysis. Thus, in Figure 14-6, one half of the supervisor's time and one eighth of a typist's time are taken by the preparation of the charge-account bills, but five full-time clerks are required. The total cost is shown in the cost field when the number or quantity of the resource in the amount field is greater than one. In this instance, $25,500 is the sum of the annual salaries of the five clerks. Actual costs are also shown for the supervisor's and the typist's time, and for a one third use of the typewriter. It should be noted that these specified resources are estimates of what is *required* in the new system. Unless they are imposed on the new system design, however, they should not be stated explicitly because this would imply the concept and procedures to be used.

Necessary materials—in this case blank-form customer record cards or some such recording device—are also summarized. Information resources are listed on the resource sheet; Figure 14-6 lists the customer file, with its annual cost.

A close analysis of this resource sheet, supported by the resource usage sheet from Phase I, may lead the analyst to refine this first approximation of the resources required to achieve the activity goal. For example, preparing the customer record in duplicate in the first place might cut the equipment and clerical costs for only a slight increase in material costs. Since the copiers by which the customer

Resource Sheet

NO.	NAME AND DESCRIPTION	AMOUNT	COST	NOTES
PO1	CLERK	5	$25,500/YR	
PO2	SUPERVISOR	1/2	$5000/YR	
PO3	TYPIST	1/8	$ 700/YR	
E1	COPIER	2	$3100/YR ①	① FIXED CHARGE OF $40 PER MO ; VARIABLE USE CHARGE OF .01 PER COPY.
E2	TYPEWRITER	1/3	$ 90/YR	AMORTIZED ON 5-YR BASE.
V1	CUSTOMER RECORD CARDS	5 M/YR	$.02/UNIT	4 IDEN. FIELDS , 5 TRANSACTION FIELDS – AVG, 409 CHARACTERS PRINTED.
V2	CUSTOMER FILE	1	$145 K/YR	

DATE   ANALYST   CHARGE ACCOUNTS   ASSOCIATED RETAILERS INC.   01
   ACTIVITY   STUDY   PAGE

Figure 14-6 Example of a completed resource sheet for a nonmechanized system—charge accounts.

record is presently prepared are rented, such a move, if it did present savings, would not meet management resistance because there was no capital investment.

In general, the resource sheet summarizes the characteristics of resources without mentioning actual equipment—unless the equipment has been imposed as a requirement. Only during the design of the system does the analyst consider actual equipment.

The form and content of critical inputs and outputs, or of those input and output items whose characteristics are predetermined, may be described in message sheets, which then become supporting documentation for the input-output sheet. Similarly, the resource sheet may be supported by descriptive file sheets wherever the operational characteristics of the file are imposed or otherwise known in advance. Supporting documents for required operations sheets include the operation sheets from Phase I; additional support may be provided by displays of operations logic to show the interconnection of inputs, outputs, and resources, and decision logic to show what happens in the operation. Flowcharts and decision tables are useful tools for this display.

The three summary forms, plus supporting documentation, guide the analyst to a valid determination of what the system will be required to do to produce a required output. Operational requirements, and the necessary inputs and resources, are inferred. Conditions imposed by logical necessity, the environment, or management are duly considered; where no preference exists, a new operational path is designed, or the most efficient existing path is selected.

Now let us turn to the use of the three documentation forms for a mechanized activity. The reader is urged to review the preliminaries of this case in Section 8-9.

14.7   REQUIREMENTS OF A MECHANIZED SYSTEM

Two operations—preparing the invoice and preparing the picking ticket in the mechanized order-processing system discussed in Section 8-9—are logical candidates for analysis, if only because of the volume of work involved. The operation sheet, prepared while the analysts were studying the existing activity, tells us that both are prepared at the rate of 475 a day (*see* Figure 8-11). Besides, the expeditious movement of orders is critical to the business because of the importance of rapid service to the customer; the preparation of the picking ticket is the necessary intermediate step between receiving the order and getting the merchandise together for shipment. The invoice-preparation step is important also because customers normally do not pay for the goods they receive until they have the invoice.

The input-output sheet in Figure 14-7 summarizes the input and output requirements associated with the preparation of the picking ticket and the invoice. We can assume that some external influence—probably the habitual preference of either the company or its customers—has dictated an $8\frac{1}{2} \times 11$ form as the medium for the invoice, just as the fixed format and content of the input sales order dictates the characteristics of its medium. The present mechanization level indicates punched cards as the medium for name-and-address and line-item cards, but flexibility of approach is permitted by the note that the medium may be changed. Only the picking ticket is of unspecified medium. Again, the volumes, sources and destinations, and other required characteristics are entered.

On the required operations sheet, Figure 14-8, the narrative description for the "prepare invoice" operation suggests that a proportionately large amount of calculation is performed in this operation. This is borne out by the estimate of processing

									Input-Output Sheet
NO.	NAME	RATE	MEDIA	SOURCE DESTINATION	NO OF FIELDS	NO. OF CHAR	FORM	CONT	NOTES
I1	SALES ORDER	2330/WK	8½ x 11 FORM	SALESMAN	① 112	① 1010	X	X	① SALES ORDER HAS: 22 "FIXED" FIELDS-500 CHAR. 6 "ITEM" FIELDS- 34 CHAR. PER ITEM - AVG. OF 15 ITEMS PER ORDER.
R1	PICKING TICKET	2500/WK	①	STOCKROOM	103	900			① NO SPECIFICATION.
I1	PICKING TICKET	2500/WK	①	STOCKROOM	118	950			① NO SPECIFICATION.
I2	NAME AND ADDRESS CARDS	1700/WK	IBM CARD	N & A FILE	7	73			MEDIA MAY BE CHANGED.
I3	LINE ITEM CARD	25.5K/WK	IBM CARD	SALES ORDER	19	80			MEDIA MAY BE CHANGED.
R1	INVOICE	2400/WK	8½ x 11 FORM	CUSTOMER	① 132	① 1070			① INVOICE HAS: 12 "FIXED" FIELDS- 320 CHAR. 8 "ITEM" FIELDS- 50 CHAR. AVG. OF 15 ITEMS PER INVOICE.

DATE   ANALYST   ORDER PROCESSING ACTIVITY   ATLANTIC DISTRIB. INC. STUDY   1 PAGE

Figure 14-7   Example of a completed input-output sheet for a mechanized activity—order processing.

steps in the "process summary." The invoice-preparation sequence also works from a relatively large number of inputs and resources, as suggested by the entry of 105 under "input factors." By comparison, the preparation of the picking ticket is fairly simple.

The resource sheet in Figure 14-9 summarizes the equipment, personnel, facili-

					Required Operations Sheet
NO.	OPERATION NAME	INPUT FACTORS	OUTPUT FACTORS	FREQUENCY OF EXECUTION	PROCESS SUMMARY
22	PREPARE PICKING TICKET	47	60	2500/WK.	18 RELATIONAL
	USING ITEM NUMBER, DETERMINE STOCK LOCATION.				25 LOOKUPS
	USING CUSTOMER NAME, DETERMINE CUSTOMER				40 EDITS
	ADDRESS. SEQUENCE BY LOCATION AND PRINT				
	PICKING TICKET.				
23	PREPARE INVOICE	105	135	2400/WK.	70 ARITHMETIC
	USING ITEM NUMBER AND QUANTITY SHIPPED,				12 RELATIONAL
	DETERMINE UNIT AND TOTAL COST, UNIT AND TOTAL				10 LOGICAL
	GROSS MARGIN, UNIT AND TOTAL PRICE, AND INVOICE				30 LOOKUPS
	PRICE. USING INVOICE PRICE AND CUSTOMER				35 EDITS
	NUMBER, DETERMINE DISCOUNT, EDIT AND PRINT				
	INVOICE.				

DATE   ANALYST   ORDER PROCESSING (ACTIVITY)   ATLANTIC DISTRIB. INC. (STUDY)   04 (PAGE)

Figure 14-8   Final page of a completed required operations sheet for a mechanized activity—order processing.

ties, materials, and files required by the two operations undergoing analysis. It lists the costs projected by the wholesale distributor for three card punches and an accounting machine with six wiring panels, plus the salaries of their operators and a full time supervisor. Location and rental cost of the single facility are noted. Materials—blank-form line-item cards, picking tickets and sales orders—are listed,

Resource Sheet

NO.	NAME AND DESCRIPTION	AMOUNT	COST	NOTES
PO1	KEY PUNCH OPERATOR	3	$16000/YR	
PO2	TAB MACHINE OPERATOR	2	$14500/YR	
PO3	SUPERVISOR	1	$10,200/YR	
EO1	KEYPUNCH WITH CARD INSERTION DEVICE	3	$195/MO	
EO2	ACCOUNTING MACHINE MOD A2	1	$835/MO	
EO3	ACCOUNTING MACHINE PANEL	6	$84/YR	$70/PANEL DEPRECIATED ON 5-YR BASIS
F1	TAB ROOM	430 SQ.FT. ①	$95/MO RENT	① IN OFFICE BLDG, 272 WILLOW ST
			$170/MO UTILITIES	
V1	LINE ITEM CARDS	1.35 M/YR	$3.10/K	
			$4200/YR	
V2	PICKING TICKET	125 K/YR	$.05/UNIT	
			$7000/YR	
V3	MASTER ITEM FILE	3	$21000/YR	32000-37000 ITEMS
V4	NAME AND ADDRESS FILE	1	$1275/YR	1700 CUSTOMERS
V5	SALES ORDER	120 K/YR	$.07/UNIT	
			$8400/YR	
VI	CATALOG ① - 32000 TO 37000 ITEMS 700 TO 820 pp.	2000/YR ②	$4.20/UNIT	① INTERNAL CATALOG MAY BE SUPPLANTED BY OTHER TYPE OF FILE.
			$8400/YR	② SUPPLEMENT ISSUED QUARTER-LY 40 pp. PER SUPPLEMENT @ $1400 PER ISSUE TOTAL $5600/YR.

DATE ___ ANALYST ___ ORDER PROCESSING ACTIVITY ___ ATLANTIC DISTRIB. STUDY ___ PAGE 1

Figure 14-9 Example of a completed resource sheet for a mechanized activity—order processing.

as are the two files which are referenced by the operation. The constraints on re-sources implicit in the resource sheet in Figure 14-9 indicate that the company has stipulated the means for performing this operation.

The sales catalog is shown as an additional reference or information resource. It is used in preparation of sales from telephoned orders or customer-purchase orders, and is occasionally referenced in other operations.

14.8 DYNAMIC USE OF FORMS

The summary forms, in the first approximation of the analysis of system requirements, serve as recording forms for the logical collection and organization of data. As the flow of the activity emerges during the information gathering and manipulating process, the analyst gains new insights into what the requirements actually are, and frequently rewrites his forms to summarize the requirements from his new point of view. The technique of successive approximation, and the willing-ness of management and the analysts to try new approaches, are vital to the dy-namic process of determining the actual requirements of the system.

It is neither easy nor straightforward to develop the true requirements of a busi-ness system. Rigid rules or step-by-step procedures are impossible. Since informa-tion gained at one point will almost invariably necessitate reevaluation of a pre-viously acquired conclusion, a series of successive approximations is necessary.

Several general procedures have been evolved through experience to guide the analyst in making these successive passes at the system. In these procedures, the three summary forms are used to define the requirements as they are deduced. The five descriptive forms from the Phase I survey (or equivalent information sources) serve as the initial inputs to the analytical phase; two of them—message and file sheets—are valuable as supporting documents to the Phase II summary forms to describe newly evolved inputs, outputs, and files.

Principal inputs and outputs are those which are related to the external environ-ment. Others are those which are logically imposed, or which are specified by management. These inputs and outputs are a logical starting point for the analytical process.

In first sketching out the requirements of the system, a rough requirements model is valuable. This model first displays all the imposed activity characteristics and their necessary interrelationships. From these can be inferred other activity requirements. A customer-service department, for example, must accept telephone calls; from this, telephones can be inferred as a required resource. An order-processing activity normally must calculate costs; a merchandise catalog or file can be inferred as a necessary information resource.

From the model of the system, the observer can begin to specify requirements. The activity output is defined first; what operations are required to produce it? These operations are listed and described; what resources and inputs are required? When these are defined, they may require or suggest changes in operation logic; a new approximation will suggest further changes, and so on.

In aggregating operations into larger groups—to be defined in the subsequent system as activities—logical grouping is of prime importance. Operations can be related causally, sequentially, or chronologically.

Causal dependence refers to operations required because of the outcome of another operation. In the charge-account activity, the recording of the sale and the posting of the file are causally dependent on the sale.

Sequential dependence is fixed when one operation must follow another. In the order-processing activity, the order is received, the picking ticket prepared, the stock selected, packaged, and shipped, and the invoice prepared. The invoice is generally not prepared before the other steps are completed, stock cannot be shipped until selected and packaged, and the selection process must follow the preparation of the picking ticket—this is a sequentially dependent set of processes.

Chronological dependence requires performance of several operations either simultaneously or at fixed intervals. In the "select stock" operation of the order-processing activity, the back order—if one is required—can be generated only at the time the stock-selection process discloses inadequate stock. At no other time is the information available to enter the system.

If the team is analyzing a single activity, the mutual interrelationships among the operations will be clearly established. In determining the requirements of larger segments of a business, or of a whole business, however, the analyst must be alert to the various types of operational dependence, and group the operations logically. He must also avoid, in studying system characteristics, the possibility of being misled by merely incidental relationships.

There are two ways to develop the decision logic of a system. The more important involves the use of imposed inputs and outputs—and resources—as limiting factors, and the construction of a logic to connect them, with inputs and resources added where needed. This procedure places great demands on the resourcefulness and imagination of the analyst, but may in the long run produce a more valid statement of true requirements. The second way is to extract the basic decision logic from present operations, as displayed on the activity and operation sheets from the Phase I survey, then modify it by interviews with management.

The decision logic evolved through the process of inference within imposed restraints must be tested in operational models. The test procedure can be as simple as tracing an input rigorously through the system as inferred; missing operations and resources will be disclosed in the process. The procedure is not unlike debugging a computer program.

At each step, or for each of the several successive approximations, the requirements are summarized on input-output, required operations, and resource sheets. At the final analysis, the sheets are grouped together in their logical relationship and recast. The supporting documentation is then prepared from preliminary sketches, in the case of flowcharts and decision tables; and message and file sheets are drawn up for critical inputs, outputs, and resources.

The summary of requirements present in the three forms and supporting documents now becomes the guide to the design and description of the new system. This is the third phase in the study and design stage of the life of a business system. It is discussed in Part 4 of our book. To complete Part 3, we present a detailed discussion of the construction of the report of requirements followed by our continuing case study, Butodale, in which the forms described in this chapter are illustrated in the fuller context of this case study.

SUMMARY

Three forms may be used to document the specification of the requirements of a system—input-output sheet, required operations sheet, and resource sheet. The input-output sheet is a summary form for recording the required characteristics of inputs and outputs. Detailed descriptions, where needed, are displayed on supporting message sheets. The required operations sheet summarizes the input factors, output factors, and frequency of execution of each logically necessary operation. A narrative description outlining what the operation logically must do is entered on the form. The resource sheet summarizes the material and informational resources that are either logically necessary or imposed on the operation. All resources are summarized: types of people, present or projected equipment, facilities, and files. *The general and summary character of the three documents guides the analyst to look more closely at what is to be done than at how it is to be accomplished.*

15

Preparing the Report of Requirements

15.1 INTRODUCTION

Except for preparing summary statements and cost analyses covering all activities as a whole, requirements analysis is now complete. The remaining task is to draw the data into a cohesive specification of requirements.

There is no established rule on how many passes are necessary to develop a satisfactory statement of system requirements. One or two may be sufficient for mechanization or improvement studies; as variability increases and constraints are fewer, analysis is more complex and more passes are required. Even in creative studies, however, a number of activities may be fairly straightforward and consist only of a single chain of decision logic. For example, in automated manufacturing planning, analysts must develop the logic chain between parts characteristics and operator or machine instructions. Complexity arises from the individual analysis of the many thousands of parts there may be in a product line.

To review, a report of requirements documents Phase II results, activity by activity, under three major headings: general, operations, and measurement. A summary should be used to tie the individual activity packets together. The reader may wish to reread Section 11.3 before continuing.

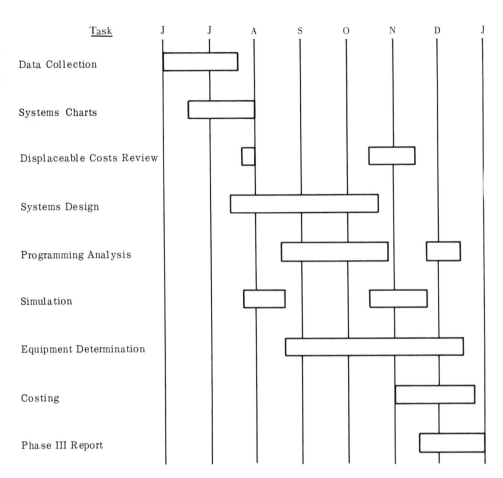

Figure 15-1   Gantt chart showing a tentative schedule of work for a study team designing a new system. Time is shown by month from June to January.

15.2   GENERAL CONSIDERATIONS

A common procedure for preparing a report of requirements is to start with activity packets, then compile the summary section.

A number of important considerations that materialized during Phase II, however, may not fall within any activity. These relate usually to policy statements and management decisions about implementation of the system, and are shown in a section of the summary entitled "General Considerations." Included can be such topics as rental or purchase of data processing facilities, financial limitations on overall system implementation and operating costs, location of equipment, and how the changeover is to be performed.

The statement of general considerations, noted below, is taken from the Custodian Life report:

Cost

The present total cost for each activity is a tentative upper cost limit for any new design applying to that activity. This includes personnel, equipment, and facilities used to perform the work normally associated with data processing.

Policies

The standards used by the underwriters in determining the acceptability of an applicant are defined by the management of the company. These standards are the guideposts in the selection of risks, and must be adhered to in the underwriting decision.

Custodian Life both leases and purchases data processing equipment; the plan most advantageous at the time is selected.

Location

Data processing is performed at the home office. Any new system would utilize the facilities and resources at this location, rather than possible facilities at the general agencies.

Conversion and Implementation

Any proposed system will be run in parallel, as much as possible, and results compared in detail with the existing system output. The period of parallel operation will last only so long as needed to prove out the results of the new system but in no case will be less than one accounting period.

It is important that any new system provide for information on the status of a customer application at all times as it goes through the new-business processing.

The study team can also show for management's approval a tentative schedule for designing the new system. The estimated start, elapsed time, and completion dates can be displayed on a Gantt chart similar to that shown in Figure 15-1.

Now we turn to a consideration of each of the three main sections of each activity's packet in the report—general, operations, and measurement. Following these three items we discuss the report's Appendix and its overall summary.

15.3   THE GENERAL SECTION

The general section of each activity packet describes business goals and objectives as they relate to that activity, its scope and boundaries, and any applicable general considerations.

Phase I business goal statements were refined and documented early in Phase II, in order to direct the requirements analysis properly. A full narrative goal definition for the entire business is included in the summary section of the report of requirements; individual goals appropriate to single activities are placed in the general section of each activity packet.

Activity definitions were resolved as the goal statement was prepared. Minor revisions may have been made to scope and boundary statements during Phase II analysis; therefore, the original statements are revised and entered in the general section in the form described in Chapter 11.

Most of the general considerations have impact on the entire business and therefore are contained in the summary section as described earlier. General considerations applying only to one activity should be placed in the general section for that activity.

15.4 THE OPERATIONS SECTION

The operations section specifies what each activity is required to do: what inputs must be accepted, what operations must be performed, what outputs must be produced, and what resources must be employed.

All four elements—inputs, outputs, operations, and resources—are described briefly in an activity requirements model similar to that shown in Figure 12-1. This model, used throughout Phase II as a working paper to portray activity elements, was subject to revision as changes occurred during analysis. Now these changes are introduced and the model produced in final form to show both imposed and logically determined requirements.

The input-output sheet, used earlier as a working paper, is now revised to summarize important features of required inputs and outputs emerging from requirements analysis.

The required operations sheet describes transformations which convert inputs to outputs. In operations documentation, emphasis is placed on identifying the decision logic rather than on describing the operation with a procedure statement. Any internal relationships, time dependencies, and required sequencing are noted in the description. Decision logic shown on decision tables and flowcharts is contained in the Appendix of the report. Special studies conducted to test operational validity, such as simulation runs, may be described there.

The resource sheet shows personnel, equipment, facilities, information, and physical inventories required by the activity. Resources may remain relatively unchanged if management imposes many constraints. More frequently, there will be important changes in resource requirements.

When positions and jobs of personnel are altered in content, the new work elements are outlined to show how they differ from previous job descriptions. Where the job title suggests the work content (computer programmer, transactions auditor, and so on), this is sufficient explanation. Position guides for new and revised jobs are prepared while the new system is being designed.

A map of an existing communications network could be placed in the Appendix after it is revised to show network requirements resulting from Phase II traffic analysis.

15.5 THE MEASUREMENT SECTION

Measurement factors and scales for evaluating the effectiveness of alternative Phase III system designs are shown in each activity packet's measurement section. Factors are displayed graphically, similar to the examples of Chapter 13. Definitions of each factor should be prepared and placed in the Appendix. In addition to their role in judging alternatives in the design of systems, measurement factors serve a useful purpose in evaluating the final system through the implementation and operation stages in the life cycle of the system.

15.6 APPENDIX OF THE REPORT

The content, layout, and forms of the report of requirements are aimed at stating systems requirements clearly, and briefly. Any analysis which cannot be readily condensed is consigned to the Appendix. The Appendix includes items such as simulation details, extensive equipment lists, message and file sheets (where they are needed to describe imposed inputs, outputs and resources), definitions of measurement factors, and the like.

15.7 SUMMARY SECTION

The summary section integrates the activity packets and appraises the impact of the study on the entire business.

General considerations affecting more than one activity (for example, management policy, new systems cost, and location) appear here. The statement of the overall goals for the business is located in this section.

Although activities are relatively independent in structure and content, outputs from some activities serve as inputs to others. There may be points of overlap, particularly in the use of common facilities. Interactivity relationship is described in this section.

A preface introduces the objectives and content of the report, and the sequence in which information is presented. The following paragraphs are excerpts from the introduction to the Commercial National Bank report:

> This report is a specification of systems requirements which describes the present and future requirements for a business system at the Commercial National Bank, and establishes the measurements by which the performance of the new system is to be evaluated.
>
> Several changes have taken place since the Present Business Description report was published. The goal statement has been expanded to reflect the anticipated growth of this institution, and introduction of many new customer services. The activities (activities are sometimes referred to as subsystems) have been clarified both in definition and scope. Management also decided to include only those activities which have good growth potential and high transaction volumes in the new system. Consequently, five activities were selected and these five constitute the major sections of the requirements report.

The introduction continues by pointing out that management wanted the most advanced system design possible, and therefore had placed very few constraints on the study team. The team leader devoted several paragraphs to an explanation of why requirements analysis is critical to systems design, and what the difference was between an existing system and a required system. The main report of requirements was then introduced.

SUMMARY

A report specifying requirements documents Phase II results, activity by activity, under three major headings: general, operations, and measurement. An overall summary entitled General Considerations may introduce the complete report and may include topics such as financial limitations on overall system implementation and operating costs, location of equipment, rental or purchase of data processing facilities, and how the changeover is to be accomplished. A tentative schedule of Phase III may also be included. The general section of each activity packet describes business goals and objectives as they relate to that activity, activity scope and boundaries, and applicable general considerations. The operations section specifies what each activity is required to do in terms of what inputs must be accepted, what operations performed, what outputs produced, and what resources employed. All four elements are related in an activity requirements model. The measurement section shows measurement factors and scales for evaluating the effectiveness of alternative systems designs. The report may include an Appendix containing simulation details, equipment lists, message and file sheets, and definitions of measurement factors.

16

Specifying Requirements for Butodale

16.1 INTRODUCTION

This chapter presents a continuation of our Butodale case study. Chapter 10 contains an adaptation of the actual report prepared by the systems analysts who studied Butodale as an existing organization. The report was accepted by management who authorized the study team to probe deeper into Butodale, but to concentrate on two activities—provide product demand and provide end products. The material will provide the essential features of the kind of work a study team must do in order to obtain a satisfactorily complete picture of the requirements of a system.

16.2 GUIDE TO THE SYSTEM REQUIREMENTS REPORT

Our first recommendation is that the reader examine the several sections of the report, noting the general form of the presentation. For comparison, he should again glance through Chapter 10.

After examining the sections briefly, the reader should go through the report, page by page, at whatever speed he desires, and with the complete report in mind, he may wish to study the following points more closely.

1. The introduction states that by agreement between the analysts and management only the provide product demand and provide end products activities are to be studied.

2. The reader might well review Section 10.3 concerning goals and objectives and compare them with their restatement in the present report.

3. Notice the time and money constraints in the section on general considerations.

4. The general section of the provide product demand activity carefully outlines the goals the activity is to satisfy and specifies the scope of the activity. These statements are of critical importance to the analyst because they are normally set by a series of conferences between the analyst and those concerned with the activity; they become the criteria against which the requirements are matched. The reader should consider them carefully.

5. The model exhibiting Butodale's requirements for the activity of providing product demand is of central interest during the presentation of the report to management for it gives a complete picture of the structure of the activity in a form easy to understand. The reader should give this model careful attention.

6. The input-output sheet, required operations sheet, and resource sheets for the provide demand activity should be examined in some detail and their relations with the Appendix of the first report explored.

7. When we review the measurement section, we see that the new system is required to perform as well as, or better than, the existing system. The reader should examine the exhibits in this section and then try to visualize their meaning and later use.

8. The reader should take time to examine the explanation of measurement factors for the provide demand activity in the Appendix. There he will see how the analysts arrived at the figures for their measurement scales. After the system is in operation there will be many ways to measure time and cost, for example. The analysts, management, and others involved in the activity have foreseen this problem, and to provide an unequivocal method for the measurement they have presented the formula in the report itself.

Here now is the complete case.

16.3 SYSTEM REQUIREMENTS SPECIFICATION: A REPORT FOR BUTODALE

SUMMARY SECTION

Introduction

This report, the System Requirements Specification, describes the present and future requirements for a business system at Butodale Electronics Company, and establishes the measurements by which the performance of the new system is to be evaluated.

Several changes have taken place since the Present Business Description report was published. The goal statement has been expanded to reflect anticipated growth and modification of the business and introduction of new products. Activities have been sharpened and clarified both in definition and scope. A decision was reached with Butodale management during this redefinition process to analyze only the Provide Product Demand and Provide End Products activities at this time, since these are the critical activities in the main line operation of the business.

Prime emphasis has been placed by Butodale management on considerations of the future so that the new system will have sufficient flexibility for development and manufacture of new products and product lines and still react quickly to customer needs. Present policies and practices, therefore, are to have a minimum influence.

Goals and Objectives

Goals and objectives of the Butodale Electronics Company are as follows:

1. Manufacture and sell standard computer equipments and accessories.
2. Design and manufacture special computer models and accessories to satisfy individual specifications and requirements.
3. Offer computation services and engineering consultation on a fee basis to industry, commerce, and schools, among others.
4. Manufacture spare parts and components for sale to the trade.
5. Repair and maintain installed equipments.
6. Conduct research on new products and services to support present lines and initiate new ones within Butodale's area of knowledge and proficiency.
7. Compensate employees and suppliers for services, and provide a satisfactory return for investors.
8. Demonstrate competence and quality in every product to clearly show advantage over competitive equipment.

General Considerations

Technological advances in the computer industry are rapidly developing needs for new products and new product characteristics. Manufacturing processes and skills will probably follow existing trends but physical nature and end usage of products may shift radically. A system to perform Provide Product Demand and Provide End Products activities must be flexible enough to control more complex and more highly specialized products for a wider range of customers. For example, developments in microminiaturization and vibration engineering will alter manufacturing and testing techniques, and the space industry has specified severe environmental requirements.

Expansion and specialization of products means that a higher percentage of orders will require engineering design. To remain competitive, the cycle times for bid/quote, design, and manufacturing must improve over current cycle times.

COST

The combined data processing costs for operation of the new system (Provide Product Demand and Provide End Products Activities) should not exceed 110% of current costs. Implementation and conversion costs are to be analyzed on the basis of a seven year amortization plan. Current system costs, based on current volumes, and new system costs, based on future volumes, are to be used.

Analysis must include purchase versus rental options available.

CONVERSION AND IMPLEMENTATION

All actions and plans shall be based on 80% of available workload to be operational under the new system within twenty months after implementation begins.

Source language for programming the equipment designated for any new system will be Fortran.

Activity Definitions and Relationships

Provide Product Demand is the interface with Butodale's customer market. Inputs from this part of the environment enter directly (requests for quotation and bids, inquiries, orders, etc.) and outputs from Provide Demand directly enter the environment (quotations, bids, acknowledgments, and so on). Provide Product Demand interfaces with Provide End Products through the new order schedule. Provide Product Demand furnishes customer orders to the master scheduling operation of Provide End Products; this operation furnishes delivery dates to Provide Product Demand. Interfaces with other activities are limited to commonly-used files of basic product, customer, and order information.

Provide End Products is the product assembly function of Butodale. This activity interfaces with the environment through outputs of finished products and invoices, but does not follow up on these outputs through control of receivables. Significant interfaces with other Butodale activities (and areas not at present classified into activities) are:

Provide Product Demand, through the master scheduling operation and supplying of order status data as requested.

Provide Material through inputs of material cost records, subassemblies and parts and outputs of production schedules and work in process reports.

Engineering, through inputs of production standards, quality control and testing standards and procedures, and facilities planning data; outputs of standard and variances, testing results, and modification requests.

Accounting (Management Control) through inputs of work-in-process controls and outputs of certified labor records, work-in-process data, disbursements for additional (subcontracted) facilities, and invoices.

Other interfaces are only through shared files and file data.

PROVIDE PRODUCT DEMAND ACTIVITY

GENERAL SECTION

Goals and Objectives

The prime goal of the Provide Product Demand Activity is to communicate customer requirements and specifications for the manufacture of end products and spare parts. This is to be accomplished by meeting the following objectives:

1. Satisfy customer information requests.
2. Determine need for and carry out engineering design.
3. Supply information for cost accounting and management control.
4. Inform customers of order disposition and schedules.
5. Arrange for manufacturing.

Scope and Boundaries

This activity is concerned with accepting customer orders and preparing bids and quotations for potential customers. Requests and orders are received from company salesmen, manufacturers' representatives, or are placed directly by the customer. They include orders for standard and custom-designed equipments and spare parts, but do not include requests for computation services. Standard equipments are processed routinely and the customer is furnished documents including price quotations, descriptive data, layouts, diagrams, and other information necessary to make the purchase decision.

Where the equipment is special, this activity includes management and engineering reviews, engineering design and layout, and the compilation of special cost data.

After receipt of a firm order, the contract is edited and clarified for communication to engineering and manufacturing. The present volume of requests averages 15–20 weekly for standard products, and 3–4 for engineered products. In the near future this could rise to a combined total of 25–30 per week.

Provide Product Demand does not include market forecasting, determination of plant schedules (this is actually worked out in conference with manufacturing when available capacity does not conform with customer requirements in regard to requested shipping dates), or the calculation of costs and prices.

The principal inputs, then, to this activity are customer orders or requests for quotation, and the principal outputs are quotations and specifications to the customer and communication of accepted orders and product specifications to manufacturing.

PROVIDE END PRODUCTS ACTIVITY

GENERAL SECTION

Goals and Objectives

Goals and objectives of the Provide End Products activity are:

1. Develop and control production schedules to achieve maximum customer satisfaction. In event of conflicting orders, preference is given to:
   a. standard products orders
   b. order acceptance date
   c. prime customers
2. Manufacture end products and components in accordance with Butodale quality standards.
3. Provide basic information for control of work in process, receivables, direct labor payroll, and end product shipping.

Scope and Boundary

Provide End Products includes the functions of:

Production scheduling and dispatching
Component assembly and test
End product assembly and test
Maintenance of production and quality standards (material and labor)
Control of work in process
Providing certified labor records for direct payroll
Routing, packing, and shipping
Invoicing

Functions not included in Provide End Products are:

Establishing production standards
Establishing testing standards or procedure
Fabrication
Accounts payable (or disbursement)
Accounts receivable (or cashier)
Purchasing or subcontracting
Personnel or payroll administration
Transportation claims or administration
Facilities planning

Prime inputs are the Order Acknowledgment (R-3050) and New Order Schedule (F-4080); prime outputs are end products and components, Invoice (R-2100), and Shipping Report (R-3070).

General Considerations

Complexity of the production schedule is expected to increase as a result of technological advances leading to more complex products. System flexibility to handle a broader general-purpose product line and (simultaneously) a more specialized product line is therefore mandatory.

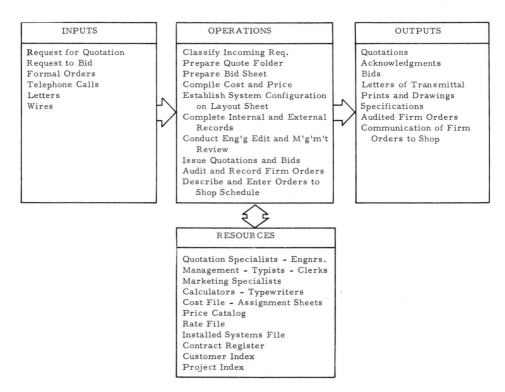

INPUTS	OPERATIONS	OUTPUTS
Request for Quotation	Classify Incoming Req.	Quotations
Request to Bid	Prepare Quote Folder	Acknowledgments
Formal Orders	Prepare Bid Sheet	Bids
Telephone Calls	Compile Cost and Price	Letters of Transmittal
Letters	Establish System Configuration	Prints and Drawings
Wires	on Layout Sheet	Specifications
	Complete Internal and External	Audited Firm Orders
	Records	Communication of Firm
	Conduct Eng'g Edit and M'g'm't	Orders to Shop
	Review	
	Issue Quotations and Bids	
	Audit and Record Firm Orders	
	Describe and Enter Orders to	
	Shop Schedule	

RESOURCES

Quotation Specialists - Engnrs.
Management - Typists - Clerks
Marketing Specialists
Calculators - Typewriters
Cost File - Assignment Sheets
Price Catalog
Rate File
Installed Systems File
Contract Register
Customer Index
Project Index

Figure 16-1 The provide product demand activity requirements model for Butodale.

NO.	NAME	RATE	MEDIA	SOURCE DESTINATION	NO. OF FIELDS	NO. OF CHAR.	F O R M	C O N T	NOTES
I1	REQUEST FOR QUOTATION (R-2000)	50/W	WIRES TELEPHONE LETTERS	CUSTOMER					AVG. PEAK STD SYSTEMS 22 30 207 - 217 20 27 OTHER 8 13
I2	REQUEST FOR BID (R-2010)	10/W	LETTERS	CUSTOMER					PEAK VOLUME 12/W 10 WKS A YEAR
I3	CUSTOMER ORDERS (R-2020)	17/W	8½x11 4 PART	CUSTOMER					PEAK 20/WK 6 WEEKS A YEAR
R1	QUOTATIONS * (R-3000)	15/W	8½x11 4 PART	CUSTOMER				X	PEAK 20/WK 10 WEEKS A YEAR
R2	ACKNOWLEDGMENTS (R-3050)	17/W		CUSTOMER SHOP (PROVIDE END PRODUCTS ACTIVITY)			X	X	NO PEAKS
R3	NEW ORDER SCHEDULE (F-4080)	17/W		SHOP (PROVIDE END PRODUCTS ACTIVITY)				X	COMMUNICATES DATA ON FIRM ORDERS
R4	CUSTOMER ORDER (R-2020)	17/W		SHOP				X	DETAILS OF FIRM ORDER ARE ENTERED ON CONTRACT REGISTER

*INCLUDES LETTERS, DRAWINGS, SPECIFICATIONS, LAYOUTS AS NECESSARY TO SUPPLEMENT QUOTATION

R.L. CASEY	DEMAND	BUTODALE	1
DATE ANALYST	ACTIVITY	STUDY	PAGE

Figure 16-2   Input-output sheet for the provide product demand activity.

NO.	OPERATION NAME	INPUT FACTORS	OUTPUT FACTORS	FREQUENCY OF EXECUTION	PROCESS SUMMARY
01	CLASSIFY INCOMING REQUESTS ALL REQUESTS FOR BID (R-2010) OR QUOTATION (R-2000) ARE SEPARATED INITIALLY INTO 3 GROUPS: STANDARD END ITEMS, STANDARD SYSTEMS, AND ENGINEERED PRODUCTS.	5	10	60/W	7 LOOKUP 3 EDIT 6 RELATIONAL
02	PREPARE QUOTE FOLDER (F-4050.1) A FOLDER IS PREPARED FOR EACH REQUEST TO HOLD CUSTOMER PAPERS AND DOCUMENTS GENERATED WITHIN BUTODALE TO FILL THE ORDER.	7	12	15/D	2 LOOKUP 4 EDIT 3 RELATIONAL
03	PREPARE BID SHEET (R-3000) A BID SHEET IS PREPARED FOR EACH REQUEST FROM PRICE, COST, AND INSTALLED SYSTEMS FILES DEPENDING ON THE TYPE REQUEST, EACH IS PRO- CESSED SOMEWHAT DIFFERENTLY. A GPAC* HAS APPROXIMATELY 13 MAJOR INTERCONNECTED COMPONENTS AVAILABLE IN DIFFERENT GROUPINGS. INPUT-OUTPUT DEVICES ARE OPTIONAL IN 6 MODELS. ALTHOUGH CONSOLE AND GROUPS DESCRIPTIONS ARE STANDARD, THEY MAY BE MODIFIED AT CUSTOMER REQUEST.	15	20	45/W	10 ARITHMETIC 50 LOGICAL 30 LOOKUP
04	DETERMINE SYSTEM LAYOUT A GPAC MAY HAVE ANY ONE OF SEVERAL CON- SOLES, AND ANY ONE OF SEVERAL RACK CONFIGURATIONS. *GENERAL PURPOSE ANALOG COMPUTER	27	38	12/W	60 ARITHMETIC 32 LOGICAL 5 EDIT 15 LOOKUP

R.L. CASEY   DEMAND   BUTODALE   1 OF 3

DATE   ANALYST   ACTIVITY   STUDY   PAGE

Figure 16-3   Required operations sheet for the provide product demand activity.

NO.	OPERATION NAME	INPUT FACTORS	OUTPUT FACTORS	FREQUENCY OF EXECUTION	PROCESS SUMMARY
05	DECIDE BID STATUS ON ENGINEERED PRODUCTS, A MANAGEMENT CONFERENCE IS HELD TO DETERMINE SPECIAL CONSIDERATIONS, PRICES, AND PROMISED DELIVERY.	40	70	40/M	30 LOOKUP 50 RELATIONAL 80 LOGICAL 10 ARITHMETIC
06	DESIGN SYSTEM LAYOUT ON ENGINEERED PRODUCTS, ENGINEERING DESIGN AND DRAFTING IS REQUIRED TO LAY OUT ALL SPECIAL REQUIREMENTS.	200	600	20/W	700 LOOKUP 200 LOGICAL 50 ARITHMETIC 40 RELATIONAL 300 EDIT
07	COST SPECIAL COMPONENTS FOR EACH SPECIAL ITEM, COSTS AND PRICES ARE ESTABLISHED TO SUPPORT THE FINAL QUOTATION.	10	18	150/W	4 LOOKUP 16 ARITHMETIC 10 RELATIONAL 8 EDIT
08	PREPARE QUOTATION (R-3000) THE CUSTOMER IS SUPPLIED A DOCUMENT DESCRIBING THE PRODUCT, ITS RACKS AND ATTACHMENTS, AND THE TOTAL PRICE, WITH OPTIONS.	75	100	20/W	30 LOOKUP 10 LOGICAL 100 EDIT 200 POSTING
09	ESTABLISH INTERNAL RECORDS DETAILS OF THE PROPOSAL ARE RECORDED ON INTERNAL DOCUMENTS AND IN THE CONTRACT REGISTER FILE. (F-4050)	200	800	20/W	10 LOGICAL 10 LOOKUP 500 POSTING 20 EDIT

DATE _____   ANALYST R.L. CASEY   ACTIVITY DEMAND   STUDY BUTODALE   PAGE 2 OF 3

Figure 16-3   (continued)

NO.	OPERATION NAME	INPUT FACTORS	OUTPUT FACTORS	FREQUENCY OF EXECUTION	PROCESS SUMMARY
10	TRANSMIT QUOTATION (R-3000) THE QUOTATION IS MAILED TO THE CUSTOMER WITH SUPPORTING DATA INCLUDING A LETTER OF TRANSMITTAL, PRINTS, DRAWINGS, LAYOUT, SPECIFICATIONS, ETC.	10	10	20/W	25 LOGICAL 10 LOOKUP 10 EDIT
11	EDIT INCOMING ORDERS (R2020) FIRM CUSTOMER ORDERS ARE EDITED AGAINST THE CONTRACT REGISTER FILE (F-4050) AND POSTED TO THE CUSTOMER (F-4060) AND PROJECT INDEX. (F-4070)	150	30	16/W	10 LOOKUP 150 EDIT 75 POSTING
12	PREPARE & TRANSMIT ACKNOWLEDGMENT (R-3050) THE CUSTOMER IS NOTIFIED OF THE ORDER RECEIPT, AND ACCEPTANCE AND DELIVERY DATES ARE RECONFIRMED.	30	30	16/W	10 LOOKUP 15 ARITHMETIC 30 EDIT
13	COMMUNICATE ORDERS TO SHOP THE CUSTOMER ORDER IS POSTED TO AN ASSIGNMENT SHEET (F-4080) AND PREPARED FOR SHOP RELEASE, OR TO ENGINEERING. SPECIAL CONDITIONS AND TERMS ARE COMMUNICATED TO INTERESTED PARTIES AT THIS TIME.	10	15	20/W	10 LOOKUP 20 POSTING 10 LOGICAL 10 EDIT

_____ DATE   R.L. CASEY ANALYST   DEMAND ACTIVITY   BUTODALE STUDY   3 OF 3 PAGE

Figure 16-3   (continued)

Resource Sheet

NO.	NAME AND DESCRIPTION	AMOUNT	COST	NOTES
P1	MANAGEMENT (PARTIAL)	2	$24,000	REVIEW QUOTATIONS
P2	SALES AND SERVICE MANAGER, SALESMEN, SERVICE ENGINEERS, SECRETARIES, CLERKS	56	$448,000	
P3	ADMINISTRATION & ADVERTISING MANAGER, MEDIA SPECIALISTS, SECRETARIES CLERKS, ANALYSTS, SUPERVISORS	14	84,000	
P4	COST CLERKS	2	9,000	
P5	ACCOUNTS RECEIVABLE CLERKS	4	19,000	
P6	PRODUCT ENGINEERS	3	26,400	
P7	ADMINISTRATIVE ENGINEERS	2	13,400	
P8	PUBLICATIONS SPECIALISTS	3	20,100	
E1	VEHICLES		10,100	DEPRECIATION & RENTAL
E2	TYPEWRITERS	15		
E3	CALCULATORS	2		
E4	DICTATING MACHINES	2		

R.L. CASEY   DEMAND   BUTODALE   1 of 1

DATE   ANALYST   ACTIVITY   STUDY   PAGE

Figure 16-4   Resource sheet for the provide product demand activity.

MEASUREMENT SECTION

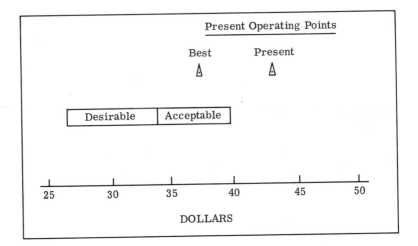

Figure 16-5   Average order processing cost.

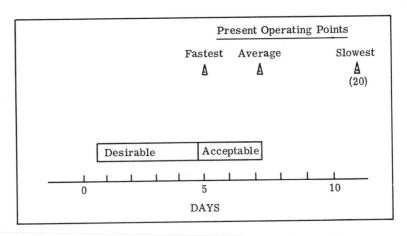

Figure 16-6   Order acknowledgment.

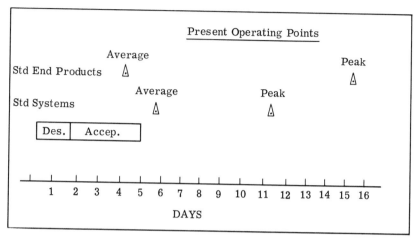

Figure 16-7   Response time for quotation.

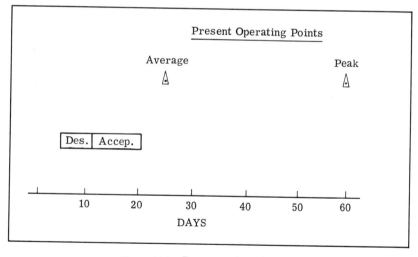

Figure 16-8   Response time for bid.

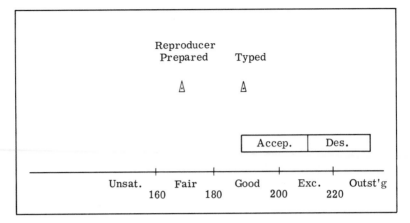

Figure 16-9   Quotation (bid) appearance.

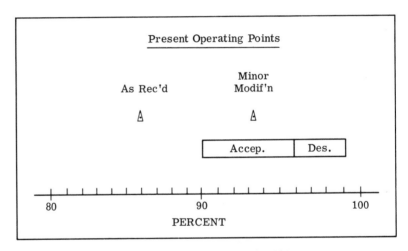

Figure 16-10   Processable request for bid/quotes.

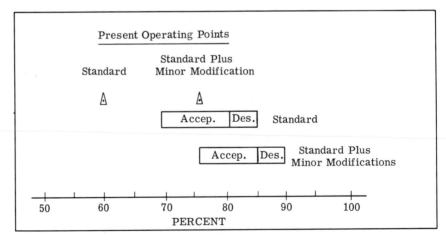

Figure 16-11   Standard products requested (compared to total requests).

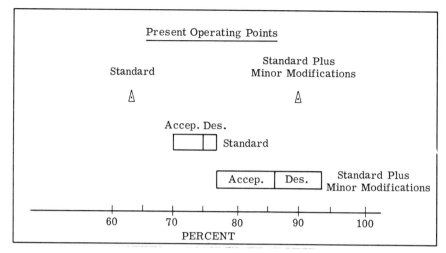

Figure 16-12   Percent relating dollars of standard product orders to dollars of total orders.

OPERATIONS SECTION

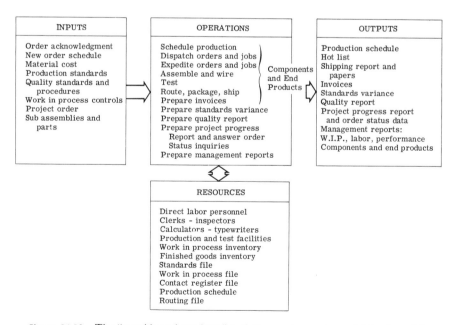

Figure 16-13   The "provide end products" activity requirements model for Butodale.

Input-Output Sheet

NO.	NAME	RATE	MEDIA	SOURCE DESTINATION	NO. OF FIELDS	NO. OF CHAR.	F O R M	C O N T	NOTES
I 1	ORDER ACKNOWLEDGMENTS (R-3050)	17/ω	LETTER	PROVIDE DEMAND ACTIVITY			X	X	NO PEAKS
I2	NEW ORDER SCHEDULE (F-4080)	1/ω		PROVIDE DEMAND ACTIVITY				X	MASTER SCHEDULE FOR END PRODUCT SHIPMENTS
I3	MATERIAL COST (R-3010)	100/D		PROVIDE MATERIAL ACTIVITY				X	COSTED MATERIAL WITHDRAWALS
I4	PRODUCTION STANDARDS	25/ω		ENG'G STDS PRODUCT'N TOOLING					ENGINEERING AND MFG MEMORANDA
I5	QUALITY STANDARDS	5/ω		ENG'G STDS					ENGINEERING MEMOS
I6	QUALITY PROCEDURES	5/MO		QUALITY CONTROL			X	X	ENTERED INTO QUALITY SECTION OF STANDARDS FILE
I7	W.I.P. CONTROLS	1/M		COST ACCT'G					
I8	PROJECT ORDERS	17/ω		MARKET&					SALES AND BUILD ORDER FOR END PRODUCTS AND COMPONENTS
R1	PRODUCTION SCHED.	1/ωۇ	TAB LISTING	PRODUCT'N DEPTS			X	X	DETAIL BY PRODUCT. DEPT. AND PROJECT
R2	HOT LIST (R-3030)	1/D — 30-50 LINES	TYPED	PRODUCT'N DEPTS			X		

R.L. CASEY   END PRODUCTS   BUTODALE   1 of 2
DATE   ANALYST   ACTIVITY   STUDY   PAGE

Figure 16-14   Input-output sheet for the provide end products activity.

Input–Output Sheet

NO.	NAME	RATE	MEDIA	SOURCE DESTINATION	NO. OF FIELDS	NO. OF CHAR	F O R M	L O N ?	NOTES
R3	SHIPPING REPORT (R-3070)	1/DAY 4-12 ITEMS	TYPED	SUPT				X	
R4	INVOICE (R-3100)	20/ω		CUST & ACCTG				X	INCLUDES SHIPPING PAPERS
R5	STANDARDS VARIANCE	10/D		PRODUCT ENG'G					INSPECTION AND TEST MEMOS
R6	QUALITY REPORT (R-3040)	1/D 5-20 ITEMS	TYPED	Q/C					ACTION REPORT
R7	PROJECT PROGRESS REPORT	1/D 100 JOBS*		SUPT					COMBINED R-3020 AND R-3070 * EXPECTED TO GROW
R8	WORK IN PROCESS REPORT	1/ω		GEN'L ACCTG					DATA AVAILABLE IN F4120
R9	LABOR REPORT	1/ω		SUPT					ANALYSIS OF F4100
R10	PERFORMANCE REPORT (R-3080)	1/D		SUPT					
R11	ORDER STATUS INQUIRY DATA	3/D	PHONE	MKTG					FURNISH WITHIN 1 HOUR

MO8-4606-1

DATE ___ R.L. CASEY ANALYST ___ END PRODUCTS ACTIVITY ___ BUTODALE STUDY ___ 2 of 2 PAGE

Figure 16-14   (continued)

Required Operations Sheet

NO.	OPERATION NAME	INPUT FACTORS	OUTPUT FACTORS	FREQUENCY OF EXECUTION	PROCESS SUMMARY
01	SCHEDULE PRODUCTION	420	1200	1/W	750 LOOKUP
	BASED ON NEW ORDER SCHEDULE (F-4080)				1500 ARITHMETIC
	PREPARE DETAIL PRODUCTION SCHEDULE				150 LOGICAL
	FOR ASSEMBLY, WIRING, AND TEST AREAS. DETAIL				1500 RELATIONAL
	BY PRODUCT, DEPARTMENT, AND PROJECT				2400 POST
	(TWO TYPES OF PROJECTS ARE IN THE NEW				
	ORDER SCHEDULE: SALES PROJECTS, WHICH				
	HAVE A CUSTOMER ORDER, AND BUILD				
	PROJECTS, WHICH DO NOT).				
	DECISION RULES FOR PRIORITY IN				
	PRODUCTION SCHEDULING:				
	1. SALES PROJECT				
	2. STANDARD PRODUCT				
	3. PRIME CUSTOMER				
02	DISPATCH ORDERS	2700	4500	1/D	700 LOOKUP
	REQUISITION SUB ASSEMBLIES, PARTS, AND				250 ARITHMETIC
	TOOLS. RELEASE PROJECTS TO ASSIGNED ASSEMBLY				450 LOGICAL
	AREAS. ADVANCE ASSEMBLED AND WIRED PROJECTS				80 RELATIONAL
	TO TEST. MOVE COMPLETED PROJECTS TO FINAL				400 EDIT
	CLEAN UP AREA.				300 POST
03	EXPEDITE ORDERS	1600	200	30/D	1000 LOOKUP
	CHECK PROGRESS TO SCHEDULE. RE-ALLOCATE				300 ARITHMETIC
	MANPOWER, EQUIPMENT, AND SPACE AS NECESSARY				400 LOGICAL
	TO MEET COMPLETION DATES.				120 RELATIONAL
	EXPEDITE PARTS SHORTAGES.				200 POST

R.L. CASEY   END PRODUCTS   BUTODALE   1 of 3

DATE   ANALYST   ACTIVITY   STUDY   PAGE

Figure 16-15   Required operations sheet for the provide end products activity.

Required Operations Sheet

NO.	OPERATION NAME	INPUT FACTORS	OUTPUT FACTORS	FREQUENCY OF EXECUTION	PROCESS SUMMARY
04	ASSEMBLE AND WIRE PROJECTS USING STANDARDS DATA, PROJECT ORDER, AND SPECIAL ENGINEERING INSTRUCTIONS, PERFORM REQUIRED ASSEMBLY AND WIRING OPERATIONS. INSPECT FOR QUALITY OF PHYSICAL CONFORMANCE TO SPECIFICATIONS.	1800	300	1/D	3100 LOOK UP 600 ARITHMETIC 3100 LOGICAL 1600 RELATIONAL
05	TEST PROJECTS USING STANDARD TEST DATA, PROGRAMS, AND SPECIAL TESTING EQUIPMENT, CHECK OUT PROJECTS TO PERFORMANCE SPECIFICATIONS AND MAKE NECESSARY ADJUSTMENTS TO MEET OR EXCEED STANDARDS.	2700	400	1/D	3100 LOOK UP 2000 ARITHMETIC 3100 LOGICAL 1500 RELATIONAL 600 EDIT 600 POST
06	FINAL CLEAN UP, ROUTING, PACKING, AND SHIPPING. PERFORM HOUSEKEEPING ON COMPLETED PROJECTS. LOOK UP TRAFFIC ROUTES AND CARRIERS. PACK ACCORDING TO CARRIER INSTRUCTIONS. PREPARE SHIPPING PAPERS. MOVE EQUIPMENT TO TRANSPORT.	120	350	17/W	250 LOOK UP 170 ARITHMETIC 550 LOGICAL 250 RELATIONAL 170 EDIT 350 POST
07	PREPARE INVOICES USING PROJECT ORDER, SHIPPING PAPERS, AND CONTRACT REGISTER (F-4050), PREPARE INVOICE (R-3100). POST UNIT AND TOTAL PRICE, TRANSPORTATION PRICE, PAYMENT TERMS. COMPUTE DISCOUNT. EDIT INVOICE.	300	300	17/W	100 LOOK UP 50 ARITHMETIC 30 LOGICAL 200 POST 300 EDIT

DATE _____   ANALYST R.L. CASEY   ACTIVITY END PRODUCTS   STUDY BUTODALE   PAGE 2 of 3

Figure 16-15   (continued)

Required Operations Sheet

NO.	OPERATION NAME	INPUT FACTORS	OUTPUT FACTORS	FREQUENCY OF EXECUTION	PROCESS SUMMARY
08	PREPARE STANDARDS VARIANCE USING STANDARDS DATA (F-4110), INSPECTION AND TEST DATA, AND ACTION MEMOS, PREPARE STANDARDS VARIANCE MEMOS (ON DEVIATIONS FROM CONFORMANCE AND PERFORMANCE SPECIFICATIONS) FOR ENGINEERING. INCLUDES VARIANCES AUTHORIZED BY ENGINEERING.	2100	600	10/D	800 LOOK UP 50 ARITHMETIC 1200 LOGICAL 300 RELATIONAL 600 POST
09	PREPARE QUALITY REPORT REPORT ON QUALITY PERFORMANCE WITH DETAIL ON REASONS FOR REJECTIONS.	350	175	1/D	350 LOOK UP 700 LOGICAL 200 POST
10	PROGRESS REPORTING PREPARE PROGRESS REPORTS ON PROJECT STATUS, WITH DETAIL ON UNITS AHEAD OR BEHIND SCHEDULE. ANSWER STATUS INQUIRIES AS RECEIVED.	1800	600	1/D	600 LOOK UP 1800 ARITHMETIC 1800 RELATIONAL 300 EDIT 900 POST
11	PREPARE MANAGEMENT REPORTS COMPILE WORK-IN-PROCESS, LABOR, AND PERFORMANCE REPORTS, INCLUDING EXPENDITURES OF TIME AND MATERIAL AS ALLOCATED TO PROJECTS.	3600	1200	1/W	300 LOOK UP 3600 ARITHMETIC 1800 EDIT 2400 POST

DATE _____ ANALYST R.L. CASEY   ACTIVITY END PRODUCTS   STUDY BUTODALE   PAGE 3 of 3

Figure 16-15   (continued)

Resource Sheet

NO.	NAME AND DESCRIPTION	AMOUNT	COST	NOTES
P1	DIRECT LABOR	450	$2.6 MILLION / YR.	#SHOULD REMAIN CONSTANT
P2	CLERKS	30	$135,000	@ $4,500/YR.
P3	INSPECTORS	85	$425,000	@ $5,000
E1	CALCULATORS	3	$100/MO	RENTED
E2	TYPEWRITERS	25	$1,200	DEPRECIATED VALUE
F1	PRODUCTION AND TEST FACILITIES	130,000 SQ. FT.		
V1	WORK-IN-PROCESS INVENTORY		*$2,830,000	PORTION OF W-I-P INVENTORY COMMITED TO END PRODUCTS ACTIVITY. TRANSFERRED TO FINISHED GOODS INVENTORY AT END OF TEST.
V2	FINISHED GOODS INVENTORY		*$1,210,000	ON-THE-SHELF PRODUCTS LIQUIDATED THROUGH CUSTOMER BILLING
				*DEVELOPED BY USING SHOP DECISION RULES IN SIMULATION AT SALES VOLUME OF $22,700,000.

R.L. CASEY   END PRODUCTS   BUTODALE   1 of 2
DATE   ANALYST   ACTIVITY   STUDY   PAGE

Figure 16-16   Resource sheet for the provide end products activity. (Figure continued on following page.)

Resource Sheet

NO.	NAME AND DESCRIPTION	AMOUNT	COST	NOTES
V3	**DECISION RULES**			
	(1) PRODUCTION SCHEDULING			
	END PRODUCTS ARE BUILT TO NEW ORDER SCHEDULE (F-4080) WHICH INCLUDES BOTH SALES AND BUILD PROJECTS. INCOMING CUSTOMER ORDERS ARE ASSIGNED TO BUILD PROJECTS USING PRIORITY RULE (BELOW).			
	(2) PRIORITY			
	a. STANDARD PRODUCTS ORDERS			
	b. ORDER ACCEPTANCE DATE			
	c. PRIME CUSTOMER			
	(3) DISPATCHING			
	DISPATCHED ACCORDING TO DEPT. COMPLETION DATE. SALES PROJECTS RECEIVE PRIORITY OVER BUILD PROJECTS. WITHIN SALES PROJECTS, PRIORITY RULES (ABOVE) APPLY.			
V4	STANDARDS FILE (F-4110)	6,000 ITEMS		
V5	WORK-IN-PROCESS FILE (F-4120)	600 TO 800 ITEMS		
V6	CONTRACT REGISTER (F-4050)	2100 ITEMS		
V7	PRODUCTION SCHEDULE			KEPT BY EACH DEPT. CLERK
V8	ROUTING FILE (F-4090)	4 VOLS	$1,200/YR SUBSCRIPTION	COMMON CARRIER REFERENCE MANUALS

DATE	R.L. CASEY ANALYST	END PRODUCTS ACTIVITY	BUTODALE STUDY	2 of 2 PAGE

Figure 16-16   (continued)

APPENDIX

Measurement Factors for the Provide Product Demand Activity

1. Average Order Processing Cost

   Total of costs attributable to processing an order divided by number of orders per year.

   Costs for order processing are based on sales salaries, field administration expense, and central marketing and engineering costs.

   Present system—

   Average of 16 orders/week; 800/year.

   Departments directly affected are Marketing Administration (Sales Administration, Quotations, Engineering Sales) and Engineering Administration.

   Present costs—

   12% of Marketing Administration.

   10% of Product Engineering costs in Provide Product Demand activity.

2. Order Acknowledgment

   Elapsed time *from* receipt of a customer order by Marketing Administration (by mail, telephone, wire, and so on) *to* mailing of a written acknowledgment to customer.

   Statistics directly obtainable.

3. Response time for quotation

   Elapsed time *from* receipt of a request for quotation by Marketing Administration (by mail, telephone, wire, and so on) *to* mailing of a written quotation to customer.

   Wide variation between shortest, average, and longest performance on standard end items and on standard systems due to nonstandard nature of product.

4. Response time for Bid

   Same as for quotation.

   Note: Bid cycle, in the opinion of Butodale management, must not lengthen under any new system; due to increased competition in Butodale's broadened future market, cycle decrease is desirable. Since future products are expected to be significantly more complex, the engineering design portion of the bidding cycle will probably lengthen; this lengthening must at least be compensated for by shortening the information processing response time by an equal amount.

5. Quotation (Bid) Appearance

   The following characteristics have been agreed upon as pertinent to appearance of a quotation or bid (along with their relative importance). In evaluating appearance, a Quotation (Bid) is judged on each characteristic on a scale from 10 (best) to 1 (worst); the points are weighted by relative importance and the total is matched to the description on the overall scale in the Measurement section.

Characteristic	Relative Importance	
Errors	5	There should be no typographical errors such as misspellings or incorrect numbers.
Six copies	5	Six legible copies must be produced.
Reference	4	There should be ready reference to prime fields of reference number, item numbers, quantity, price, and delivery date.
Smudges	3	There should be no carbon or ink smudges or edge impressions.
Linearity	3	Lines of print should be neat and straight.
Symmetry	2	Symmetry between numbers and letters is an important feature of the character set, since description is a mixture of alphabetic and numeric characters.
Impression	2	Print impression should be constant: no hollow letters or varying strength of impression.

Descriptions on the over-all scale in the Measurements section correspond to these point totals:

Outstanding	220 and above
Excellent	200-220
Good	180-200
Fair	160-180
Unsatisfactory	below 160

Two means of producing Quotations (under the present system) were evaluated as follows:

Characteristic	Rubberstamped and Reproduced	Typed
Errors	10(5) — 50	4(5) — 20
Six copies	10(5) — 50	10(5) — 50
Reference	6(4) — 24	6(4) — 24
Smudges	4(3) — 12	10(3) — 30
Linearity	4(3) — 12	10(3) — 30
Symmetry	5(2) — 10	5(2) — 10
Impression	2(2) — 4	10(2) — 20
	162 (Fair)	184 (Good)

6. Processable Requests for Quotes/Bids

> Two general categories of errors delay processing of quotations and bids. The first category requires inquiry back to the customer or salesman submitting the request, and no processing can be done until an answer is received. The second category requires further investigation, but (while this investigation is going on) the request can be processed.
>
> Processing stops if the request has:
>> incomplete product information, such as missing specifications, no power supply, etc.
>>
>> illogical specifications, such as 110-volt power supply feeding a 220-volt amplifier.
>>
>> unacceptable description of unit or an incorrect identification or item number.
>>
>> illegible information.
>
> Further investigation is required if the request has:
>> improper customer designation such as incomplete name or missing address.

7. Standard Products Requested (compared to total requests)

> A minor modification is substitution at the subassembly level or higher; below the subassembly level, modification is considered a design function.
>
> Standard products are combinations of catalog and end product items with no substitutions.
>
> Percent of standard products requested may be increased by:
>> broadening the Butodale product line.
>>
>> a higher price differential between standard and nonstandard products.
>>
>> more products of a general purpose nature.
>
> A higher percentage of standard products means that usage of standard parts will increase (with attendant lowering of production unit cost); this permits design flexibility with fewer items in inventory (again affecting production cost) and application of consistent design practices. An important benefit of standardization is the ability to expand or contract the product line without significantly affecting administrative (processing) costs.
>
> No more than 90% standard products plus minor modifications is desired. The remaining 10% represents products requiring engineering design effort; it is the breakpoint for supporting sufficient design capability to create new commercially acceptable products.

8. Dollars of Standard Product Orders (compared to dollars of total orders)

> Definitions of minor modifications and standard products are the same.
>
> It is important to note that the Acceptable/Desirable range for minor modifications lies outside the range for standard products. This supports the the price differential desired by Butodale: modified products will result in somewhat greater comparable revenue.

PART 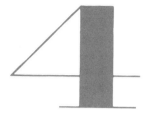 4

DESIGN THE NEW SYSTEM

Part 4 discusses how to conduct the third phase of a system study, "Design the New System." Design alternatives are formulated initially around design concepts for one activity. Other activities should be investigated for possible consolidation. Equipment configurations are analyzed for each alternative and refined into a system solution. Implementation costs are compiled, added to projected operating costs, and compared to system benefits to determine the economic impact on the business. Design data is organized into a final report entitled new system plan.

New system design is concerned with the development, evaluation, and description of a business information system that best fulfills the requirements established in the Phase II system requirements specification. During Phase III, various design approaches are considered. For each alternative, a broad class of equipment is specified and evaluated against the requirements that were specified. The most promising solutions are further defined in terms of a specific equipment configuration; finally, the best solution is recommended to management.

The general concepts are illustrated in our case study, Butodale, for which we present the third report in Chapter 20.

CHAPTER

Basic System Design

17.1 TASKS OF THE DESIGN

Several major tasks have to be performed in the design of a new system:

1. Develop a basic system design.
2. Analyze the interaction of multiple activities.
3. Specify the equipment configuration.
4. Prepare a preliminary plan for system implementation.
5. Determine the impact of the design on profitability of the business.
6. Document the new system design.

The analysts accomplish these tasks by starting with the requirements report and ending with a report containing the plan for a new system.

The requirements report is a significant input to the work of the analysts because design alternatives are accepted or rejected on their ability to satisfy specific requirements appearing in the requirements report. The statement of business goals in that report shows what the new system is expected to accomplish. The statement of activity scope and boundary defines the size and content of each activity for design purposes. Input-output, required operations, and resource sheets amplify requirements such as (1) the number of characters and fields in inputs and outputs,

285

(2) the rate at which information must move through the system, (3) a summary of processes in each operation and frequency of their execution, and (4) file characteristics and content. As designs evolve, measurement factors appearing in the report of requirements can be used to evaluate design alternatives.

In designing the new system, the analysts usually center their attention on the single predominant activity of the business according to its size, potential savings, or special characteristics. Initially, various input, output, processing, and file possibilities are hypothesized. The possibilities are then merged into alternative system designs using different design approaches. Several alternatives are formulated and, through evaluation and selection of the most reasonable, are successively reduced to a manageable two or three.

The final major task in actual design is the selection and refinement of an equipment configuration. Specific equipment solutions can then be postulated for each design alternative retained up to this point, and these equipment possibilities are evaluated by performing a rough timing and cost analysis. The best solution for each design alternative is then compared with the others in order to arrive at a final solution and designation of a complete equipment configuration. Finally, detail run timing and cost figures on this solution are reviewed to ensure validity of the decision.

While system implementation itself is outside the scope of this book, it is necessary to know and show the numbers and types of people required to put the system into operation, when they will be needed, and how long it will take to complete the transition from the final design to full system operation. Major preparation costs involved in system implementation and time schedules should be prepared. These costs include:

1. Detailed system design
2. Programming and program testing
3. Installation (physical)
4. Conversion and test
5. Personnel selection and training

As the design of the new system evolves, the analysts use the measurement factors from the report of requirements to evaluate the performance of alternatives. For the final design selected, the system is appraised on the basis of its total worth to the business. Business profits, operating expenses, return on investment, and cash flow (projected over the estimated life of the new system) are typical factors used in this analysis.

At the completion of these tasks, the new system design is organized and documented in a final report entitled the new system plan.

17.2 NEW SYSTEM PLAN

Although Chapter 19 covers in some detail the contents of this present section, the brief discussion here will help clarify some of the concepts in Part 4. The report containing the analysts' recommendations is intended to be a concise and complete description of the new system, with an objective judgment of the system's immediate and future value to the business. The report normally contains a preface and five major sections:

1. Management abstract
2. New system in operation
3. Implementation plan
4. Appraisal of system value
5. Appendix

Each section of the report is directed to a particular audience. The management-abstract section outlines key recommendations of the study and summarizes the system design for top management. The new system in operation section conveys to operating management the special features of the system as it will function after installation. The implementation plan section shows the cost and time required to put the system into operation, and the appraisal of system value section reveals the cost and profit impact of the system on financial and operating personnel. Finally, the Appendix contains data useful for implementation and for operating personnel.

Let us turn to some of the initial steps in designing a new system.

17.3   MAJOR STEPS IN DESIGNING A SYSTEM

In system design, a study team should lay out a master plan for a new system, first concentrating on the single most important activity of the business. Possibilities for inputs, outputs, operations, and files are identified. The best possibilities among these elements are fused into a few specific design alternatives, using various design concepts. Each alternative should be described at a generic system level, with appropriate supporting narrative description.

System design involves five major steps:

1. Activity selection   The activity that is judged to be dominant by management and the study team is selected for initial design.

2. System element analysis   Various element possibilities (different inputs, outputs, processing operations, and files) are identified and evaluated for this activity.

3. Design alternative formulation   Design alternatives are synthesized and evaluated; the best two or three are accepted for further analysis.

4. System description   The selected design alternatives are documented with a system description.

5. Multiactivity integration   Other activities undergo a similar process. Relationships among design alternatives for the activities are then analyzed, and appropriate compromises and consolidations are made. A few realistic design alternatives are carried forward for selection of specific equipment.

System design requires a high level of creativity, but it is more fruitful if it is a disciplined effort. Thinking in terms of design concepts—independently of specific equipment configurations—is a major key. Imagination in the application of design concepts can lead to the major improvements a study team seeks.

The idea of building a design around concepts or ideas can be illustrated by one of our case studies. The National Bank of Commerce, like many other banks, offered its customers a complete range of banking services (checking accounts, Christmas Club, and so on), yet it processed the information for each one in separate, specialized routines. One design concept considered was the use of an integrated banking information service, producing one monthly statement for each customer covering the entire range of banking services used. Discussion and analysis showed that a consolidated monthly statement of transactions and balances was feasible. The "one customer, one statement" concept led to important changes in element requirements. Since much similarity existed in the separate file requirements among the several activities, a central file was postulated to handle all data. Similarity of input data requirements for the checking and savings accounts led to the use of a check-like document issued by the bank (or written by the customer) rather than the conventional deposit and withdrawal slips. Review of proposed legislation which would modify the requirement for a savings passbook showed that there was a good chance that the practice of mailing this document to the customer could be discontinued. This meant that the bank could mail out a monthly or quarterly statement of customer balance and interim transactions. Furthermore, with the central-file concept, up-to-the-minute statistics by teller, by branch, or for the entire bank could be made available to direct inquiry from remote locations.

Developing a system design in terms of a concept (in the above case, the central file concept), and independently of equipment, applies to all types of studies. Design quality depends on applying sound technical and business judgment based on broad knowledge of equipment characteristics and capabilities, an awareness of outstanding design concepts developed in previous studies, a thorough training in programming principles, and solid experience in the use of management science and other technical tools.

17.4   ACTIVITY SELECTION

The initial activity for the design of a system is selected on the basis of one or more of the following factors:

1. *Dominant performance criteria*   A single performance requirement (response time to customer inquiries and orders, for example) makes the activity so important that it overrides other activities.
2. *High affectable dollars*   A potentially large savings is involved.
3. *Large size*   The activity is large either in input-output volume or in computing complexity.
4. *Inefficiency*   The activity is the most inefficient area of performance in the present system.
5. *Management preference*   Management may have its own special reasons for selecting the activity.

Let us assume that the analysts and management have now selected the initial activity.

17.5 SYSTEM ANALYSIS

After an activity is selected, the analysts must decide on the specifics (inputs, outputs, processing operations, and files) that are to constitute the activity. The operations section from the requirements report is particularly helpful in identifying and evaluating possibilities. Penetrating and specific questions must be asked about each. If punched card input is under consideration, the volume of information, the handling of this information, the time it would involve on representative equipment, and accuracy or verification requirements must be examined before concluding that punched cards are the best input. Each possibility must be realistic—in terms of the available money and implementation time. If the use of optical or magnetic ink coded input, for instance, departed from established industry practices, prior acceptance by governmental agencies or industry associations might be required. Many specific possibilities are usually rejected at this point: known equipment capabilities may not permit economical use of the proposed input or output form, or provide the access frequency required for the file, or have the computation speed demanded for the proposed method of processing.

For the above reasons, throughout the analysis of design possibilities, the study team must constantly consider the dominant characteristics of the activity; frequently, input-output volumes and specifications indicate such dominance.

As far as inputs are concerned, they often have to be accepted in the form in which they are received from the outside (or from another activity); thus it frequently happens that input design is really a task of conversion to machine-usable form. For outputs, design frequently involves producing a form acceptable to the environment (or to another activity). This may require several intermediate steps, as in an activity using a communications network. In such an activity, inputs may be received originally in oral or handwritten form, converted to punched-paper tape, transmitted over a circuit to a data-processing center which again produces punched-paper tape, converted from paper tape to cards, and finally edited and processed on a small computer to produce magnetic tape for further large computer operations.

Typical considerations in analyzing input possibilities are:

1. Does each input have to be handled on an as received (usually a unit) basis, or can inputs be processed in batches?
2. Should inputs received in nonprocessable form be converted, edited, and machine entered, or should they be manually entered?
3. Can inputs be processed randomly as received, or should they be sequenced by designated control fields?
4. What is the significance of input volume variation on system performance criteria, particularly during peak periods?
5. Is interruption to be allowed or not? How does this affect reliability requirements?

Output possibilities are similarly examined:

1. Are reports to be printed or punched, or is the output to be in some form of audio or direct display (such as voice answerback or direct display of blueprints)?

2. How much of output content is to be summarized? detailed? listed by exception?

3. Which reports must be generated on schedule? on demand? on exception?

4. What are the general requirements on format, readability, and number of copies?

5. Are standard forms required, or may non-standard forms be used?

6. Can output printing be offline?

7. Will output data be reused?

8. Will output go to another activity as a signal, tape record, or other machine-usable form?

After these possibilities have been explored and the inappropriate, unlikely, and unacceptable ones set aside, possible inputs and outputs can be stated as "punched cards," "magnetic tape," "machine sensible" for optical scanning (or magnetic ink character recognition) and the like. This selection of reasonable possibilities takes into account such factors as time restrictions or equipment capabilities, while not explicitly specifying input-output equipment.

The selection of input-output media is far from simple, and part of the decision depends on the alternatives permitted or available for organizing data files. In analyzing files, as in other activity elements, the analysts must isolate and evaluate the dominant characteristics of the activity. Five important questions may be used for a checklist:

1. To what extent do separate files contain the same data? Can they be consolidated?

2. How frequently is a file referenced for inquiry?

3. What is the frequency of file change or updating?

4. How many ways is a file referenced? If it is in one order, will it be necessary to sort and resort the files when they are used in different operations?

5. What is the growth rate of the file?

After the analysts have found answers to these questions, they will have a description of file alternatives in terms of file size, average access time, maximum access time, etc.

When they explore the conceptual aspects of the mechanism that can be used for processing data, the analysts' primary concern is the magnitude and complexity of operations and the impact of these items on the system design. Such points as the following should be analyzed:

1. Should processing be random or sequential?

2. How frequently are operations executed?

3. What are the predominant characteristics in operations—arithmetic? logical? relational? edit? lookup?

4. If high in mathematical processes, is floating point arithmetic necessary?
5. How complex is operations logic (in terms of computing time)?
6. Can processing include main-line operations only, or must it include all exceptions? some exceptions?
7. Will operations require significant restart and checkpoint routines?
8. How automatic (man-independent) is the system to be? Is manual override necessary, or can the system operate automatically without intervention?
9. What kind of audit trail should be provided?
10. Must error corrections be made immediately, or can errors be recycled for later processing?

When they finish answering these ten questions, the analysts should have arrived at a set of possible processing characteristics which will make it possible to transform data inputs into data outputs. In fact, the information they now possess on input-output, file, and processing characteristics should be sufficient for designing many alternative kinds of systems to handle the information for the activity.

17.6 DEVELOPING DESIGN ALTERNATIVES

A design alternative is a specifically stated combination of various input, output, processing, and file element possibilities. Each design alternative is built around a design concept: the way in which the information processing will be carried out. A design concept is the force that holds together the separate elements in a design alternative; a design alternative describes how the concept is applied using the elements. In many cases, design alternatives can be built upon a concept or approach that has proved successful in previous installations in the type of business under study. Where pioneering is required, greater design time is usually needed. However, possible design alternatives often have to be discarded because of timing imbalances or obvious cost constraints; with a solid knowledge of equipment capabilities, analysts can usually judge design alternatives intelligently without the time or expense of detailed system design and run timing. The measurement factors outlined in Chapter 13 can be used to evaluate the several design alternatives the study team creates. From the designs examined, two or three are selected as basic system designs. The practicality of an appropriate design concept determines to a great extent how the individual possibilities are combined into a system. Four of the many varieties of design concepts are illustrated here.

1. Regeneration

Instead of retaining a large number of answers in memory, it is often possible to store the decision logic necessary to compute or generate each answer as it is needed. When the regeneration (rather than the file reference) principle is used extensively, files can usually be reduced, search eliminated, and access speeds increased.

2. Transaction-file reversal

Transaction-file reversal shows how good solutions evolve by considering extremes or opposites. In a manufacturing business, for example, gross parts and materials requirements are often established by successive explosion of bills of material through several levels of the product structure. Product requirements are considered the transactions, and the bills of material are the files. This approach is often cumbersome and time-consuming. However, by completely reversing the procedure and by considering where-used bill of material records as the transactions to be passed against the product requirements (as the file), it may be possible to accomplish the same result in a single pass through the computer at significantly lower cost.

3. Unified services

In multiservice or multiple-location operations, a decision must be made whether to design several independent systems or to consolidate data processing operations into a single system. In a company with a widespread network of warehouses, for example, the system can be warehouse-oriented or total-network-oriented. Such a decision depends on many different factors: type of products stocked in each warehouse, nature of the market, and characteristics of the distribution system. The unified services concept would consider the entire span of requirements for each warehouse in a single system.

4. Real-time response

Entire systems can be built around real-time response to each transaction received; the system becomes the "sum of the transactions." Real-time systems typically involve communications networks and are highly equipment-dependent; for example, systems designed for airlines and brokerage firms would not have been possible without data processing communications equipment and direct access files.

In many industries there are particular concepts that are suitable and around which such design alternatives can be developed. Online processing, daily cycling, periodic status review, exception reporting, and centralized data processing are a few examples of frameworks upon which design alternatives can be built. If a standard application program pertains directly to an activity, the concept behind that program can certainly be considered as one of the principal options.

At the outset of design, the study team deals with pieces and parts (inputs, operations, and so forth). Now, in formulating design alternatives, the team approaches design from an integrated and unified standpoint; a design, instead of being an aggregation of parts, is an entity. Creative effort has been applied to build the system around a design concept. A large number of design alternatives may result from this process; typically, some are fairly similar, others quite different. Alternatives for the activity are compared with each other, and similar ones are combined until the best two or three basically different alternatives remain.

17.7 SYSTEM DESCRIPTION

At this point, sufficient information has been accumulated to prepare a system description, which is essentially a statement of the major inputs, outputs, processing operations, and files needed. No detailed computer run design is formulated and no attempt is made to state how many card readers, tape units or printers are desired, or what size memory is desired. The purpose of the system description is to show the logical flow of information and the logical operations necessary to carry out the particular design alternative. Figure 17-1 is a system description for a multiple warehouse inventory control system. The activity sheet is convenient for this documentation, since it shows a system flow diagram along with information on volumes, time relationships, and specific functions or requirements.

The following narrative, taken from our Atlantic Distributors case, indicates the kind and level of information that should be available at the end of basic system design.

Warehouse Inventory Control Activity

This activity is concerned with an inventory control system for a finished goods warehouse. There are many relatively small items stocked in the central warehouse with which the information processing system is associated. Five other auxiliary warehouses, from 100 to 500 miles away, place orders on the central warehouse and may require rapid delivery of critical items. There are four major groups of operations within the system: *updating stock status,* based on actual transactions; *response to inquiries* from auxiliary warehouses and central warehouse; *reorder analysis,* including purchase order preparation; and *weekly analytic reports* to show slow-moving items, major changes in usage rates, behind-schedule reports, and economic lot sizes.

A. *Update Stock Status*

1. As material is received, the enclosed paperwork is marked to indicate the quantity received and quality acceptance. The bill of lading or packing skip is then passed against the receiving order file to withdraw the appropriate receiving record (a prepunched card) for each item. Actual quantity received, date received, and quality acceptance code are keypunched, and the card information is then transmitted to the data processing center.

2. After each customer order is filled, a card is keypunched for each item on the marked-up order, showing actual quantity delivered, customer number, item number, date, and quantity. These withdrawals are transmitted to the data processing center.

3. A variety of miscellaneous transactions are initiated by the warehouse, the receiving area, and purchasing: returns, rejects of incoming material, recounts, back orders, substitution, and scrap items. A card is prepared for each such transaction with the appropriate code for the transaction: item identification and quantity information are then inserted in the card. These cards are also transmitted to the data processing center.

4. Transactions are received throughout the day at the data processing center. As each transaction is received, it is processed against the master stock file (on a direct access device) to update the status of each item. Validation checks are made during this operation to ensure that the item number is correct and that the quantity of the transaction is within reasonable limits. Invalid transactions are printed as typewriter output.

B. *Remote Orders and Stock Status Inquiry*

5. The order-filling area (in the central warehouse) and the auxiliary warehouses have direct keyboard input to the data processing center by which

				Activity Name	INVENTORY CONTROL						

UPDATE STOCK STATUS
Freq: As transactions received
Inputs: 2000, 2010, 2020

Key	Time	Note
1–4	2 HR	
2–4	2 HR	1000
3–4	4 HR	

RESPONSE TO INQUIRY
Freq: As received
Inputs: 2030

Key	Time	Note
5–6	1 MIN	1000

REORDER ANALYSIS
Freq: Daily
Inputs: 4010

Key	Time	Note
7–8	6 HR	1000
8–10	2 HR	1000

REPORTING
Freq: Weekly
Inputs: 4010

Key	Time	Note
11–12	8 HR	1000

INPUTS

Key	Name	Volume
2000	Receipts	500/Day
2010	Withdrawals	10,000/Day
2020	Misc Trans	1,000/Day
2030	Inq's & Ord's	2,000/Day

OUTPUTS

Key	Name	Volume
3000	Stk Status	1,750/Day
3010	Invalid Trans	-
3020	Ship Instr	500/Day
3030	Recv'g Cards	500/Day
3040	Purch Ord	100/Day
3050	Exceptions	1,000 Items/Day
3060	Stock Status	20,000 Lines/wk

FILES

Key	Name	Size	Access Rqmts	Note
4000	Recv'g File	20,000 Records	Randm – 5 Min	
4010	Master Stock	20,000 Records	Randm – 10 Sec	
4020	Commodity	200 Records	Seq – Daily	1050
4030	Vendor	1,000 Records	Randm – 3 Min	1050

Activity Sheet

NOTES

1000 - Maximum allowable per
　　　 requirements report.

NOTES

1050 - Commodity file is section of vendor file

Figure 17-1 A system description for the inventory control activity for a wholesale organization.

Activity Name	INVENTORY CONTROL

UPDATE STOCK STATUS

Freq: As transactions received

Inputs: 2000, 2010, 2020

Key	Time	Note
1-4	2 HR	
2-4	2 HR	1000
3-4	4 HR	

RESPONSE TO INQUIRY

Freq: As received

Inputs: 2030

Key	Time	Note
5-6	1 MIN	1000

REORDER ANALYSIS

Freq: Daily

Inputs: 4010

Key	Time	Note
7-8	6 HR	1000
8-10	2 HR	1000

REPORTING

Freq: Weekly

Inputs: 4010

Key	Time	Note
11-12	8 HR	1000

INPUTS

Key	Name	Volume
2000	Receipts	500/Day
2010	Withdrawals	10,000/Day
2020	Misc Trans	1,000/Day
2030	Inq's & Ord's	2,000/Day

OUTPUTS

Key	Name	Volume
3000	Stk Status	1,750/Day
3010	Invalid Trans	-
3020	Ship Instr	500/Day
3030	Recv'g Cards	500/Day
3040	Purch Ord	100/Day
3050	Exceptions	1,000 Items/Day
3060	Stock Status	20,000 Lines/wk

FILES

Key	Name	Size	Access Rqmts	Note
4000	Recv'g File	20,000 Records	Randm-5 Min	
4010	Master Stock	20,000 Records	Randm- 10 Sec	
4020	Commodity	200 Records	Seq - Daily	1050
4030	Vendor	1,000 Records	Randm-3 Min	1050

Activity Sheet

NOTES

1000 - Maximum allowable per requirements report.

NOTES

1050 - Commodity file is section of vendor file

Figure 17-1   (continued)

online inquiries can be made. Availability (or planned availability) for all items can be obtained on an online basis by keying the item information, quantity desired, and nature of the request.

6. The data processing center interrupts its other processing on receipt of an inquiry to determine stock status and to answer the information request. This is then transmitted back to the proper station. If a reservation or a request to ship is made, appropriate paperwork is prepared and the master stock file modified to show the reservation or withdrawal.

C. *Reorder Analysis and Purchase Order Preparation*

7. Each night, after all transactions have been posted, the entire master stock file is reviewed. Each item's current balance and planned availability balance are analyzed against expected day-by-day requirements and desired protective stock levels. Where appropriate, reorder quantity is calculated and reorders are made. The planned due date is set, based on normal delivery cycles. If normal reorder quantity does not give adequate coverage, a specific indication is made.

8. All orders are then sorted by commodity code. Total dollar volume is summarized by commodity.

9. For each commodity code the approved vendor list is reviewed and individual orders are assigned to vendors on the basis of planned participation rates on specific items being ordered, dates required, and current quality-and-date performance by the vendor. Purchase orders are then prepared, and items ordered from the same vendor are grouped together by commodity code. Individual receiving cards are prepared for each item, sent to receiving, and placed in the receiving file. The vendor file is updated to note volume or orders placed and items ordered.

10. The purchase orders are reviewed by the purchasing agent or buyer on the following day, and each is approved and signed. Where changes are required or special decisions needed, the purchasing agent can request detailed information from the master stock file.

D. *Stock Status Analysis*

11. Weekly, the master stock file is reviewed to determine whether actual usage rates have changed significantly from expected usage rates and to carefully compare current stock status with revised usage. This identifies excessive stocks, overdue orders, and other specific relationships that require management attention. An item-by-item stock status report is issued with an exception report indicating usage and status of each item whose balance or open order is outside planned control limits.

17.8 MULTIPLE ACTIVITY INTEGRATION

Where system design encompasses several activities, alternatives are formulated for the others in the same manner as described above. The resulting best design alternatives for each are then compared with the major activity for resolution of conflicts or incompatibilities. Activities are also reviewed as a group to determine the potential for consolidation among inputs, outputs, operations, and files. Of course, such consolidation must ensure the compatibility of all the elements in the design of the system.

It sometimes happens that the characteristics of the dominant activity are so overriding that other considerations are subordinated and alternatives for the remaining activities tailored to fit the design. Systems for investment houses and airlines are examples of this kind of dominance; the system is designed around the real-time activity (order and inquiry processing), and other activities are accommodated offline as equipment capacity and available processing time permit (though additional features and components may well be added to the system).

Developing an efficient solution for activities with diverse profiles can significantly increase equipment requirements. One activity, for example, might call for a very large direct access storage device; another might need a central processing unit with complex, high-speed logical and arithmetic commands. Properly designed, a system using a computer with both tape and direct access files might handle both activities efficiently; conversely, separate smaller machines with specialized files might prove to be a more economical solution.

Sometimes a "balancing" activity is added to take advantage of the higher price-performance ratio of larger equipment. An activity requiring extensive computation and limited input-output can be combined with another activity having high input-output volumes and relatively little computation. Later, when equipment is selected, these two activities together could represent a better total equipment utilization than would be possible for either one alone; hence, the installation is more profitable to the user.

Even the proposed implementation schedule can influence multiple activity decisions. Complexity of installation and lack of trained programmers and analysts often make an extended implementation period necessary. When this occurs, effort usually has to be first directed to the dominant activity scheduled for initial implementation, with only a compatibility check made to ensure that the systems for the later activities will be compatible with the system implemented first.

17.9   CONSOLIDATION OF FILES

To this point, activities have been treated as relatively independent entities. However, the new design may permit further opportunities for consolidation, especially in regard to common usage of files.

Files having common characteristics, content, and application should be consolidated wherever feasible. Consolidation possibilities were shown by several files in the Butodale study. In that company, engineering maintained a large parts file containing data on manufactured and purchased parts, costs, and commodity codes for compiling quotations on requests to bid; three manufacturing sections (standard products, custom-designed products, and spare parts) each supported cost files for preparing product costs; and accounting used another cost file for pricing purposes. This last file was sequenced by part and assembly number, and it showed both part cost and part selling price. A good possibility for file consolidation existed among these three files, as long as each activity had proper access to the data.

Similar kinds of consolidation possibilities exist among inputs, outputs, and operations. One activity may use the same or similar inputs, or it may produce outputs similar to those of another activity, as demonstrated in the "one customer, one statement" approach of the National Bank of Commerce mentioned in Section 17.3. Output from one activity is often input to another. Inputs and outputs of the several activities, therefore, are examined for consolidation (or even for combining two sequential activities by eliminating the input-output junction); care must be taken to resolve incompatibilities of form, content, timing, or accuracy of data between activities.

Operations are normally less susceptible to consolidation than inputs, outputs, or files. Nevertheless, they should be checked for possible multiprocessing and multiprogramming when there is a dissimilarity of basic design concepts. Two examples of such dissimilarity are: (1) One activity with low-volume real-time operations, the other a high-volume batch activity, and (2) One activity with high input-output and low computation, the other with high computation. Note that one consolidation often opens up other consolidation possibilities. The use of a common transaction document for inputs at National Bank of Commerce made possible the combining of operations among the affected activities by taking advantage of the differences in operation volume and frequency of execution.

After reviewing the various possibilities, two or three integrated design alternatives should be put together on activity sheets. Both these integrated design alternatives and the earlier individual activity alternatives are the basis for the actual selection of a system.

SUMMARY

The process of system design leads to the definition of alternative systems. These alternatives become the base from which the selection of a specific system takes place. Experience, of course, is required to find out where basic design should be stopped in order to avoid becoming involved in implementation details.

Some analysts find it more convenient to go through system selection for a single design alternative before developing additional alternatives. This is perfectly reasonable and does not at all conflict with the guide to design of systems developed in this book.

When a creative basic system design has been carried out, the opportunity exists for efficient system selection from reasonable alternatives which will meet business goals and objectives. Frequently, considerable consolidation and elimination of duplication among files and activities is possible.

18

System Selection, Implementation Planning, and Evaluation

18.1 INTRODUCTION

The development of a system includes the process of selecting an efficient equipment configuration for a particular design alternative. Implementation planning for a system involves a thorough analysis and documentation of the expected investment required to install a system. Evaluation of a system involves management's appraisal of the system's value measured by how well it conforms to the cost and performance criteria previously established for it in Phase II. These three topics are so closely intertwined they are considered in conjunction with one another in this chapter.

In the remainder of our book it will often be necessary to refer to makes and models of computers. For this purpose we shall use XYZ to represent any computer make. For model identification we shall use capital letters. Thus, XYZ/A is the A model of the XYZ computer.

18.2 THE PROCESS OF SELECTION

The selection of a system is an iterative, trial-and-error process. After a system is selected, the very evaluation of equipment solutions frequently results in further changes in the configuration or features and even in the design alternative structure. Equipment selection affects and is affected by the design of computer programs. Modification of one directly influences the other and may, in turn, influence alignment of equipment with design alternatives.

These design alternatives plus other system requirements provide the framework within which system selection is performed. These requirements may be quite explicit and may significantly limit equipment choice. For example, suppose the following three requirements were set for the computing element of a particular system:

1. Must provide magnetic ink character recognition for input of transactions.
2. Must create a magnetic tape output which is compatible with file requirements on an XYZ/R.
3. Must provide for immediate inquiry for master file records.

Each of these three requirements implies either that certain components must be included in the final system, or that certain components may not be included— which may simplify system selection, but which may also build undesirable rigidities into the system.

There may also be qualitative boundaries within which the system must operate to be acceptable. For example, consider the following five constraints:

1. Operating time must not exceed two shifts per day, five days per week.
2. Operating cost must be less than a certain limit; or the new system cost should not exceed the operating cost of the old system.
3. A particular report must be available to management at a given time.
4. Cycle or turn-around time must be within a specified limit; transactions received by a certain time must be processed the same day.
5. Availability requirements must be satisfied; the system cannot be inoperative for more than two minutes during any hour.

A dollar value is often associated with bringing a factor further inside the boundary limit: for example, decreased cycle time may result in a decrease in open accounts receivable. The choice between equipment configurations meeting all restrictions may be based on the degree to which boundary limits are bettered. Boundary restrictions often limit equipment. Cost may eliminate certain large systems; reliability may require the duplexing of some components.

Initial evaluation of both the requirements and the boundaries defines the framework within which equipment can be selected. This does not mean that the requirements have become inviolate. The realities of system selection may show that some requirements are so expensive to satisfy that they should be relaxed. A stipulation, for example, that a report be available by 4:00 P.M. one day, rather than 8:00 A.M. the next day, may be the only factor which forces the selection of a large computer operating one shift per day, rather than a less costly computer operating two shifts per day. Such a requirement must be examined in light of the additional expense directly attributable to it. Since the requirements have already been reviewed and approved, any such change must be cleared before it is adopted.

System selection, then, is essentially a serial, iterative process aimed at satisfying design requirements and constraints. These restrictions should be sequenced in order of importance or difficulty, so that there is a basis for choosing to improve upon one of the factors rather than another.

System selection involves iteration through the following steps:

1. Specify equipment to satisfy a design alternative.
2. Define computer runs using the specified equipment.
3. Time the configuration for each run, beginning with the longest run, until a requirement is violated or until all runs have been timed.
4. Iterate, modifying the equipment configuration (or the system design), to remove the violation or to improve its relationship with boundary factors. More components may reduce running time and extra shift rental; fewer components may increase running time but decrease prime and extra shift rental.
5. When the best joint solution for equipment and computer runs has been found, specify a new equipment solution for that design alternative.
6. After two or three feasible equipment and run solutions have been timed, go to the next design alternative.
7. When all design alternatives have been evaluated, select the best equipment/ design combination based on requirements, running time, cost impact upon the business, and implementation and operating costs of the proposed systems.

18.3   EQUIPMENT SPECIFICATION

The postulation of successive equipment alternatives includes the consideration of peripheral characteristics of the equipment and its support: modularity, compatibility, programming languages, and application programs. Let us consider these four points.

Modularity   When people talk about modularity they usually refer to a feature of computer design that permits the easy addition or removal of component parts of the equipment.

If a large activity is gradually to be converted to a computer system, modularity allows an initial installation of a less expensive, slower system with faster or larger components added as volume warrants. Modularity is also significant if volume is expected to grow substantially with little or no change in system objectives.

The substitution of faster components for slower ones with no programming change is a most important consideration; an example is the substitution of a faster processing unit for a slower one. Nearly as useful is modularity which only requires program recompilation, such as substitution of a disk unit for a tape unit. Recompilation may be necessary for proper input-output commands, but the program otherwise would remain unchanged. Also valuable is the ability to add components (more tape units or more core storage), even though taking full advantage of such modularity may require reprogramming of the longest runs if the additional components are to affect running time.

Compatibility   For many years the installation of one computer to replace another meant that the computer programs had to be rewritten by programmers. Thus, if a given computer configuration had become too slow to fulfill its role in the management system, its replacement by a newer computer configuration often meant an overload for the programming staff, and occasionally a loss of management's confidence in computers. The design of modular computers has helped to reduce this problem. Computer scientists designed computers that were compatible in three ways.

First, the computers were of a multi-purpose design permitting them to be used with equal facility for data processing, communications, and scientific calculations. Second, the design permitted programs to be used for a wide family of computers so that programs, written for any one model, could be used for all models. Third, computers were made compatible by emulation and by simulation programs. These features permit computer programs written for one computer to be run on an entirely different computer.

In designing a management system, compatibility usually plays an important part in selecting the equipment and the features. Proper selection can significantly reduce the conversion cost and transition time.

Programming Languages   Although programming does not take place until the system is being implemented, the selection of a programming language affects the equipment choice. The equipment configuration, for example, must be sufficient to compile programs written in the language chosen.

The most widely used languages are Fortran, Cobol, assembly languages, PL/I, Algol, and Report Program Generator. Several factors should be assessed in reaching a decision on a language:

1. Will the workload consist of many one-shot jobs, resulting in a heavy load of programming and compilation—or will relatively few, repetitive programs utilize the system? High-level languages tend to reduce programming costs but they usually increase compilation costs and many produce programs which are somewhat less efficient in space utilization and running time.

2. If the system is input/output-dominated, an efficient input-output control system is vital.

3. Will programming be done by many people scattered throughout the organization (open shop) or by a centralized group of programming specialists (closed shop)? Fortran, for example, is easier to teach and use in solving scientific problems, but more efficient complex programs may be obtained by writing in assembly languages.

In addition to these points, the previous comments regarding compatibility with existing programs also are relevant as far as languages are concerned.

Application programs   The availability of standard computer programs can represent an important factor in the selection of computer equipment. For example, if an organization is going to install a management system and if another organization has an excellent system already operating, it may be possible to acquire and use all of their programs merely by installing identical or compatible equipment. Of course, many computer manufacturers will furnish' the user of computer equipment with a set of programs that will perform many standard kinds of work for the organization. These include such things as computer programs that will schedule the operation of the computer system itself, programs that will sort records, merge files of records, and such routine operations. Other packages of programs include sets of subroutines that will do many kinds of statistical and scientific operations with a minimum of programming effort, or provide programs for particular industries or technical applications like inventory control or linear programming.

Even when it is necessary to modify these application programs to meet individual systems requirements, the time expended on the detailed design of record layouts, file organization, indexing schemes for records, and samples of outputs, can be reduced.

18.4   RUN DEFINITION

The effectiveness of an equipment configuration is determined mainly by analyzing the time and cost of processing data. A first step, therefore, is the organization of the system into computer runs which break the job down into manageable portions.

Most systems have natural segmentation points for initial run timing. In a serial system, for example, natural segments would be:

1. Input conversion and data validation
2. Sorting
3. Master file updating
4. Output editing and conversion

For a real-time system, the segments differ somewhat and could be:

1. Input
2. Transactions (batch, single)
3. Inquiries
4. Control functions
5. Outputs
6. Reports

Runs are generally defined in descending order of their impact on total running time. As runs are defined, other aspects arise:

1. On smaller systems, both the maximum possible configuration and the minimum configuration are restrictions. Even on large-scale systems, where the theoretical maximum configuration of input-output devices may exceed the realistic requirements of any one activity, a maximum core storage restriction exists. Even where enormous direct-access storage devices are available, the high costs or relatively slow access constitute a barrier for the typical organization.
2. Where multiple input-output devices are attached to a single control unit, the maximum number that a control unit can handle acts as a ceiling on the configuration. With additional control devices (at additional cost) the ceiling may be raised up to the limit of the number of feasible devices.

3. Volume must be analyzed when converting from source media to magnetic tape (and from magnetic tape to punched card or printed output) to determine whether to convert online or through a supporting system. Special requirements such as optical scanning, MICR (magnetic ink character recognition) reading of input documents, or production of special-media outputs also affect this decision.

After the runs have been defined, a system chart (or run organization chart) showing the flow of information through the system and the relationship of the runs to files must be prepared to illustrate the magnitude and scope of the computer runs.

After run definition, the study team selects the number and models of direct access units, tape drives, printers, readers, punches, and other components. Equipment features should be identified completely, including a list of the standard and special features needed to fulfill the objectives set for the processing system. If the system is to be handled by equipment already installed, then equipment configuration is fixed and the runs must be designed to fit the existing equipment.

18.5 RUN TIMING AND COSTING

Each equipment configuration should be evaluated for performance and cost by comparing the times and costs of all the configurations. This requires the identification of equipment features, a more detailed description of file organization, and a review of noncomputer-oriented factors.

File definitions are normally expanded to show:

1. Restrictions on file format, such as block size limitations and compatibility requirements.
2. Record formats, recognizing:
   a. core storage characteristics (word size and extra control characters).
   b. Magnetic tape unit characteristics (suppression of leading blanks and zeros and extra control characters).
3. Average record length of each file (in characters or digits for tape, in words or bytes for core storage).

The approximate tape-passing time and the number of reels required can be calculated for each file on the basis of volume, tape density, and a tentative record-blocking factor. Tape drives are assigned to achieve a balanced channel condition, and provision is made for error and exception routines.

Utility runs, such as sorts and mergers, can be timed from published formulas. For other types of runs, timing is based on tape-passing time and internal processing time (considering core storage and tape-interference time). If the system is unbuffered, run time is the sum of tape-passing time and internal processing time; if the system is buffered, run time is the greater of internal processing time or tape-passing time on the channel with the heaviest load.

In analyzing run times for direct access storage, the time required to locate a record is often critical. Various file-organization schemes should be studied to determine which will minimize through-put time.

Runs are reviewed for improvement in order of total running time. It may be possible to reduce the number of tape or disk drives, combine short runs, or split long runs for greater efficiency.

The best equipment configuration for a design alternative is determined from run time results and from a careful review of other system costs.

System cost is constructed from unit costs for system components, special features, operating supplies, and personnel requirements. We must remember of course, that a system comprises people, procedures, and equipment. System selection to this point has been concentrated on equipment. Associated procedures also must be examined to take advantage of file organization, better concepts of information storage and retrieval, new transmission equipment, and the like.

There must also be an estimate of the cost of personnel to operate the system after it is fully installed. Salaries and clerical support costs are developed from actual payroll data (or industry averages, for new jobs) projected over the useful life of the operating system. Combined with timing and cost data for the equipment, this produces a total operating cost for the new system.

18.6   FINAL SYSTEM SELECTION

The process just described for equipment specification, run definition, and timing and cost analysis may be repeated for two or three equipment solutions (where practical) for a given design alternative. The best solution for that design alternative is then selected. The process is executed for each design alternative until a final choice can be made among the best solutions for each alternative.

In the final selection process several additional business factors must be reviewed:

1. Growth of the business.
2. Need for system flexibility.
3. Other applications and activities.
4. Ease of implementation.
5. Selection and training of personnel.
6. Availability of assistance by computer specialists from the equipment manufacturer.

One particularly important consideration in system selection is evaluation of the several prospective solutions as they affect implementation costs and the general operations of the business. This is necessary in order to understand the complete system cost and thus avoid the error of making the ultimate decision solely on the basis of equipment rental. When these topics have been examined in conjunction with the special advantages of each system configuration, the final system decision should be the one that is best for the total business, both now and in future years.

With the designation of a system solution, run description and timing data are reviewed once more to ensure that the best possible run design exists prior to final documentation.

Separate activity sheets may be filled out for each system run, or they may be combined on a single system flowchart. Volumes, time relationships, frequency, and other significant data are noted in the tabular area; the system flowchart may be drawn on the right side of the form, showing inputs, outputs, operations, and terminations.

Message, file, and operation sheets may be used where appropriate. Selective detail is the keynote to documentation; critical areas may require some detailing, but most areas can be treated on a general level.

A summary activity sheet is usually desirable to display the system as an entity, with separate descriptions of equipment configuration and personnel requirements.

18.7   SYSTEM SELECTION EXAMPLE

Since the process of system selection involves a certain amount of re-cycling and iteration, it is illustrated further in the following example of a finished stock control and warehousing activity from a multiplant manufacturing concern. In order to demonstrate system selection, we occasionally refer to decisions arrived at during basic design and system integration. Our discussion will center on four topics: (a) general data, (b) a decentralized design alternative, (c) a centralized design alternative, and (d) the actual system design selected.

a) *General Data*   The company in our example maintains 20 finished stock warehouses and distribution centers at widely dispersed points throughout the country, each one differing in size and type of items stocked. The study team formulated two basic design alternatives: one for a decentralized, local control system, and another for a completely centralized system. During their study of the existing organization, the analysts had found that orders were received at the several warehouses by telephone, in the mail, or on handwritten forms.

b) *Decentralized Concept*   Under the decentralized design alternative, manual documents would be converted to punched cards and processed in a computer at least four times a day at each warehouse. A direct access file would be maintained for inventory item balances and pricing data. Output would be in two forms: a printed listing of transactions and updated balances, and a card for order picking. Reorder point analysis was scheduled for once-a-day review.

Three general computer equipment configurations were postulated for this alternative, each with direct access storage units:

1. XYZ/A card system with an online printer.
2. XYZ/B card system with an online printer.
3. XYZ/S system. The acceptance of this configuration would depend largely on the volume of complex calculations.

A fourth possibility was the use of tabulating equipment in conjunction with tub files. Because the study team had to contend with different volumes at different warehouses, there was a chance that any one of these configurations might be appropriate in individual situations.

Starting with the knowledge that the design concept is decentralized and with the fact that several generic equipments have been specified, what implications can be made in regard to each system? In the XYZ/A system, for example:

1. Can sufficient disk files be provided to allow real-time response?

or

2. Does the inflow have to be considered in batches?

In regard to files:

1. What files are needed?
2. How many transactions occur per day, distributed in time?
3. How many characters are there in each transaction?
4. Can name and address be coded or does it come direct?
5. How big is the inventory file?
6. Can the inventory file be combined with the pricing file, or name and address file?
7. Is discount data a separate file, or can this·be put alongside each item?

With regard to the batching of work, the analysts had to answer the following seven questions:

1. Is inventory reorder point data separate or combined with another file?
2. Are orders separated by geographical location to take advantage of full carloads?
3. Are orders filled by breaking packs, or only to full-unit packs?
4. How are modifications handled?
5. What kind of sales records are submitted and maintained?
6. Is accounts receivable part of this activity or is it separate?
7. Does credit have to be authorized on each order?

All these questions are directed at determining the number and size of files. After they defined the files, the analysts decided on batch processing for this activity. Their next step involved an identification of runs, as follows:

1. Sort transactions by item or customer number.
2. Review credit by customer name or number.
3. Sort by geographic location code.
4. Group items into carload lots.
5. Sort carloads by item number.
6. Pass item numbers against the inventory file to produce picking tickets.
7. Sort picking tickets into sequence by location for carload accumulations.
8. Price the items from price charts.
9. Resort by customer.

10. Perform a discount analysis.
11. Produce an invoice and accumulate to accounts receivable.

This first pass run designation was then reanalyzed to improve its overall efficiency, and the amount of processing was defined to some extent for each run.

Next, the equipment configuration was expanded in detail by answering four questions.

1. How many disk drives?
2. What speed card reader is needed?
3. What line speed is required for the printer?
4. How many cards are being punched on each run?

Finally, a run timing and costing analysis was prepared for each run, which led to further run modifications. This entire process was repeated for the other two proposed equipments: XYZ/B and XYZ/S. On the basis of the run timing and costing results of each equipment configuration, a decision was made on the most feasible one for the decentralized design alternative: one XYZ/A system for each finished stock warehouse and distribution center, and one central XYZ/S system for invoicing.

c) *Centralized Concept*   The same general approach was applied to the design alternative built around centralized control.

Equipment networks were postulated to answer such questions as:

1. What kind of terminals would be needed? What kind of lines?
2. How many miles of lines?
3. What would line rates be?
4. Would lines be one way or two way?
5. Would there be punched card or tape input terminals, or job-oriented terminals?
6. Centrally, would a computer be used for message exchange, or would some other type of standard communications equipment be used?
7. Are reliability requirements such that equipment must be duplexed, or is there an adequate fallback procedure, or is degraded service acceptable?

As to files, additional questions might be:

1. How many logical files are there?
2. How are files organized?
3. How are files addressed? That is, are files controlled by warehouse or by part number for all warehouses?

These and similar questions were reviewed until a detailed specification of inputs, outputs, and files had been completed.

The run designations were quite different from the decentralized alternative, since the system would operate on a real-time basis. Eight or nine major operations were specified for processing transactions and for the associated batch or clean-up runs. A system simulation was considered necessary to evaluate the complexities of interactions, queuing, and overlap seeks. The analysts used a general purpose simulation system which they found to be effective for this purpose.

Once all these considerations had been weighed, equipment configurations were postulated:

1. Back-to-back XYZ/A's
2. Single XYZ/E with an XYZ/B for input-output.
3. XYZ/B system for input-output; XYZ/S to handle complex calculations

The configuration was then detailed to show:

1. Features of the equipment
2. Numbers and speeds of tape drives
3. Numbers and sizes of disk files
4. Number of channels between the input-output device and the computer

Run timing was considerably more complicated for these alternatives and again the systems simulator was used. On the basis of run time and cost comparisons, the study team decided on an XYZ/C—XYZ/B combination as the ideal solution, even though this particular configuration had not been specified originally. This solution illustrates how equipment alternatives become modified and blended through successive iterations. This last configuration provided the best compromise since the XYZ/C's high calculating capability, in conjunction with the high input-output capability of the XYZ/B could also handle the scientific computations of an engineering activity. The remainder of the equipment specification included six tapes, four terminals at each location, and two-way lines.

d) *System Selection*   The centralized equipment solution was compared with the solution under the decentralized concept. The evaluation of these two included examination of many factors specified in system requirements plus some new, equipment oriented elements:

1. Future business growth
2. System flexibility
3. Ease of implementation
4. Training of personnel
5. Programming languages, operating systems, application packages
6. Effect of other applications
7. Cost

When these factors were fully examined and both of the alternatives reorganized and rearranged, the study team made a final recommendation, as follows:

1. Three high-volume warehouses were assigned separate XYZ/A's, although invoicing was to be performed centrally.
2. The other 17 warehouses were unified under a central XYZ/C—XYZ/B system with a one-hour batch time to eliminate possible queues in the system.

The complete design solution was documented as a final step to show the detail on the equipment, individual run descriptions, files, inputs, and outputs. Then the problem was to plan for the implementation of this proposed system.

18.8   PLANNING TO IMPLEMENT THE SYSTEM

An implementation plan thoroughly documents the expected investment in systems installation as an important element of total systems cost. Estimated time and cost to execute the plan are of primary relevance here, rather than the substance and detail of the actual work of implementation.

System implementation planning has a parallel in physical facility planning. Before a commitment is made to proceed with the building of a new plant, management must know what costs are entailed, how long the construction will take, and what the cost of the product will be when produced by the new facility. Only then can a reasonable comparison be made between required investment and the benefits to be derived from making this investment.

A substantial investment in time and money is required to transform a drawing-board solution into a fully operating system. Investment in implementation is as much a part of the total cost of a new system as the rental or purchase price of equipment. Therefore, it is necessary to prepare an accurate estimate of these costs for management review as part of system recommendations.

In many studies the estimate should reflect the fact that complete systems are rarely installed simultaneously. For instance, an implementation schedule for replacing a tape system with a complex computer network of communications equipment and a disk system may call for a four-step program extending over a period of two to three years:

1. The present application programs and reference tables are converted to the logic of the new computer and stored in one of the new system's disk files. Transactions are still batched on tape and processed against tape master records.
2. All master records now on magnetic tape are converted to disk master records; additional disk file units are installed at this point. Transactions would enter the system from tape in random sequence and be processed against disk file master records.
3. "In-house" or home office inquiry stations and the control unit are installed. The control program, under design since the first phase, must be operational at this point. Operating programs are now put into final form. Checkpoint and restart procedures are tested.
4. Terminal units are installed in field offices (starting with offices that transmit the greatest diversity of transaction types in order to fully prove system logic).

There is no complete check list that will apply to every implementation program. There are certain checkpoints, however, that are encountered in most schedules. These are useful when incorporated into a specific preinstallation plan:

1. Establishment of an organization for system implementation
2. Initial education program
3. Physical installation plan
4. Detailed system design
5. Completion of first test
6. Establishment of conversion procedures
7. Machine-room layout and cable order
8. Selection and training of operating personnel
9. Conversion, testing, and pilot runs

Two special planning tools or techniques, PERT (Program Evaluation and Review Technique) and CPM (Critical Path Method), both based on the critical path method of analysis, have been used in planning preinstallation schedules. If either PERT or CPM is employed, its use at this point should be confined to an overall description of implementation plans; later, when implementation has actually begun, a more detailed network may be developed.

18.9   COST PLANNING

Implementation itself takes place after the report containing the new system plan is approved. Initial planning for implementation, however, must begin before recommendations are submitted—in order to consider the implementation schedule and cost. Implementation cost planning covers five major tasks:

1. Detailed system design
2. Programming and program testing
3. Physical installation
4. Conversion and system testing
5. Personnel selection and training (performed concurrently with other tasks)

For each of the five tasks an estimate must be prepared showing how long it will take, how many trained personnel are needed, how much training each person will require, and how much it will cost.

18.10   COST OF DETAILED SYSTEM DESIGN

The new system must be described at a procedural level (during detailed system design) before programming can begin. When developing the implementation plan, however, the concern is not with the techniques of detailed design, but with the time and cost implications of performing this task: How long will it take? How many trained specialists will it require? How much will it cost in total? These considerations are answered by compiling individual estimates for separate assignments within detailed system design: flowcharting, detailed run design and run book preparation, forms design and layout, report content and layout, detailed file design, and manual procedures.

Figure 18-1 An illustration of how the time and cost plan for implementing the detailed design of a system may be exhibited.

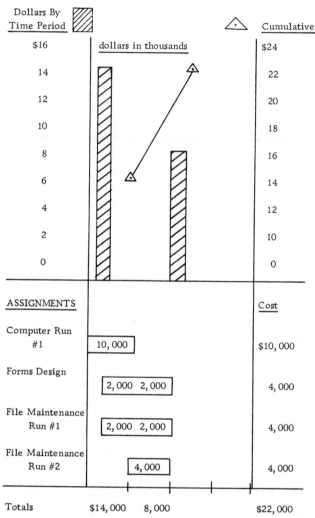

Estimates are prepared by sampling representative routines, applying experience from comparable prior designs, using appropriate standards, or conducting small-scale desk tests. After individual estimates have been completed for all assignments, they are reviewed and modified, and then an overall plan is prepared.

One method of displaying this data in compact form is illustrated in Figure 18.1. The upper bar graph shows total dollar expenditures in a particular time period; the line graph (connecting the triangles) shows cumulative total dollars as of that time period. The lower horizontal bar graph portrays the period of time over which the assignment is to be performed and the dollars required for the assignment.

18.11 ESTIMATING THE COST OF PROGRAMMING

As segments of the detailed system design are completed, programming will be initiated. Here we include program flowcharting, coding, creating test data, desk checking, and testing. In planning the implementation cost for the new system, the analysts should estimate the time and money cost of these several tasks of programming.

After the basic logic and flow have been defined, a programmer will normally analyze and rearrange operations to take maximum advantage of computer (and peripheral equipment) characteristics. This reorganization involves evaluation of a number of computer-oriented design considerations which have an important effect on system performance and efficiency: tape blocking, channel assignment, program overlays, use of subroutines, reference tables, multiple printers, work areas, overlapping and sequence of seeks, and similar technical aspects of data processing. The introduction of these factors will undoubtedly cause some changes in the detailed design. An appropriate cost allowance for this work should be included in the programming estimate. The magnitude of the cost will depend largely on the quality of the design that the analysts prepare for the programmer.

Time and cost estimates must also be developed for creating test data and for desk-checking the program prior to machine testing. In machine testing and debugging, automatic testing packages improve machine utilization and enable more programs to be tested in a given length of time. Waiting time should be allowed for during debugging, since a computer may not always be immediately available.

After individual segments (routines or runs) are debugged, they must be linked with other segments. An adequate safety factor is necessary here: debugging of individual segments can be predicted with a fair degree of accuracy, but when several programs are integrated into a system, their interaction may be very high—and the higher the interaction, the more sharply debugging time increases.

Total programming time can be reduced by using programming systems: generalized programs, utility programs, and program testing aids. Often application programs can materially reduce programming time—whether the package is used intact, modified, or used as detail support (system runs, file organization, indexing schemes, and record layout).

Actual costs from installed systems and suggested time allowances can be studied for guidance in calculating programming estimates. In addition the analysts should draw upon the experience of programmers.

When summarizing the information for management, the analysts may wish to consider a graph with a format similar to that outlined earlier in Figure 18-1.

18.12 PLANNING THE COST OF THE PHYSICAL SITE

Various aspects of physical planning (site selection and construction, air conditioning, equipment and office layout, and electrical and cable requirements) have been thoroughly discussed in other literature. Thus, detailed guides are available on both the general subject and individual systems. The reader is referred to the bibliography which lists a book on this subject by Canning.

The main concern in establishing a physical installation time and cost plan is to provide an adequate time schedule and sufficient construction funds for the work.

The installation estimate can be reported in a form similar to that shown in Figure 18-1, from data supplied by subcontractors or the organization's internal facilities group.

18.13 PLANNING THE COST OF CONVERSION

The size of the conversion task depends on how large a part of the total system is included in the initial change and on how much is consigned to later implementation. A variety of assignments are reflected in the time and cost estimate for conversion:

1. Preparing and editing files for completeness, accuracy, and format.
2. Establishing file maintenance procedures.
3. Providing training in system operation for using departments and for source-data departments.
4. Compiling schedules for the change to the new computer.
5. Planning for pilot or parallel operation. (In parallel operation, the old and new systems are operated simultaneously for a time on current data; in pilot operation, the new system is checked out extensively, using data from a prior period, before it takes over processing current operations.)
6. Coordinating the conversion.

A realistic schedule is based on the amount and type of work to be done and on the availability of personnel to handle it with dispatch. Appropriate time and costs can be summarized in a form similar to that of Figure 18-1.

18.14 PLANNING THE COST OF PERSONNEL

Each of the foregoing tasks included some personnel cost for doing the work. Since salaries and associated overhead constitute a large part of implementation expense, it is often helpful to show in a separate summary the personnel build-up (by job categories) for all the tasks. Figure 18-2 shows requirements for each position, broken down by experienced personnel (E) and trainees (T). The upper numeral in a box indicates the number of persons to be added or released during a stated time period, while the lower numeral reveals the cumulative number in that position at any one time.

Another personnel expense, other than the salaries of implementation personnel, is that of testing and selecting these individuals, then training them in the classroom and on the job. Time must also be allowed for interviewing, testing, rating, and selecting these personnel.

Extensive educational programs are offered on specific data processing systems for those who will perform systems analysis, programming, and machine operations jobs, as well as for installation personnel and operation supervisors. Job training for tape librarians, console operators, and auxiliary machine operators is also required. Availability of this training is an important factor in accomplishing a smooth transition to routine systems operation while meeting tight schedules.

Identifying and scheduling personnel selection and training and summarizing time and cost are the final steps in implementation planning. Figure 18-3 illustrates one way of displaying these costs and their time relationships.

Number of People

30

25

20

15

10

5

Figure 18-2 A method for showing the number of people needed to implement and operate the computer portion of a new management system.

Time Periods		1	2	3	4	5	6
		IMPLEMENTATION				OPERATION	
Coordinator	E	+1	0	0	0	0	0
		1	1	1	1	1	1
Systems Analysts	E	+4 E	-2	-1	-1	0	0
		4	2	1	0	0	0
Programmers	1/2 E	+10	-4	-3	-2	0	0
	1/2 T	+10	6	3	1	1	1
Coders	T	+2	0	0	-2	0	0
		2	2	2	0	0	0
Machine Operators	1/2 E	+4	+2	+2	+1	0	0
	1/2 T	4	6	8	9	9	9
Maintenance	E	+2	0	0	0	0	0
		2	2	2	2	2	2
Time Periods		1	2	3	4	5	6

E — Experienced
T — Trainee

This concludes the discussion of planning the implementation, and we now turn to methods for estimating the value of the new system as it should be after the actual implementation.

18.15 APPRAISAL OF SYSTEM VALUE

Normally the value of a new system to an organization is determined by the management of that organization. Management usually appraises the value of a new system by how well it compares to selected decision-making yardsticks, asking: How will the system affect profits and markets for the next few years? Are

Figure 18-3 A method for showing the time and cost relations for training the computer personnel of a new system.

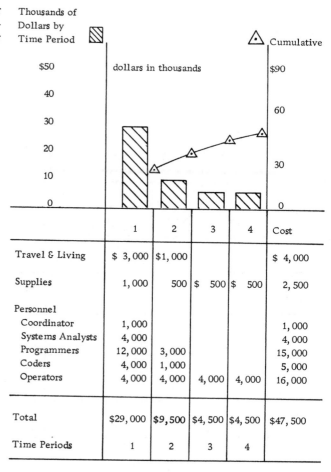

	1	2	3	4	Cost
Travel & Living	$ 3,000	$1,000			$ 4,000
Supplies	1,000	500	$ 500	$ 500	2,500
Personnel					
Coordinator	1,000				1,000
Systems Analysts	4,000				4,000
Programmers	12,000	3,000			15,000
Coders	4,000	1,000			5,000
Operators	4,000	4,000	4,000	4,000	16,000
Total	$29,000	$9,500	$4,500	$4,500	$47,500
Time Periods	1	2	3	4	

there sufficient funds to support the initial installation, or does money have to be borrowed? If so, for how long? What is the economic worth of the system besides higher operating efficiency and greater flexibility? To answer this latter question, a study team should also examine the proposed system in terms other than cost to find out what its ultimate payoff will be.

For this reason, an appraisal of system value must have multiple dimensions to satisfy management. In addition to cost, there should be comparable appraisals for time, flexibility, volume, and accuracy values. It is often difficult to assign values to less tangible measures, yet these must be evaluated on an economic basis to provide management with explicit information for making sound judgments.

Most of the measurement factors were outlined in the report on requirements, and they have already served individually as guideposts for system design. Now the problem is one of establishing the system's total economic effect on the business. This approach can be illustrated by the study involving one of our cases, the National Bank of Commerce. The real value of a unified banking system is not just that "the depositor is better served and more satisfied." A substantive statement of this value would say:

1. System accuracy, flexibility, and expandability accommodate planned increases (4 percent annually) in the number and amount of deposits. These extra funds will then be available for reinvestment in income-producing endeavors.
2. The system encourages depositors to combine their other banking requirements with this institution. This will lead to increases from profit-generating services.

These advantages can be further refined with forecasts of change in assets and revenue due solely to the new system.

To prepare a comprehensive appraisal of system value, four types of data are needed:

1. New system operating costs, projected over the estimated useful life of the system.
2. Present system operating costs, projected over the same period.
3. Investment required to bring the new system into full operation (implementation costs).
4. Basic values the new system offers to the organization, expressed in economic terms.

Costs should then be related to values to show the impact of the total system. Comparisons should be made to a consistent base at all times; this base is generally the projection of present system costs. The approach is especially helpful if two or more recommended designs (for example, an online and an offline system) are analyzed in terms of system value. In this situation, the study team makes an evaluation of each possible system against the common denominator of the present system—instead of the less conclusive evaluation of one new system against another.

In the following four sections we shall discuss the types of data just mentioned, followed by a section relating costs and values.

18.16 NEW SYSTEM OPERATING COSTS

One of the outputs from system selection is a description and summary of operating costs for the proposed system. As discussed in Section 18.5, costs were compiled for the equipment, material, and personnel required. If these figures were not then projected into the future, an estimate of direct operating expense is now developed to cover the useful life of the system—recognizing factors such as anticipated growth and planned expansion.

Estimated equipment, personnel, and other costs are influenced by the potential growth of the business and by the decisions on implementing the system progressively over some period of time. A sales forecast and the implementation schedule are necessary resources for preparing a cost summary. Marketing forecasts of sales or service levels as developed for other business planning applications can be used. If desired, the potential variation in forecast accuracy can be accounted for by

0–1		2–3		4–5		6–7		8–9	
Prob.	Am't*	Prob.	Am't*	Prob.	Amt't*	Prob.	Am't*	Prob.	Am't*
.1	12.5	.1	16.5	.1	20.0	.1	25.0	.1	30.0
.4	13.5	.4	17.5	.4	21.5	.4	26.5	.4	31.5
.5	15.0	.5	18.0	.5	22.5	.5	28.0	.5	32.5
	14.15**		17.65**		21.85**		27.10**		31.85**

* millions of dollars
** weighted average

Figure 18-4   Probabilities and estimated revenues for the ten-year period (0 through 9) after implementation begins for a proposed system, in two-year intervals.

stating future expected sales on a probability basis. This method is shown in Figure 18-4. The data represent total revenues for two-year periods. The probabilities, usually set after consultation with management, are used to get a weighted average of estimates. For example, for the two year period, 0-1, it was estimated that the probability is .1 that revenues will be $12,500,000; that the probability is .4 that revenues will be $13,500,000; and that the probability is .5 that revenues will be $15,000,000. The weighted average is $14,150,000. This weighted estimate then can be used for forecasting. The other sets of figures are similarly interpreted.

The implementation schedule, although emphasizing only the initial installation, should also contain plans for implementing other activities. The cost estimate is prepared with due recognition to equipment and personnel buildup required to support the additional workload.

Equipment costs have to reflect the decision to rent or to purchase. With rental, monthly charges are carried as expense; with purchase, a schedule is set up for monthly depreciation charges and related costs (such as the interest on money borrowed to finance the purchase). If no decision has yet been reached, parallel descriptions are prepared to show the different cost impact during a system's life.

Figure 18-5 is an example of a new system operating cost summary. Ordinarily, the data are projected on an annual basis, but where the time span is longer than five years, the figures can be aggregated in two-year sums.

As cost data is compiled, a study team often finds that special analytical techniques are needed to derive valid data.

Logical analysis techniques are appropriate for constructing operating costs in some areas of the system (number of operators required to run communications terminals, for example). For collecting samples of performance, statistical methods are useful. Finally, techniques of experimentation and observation can sometimes be applied.

Experimentation involves the manipulation of situations under controlled conditions so that results closely approximate those found in the real world. Experimentation, however, is expensive and should be confined to a limited number of

Item \ Year	0–1	2–3	4–5	6–7	8–9
Data Processing Equipment	215	240	260	295	295
Personnel	85	85	95	95	105
Materials	120	65	35	35	40
All Other	90	85	90	95	120
Totals (in thousands of dollars)	510	475	480	520	560

Figure 18-5   Estimated costs for a proposed system in two-year intervals, projected over ten years.

special problems. Simulation, one form of experimentation, may have been employed earlier (especially in design of real-time systems); and if a simulator is already constructed, it can be reused to provide information that will be of assistance in projecting costs.

Direct observation and the extrapolation of results from known data may also prove to be useful methods for estimating costs. The method consists of setting up a test situation to evaluate the length of time a series of operations takes, or to determine what the displaceable costs amount to for certain current operations.

18.17   PROJECTING THE COST OF THE EXISTING SYSTEM

A third category of costs necessary for the appraisal of the value of the new system is an estimate of how much the *present* system would cost to operate if maintained over the expected life of the *new* system and with the expected volumes. The cost data that should be included are the present personnel, equipment, and other related costs that would be superseded by each new activity. The compilation would cut across conventional departmental boundaries and would reflect the progressive implementation of activities in the business. This makes the costing process complex, but only in this way can costs be compared on a common base.

Balance sheets of financial operations, income and expense statements, and resource usage sheets from the description of the present business are sources for the needed data. Expenses should be projected from current operations to determine how much personnel and equipment costs would be when extended to the higher anticipated volume of future years. Allowances must be made for wage increases, changes in material costs, and trends in cost reduction.

For management review, cost can be summarized and plotted on a graph such as the one in Figure 18-6 to show the difference between projections in present and proposed system operating expense for a ten-year period.

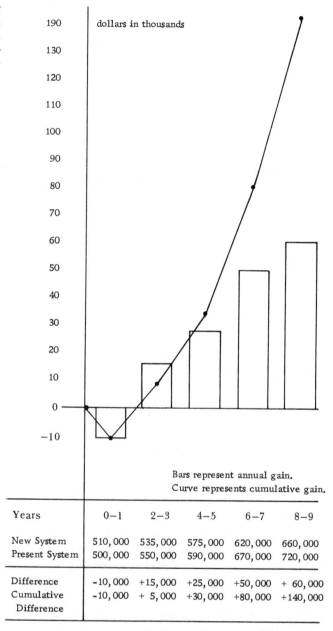

Figure 18-6 A representation of the cumulative cost difference between an existing and a proposed management system, for a ten-year period by two-year intervals.

dollars in thousands

Bars represent annual gain.
Curve represents cumulative gain.

Years	0−1	2−3	4−5	6−7	8−9
New System	510,000	535,000	575,000	620,000	660,000
Present System	500,000	550,000	590,000	670,000	720,000
Difference	−10,000	+15,000	+25,000	+50,000	+ 60,000
Cumulative Difference	−10,000	+ 5,000	+30,000	+80,000	+140,000

18.18   COSTS AS INVESTMENT

We have shown in this chapter that, after determining the new system operating costs, an estimate was established for implementation costs. Although implementation is a cost in the accounting sense, it also can be viewed as an investment. Management must weigh its value in the same manner as new plant construction costs or other projects competing for investment funds. For this reason, implementation costs are customarily regarded as an element of investment during system appraisal.

18.19 ECONOMIC VALUE OF THE NEW SYSTEM

Aside from costs, a study team should consider some of the less tangible ways a new system affects the business. What is it worth, for example, to achieve 99 percent accuracy in certain operations rather than 93 percent? A general explanation is not enough; to effectively demonstrate the real value of such an improvement, accuracy must be discussed in economic terms. One approach is to look at business lost because of invoice or statement errors. If a company loses .3 percent of its customers annually because of statement errors, and if the new system prevents such errors, this .3 percent can be saved; the effect is a .3 percent annual gain in customers for the company. The analyst, using additional sales statistics, could then translate this .3 percent gain into actual dollars of gross sales.

This type of analysis is applied to each of the factors outlined in the report on requirements (and to any other factors added since that report was presented). The results explain how the new system will perform in regard to each factor, and what economic value is assigned to this performance. Some factors to consider are:

1. Decrease in the length of a product or service processing cycle.
2. Improvement in product or service quality.
3. Shortened response time to inquiries from prospective customers.
4. Effect on other classes of investment and resources (for example, accounts receivable, utilized floor space, and inventories).
5. Increased employment stability.
6. Better maintenance of delivery promises to customers.
7. Greater stock availability to service a variable demand.
8. Effect of cost reduction, elimination of spoilage and waste, and obsolete materials.

This concludes the discussion of the four types of cost and value data listed in Section 18.15. Now we consider ways to relate the costs and values.

18.20 RELATING COSTS TO VALUE

In a final step, the several analyses of cost and value are drawn together to present a complete and integrated appraisal for the new system. This is best accomplished through displays that have been found to be meaningful to management: profit and loss, return on investment, and cash flow statements. We discuss these three topics in this section.

Profit and Loss Statement   The cost-value relationship can be portrayed in financial report style with a summary-of-operations statement for the entire business or for some selected part of it. Figure 18-7 illustrates this method of presentation. This method requires the projection of data to develop additional information.

(4-year average - $ in 000)			
	Present	Proposed	Difference
Net Sales Billed	$8710	$8830	+$120
Cost of Sales	7560	6950	- 610
Direct Material	3280	3040	- 240
Data Processing Equipment	30	110	+ 80
Other Indirect Costs	430	350	- 80
Non-Qualifying Costs*	1930	1930	-
Gross Income	1150	1880	+ 730
Federal Income Tax	600	980	+ 380
Net Income	550	900	+ 350
% to Sales	6. 3	10. 2	+ 3. 9

*Expenses not affected by new system.

Figure 18-7 An illustration of the financial report style statement portraying the cost-value relationship between an existing and a proposed management system.

Estimates of future conditions and events must be conservative, reasonable, and believable. The sales forecast is a case in point. If, for example, one benefit from the proposed system is reduced cycle time or faster response to customer inquiries, what direct effect will this have on future markets? material costs? selling price? Unless the impact of this benefit can be predicted with assurance by the marketing department, the conservative approach is to use the same sales forecast for both present and proposed systems.

In the compilation of cost data, projection can be simplified by separating from the computations those costs that are not affected by the change in the system. Within the other cost areas, the analysts establish dollar figures for factors such as personnel changes, cost reduction improvements, waste and spoilage reductions, quality improvements, and differences in fixed and variable costs. One study team conducted a broad analysis of this type by interviewing each department head. Supervisors were asked to pinpoint how their costs would change with the new system—down to individual job classifications and related-expense areas. Costs that were not affected were set aside, and the supervisors' estimates were adjusted for the greater volumes anticipated over the next few years. Results were then organized in an operations statement similar to Figure 18-7.

Return on Investment Another form of value appraisal is the computation of

Time Periods		1	2	3	4	Total
Present System	(1) Operating Costs	$300,000	$330,000	$370,000	$450,000	$1,450,000
	(2) Inventory Level	2,000,000	2,200,000	2,400,000	2,800,000	9,400,000
New System	(3) Operating Costs	350,000	300,000	300,000	350,000	1,300,000
	(4) Inventory Level	1,200,000	1,200,000	1,300,000	1,500,000	5,200,000
	(5) Operating Costs Difference (1) - (3)	-50,000	+30,000	+70,000	+100,000	150,000
	(6) Inventory Level Difference (2) - (4)	800,000	1,000,000	1,100,000	1,300,000	4,200,000
	(7) Value of Inventory Reduction 25% of (6)	200,000	250,000	275,000	325,000	1,050,000
	(8) Net Operational Improvement (5) + (7)	150,000	280,000	345,000	425,000	1,200,000
	(9) Implementation plus Equipment Costs	1,200,000				
	(10) Return on Investment	25% per year				

Figure 18-8　An illustration of how return on investment estimates for an existing and a proposed system can be prepared for management review.

the return on investment in the new system. This form of analysis is designed to demonstrate the value of a proposed investment in terms of earnings by measuring present system cost, new system cost, and investment differences.

Figure 18-8 shows the result of such an analysis. Year-by-year system operating costs were projected over four time periods, along with the level of inventory required to support the forecasted sales. (Inventory can be projected by simulations—for example, by applying significant ratios such as turnover by inventory class, and number of weeks of inventory on hand—or by calculating balances remaining from estimated shipment schedules.) Comparable data was developed for the proposed system; the differences are shown in lines 5 and 6.

The dollar value of the inventory reduction was determined on the basis of estimated savings from reduced obsolescence and deterioration, space savings, and opportunity costs. In this case it amounted to 25 percent, and is shown on line 7. The net operational improvement (line 8) was developed by adding the operating cost difference (line 5) to the dollar value of the inventory reduction (line 7) for each forecast period. Implementation costs and equipment purchase costs were totaled to show investment (line 9). Return on this investment (line 10) was found by dividing average yearly improvement by the implementation and equipment costs (line 9). Line 8 total, $1,200,000, was divided by number of time periods, 4, to produce $300,000 average yearly improvement.

Cash Flow　The display of the expected impact of the proposed system on the cash position of the business will enable management to have sufficient funds available to meet commitments as they arise.

A cash flow analysis is illustrated in Figure 18-9. Total implementation investment was calculated for the period prior to operation, and net operational improvements (same as line 8, Figure 18-8) were inserted for each following time period.

Time Periods	0	1	2	3	4
(1) Total Implementation Investment	$ 600,000				
(2) Net Operational Improvement		$ 150,000	$ 280,000	$ 345,000	$ 425,000
(3) Inventory Level Incremental Difference		800,000	200,000	100,000	200,000
(4) Purchase of Equipment	200,000	200,000	200,000		
(5) Depreciation of Equipment		80,000	120,000	120,000	120,000
(6) Net Cash Flow (2)+(3)+(5)-(1)-(4)	-800,000	+830,000	+400,000	+565,000	+745,000
(7) Cumulative Cash Flow	-800,000	+30,000	+430,000	+995,000	+1,740,000

Figure 18-9   An illustration of a method for analyzing the cash flow for an organization installing a new system. The data are from Figure 18-8.

An incremental inventory level difference was computed by subtracting each period's inventory level difference from that of the prior period (line 6 of Figure 18-8). Equipment purchase costs were included on line 4 to reflect three equal annual payments; this capital charge was depreciated for a five-year life beginning in the second period. Net cash flow is net operational improvement plus inventory level incremental difference plus equipment depreciation minus implementation investment minus equipment purchase price. Cumulative cash flow is the total of the previous year's cumulative cash flow and the current year's net cash flow.

Cash flow can be shown as in Figure 18-10. The main line in the graph shows the projected total cash outflow and inflow annually for a four-year period. An examination of the graph reveals that $800,000 additional cash is required to place the system in operation, but that funds will be generated fast enough to permit repayment toward the end of the first period of operation.

We have just presented several ways of relating the projected costs and values of a proposed system compared to an existing system. We must point out, however, that much of the information contained in the review of value depends on a proper interpretation of future events, so it is advisable for the analysts to explain in their report how the key cost-value comparisons were developed. Also, they should amplify the significance of these comparisons on the operations of the organization. Major results of the appraisal should be emphasized, particularly with regard to the time it will take for the system to pay back the initial investment, and the magnitude of future profits once the system is in operation for a given time period.

These remarks conclude our discussion of system selection, implementation

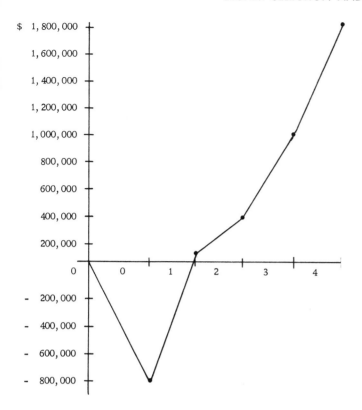

Figure 18-10   An illustration of a method for portraying the net annual cash flow projected for a proposed system for a five-year period (0 through 4).

planning, and evaluation. We next consider the preparation of the report containing the plan for the new system, the subject of Chapter 19.

SUMMARY

The selection of a system is an iterative process. Selected equipment must meet the requirements of the system as well as conform to qualitative constraints. Considerations in equipment alternatives include modularity, compatibility, programming languages, and application programs. The effectiveness of an equipment configuration is determined mainly by analyzing the time and cost of processing the data through the computer runs. A system flowchart illustrates the flow of information through the system and the relationship of runs and files. An implementation plan thoroughly documents the expected investment in system installation. Implementation planning consists of determining the cost of detailed systems design, programming, program testing, physical planning, conversion, and personnel selection and training. Graphic and tabular formats may be useful for illustrating these costs to management. Management usually appraises the value of a new system by how well it compares to selected decision-making yardsticks. A comprehensive appraisal of systems value includes new system operating costs, present system operating costs, investment required for the new system, and basic values the new system offers to the organization. A complete and integrated appraisal of the new system includes its impact on profit and loss, on return on investment, and on cash flow.

19

Describing a New System

19.1 THE DESIGN PROCESS

Automated techniques have not been developed for the design of a new business system to fulfill the requirements defined during the Phase II study. The reason is clear: design is a highly creative process, one which requires an unpredictable number of variables.

In approaching the design of a new system, the most valuable information available to the analyst is a description of the system as it is, and a summary analysis of what the new system must accomplish. The summary analysis should contain the operations and processes required; it now becomes the analyst's task to translate these requirements into a new system design which incorporates implicitly and explicitly specified equipment.

An overall system profile based on information flow, such as is shown abstractly in Figure 19-1, is also useful as a preliminary guide. Of course, to serve a particular situation, this abstraction would have to be converted to the specific terminology of the activity.

As a first attack on the problem of developing a new system, the analyst normally produces several tentative designs that possibly can fulfill the requirements. Through consultation with management, the analyst can narrow the choice to two

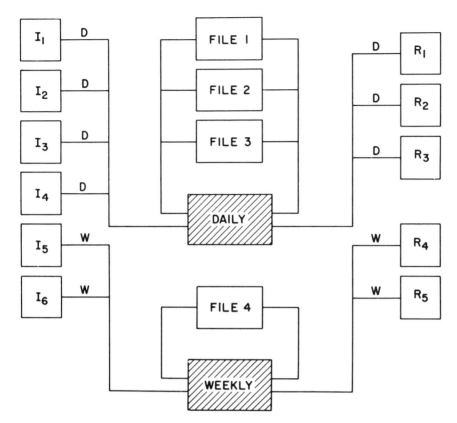

Figure 19-1   An illustration of an overall system profile based on the processing of data. The I represents input. D represents daily. W represents weekly. R represents output.

or three potential solutions. These have to be investigated in more detail until one is selected as a practical optimum.

When an acceptable design is evolved, it must be described, and for this purpose the descriptive forms from Phase I are used. In describing the projected installation, the forms are usually supported by more exhaustive documentation, and the level of detail is typically greater. The analyst should remember that the forms in the third phase will be used to set up a new system; hence complete and precise information is generally required.

The new system as designed is present initially only in the mind of the designer; the design must still be communicated to others. A description of the mechanism of the system is important to management, to other systems engineers who may help implement the system, and to the analyst himself.

The use of the basic forms described in Chapters 8 and 14 assures the designer that he has probably not overlooked anything significant. If he has, the lack should show up on the activity or operation sheets.

The principal difference between the use of the forms in a Phase I study and a Phase III description is the level of detail and the amount of supporting documentation. The aim of the Phase III description remains the same as in the earlier survey: to show what the system will do, working from what inputs to produce what outputs through the use of what resources and facilities.

19.2 DESCRIBING A NEW SYSTEM

The procedure for describing a planned system normally starts with the activity sheet (or sheets) and ends with the resource usage sheet. The first step is to prepare the flow diagram on the activity sheet. If only one activity has been considered in the study, the procedure is straightforward. If the system as designed covers an unwieldy number of operations—say, more than 25—it may be necessary to break the activity into parts and consider each part as a separate activity.

The flow diagram is the key to the validity of the subsequent documentation. The analyst should see to it that this truly represents the activity; that all inputs, outputs, and files are referenced; that no essential operation is omitted. Required operations sheets from the requirements report are valuable guides in preparing the flow diagram.

The tabular section of the activity sheet can then be filled in. Frequency of inputs to and outputs from operational sequences, and average- and peak-volume data for operations within the sequences can be obtained from input-output and required operations sheets. Notes and supporting documents are prepared and attached. The process of supporting the basic documentation continues throughout Phase III: as additional supporting data is produced, it is entered on or attached to activity and operation sheets.

The operation sheets exploding the individual boxes on the activity sheet are next prepared. All three summary documents from the phase two analysis are valuable in guiding the preparation of operation sheets. Equipment designations are noted on the sheet and specifications are attached as support. Narrative descriptions in detail are frequently valuable for unusual procedures which the operation sheet may not completely explain.

Message and file sheets are next prepared for all inputs, outputs, and information resources. Copies, document specifications, file equipment specifications, and distribution lists are appended.

The resource usage sheet is the last descriptive form to be prepared. The references to departments which appear on the activity sheet are primary inputs to the construction of the new resource usage sheet. These are the departments concerned with the activity, the ones which form the framework of the business segment within which the activity takes place.

The procedure is fairly straightforward. Selecting a common lower level if possible, the analyst should distribute the operating departments in related groups across the bottom of the upper sections of the resource usage sheet. A few short interviews will then permit him to construct the levels above the common lower level. The organizational lines should be traced back until they come together in one management box. The procedure is not unlike drawing a family tree.

The personnel quantities and costs are next gathered and entered. As in phase one, employees in any lower-level components not shown on the chart are totaled into the lower boxes, while upper-level boxes show only their own immediate employee totals.

A new cost tabulation is then prepared. For the purpose of describing a projected system, cost estimates are perfectly valid in this tabulation. Costs of personnel, machines and equipment, materials and so forth are summarized for each of the organizational components in the bottom level, and for higher-level components directly concerned in the activity. These costs are summed horizontally in the column for totals.

Costs included in the activity being described are then tabulated below the inclusive tabulation for the section of the business. These, too, are summed horizontally in the column for totals. Data such as the average amount of money invested in inventories or accounts receivable is tabulated and identified in the two unmarked columns at the far right of the resource usage sheet.

Refinement and correction of each form to bring all of them into agreement with each other, and addition of notes or appendices to support and explain peculiarities of the system, are final steps in the procedure. The end product should be a clear description of the system as it will be installed.

The basic operations of the new system are traced on the activity sheet, while the framework within which the activity takes place is displayed on the resource usage sheet. Details of processing steps and of the equipment that will perform them are described on the operation sheets. The message and file sheets provide details of the information inputs, outputs, and resources.

The descriptive forms, working with the detailed supporting documentation, should communicate all the information needed to describe the new system in operation. The five descriptive forms, coupled with the three summary forms used in phase two, thus provide a related approach by which an analyst can derive the facts needed to study a system, determine what the system should be doing, and then design and describe a system to do the required job. Now let us turn to the report itself and consider its component parts.

19.3   STRUCTURE OF THE REPORT

The report describing the design of a new system proposes a course of action for management. It has two major objectives:

1. Provide management with an understanding of the new system, stressing economic value to the business.
2. Furnish supporting data for objective evaluation by technical and functional specialists within the business.

Because of its dual purpose, the report must put the message across succinctly, with awareness of reader interest and point of view.

Liberal use should be made of charts, graphs, and pictures to illustrate complex points difficult to describe in the text, statistical data, equipment layout, work flow, and personnel organization. In addition, the five basic documentation forms described in Chapters 8 and 14 and just mentioned in Sections 19.1 should be used as necessary, since they permit descriptions from a very general level down to the detail desired. Normally, these basic documents are included in the Appendix, although the resource usage sheet and activity sheets often appear in the main body of the report.

As far as the physical report is concerned, six sections are suggested and illustrated in Figure 19-2. The sections are:

1. *Preface*   containing (1) a letter of transmittal from the study team to management, with recognition of study participants and contributors, (2) a general introduction, and (3) a table of contents.
2. *Management Abstract*   a concise, executive-level summary of key system recommendations and study results, aimed at the principal managers of the business.
3. *New System in Operation*   describing how the job will be done, and directed toward operating management.
4. *Implementation Plans*   showing time and cost of system implementation, and directed toward managers responsible for financial operations, planning and implementation management.
5. *Appraisal of System Value*   portraying economic impact and value of the new system, and aimed at financial and operating management.
6. *Appendix*   displaying selected background data on detailed procedures for methods and programming personnel.

The following sections of this chapter cover each of the six sections of the report.

19.4   PREFACE

The transmittal letter to management notes the formal conclusion of the analysts' work in designing a new system. The original scope and objectives of the study are reviewed along with any major changes in either. The composition of the study team is described and mention is made of special assistance supplied by other persons or groups.

An introduction is written for the report, and a table of contents is included for the material.

19.5   MANAGEMENT ABSTRACT

The nucleus of the new system plan is the management abstract. It should be written so that an executive can gain insight and understanding into the proposed new system quickly, without the burden of excessive detail. It describes the system at an overview level and serves as an extended table of contents for the balance of the report.

Within this critical section, management expects to see precise facts about the investment potential of the new system. Its content, then, must include a basic appraisal of essential values and advantages to the business. The subject matter must be thorough but selective, and must cover only significant facts. The principal points should be stated in an orderly and logical manner.

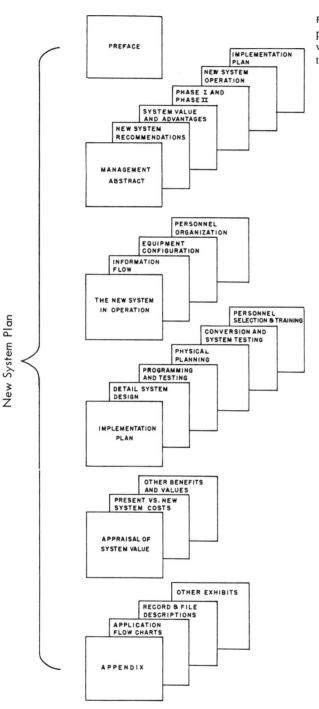

Figure 19-2 Structure of the report presenting management with the design of the new system.

However brief, an abstract should cover:

1. Recommended course of action with regard to the new system.
2. Appraisal of system advantages, benefits, and savings.
3. Review of results from the present system analysis and future system requirements.
4. New system operating costs.
5. Review of investment required during implementation.

We shall discuss each of these points next.

1. *New System Recommendations*   The system solution proposed to management is the concluding recommendation of the study team. The new system is defined and described in broad outline; general advantages are cited for its acceptance and introduction into the business. This kind of recommendation is illustrated by an excerpt from the report of one of our case studies.

> Following a thorough examination of the present business at Collins and McCabe, and specification of systems requirements, we recommend the installation of a communications system consisting of two XYZ/B computers. This data processing system will provide complete brokerage service for Collins and McCabe through integration of communications and accounting operations.
>
> The computer-based communications network will bring remotely located data to a central processing area, forward it for action, and return processed data to originating locations for prompt satisfaction of customer requirements and efficient recording and reporting of information.
>
> A complete range of brokerage operations will be handled electronically, with minimum manual intervention. The real-time nature of the system is made possible by computer control of transmission facilities. Direct access disk storage units will accept many different types of entries for processing against customer and security files.

2. *System Value and Advantages*   Since information and conclusions are presented in order of their interest to management, economic value of the proposed system is discussed next. Management generally looks first for direct dollar savings, then for intangible improvements. Value must be demonstrated by how the new system will produce added profits and how the capital structure of the business is affected over the estimated useful life of the system.

To portray value objectively, selected exhibits described in Chapter 18 are used along with a narrative explanation. Figure 19-3 shows how expected savings were graphically illustrated in the Collins and McCabe report.

Exhibits can be further supported with statements of savings and benefits in specialized areas. In so doing, each factor must be described in terms of direct economic value to the business. Faster, more accurate reports are an advantage, to be sure, but an attempt should be made to translate such intangible benefits into economic value. In the Collins and McCabe report, values were shown for:

1. Improved customer service through specific reductions in elapsed time.
2. Greater computational accuracy through error-checking procedures.
3. Capacity for growth in transaction volume—without significant increases in clerical cost.

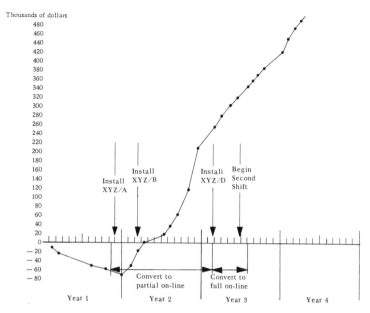

Figure 19-3 A graph taken from the Collins and McCabe case study showing estimated initial costs (negative values) and the savings by month over the first four years of a new system beginning with implementation.

4. Reductions in after-hours operation by application of direct access storage techniques for transaction and record posting.

The actual value of these and other benefits was shown to demonstrate advantages beyond savings in operating costs.

3. *Present Business Description and Systems Requirements Specification*   One or two paragraphs are inserted in the report to review distinctive features from the present business description. Brief facts on products or services, markets, present sales volumes, rate of growth, organization structure, and the like are combined into a comprehensive statement similar to the following:

> The National Bank of Commerce is located in the center of the nation's richest agricultural country. It is organized by the primary services it supplies: correspondence, service, deposits, loans, and trusts. The bank has grown at the rate of $2.5 million in deposits per year, for the last 30 years, to the present level of $250,000,000. About 75 percent of the outstanding shares in the company are owned locally. Of the 210 personnel, 65 are administrative officers and 145 are operating personnel.

Activity requirements for the future system are also outlined here in one or two pages. Goals and scope for each activity are specified in narrative form, as in the following example for an insurance company:

> This activity handles details of new business for Custodian Life Insurance Company, from receipt of an application at the home office to completion of the policy and related records for transmission to the customer. In the last three years, applica-

tions processed have increased from 8,565 to 9,811. Volume is expected to increase gradually over the next few years (no sudden increase, however, is expected).

New business applications are vital to the prosperity of Custodian. Quick and efficient processing of applications will assist greatly in stimulating even more new business and in keeping costs down.

Or, the goals and scope could be specified in a two-part list:

> *The new activity performs these functions:*
> Review application and related forms
> Request medical and policyholder history
> Underwrite applications
> Assemble application data
> Calculate premiums
> *The new activity does not perform these functions:*
> Determine outside underwriting services
> Determine underwriting standards
> Set limits on policy size
> Determine medical standards
> Determine premium rate schedule

Cost limitations, policy constraints, or any other considerations affecting the activity are noted at this point.

4. *New System Operation* This part of the management abstract describes how the new system will appear in full operation. Managerial *uses* of data are emphasized, rather than the mechanics of processing data. Discussion of operating highlights and characteristics should employ terminology used by the management audience.

The content may be organized around a summary system flowchart or around a modified flow diagram as in Figure 19-4 from Collins and McCabe. Description is focused on major inputs, operations and outputs, the mainline events, and salient features. Thus, management can acquire an understanding of the system in operation without becoming involved in detailed procedures.

Conciseness applies equally well to the equipment description. Frequently, the explanation can be blended with the system operations discussion, as in the following excerpt from our Supersonic Airlines case study:

> The data processing center is the heart of the system. Communication lines form the main arteries over which vital reservations data is transferred between agents and the center.
>
> The design of the data processing center is based on two major subsystems: the XYZ/F data processing system and a bank of disk storage units.
>
> The central processing unit performs all logical and decision-making functions required in the reservation process.
>
> The data channel is similar to a subsidiary computer and uses a semi-independent stored program to control the flow of data between the computer memory and a group of input and output devices. Several data channels may operate concurrently in the XYZ/F system.
>
> Data from communication lines enters the processing center through the transmission control unit. Among other functions, this device assembles message characters arriving on the communication lines into groups, checks these groups for errors, and moves them into the main computer storage unit.

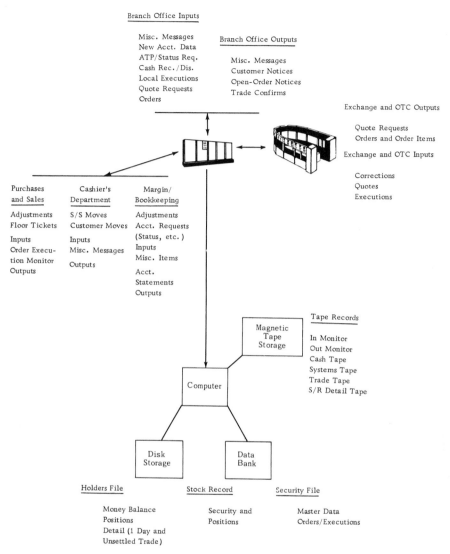

Figure 19-4   Real-time traffic flow as a modified flowchart taken from the Collins and McCabe case study.

Large-capacity disks store the reservation records. These disks contain records of seat inventory, availability, current passenger reservations, current flight information, fares, and infrequently used computer programs. Reading and recording mechanisms, operating automatically under control of the central processing unit and the associated data channels, locate records to be read or recorded at high speed.

The profile of new system operation is completed with a short summary of new positions and specialized job skills required. Personnel requirements can be illustrated graphically by means of an organization chart that shows how the new system differs from the present in positions and in alignment of duties.

Figure 19-5 An illustration of a composite summary of implementation costs prepared for the management abstract of a new system plan.

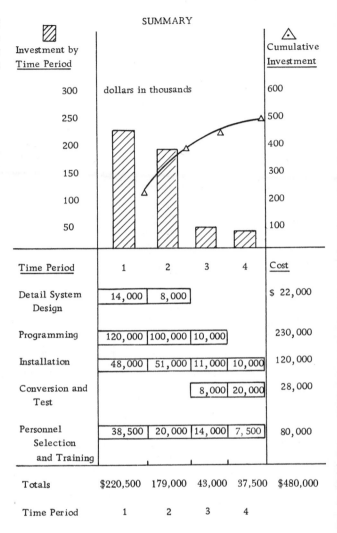

Time Period	1	2	3	4	Cost
Detail System Design	14,000	8,000			$ 22,000
Programming	120,000	100,000	10,000		230,000
Installation	48,000	51,000	11,000	10,000	120,000
Conversion and Test			8,000	20,000	28,000
Personnel Selection and Training	38,500	20,000	14,000	7,500	80,000
Totals	$220,500	179,000	43,000	37,500	$480,000
Time Period	1	2	3	4	

5. *Investment requirements* The timetable and the costs associated with implementation form the final section of the abstract. A composite exhibit is prepared from the five separate task schedules and is shown in Figure 19-5. Beginning with an estimated start date, costs and time are projected for each implementation task; detailed system design, programming, installation, conversion, and personnel selection and training. A one-paragraph description of each task is included with the exhibit, similar to the following explanation on personnel selection and training:

This task involves the selection and education of personnel capable of effectively performing functions such as systems analysis, programming, documentation, and console operation. The selection procedures will include aptitude tests, educational qualifications, and past experience reviews. Training will involve both classroom and on-the-job training.

19.6 NEW SYSTEM IN OPERATION

The new system operation as described in the management abstract is expanded to provide further information for operating managers and other personnel of the business. The principal sources for this second major report section are the individual activity sheets. Data may be condensed and summarized under three headings:

1. Information Flow
2. Equipment Configuration
3. Personnel Organization

We shall touch briefly on each of these points.

1. *Information flow*   The broad system description and pictorial diagram in the management abstract is reoriented to convey more detail on information flow for operating personnel. General terms are replaced by specialized nomenclature associated with equipment descriptions and flowcharting techniques.

Explanation, as before, is highly visual. Description may be maintained at a single level of detail, or it may work down progressively from a total system flowchart, through activity diagrams, to operation flowcharts, as illustrated in Figure 19-6 for a state tax agency study. Data for this part of the report is extracted from the activity sheets prepared earlier for designing the new system.

Narrative explanations can be attached to the flowcharts, or can be integrated into a running system description. In our Typical State case study, the diagram shown in Figure 19-6 was prepared to document the system design. A statement for the operation "correction of edit-found errors" illustrates how narrative can supplement and support the presentation in the flowchart.

> Input to the taxpayer error correction routine consists of error cards. Cards are given to clerks, who interpret them and write corrections directly on the cards (those cards that cannot be corrected are destroyed, and corrections are made at the computing center). Cards that can be corrected are of two kinds: those that can be handled locally and those that require information from the master file located at the computing center. In either case, after referring to the source document file or to the appropriate master file at the computer center, the clerks write correct data on the cards. The cards are keypunched, verified, and sorted by document number. They are now ready to be used in correcting the taxpayer error tapes, which are then sent to the computing center.

2. *Equipment configuration*   Each unit of the proposed equipment configuration is identified by name and number and related to the other equipment on a single display, unless photographs have already been used in the general system diagram. Physical characteristics and functions of units are discussed in a paragraph, as in the following description of a card read-punch:

> The card read-punch is a device particularly suited to applications requiring high-speed reading and punching of cards at reasonable cost. It is capable of reading cards at a rate of 1000 per minute and of punching cards at a rate of 500 per minute. For maximum utility in the computer system, several features are incorporated in

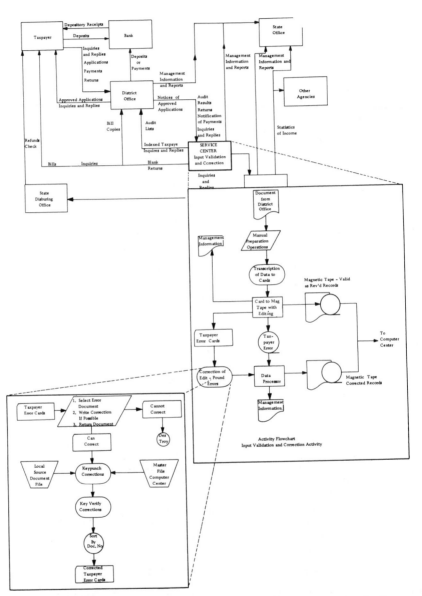

Figure 19-6 An example of a system diagram prepared for a new system in the operation section of a new system plan.

the card read punch. High reading speed is complemented by a file-feed device that allows an entire tray of 5000 cards to be loaded at one time. Cards entered into the machine on either the read side or punch side are directed to radial stackers, each with a 1000-card capacity. Each can be unloaded without interruption of other operations. For example, forms are converted from card to tape at the rate of 400,000 per eight-hour shift by the use of the exceptional reading ability of the card reader. To ensure accuracy of input information, a comparison check is made at two reading stations. This further reduces the possibility of error. The high punching speed of the card punch unit complements its reading speed by punching any cards detected in error during the editing process as exception cards without delaying the conversion process of the main file. The card read-punch combines extremely high speed with convenience and self-checking ability to provide low-cost input/output for the card-to-tape and tape-to-punch operations.

3. *Personnel organization*   A proposed personnel organization chart has already been included in the management abstract; the specific duties of each new position are outlined. Delegations of responsibility and authority are also specified, since they apply to the data-processing group and that group's relationship with external organization components.

There are generally three categories of full-time systems personnel:

1. *Systems analysts*   responsible primarily for the design of the system and acting as advisors to the programmers in systems problems; they may also serve as programmers.

2. *Programmers*   who translate the flow diagrams to machine-acceptable language. This work includes the preparation of detail flowcharts and the writing and testing of programs.

3. *Operators*
   a. *Console operators*   in charge of operations in the machine room during actual running of the equipment.
   b. *Tape librarians*   responsible for the receipt, storage, and issuance of taped records.
   c. *Data control clerks*   log and establish controls on all incoming and outgoing jobs, and who set up and maintain job schedules.

19.7   IMPLEMENTATION PLAN

Various implementation task schedules discussed in Chapter 18 are placed in this report section to expand the implementation summary of the management abstract. These exhibits, along with backup narrative, provide a sufficient amount of implementation detail, although some study teams have used PERT or critical path network diagrams to further illustrate time and cost relationships. The Collins and McCabe report, for example, contained brief narrative accounts on each of the five tasks; major cost and service events were then itemized, showing when equipment and procedures would be installed, and the cost associated with each event.

Figure 19-7 from the Collins and McCabe case study uses a somewhat different

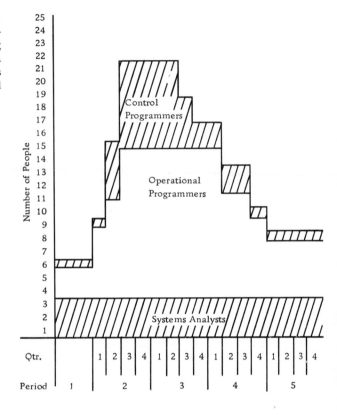

Figure 19-7 An example of a method for presenting the projected change in programming and systems personnel for a new system. The graph was taken from our Collins and McCabe case study.

technique of displaying personnel buildup during implementation as compared with the bar graphs in Chapter 18.

19.8 APPRAISAL OF SYSTEM VALUE

The management abstract emphasized economic values of the system in terms of profits, cash flow, and return on investment. In the present section, system advantages are examined as they pertain to other operating personnel in accounting, facilities, and property departments. Two kinds of information are generally included:

1. Cost comparisons between the present system projected into the future and the proposed new system over its useful life.
2. Detailed descriptions of other system benefits and values.

Personnel, materials, data processing rental or depreciation, and related expenses are drawn from the cost summaries prepared in Chapter 18. These are supplemented with narrative to indicate break-even points, trends and other important features.

Specific reasons for rejecting alternate proposals can also be noted here. At Collins and McCabe, alternate solutions for pure message switching, for message switching and order matching, and common-carrier service were evaluated and reasons listed for the rejection of each one.

A discussion of this nature leads to an evaluation of other system advantages and benefits, including such intangible values as flexibility, efficiency, improved service, reliability, and so on. Where assumptions are made in costing these factors, the basis for arriving at values should be carefully explained. Any values developed in Chapter 18 and not covered in the management abstract should be discussed here.

19.9 APPENDIX

The Appendix is a technical validation and detailing section and contains information useful primarily to methods and programming personnel. It is not merely a place for study detail that does not fit elsewhere. Emphasis is directed in particular to critical and to advanced elements of the study.

The appendix includes such subjects as:

1. Simulation data on message flow, volumes, equipment utilization, networks, and so forth.
2. Record, file and message descriptions.
3. Sample (and demonstration) programs.
4. Application flowcharts.
5. Physical planning detail.
6. Detailed equipment characteristics.
7. Disk and tape requirement calculations.
8. Derivation of formulas and calculations.
9. Training course descriptions.
10. Programming systems support.

The basic five documentations forms (resource usage, activity, operation, message, and file sheets) are included, since they permit description in the necessary depth. But certain types of data require other media for description (program flowcharts, manual procedures, and network diagrams.)

SUMMARY

The new system plan is both a description of the study team's solution to a major business problem, and a formal presentation to management for decision and action. It is the culmination of a systems study—providing management with the penetrating, thorough, and validated information to make sound decisions about future systems that will promote the short- and long-term growth of the business. The next step is management's directive to proceed with systems implementation and operation.

20

A New System Plan for Butodale

20.1 INTRODUCTION

In this chapter we present the new system plan developed for our composite case study, Butodale. Although derived basically from an actual report, the plan has been modified to conceal the company's identity and to adapt it to book form. Because of its length, the Appendix to the new system plan has not been included. The report is primarily to illustrate concepts and principles and is not designed to be analyzed for the adequacy or accuracy of its equipment recommendations.

We wish to point out that the new system plan for Butodale proposes a basic batch-oriented approach to the problem. This approach is appropriate for an organization with limited exerience with computers. With time, the system would probably evolve into an online system for immediate response.

20.2 GUIDE TO BUTODALE'S NEW SYSTEM PLAN

The reader will recall that the five main parts of the new system plan are preface, management abstract, the new system in operation, implementation plan, and appraisal of system value. Within each of these, except the implementation plan, the subdivisions of Butodale's new system plan closely follow the suggestions set forth in Section 19-4. The implementation plan intermixes topics. Analysts should find the outline in Figure 19-2 convenient for management presentations and as a check list to guide them during a study. Similarly, management and operating personnel studying the report should find the outline helpful in guiding their reading.

After an initial review, the reader might find it useful to imagine himself as J. R. Stearns, Vice-President of Engineering and chief decision maker on Butodale's computer-evaluation committee. On the basis of this report, would you, in Stearns' position, install the computerized system, retain the existing system, or take some alternative course of action? Does the letter of transmittal convey the information that permits you to capture the study team's point of view and main conclusions? Does the general introduction adequately recap the Phase I and Phase II reports? Does it provide an adequate frame of reference for the Phase III report?

Your main interest will probably be centered on the management abstract where you will find the team's recommendations. The first recommendation asks for your positive decision to proceed to implement the new system plan. Next, under the summary of system values and advantages you will find—the payoff and the cost! An economic advantage of $240,000 per year for the new system is projected—an important factor—if the report convinces you that this potential is attainable.

The remainder of the abstract should provide you with an overview of how the new system will operate and how the study team proposes to implement it.

The next few sections of the report will be of special significance to your financial and technical staff. The information flow and recommended equipment is of prime concern to your technical people to evaluate whether it will do the work necessary to accomplish the goals and objectives for the provide product demand activity. Financial management must evaluate the rental or purchase costs of the equipment, and the personnel costs of staffing the new department.

The graphic representation of the implementation plan (Figure 20-5) shows at a glance the steps needed to change from the existing system to the new system.

Figure 20-6, in the division of the report appraising the value of the new system, gives you the "net" financial picture. Column 2 carries forward the figures from the resource usage sheet of the Phase I report. This column, when compared with column 6 shows the "before" and "after" cost of the provide product demand activity. Column 7 isolates cost increases and decreases by department for this activity, with a net $240,000 reduction.

The nonfinancial benefits and values of the new system are presented in the final pages of the report. The potential benefits outlined here for your evaluation must be considered carefully as they may be of even more importance than any cost savings.

After looking at the report through the eyes of Stearns, the chairman of the computer evaluation committee, the reader should review the report as L. P. Barksdale, the chief financial executive in Butodale. In the same manner, the reader might profitably consider the report from other viewpoints, such as that of the manager of product engineering or engineering services. As soon as he leaves the top level of decision making, the reader will begin to explore the technical detail more carefully.

We conclude our guide to the case study and proceed to the report itself.

20.3   A NEW SYSTEM PLAN FOR THE BUTODALE ELECTRONICS COMPANY

Mr. Ansel T. Benson
Butodale Electronics Company
Danvers, Massachusetts

Dear Mr. Benson:

Last October, a study was undertaken to determine the extent to which computers could be used for automating Company activities. Since the presentation of our two earlier reports, our scope has centered on the activity of providing the demand information for Butodale's products. This activity involves engineering design in response to customer orders and preparing bids and quotations for potential customers. The study was completed in late April.

Briefly, our findings are as follows:

1. The provide product demand activity can be automated.
2. Utilization of a computer for this activity will result in economic savings and other tangible advantages to Butodale.
3. Special design calculations, now done manually, also can be effectively accomplished by data-processing equipment.

The attached report includes a summary of the study objectives, an analysis of the present system and a description of the proposed new system. Further, we include a proposed implementation schedule.

This report will assist you in appraising the potential value of data processing equipment in handling this part of Butodale's operations. We believe the recommendations are sound and substantiated by the information available and the various analyses that have been made.

We appreciate the excellent cooperation you and the other members of management have given us during this study. In particular, we want to commend the work of Messrs. L. K. White, T. R. Fellows, P. K. Ragonese, and K. R. Sherman for their special contributions to and cooperation with the members of the study team. Finally, we wish to acknowledge the help received from the sales representative and systems engineers of the XYZ Computer Company.

Yours very truly,

R. L. Casey
Project Coordinator

CONTENTS

I PREFACE—GENERAL INFORMATION

Six months ago a study was begun to examine the existing information processing system at Butodale, to establish requirements for a new system, and to design and propose a new system, employing automated procedures as much as possible. After the completion of Phase II, it was decided to concentrate our efforts on the provide product demand activity.

Objectives

The five objectives set for the provide product demand activity are:

1. Satisfy customer information requests.
2. Perform engineering design.
3. Supply information for cost accounting and management control.
4. Inform customers of order disposition and schedules.
5. Provide information to manufacturing.

Project Scope

Essentially, the complete activity of providing product demand involves accounting, sales and service, administration and advertising, product engineering, and engineering services functions of the company. Those operations within this activity that are directly involved in the automated aspects of the system are concerned with the engineering design for customer orders and preparing bids and quotations for potential customers. Both the requests and the orders may be for standard or nonstandard analog computers or modifications to installed computers.

Requests for standard analog computers are processed routinely and the customer is furnished information which includes price quotations, descriptions, layouts, diagrams, and other data necessary for the potential customer to make the purchase decision.

Requests for nonstandard analog computers are handled specially and involve engineering reviews, engineering design and layout, and the compilation of special cost data. The customer is furnished the same kind of data for nonstandard computers as for standard computers.

When a formal order is received from a customer, it must be edited and clarified and then detail-designed for communication to manufacturing.

In brief, this report concerns those operations involved with the receipt of customer orders, customer requests for bids and quotations, producing quotations and specifications in response to requests, and providing detailed engineering design documents in response to formal orders.

Organization of the Study

The project was organized into three phases: Phase I, which comprised the study of the existing manual system in relation to its environment; Phase II, the analysis of the product line and its specifications to determine system requirements; and Phase III, the design and evaluation of the new system.

In *Phase I,* the project team reviewed pertinent Company and industry literature in order to describe Butodale's present operations, the industry background, the major policies and practices, and the Company's principal objectives. The conclusions were verified by interviews with Company executives. Following this first step, the basic structure of the Company was outlined in the following areas:

> products and markets
> materials and suppliers
> finances
> personnel
> facilities

Finally, interviews were conducted in the sales and order processing department, the engineering department, and the manufacturing department to determine time and volume data. Historical data and actual samples of present orders were reviewed in order to arrive at accurate analyses of cost. Descriptions of all procedures, supporting documents, resources, and costs related to activities were prepared and included in the Present Business Description report, which was submitted to Butodale management.

In order to determine the requirements for the projected system, *Phase II* was organized to include 1) an analysis of customer specifications, 2) a structural description of the general-purpose analog computer, 3) a parts analysis, and 4) the definition of the design logic for selected standard and nonstandard models. An analysis of customer specifications was performed which identified each unique specification and indicated a value or range of values for each.

By reviewing Company product manuals, interviewing appropriate personnel, and perusing many blueprints, the major assemblies, subassemblies, and parts were identified and their relationships defined. This information was synthesized in a generic model list demonstrating the relationships among parts and assemblies at different structure levels.

Next, a detailed parts analysis was performed in which product and parts characteristics were identified and documented, and a value or range of values assigned to each one. Characteristics were separated into fixed and variable. The greatest effort was spent on the variable characteristics since these express the real parameters of the product line and its potential expandability.

The final step was the determination of the design logic which connects the customer specifications to the product characteristics. One approach was to group, structure, and tie parts characteristics back to individual customer specifications through the medium of the design logic. Alternately, the design logic was brought out by working first with customer specifications and progressing down to the product and parts characteristics.

Throughout the design-logic determination, it was necessary to record this information so as to be readily communicated to all concerned including engineers, analysts, and programmers. For this purpose, flowcharts and decision tables were utilized because of their ability to display complex interrelationships among data in simplified form, and at several different levels of descriptive language. We summarized our findings in the System Requirements Specifications report, which was accepted by Butodale management in February.

In *Phase III,* the final phase, the specifications of the new system were agreed upon during several conferences with management, and the system was then designed in detail. One part of this development was to restructure the existing design logic found in Phase II so that a general approach was made to each design problem. In this manner, great flexibility and breadth of coverage was included.

An evaluation of the proposed new system as compared to the present system was conducted to determine: (1) Does the new system meet the criteria set for it? (2) Is technical feasibility demonstrated? (3) What are the actual dollar savings plus intangible advantages?

In order to provide concrete proof of the feasibility of the automated design concepts and to show particular solutions to the types of problems encountered in the design of an analog computer, a demonstration for selected portions of the product was developed. This demonstration covered enough of the product line and the product to indicate that complete coverage is feasible.

Finally, the new designed ADE/BUT (automated design engineering for Butodale) System and the demonstration were fully documented.

II   MANAGEMENT ABSTRACT

New System Recommendations

For Butodale to gain the benefits of an automated system, the following steps should be taken:

1. Approve and begin implementation of the system described in this report.
2. Assign four engineers familiar with the engineering functions of the general-purpose analog computer line to participate in the implementation of the system.
3. Order the necessary XYZ equipment for installation in late September.

Each of these recommendations is documented and substantiated in this report. A detailed description of the present system and other information on the computer-programming techniques to be used is contained in the Appendix to this report.

System Value and Advantages

The proposed system offers the following advantages to Butodale:

1. Estimated direct cost savings of $240,000 per year.
2. A decrease in the elapsed time for quotation preparation from one week to one day.
3. In product engineering, the actual elapsed time in the new system will be less than three days. Under the present system, one to two months are required for new orders.
4. Clerical, computational, and design errors will be substantially reduced because of the inherent accuracy and reliability of the data processing equipment.

5. Standardization of parts and models without loss of flexibility will enable increased order quantities of identical parts for manufacturing.
6. Provide experience to Butodale so that like systems can be developed for other product lines, such as data plotters.

Phase I and Phase II

There are two main results that stand out from the present business description at Butodale.

1. The total market for general purpose analog computers is growing significantly and Butodale is capturing a large share of the market.
2. The provide product demand and provide end products activities are of such a character as to be likely candidates for automation.

After this report was presented, the study team was authorized to proceed with the Phase II study to determine the requirements for automating these two activities.

During the Phase II study, the requirements were specified for both the provide product demand and the provide end products activities. The report was presented to management in February. After this presentation, management decided to consider the provide product demand activity first. Thus, the main outcome of the Phase II study was management's authorization to proceed with the design of the ADE/BUT System for the provide product demand activity.

New System in Operation

The automated design engineering system for Butodale will consist of a man-machine complex designed to utilize most effectively the education, experience, and creativity of the engineer while relieving him of the necessity for completing tedious and routine tasks. The product lines processed will include standard and nonstandard general-purpose analog computers.

Requests for quotations and bids will be processed by entering customer requirements and pre-engineering results. These will be processed by the XYZ/C computer in order to produce the required equipment list with prices and necessary information for preparation of drawings. Results developed during this phase are retained for later use if the order is received.

The receipt of an order initiates a similar input process in which any customer changes and pre-engineering are incorporated. The results are the engineering specifications, drawing backups, information for drafting of required drawings, and a machine-readable product record describing the complete product.

This product record enables the system to handle future modifications as they are received. For computers for which there is no existing machine-readable product record, one will be prepared from the job file when the first modification order for that particular computer is received.

The cost of operating the system is $238,960 per year which is balanced against a present cost of $479,245 per year, resulting in potential savings of $240,285 per year when the system is in full operation.

Implementation Plan

It is recommended that the new system be implemented over a nineteen-month period. During this time the team will reach several "milestones."

1. Order the necessary equipment for delivery in September.
2. Establish the proper organization to implement and install the new system.
3. Prepare the physical site.
4. Provide for training the project group by XYZ personnel in the necessary programming technology.
5. Complete the analysis of the general-purpose analog computer product line and prepare the detailed logic design.
6. Begin programming.
7. Install the computer and related equipment.
8. Test and debug the programs.
9. Begin parallel operations.
10. Begin full operations of the new system.

III   THE NEW SYSTEM IN OPERATION

Information Flow

1.   SYSTEM DESIGN APPROACH

The system proposed is the result of the comprehensive study of the existing system conducted by the study team. The new system represents a unified systems approach in that the total problem was surveyed and the system then designed to fulfill a goal-directed activity of Butodale Electronics. The goal which the system will fulfill is:

Prepare for use by the manufacturing department all information necessary for the production of general-purpose analog computers in response to customer orders; prepare responses to customer requests for quotations and bids.

2.   DESCRIPTION OF THE SYSTEM

The broad aspects of the operating system are pictorially presented in two figures. Figure 20-1 is an activity model of the ADE/BUT System. Both the present manual system and the ADE/BUT System must accept as inputs customer requests for quotations, customer requests for bids, and customer orders. The new system will also accept inquiries from engineers. The system produces engineering specifications divided into computational, electronic, and mechanical sections, requests for special purchases, and a bill of materials. In the ADE/BUT System, the product-record file may be thought of as a bill of material. The answers to requests for quotes or bids are in a form which can be sent to the customer. In addition to these outputs, the ADE/BUT System provides a specification errata sheet on which are listed any customer specification errors or inconsistencies which the computer program detects and cannot resolve. This sheet can also be used for communication with the customer.

Connecting the inputs and the outputs are the operations necessary to accomplish

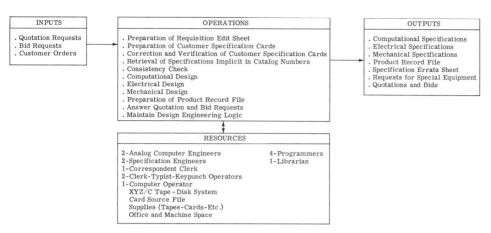

INPUTS	OPERATIONS	OUTPUTS
. Quotation Requests . Bid Requests . Customer Orders	. Preparation of Requisition Edit Sheet . Preparation of Customer Specification Cards . Correction and Verification of Customer Specification Cards . Retrieval of Specifications Implicit in Catalog Numbers . Consistency Check . Computational Design . Electrical Design . Mechanical Design . Preparation of Product Record File . Answer Quotation and Bid Requests . Maintain Design Engineering Logic	. Computational Specifications . Electrical Specifications . Mechanical Specifications . Product Record File . Specification Errata Sheet . Requests for Special Equipment . Quotations and Bids

RESOURCES

2-Analog Computer Engineers   4-Programmers
2-Specification Engineers   1-Librarian
1-Correspondent Clerk
2-Clerk-Typist-Keypunch Operators
1-Computer Operator
   XYZ/C Tape - Disk System
   Card Source File
   Supplies (Tapes-Cards-Etc.)
   Office and Machine Space

Figure 20-1 Schematic model of Butodale's automatic design engineering system for the provide product demand activity.

the goals of the system with the resources which are to be used in these operations. The operations are listed in Figure 20-1 and detailed in the following sections. The resources consist primarily of the personnel and equipment which make up the man-machine complex that is the ADE/BUT System. In addition, there are supplies, office equipment, and physical space.

Figure 20-2 is a general flow diagram of the operations listed in the previous figure. Manual operations are shown as ovals and machine functions as a rectangle. The first step is the translation of the customer orders, or bid and quotation requests, into a form which can be efficiently handled by the computer. This is accomplished by filling in a requisition edit sheet, an example of which is shown in the Appendix. In the next operation, the requisition edit sheet is used for preparation of customer specification cards to serve as input to the computer program. This is accomplished by keypunching information from the specification edit sheet and, where possible, using prepunched cards covering standard information. After the cards are completed, they are checked and verified both manually and mechanically.

The cards thus prepared are read into the XYZ/C computer and form the input data for the computer programs. One of the first functions performed by the program is to make an extensive logic and accuracy check on the customer specifications. At this point any errors or inconsistencies are printed out on a specifications errata sheet. The actual design will continue if the magnitude and nature of the errors detected permit; otherwise the design is abandoned and a customer-order rejection notice prepared.

The design proceeds serially, designing first the computational elements, then the electrical portions, and finally the mechanical components. Throughout the design, the engineering specifications are printed out, and the parts and subassemblies as generated or selected are written on the product-record file.

If any manual design is called for, the order is listed for special engineering. Engineering specifications are produced for answering quotation and bid requests; these are sent to customers after an engineering review. An engineering specification for production undergoes an engineering review and is sent to manufacturing for scheduling and advance ordering, and customer acceptance is forwarded for formal orders. The

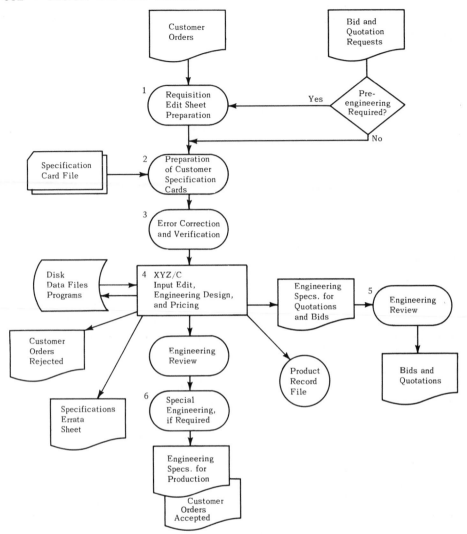

Figure 20-2   The general flow of operations shown in Figure 20-1 for Butodale's provide product demand activity.

product-record file would form a logical input to an automated inventory planning and control system.

Detailed System Flow

The following sections provide additional detail concerning the individual operations shown in Figure 20-2 and discussed in general above.

1. REQUISITION EDIT AND PREPARATION OF CUSTOMER SPECIFICATION CARDS

The first operation is pre-engineering analysis, which is required for about 10 percent of the orders to identify them for general-purpose ana'og computers and to provide key technical information. The next operation is the preparation of a requisition edit sheet from the request for quotation, request for bid, and customer order. The preparation of the requisition edit sheet serves the function of converting the customer's terminology into standard specification terminology. This is accomplished principally by checking appropriate boxes on the edit sheet to indicate the alternatives selected by the customer. In addition, it will be necessary to write in certain variables which can take on continuous or nearly continuous values, that is, ranges and catalog numbers.

From the completed requisition edit sheet, prepunched cards are pulled from the specifications card file for the standard specifications indicated on the requisition edit sheet and printed on the cards. The other values that have been shown are now keypunched into additional specification cards.

2.   VERIFICATION AND ERROR CORRECTION

The cards are first listed to provide an easy visual check. The listing is compared with both the original customer order and the requisition edit sheet to check for editing errors and pulling or keypunch errors. Detected errors are corrected and the checking procedure is repeated.

3.   COMPUTER OPERATIONS

The operations included in the computer programs are the heart of the ADE/BUT System. The size and complexity of these programs preclude any but a general description of their operations in this summary. The Appendix contains an example showing the design process in more detail. The checked and verified cards whose preparation is described above form the input to the computer. The first computer operation is to retrieve the customer specifications which are implied by the catalog numbers, values, and ranges. The individual customer specifications are next allowed to supplement and modify retrieved specifications in order to represent the total customer requirements.

An extensive internal check is now performed to insure consistency of the final specifications. If consistency errors are found, or if it is necessary to assume missing values, messages are printed to this effect on the specifications errata sheet. If design can proceed with reasonable assumptions, the order continues in the main line; if not, an order rejection notice is printed, the design process is terminated and the next order is begun.

If no errors are encountered, the design now proceeds serially designing the computational, electrical, and mechanical components. Three design techniques are used for the design programs. The first is a selection of existing parts or subassemblies and their implicit assembly according to the specific detail drawing on the basis of the customer specifications and internally generated specifications. The second technique is to use the computer for calculations of values and conditions which can be expressed mathematically. Circuit parameter calculations are an example of this. The calculated values for components such as resistors are referred to a standard circuit drawing. The third technique is to utilize the high speed of the computer to iterate using the design logic many times, and using different assumptions to develop balanced solutions. At the end of each iteration, the result is compared against acceptability criteria. If the criteria are not met, the basic assumptions are modified to improve the results and the next iteration commences.

As the design proceeds, the engineering specifications are listed on the printer and required parts and subassemblies are written on the product record file. If any special engineering is required, special cards are punched for later printing.

4. SPECIAL ENGINEERING OPERATIONS

Operations 5 and 6 in Figure 20-2 describe special engineering procedures. The engineering specifications produced in the computer phase are either sent to manufacturing (after special engineering, if required) or are used in the preparation of answers to quotation requests and bids. The product-record file could provide an input to an automated inventory planning and control system. An automated inventory system would include the ability to summarize parts and assembly requirements. This would be used for reducing inventories, checking for reorder points, forecasting, and ordering special purchased parts.

5. DESCRIPTION OF PROGRAM PHILOSOPHY

One of the prime considerations in the automation of design engineering is that the design logic is never static; rather it is in a continuing, dynamic state of change as in any other management system. Thus, the computer programs which represent this logic must reflect these changes. The ADE/BUT System is designed with this in mind. One technique for insuring this flexibility is to provide detailed documentation of the logic in a modular form. This is accomplished through the use of master flowcharts for an effective overview and detailed decision tables, which are easily understood by all interested personnel (engineers, programmers, and analysts) and are inherently modular. This procedure allows changes to be prepared and confirmed by those most knowledgeable—the engineers themselves.

Equipment Configuration

In order to implement the ADE/BUT System at Butodale, we recommend that an XYZ/C computer system be installed. This equipment will give the capacity and flexibility needed to carry out the automated program for the provide product demand activity for the general-purpose analog computer and allow compatible growth for future expansion into other product lines and activities.

Our recommendation is based on the following considerations:

1. The present unit record system in Finance is being used approximately one full shift, amounting to almost 176 hours of usage a month. Additional applications in the area of cost and inventory control are already planned for this equipment. For both technical and workload reasons, it is not feasible to plan on using this punched-card system for a project of such large scope and complexity as ADE/BUT. As a future project, this equipment should be replaced with a computer compatible with the XYZ/C or on a shared basis with a larger XYZ computer.

2. We estimate that the ADE/BUT System will utilize the XYZ/C tape-disk system an average of 4 hours per day to process the current volume of requests and orders for general purpose analog computers. On peak days, processing of current requests

Qty.	Type	Model	Description	Monthly Rental	Purchase Price
1	XYZ	C	Processing Unit (32K)	$ 3,280	$ 176,000
1	XYZ	3	Inquiry Station	180	9,000
1	XYZ	500	Card Read Punch	500	25,000
1	XYZ	1000	Printer	795	39,750
2	XYZ	10	Disk Storage	1,200	46,000
4	XYZ	9	Magnetic Tape Units	1,160	54,000
			TOTAL	$ 7,115	$ 349,750

Figure 20-3   Recommended equipment configuration for ADE/BUT in the provide product demand activity.

for quotations and orders may fill an entire 8-hour day. In addition, the time not utilized on the machine by processing current orders will be used for modifying, expanding, and testing the ADE/BUT System for the general-purpose analog computer line.

3. One of the most important considerations is the need to recommend a system which will have the capacity to expand this computer-application concept to other product lines and other applications. The knowledge gained in implementing the ADE/BUT System for the general-purpose analog computer line will give the capability to expand into other important areas, such as forecasting and cost estimating. Figure 20-3 is a summary of equipment costs.

Organization

The automated design-engineering system will occupy a position of considerable importance in Butodale operations. For this reason, it is recommended that a separate organizational group be created to implement and operate the system.

The most important justification for such an organization is that the people operating and implementing the system must be familiar with its procedures, capabilities, and limitations. By organizing these people into one group, the communication of necessary information is facilitated.

Also, these personnel can and essentially will be interchangeable in that they will be involved in both implementation and operation. This interchangeability increases the flexibility of the system and enables it to more effectively meet peak demands.

Personnel requirements will vary throughout the stages of implementation and operation. In the initial implementation stage, four engineers familiar with the general-purpose analog computer line will be required. Only one engineer will be required for operations.

After about six months, the program will be partially implemented. By then a portion of the system will be operational and the remainder will be in the process of completion. During this time, the personnel will be split into two groups. The plans for personnel are summarized in Figure 20-4.

Column 1 of Figure 20-4 lists the personnel needed for implementation and operation of the new system. These are principally Butodale personnel with some participation

PERSONNEL NEEDED	During the 19 months of implementation	Annually for full operation after implementation
Analog Computer Engineers	4	1
Programmers	4	2
XYZ/C Operator	1	1
Correspondent Clerk	1	1
Keypunch Operators	2	2
Librarian	1	1
XYZ Systems Engineers	2	
NUMBER		
Butodale Personnel	13	8
XYZ Personnel	2	
COST		
Butodale Personnel	$ 182,000	$ 75,500

Figure 20-4   Personnel needed during the implementation and full operation of the ADE/ BUT system.

by XYZ personnel. Column 2 gives the full-time equivalents of personnel during the 19 months of implementation.

Column 3 contains the full-time equivalents for personnel after the system is in full operation.

IV   IMPLEMENTATION PLAN

The transition period during which a new system is being installed can be difficult and expensive. For this reason, it is necessary to plan thoroughly the tasks to be accomplished. This section details a recommended plan for the implementation of the Butodale ADE system.

The plan covers a period of 19 months. At the end of this time it is anticipated that the major implementation effort will have been completed. Due to the dynamic nature of the system, however, there will be continued implementation, modification, and maintenance of the system throughout its life.

Figure 20-5 presents a pictorial representation of the plan, detailing major tasks with estimated times, and indicating "milestones" in the implementation of the system. The duration and calendar times allotted for the tasks are indicative of the expected requirements.

The plan is organized to provide an orderly transition from the existing manual system. Throughout this period, portions of the product line will be in the process of conversion to the automated system. Thus, the transition will be gradual and will produce minimum disorder in both the new and the old system.

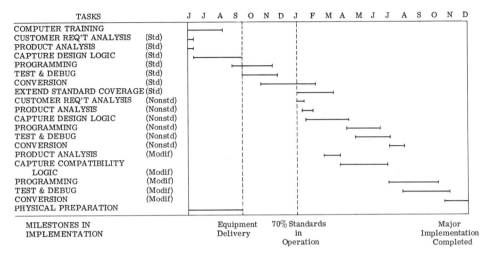

TASKS		J J A S O N D J F M A M J J A S O N D
COMPUTER TRAINING		
CUSTOMER REQ'T ANALYSIS	(Std)	
PRODUCT ANALYSIS	(Std)	
CAPTURE DESIGN LOGIC	(Std)	
PROGRAMMING	(Std)	
TEST & DEBUG	(Std)	
CONVERSION	(Std)	
EXTEND STANDARD COVERAGE	(Std)	
CUSTOMER REQ'T ANALYSIS	(Nonstd)	
PRODUCT ANALYSIS	(Nonstd)	
CAPTURE DESIGN LOGIC	(Nonstd)	
PROGRAMMING	(Nonstd)	
TEST & DEBUG	(Nonstd)	
CONVERSION	(Nonstd)	
PRODUCT ANALYSIS	(Modif)	
CAPTURE COMPATIBILITY LOGIC	(Modif)	
PROGRAMMING	(Modif)	
TEST & DEBUG	(Modif)	
CONVERSION	(Modif)	
PHYSICAL PREPARATION		

MILESTONES IN IMPLEMENTATION	Equipment Delivery	70% Standards in Operation	Major Implementation Completed

Figure 20-5   A graphic representation of the major tasks, estimated times, and milestones during the implementation phase of the ADE/BUT system.

One of the major objectives of this implementation plan is to endeavor to place a substantial portion of the product line into operational status as rapidly as possible. This is desirable from a number of standpoints.

(a) First and primarily, it is anticipated that this portion will help cover the cost of the continued implementation of the system, thus insuring Butodale a maximum and rapid return on the out-of-pocket investment.

(b) It will provide maximum training to Butodale personnel, as they will have been exposed to the full spectrum of the tasks involved in implementation.

(c) It will make maximum utilization of the time and assistance provided by the XYZ systems engineers.

In order to insure the above advantages it is recommended that Butodale provide a total of four engineers familiar with the engineering functions within the general-purpose analog computer line. In addition, it is recommended that a keypunch operator-clerk and a programmer be added as soon as implementation begins. These personnel will form the nucleus for the continued implementation and operation of the ADE/BUT System.

For its part, XYZ personnel will provide continued support and will also provide additional technical support as needed during implementation.

The first "milestone" is the installation of the XYZ equipment necessary for this application. The next is the completion of the implementation of the first portion of the standard-product line. The operation of this portion will provide savings to help offset its own costs and the continued implementation costs. The final "milestone" shown is the point at which the major implementation effort will have been completed. The proposed system will then be in operation.

Key steps in the implementation plan are:

1. *Schools*—It is desirable to have the Butodale implementation and operating per-

sonnel thoroughly familiar with all aspects of programming and operating the system. For this reason, it is planned for all personnel to attend classes during June and July at the XYZ Education Center in Boston. These 2- to 8-week schools will provide a knowledge of the equipment and a background for the programming languages needed.

2. *Analysis and Design Logic*—During this step the design-logic and system approach used for the preliminary demonstration will be reviewed and modified as necessary to fit the operating system. In addition, those areas not covered by the example in the Appendix will be thoroughly analyzed and recorded in the form of flowcharts and decision tables.

3. *Programming*—In parallel with the analysis, as sections of the design logic are completed, conversion of flowcharts and decision tables into programs will commence. In the latter stages of the programming step, it will be necessary to add another keypunch operator to the group. In addition to her keypunch duties, she will perform many clerical duties which will arise in the analysis and conversion.

4. *Test and Debug*—The magnitude and complexity of the programs involved in the ADE/BUT System will dictate extensive testing and debugging. It is XYZ policy to provide a number of hours of free test time prior to installation of a system. The XYZ/C Tape-Disk system for this test time is located in Boston. In the 90 days prior to the delivery of the computer, a number of trips to the data center will be necessary to test the programs. As each new section of the system is described in modular form and coded into Fortran, it can be independently checked out with sample problems. In this way the analysis, flowcharts, decision tables, coding, and design logic can be tested as a unit, thus minimizing total test time.

An additional recommendation is that a limited parallel operation be started immediately and continue through installation. Once or twice a month a number of current customer orders should be put through the sample system as it is expanded to include the newest proven additions. This will aid in further testing the selected computational, electrical, and mechanical assemblies as they are programmed. This will also aid in pointing out the more common inconsistencies and errors so that these may be added to the specification-consistency check program. In this way an even more powerful checking feature can be built into the system prior to installation, and the system when installed will be that much more error free and efficient.

In addition to the initial test of the programs, the arrival of the computer system will initiate a period of intensive testing and debugging. At this time, a machine operator should be added to the team to free the engineers and programmers from these operations. This operator will continue with the system during full operation.

5. *Conversion*—As the programs begin to approach a debugged state, parallel running of the ADE/BUT System with the present system should commence. This will be concurrent with continued testing and debugging. Parallel runs of one to one and a half months should bring the system to the point where productive output can be expected. At that state, it is anticipated that 70% of the standard general-purpose analog computers will be designed completely. Other portions of the line will be designed to various stages by the ADE/BUT System with manual intervention to complete the designs. At this time, the return will begin to equal the operating cost.

Continued addition of the logic for the portions of the remaining line will bring the system coverage to the estimated 95% in an additional period of two months. As more and more of the line is added to the system, the advantages and savings to Butodale will reach their full potential.

6. *Physical Planning*—Prior to the actual arrival of the system, facilities for it must be prepared. These facilities take the form of an air-conditioned room, preferably with a raised floor to accommodate cables. It has been estimated, based on experience of other users and advice from the XYZ Company, that such a room will cost approximately $15,000, this low cost being due to the extensive facilities available.

V   APPRAISAL OF SYSTEM VALUE

Present vs New System Cost

The analysis of the present system conducted during the first phase of the study by the study team provides the background against which the new system can be evaluated. In most systems comparisons, it is unusual to have the wealth of detail which has been made available by Phase I of this study. In the evaluation, full use of these figures and examples has been made. The results represent the best estimates of the existing conditions and projections of the future system in operation that can be made by the team members.

1.   PRODUCT LINE COVERAGE

It is anticipated that the proposed system will be capable of processing approximately 95% of the engineering effort involved in the general-purpose analog computer line. The remaining 5% consists of such types as export orders and other complex or unique installations.

Also significant to Butodale is the inclusion of modifications to existing configurations. As the market in analog-computer equipment is growing, the ability to process these jobs automatically will become of increasing importance to help customers grow with their existing equipment.

2.   COST COMPARISONS OF OPERATING SYSTEMS

The prime justification for the proposed system is the direct-cost savings made available by allowing the computer to assume the many routine, repetitive tasks involved in this area. The Appendix contains the detailed analysis of the costs associated with the present system. Figure 20-6 summarizes the overall costs associated with the activity of providing product demand.

The seven columns in the figure are explained below, column by column.

1. Under the new system, in addition to the six departments involved in providing product demand, it will be necessary to set up a new department, the ADE computer department.
2. The cost of providing product demand was presented in the report from Phase I. These are the same cost figures as in the resource usage sheet of Phase I.
3. The costs in this column represent all of the old system costs that will be eliminated by the installation of the new system.

	1	2	3	4	5	6
Department	Old provide product demand annual cost	Eliminated costs from present system	Remaining functional costs	Added costs under new system	New provide product demand annual cost	Annual savings of ADE/BUT
Management	24	8	16		16	8
Accounting	32	7	25		25	7
Sales and service	1,052	282	770	108	878	174
Administration	265	104	161	10	171	94
Product engineering	126	106	20	41	61	65
Engineering services	152	120	32	32	64	88
ADE computer department				196	196	−196
Total	1,651	627	1,024	387	1,411	240

Figure 20-6 Summary cost and savings analysis for the provide product demand activity under the present system and under ADE/BUT. All figures are in thousands of dollars.

4. The cost figures in this column represent the remaining functional costs within Butodale which are not affected by the installation of ADE/BUT.
5. Each cost figure in this column represents the added costs after the computer system is installed. Of special interest here is the cost of machine rental, personnel, and other costs that arise with the new computer department. This $196,000 increase represents a new cost item.
6. This column shows the total costs of providing product demand among the six old departments and the new computer department under the ADE/BUT System.
7. The figures in this column represent the cost savings of ADE/BUT, department by department. We show the new costs associated with the system as a negative savings (—$196,000). The main factor in this column, and indeed in the entire table, is the overall cost saving of $240,000 per year to Butodale if ADE/BUT is implemented.

3. IMPLEMENTATION COSTS

There are three main aspects to the costs of implementation. First to be considered are the personnel, then the equipment, and finally, supply and other costs. During this period there will be some overlap between the operations under the present system and those under the new one.

We summarize the implementation costs for 19 months as follows:

Butodale personnel	$182,000
Equipment rental	106,725
Other conversion costs	78,370
Total cost	$367,095
Estimated net operational savings during implementation	143,756
Net implementation cost:	$223,339

From these figures, we see that Butodale must expect to spend a net of $223,000 during the 19 months of implementation. Thus, at the rate of $20,000 monthly savings under ADE/BUT, it will require 11 months after implementation to recover the capital invested, not including interest on the investment. There is a total of 30 months therefore until Butodale begins to realize a net savings from ADE/BUT for the provide product demand activity. After that, the cost savings will be approximately $240,000 per year. A fuller breakdown of these cost and savings figures may be found in the Appendix. They were developed by the study team and represent estimates using the best available data and conservative projection methods.

Other Benefits and Values

1. FASTER RESPONSE TIME

An area of great potential value to Butodale is the reduced elapsed time associated with orders processed in the automated system.

One particular advantage is that the reduced proposal time will encourage the transmission of increased numbers of field requirements for proposals to the plant. This will serve to allow the sales engineer in the field to spend more time with customers and potential customers. In addition, reduced engineering time for orders will result in decreased lead time and an improved competitive position for Butodale.

The ADE/BUT System has provided sufficient personnel in order to respond to proposals and orders on an average of one day each. However, it is recognized that there must be sufficient lead time prior to manufacturing to enable proper shop loading. This time is considered to be approximately one week.

2. ACCURACY AND CONSISTENCY

"To err is human" and, because of this, every manual system endeavors, with varying degrees of success, to cope with the human element. The larger and more complex the operation, the more human error will tend to compound itself. In the present system, it is difficult to assign a dollar value to the errors existing. It is, however, recognized that they are substantial.

Errors may arise from such sources as transposition of digits, incorrect transcription, calculation, and many other sources. In the proposed system such errors are virtually eliminated due to the inherent reliability and accuracy of electronic data-processing equipment.

Typically, for a product as sophisticated as a general-purpose analog computer a number of engineering solutions exist for a given set of customer requirements. Thus, there is no guarantee that two engineers doing the same job would come up with the same result. However, a best approach does exist. It is this best-design solution for which the logic will be incorporated in the ADE/BUT System. The result is that the best-engineering solution is consistently produced without sacrificing the flexibility of the system.

It has been estimated by the Butodale operating personnel that, under the existing manual system, 75% of all orders reaching manufacturing contain some form of error. These errors take on many forms but most can be traced to the human element. One prime source of error is in the material being selected for manufacturing.

Material errors can arise in several ways:

a. Engineering errors—either through the specification engineers or through the bill of material clerks.
b. Incorrect updating of bill of material or drawings.
c. Typing or selection errors in the factory-order preparation.
d. Storeroom material selection errors.

All of these errors except (d) can be greatly reduced by the ADE/BUT System with its elimination of much of the human element and its extensive programmed and manual checks.

These problems are easily solved by a man-machine complex such as the ADE/BUT System. Calculations are completed rapidly and accurately by the computer. In the design and updating of the programs, the best criteria are selected for each case from all of the approaches presently being used. Thus, under the ADE/BUT System, the design produced for a given set of specifications would be consistently the same unless altered by later engineering changes. It would represent the best design philosophy available, produce mathematically and logically accurate results, and would be done at computer speed.

If it were necessary to present justification for the ADE/BUT System on the basis of only one area, the increased accuracy, reliability, and consistency of the system would have been selected as the one with the most potential value to Butodale.

3. FLEXIBILITY

One of the prime objectives of the design of a system is to insure flexibility. Engineering applications are by their very nature dynamic; new technologies are constantly being developed, new engineering procedures and standards are evolved. Also, for a semicustom-engineered product such as analog computers, the system must be capable of responding to a large percentage of the wide range of nonstandard requirements that the customer may specify.

These criteria have been considered in the design of the ADE/BUT System. In order to insure the necessary flexibility, a number of procedures and techniques have been employed. In computer programs, ease of modification is achieved by modularity, by use of higher level programming languages, and by thorough documentation of the programs. The ADE/BUT System programs will be written primarily in Fortran. Fortran is a largely machine-independent computer language closely resembling the ordinary language of mathematics. This resemblance makes Fortran programs particularly easy to understand and hence to modify, especially in engineering applications.

The goals of modularity and documentation are advanced through the use of a logic-recording technique referred to as decision tables. This is a method of describing and recording complex logical situations which contains better structured information than the more conventional narrative or flowchart means of documenting logic. Furthermore, decision tables are easily understood by programmers and engineers alike. Not only are they ideal for capturing and recording logic for programming, but they serve as their own documentation.

The structure of decision tables is such that related logic tends to group naturally into modules. This inherent modularity will be preserved in the programs. Engineering changes dealing with a particular portion of the design logic can be made by changing only those tables involved.

By the use of these techniques, and by keeping the need for modularity and documentation firmly in mind during the implementation period, the flexibility so necessary for an automated system will be achieved.

4. FUTURE EXPANSION

The ADE/BUT System as proposed will be a continually expanding system. As it progresses through its various stages of implementation, the system will grow to encompass essentially the total scope of the general-purpose analog computer line.

An area for which there is great potential for future expansion is that of digital plotter systems. At the present stage of development, plotter engineering is primarily of a prototype nature. That is, design, criteria, and procedures are in the process of being established. Each system at this time is relatively unique. In the future, as plotter systems begin to replace the electromechanical systems, they will move from a prototype status into an engineering procedure similar to the analog computer.

The initial introduction of a new product is a particularly advantageous stage for utilization of automated design engineering. The design logic is fresh and easily captured. It can in fact be developed with a computerized system in mind. There is no background of historical results with which the new system must cope. In particular, the system can be designed to handle automatically future additions to engineered products.

The experience gained by Butodale in implementing and operating the automated system will be of great value in future expansions to other product lines.

The second area for expansion is to extend the boundaries of the system to include many of the functions now performed in manufacturing, engineering, order control, and scheduling.

In addition to the above, there are other types of applications which, while not a part of an ADE/BUT System, are its logical outgrowths. One such is an inventory system that could be used with the ADE/BUT System. Other possibilities exist in the financial and accounting control areas.

It is likely that there are other areas of management in which the computer sophistication and system analysis ability gained by Butodale personnel will be profitably used in the future.

21

Stages 2 and 3: Implementation and Operation

21.1 RELATIONSHIP OF THE THREE STAGES

The three stages in the life cycle of a system—study and design, implementation, and operation—are repeated in Figure 21-1. We have now covered Stage 1 in detail. This final chapter will provide an overview of Stages 2 and 3. Although each has its own characteristics and methods, no one stage can be considered independently of the others. The three stages are interdependent and require coordination of the study team, the implementation team, and the operating personnel if they are to accomplish the goals set for the system.

After reviewing and approving the new system proposal, management may want the plan implemented immediately. However, a hastily installed system may well encounter difficulties and fail to accomplish its objectives as defined in the study and design stage. Careful planning and control are required for proper systems installation and operation, and the balance of this chapter provides an overview and discusses some of the more critical points of installing and operating a system.

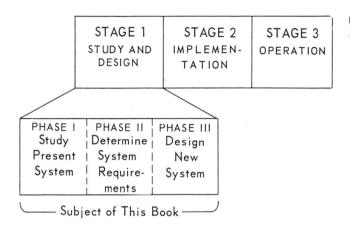

Figure 21-1   The development of a system.

21.2 RESPONSIBILITY FOR INSTALLATION AND OPERATION

Signing a lease or purchase agreement with a computer manufacturer for a set of equipment puts the responsibility for its installation and operation not with the manufacturer but with the user. The system belongs to the company. The company must live with the system, and the employees of the company must install, operate, and maintain it. Management therefore must designate those personnel who will be responsible for the installation and operation stages.

The physical site for the computer installation must also be designated by management. Power requirements, floor loads, air conditioning, and space for programming and operating personnel are factors in determining the physical site.

The equipment manufacturer can assist the company in personnel selection criteria and physical site requirements. But he should only be looked to for advice, guidance, and teaching.

21.3 PERSONNEL REQUIREMENTS

The most important personnel decision made by management is the selection of the individual who will be responsible for the installation and operation of the system. This person will also direct the computer department in converting additional applications to the equipment. (In a large facility there may be different managers involved in these two roles.)

Requirements for this position usually include a degree in business administration, engineering, or one of the sciences. In addition to the educational requirements, the person selected must have creative ability and drive. He must also be able to deal with management and supervisory personnel because it is he who will provide the primary liaison between the computer department and the other departments of the company. As additional applications are converted to the computer, this position of system manager becomes increasingly important, and in many companies he becomes one of the key management personnel.

The system manager may be either the leader of the study team or one of its members, or a present employee of the company, or he may be hired from outside. There are advantages and disadvantages to both the internal and the external source.

A present employee has knowledge of the company's operations and policies, but often must be trained in computer techniques. A new employee will be hired for his training and experience in the use of computers, but he will have to be indoctrinated in the operations and polices of the company. Whichever source is used, management must realize that the position requires the full efforts of the individual and that he must receive the complete support of company management.

The source of programming and operating personnel may also pose a problem to management. If present company employees can be made available for these positions, the equipment manufacturer may advise tests to evaluate their ability to perform programming and operating duties. If present employees are not available or not capable, then new employees must be hired. Assistance in locating qualified applicants can usually best be obtained through the company's personnel office or through personnel agencies. Many agencies now specialize in computer personnel and can generally supply lists of qualified applicants.

If company personnel are to be trained in programming and operating the equipment, the manufacturer may provide classroom teaching and home study courses. Sufficient time must be allotted for such training since programming personnel may spend several months in training before writing any programs for the new system.

Other personnel, such as department managers and supervisors whose work will be affected by the new system, should also be educated in the concepts of computers and data processing. Seminars for this purpose can usually be provided by the equipment manufacturer, by management associations, by consultants, or by universities. Proper indoctrination of this group of company personnel is important for the successful installation and operation of the system. These are the people who will supervise the preparation of the input for the system and will receive and use its output. The installation of a computer sometimes causes this group concern as to the future of their jobs or that the new system will disrupt their ability to carry out their jobs successfully. These concerns can be eliminated, or at least reduced, through proper education and communication.

21.4   STAGE 2: IMPLEMENT AND INSTALL

The second stage—implement and install—in the life cycle of a business system includes: detailed system design, file design, programming and documentation, developing test criteria, testing, parallel operation, and converting to the new system. The time and effort required for each of these steps will vary from one system to another. Each step is important and all are interrelated.

Figure 21-2 shows the sequence of steps and the feedback paths from one step to one or more other steps. These feedback paths are an important part of implementation and are discussed in the following sections in conjunction with the steps that generate the feedback.

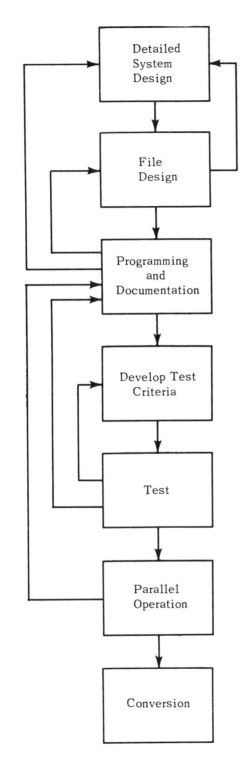

Figure 21-2   Sequence and feed-back of steps in Stage 2.

Feedback
Paths

21.5   DETAILED SYSTEM DESIGN AND FILE DESIGN

Detailed system design includes precise definitions of the logic required to control the flow of data through the system. The flow of data is in turn dependent upon the design of the files. These two steps are closely associated and must be considered in conjunction with the type of equipment that will perform the processing. Computer storage capacity, input and output media, and access methods (sequential, random, or indexed) are critical factors in these two steps. The record and file contents defined during Phase III are used to establish the basic logical flow of the data.

Systems flow diagrams, program flowcharts, and record layouts are outputs from these two steps. The sequence of processing each record in every file is defined by the flowcharts. The character-by-character contents of every record are specified by the record layouts. The flowchart for each program, together with the layouts of the files which are inputs to and outputs from the program, are used by the programmer during the programming and documentation steps.

A complete review of the total flow of data through the system is desirable before the programming step begins. This is because a change in record layout or processing in one program may affect one or more other programs. Thus, there is considerable feedback within the steps of detailed system design and file design. However, as one program is designed—input, process, output—it may be passed on for programming before all programs are defined. If this is done, any changes in processing or record layouts which affect the "upstream" programs already passed on to progamming must be made in these programs. No single rule can be applied to all cases and the judgment of the individual controlling the implementation stage must be called upon.

File design is less difficult if a system is being converted from one automated medium to another and if the file structure and content are to remain similar. Thus, if a system has been operating in a card-processing computer environment, the record contents may be fairly well-defined from past experience. If the same basic system is to be converted to a tape-processing system, the tape record layouts can be simply an aggregation of known card layouts. The combining of the records into files will change because of the change in medium. Available space should be left in the records wherever possible for future additions to the system.

When the new system is being installed to automate a manual system, or because a card-processing system is inadequate, record redesign will require more attention. The meaning of and need for each character should be clearly defined and reviewed with operating department personnel so that all required information is available in the system.

21.6   PROGRAMMING AND DOCUMENTATION

During the programming and documentation steps the program specifications developed in the preceding steps are followed to prepare instructions for the computer and to record pertinent information about each program. Instructions for the computer may be written in one of several languages, depending upon the type of program (business or scientific), abilities of the programmers, and the availability of the language for the equipment configuration. Scientific programs are usually written in Fortran, Algol, or PL/I. Business data processing programs can be written in Cobol, assembly language, report program generator, or PL/I. Languages such as Fortran, Algol, Cobol, and PL/I are best suited to magnetic tape and/or disk input-output configurations with sufficient high-speed storage for compilation. Thus, a small configuration using only cards and a printer for input-output may be confined to only one or two languages at the report program generator and assembly language level.

Regardless of the programming language used, it is extremely important that each program be properly documented. Information about each program should be recorded in a standardized format and collected into a file folder, a loose-leaf binder, or some other device for keeping the material together. Items which should be included in the documentation are:

1. A narrative description of each run or module, briefly describing its inputs, outputs, and functions.
2. Equipment operating instructions for setting up and executing the program.
3. Samples of all printouts produced.
4. A flowchart of the logic of the program.
5. Source and object program listings.
6. Record layouts of all files which are input to or output from the run or module.
7. A list of all constants in the program which require periodic updating (for example, the FICA rate) and the procedure for changing them.
8. A description of any tables used by the program and the method by which they can be updated.

Much of the documentation can be incorporated into the program through the use of "comments." Almost all programming systems provide for the entering of notations in the source program. These notes or comments are not steps in the program but are useful in providing required documentation. As an example, a comments line at the beginning of a program could state that the program contains the FICA rate which should be checked every January 1 for possible change. The line in the program which contains the FICA rate as a constant can be preceded or followed by comments describing the constant and how it can be changed.

Comments lines in the source program are one of the most valuable and most practical methods of program documentation. The comments remain with the source program and are printed in all source program listings and usually in object program listings. Thus, each time the program is assembled or compiled a new listing is automatically prepared, including comments. The comments, of course, must be updated as changes are made to the program or they will lose their value.

The use of *documentation standards* within the organization facilitates the preparation, communication, interpretation, and maintenance of the documentation. These standards include record layouts, printer layouts, flowchart symbols, operating instructions format, and the use of comments within the programs. Use of automatic flowcharting techniques is also helpful in preparing and maintaining good program documentation.

Since a complete system will include at least some manual operations, the procedures for them must be prepared and documented. These procedures for people are the equivalent of the program for the computer. Narrative, flowchart, and decision-table formats may be used for documenting these procedures. Samples of completed forms and computer input and output should be included in the procedures to give them more meaning for operating personnel reference.

Figure 21-2 shows a feedback from the programming and documentation steps to the detailed systems design and file design steps. This feedback results from changes which may be brought to light during the programming of the computer runs. The changes may affect operations logic, data flow, and file design. When such changes are made, it is important to check all other program segments to determine if they are affected by the change. Feedback at this time is not unusual and assists in developing refinements in the system.

21.7 DEVELOPING TEST CRITERIA AND TESTING

Testing the system consists of: (1) testing each program independently, and (2) testing all the programs of the system by processing sets of data through all the programs.

Each program may test perfectly by itself but still not be compatible with the other programs in the system. This can be due to inconsistencies in record layout or errors in logical dependency of one program on another.

Developing criteria and data which will test every combination of operations in the system under all possible conditions is usually an impossible task. Even when the system serves only one activity of the company, the integration of operations is typically complex and a set of inputs that will trigger all possible combinations of operations will be difficult to establish. As the number of activities that the system is to serve increases, the possible combinations of operations increases geometrically and the difficulty of developing comprehensive test criteria and data increases accordingly.

Test data may be created so that it will test all reasonable combinations of operations. Rather than creating artificial test data, it may be better to obtain real data in a machine-readable medium from previous application history.

Actual data on punched cards could serve as test data for a new system using the same information but operating on a computer with magnetic tape or disk storage. The data in the cards will probably not be in the same format as that required for the new system, but it can easily be edited into such formats through file-modification programs. Test data may also be obtained from simulation programs which imitate the external environment.

It may be desirable to test a program or the system in sections. Thus, in a complex program the programmer may prepare data to test only one module or a key group of operations. When these operations are judged as performing correctly, another set of operations can be tested. The same method can be applied to testing the system. A group of two or more programs can be tested to verify that the processing from one program to another is compatible and according to requirements. When tests on this initial group of programs are satisfactory, one or more additional programs can be added to the test. The expansion of the test group continues until the complete system has been tested. In all tests the results must be carefully audited to assure that the system performs as it was designed to perform.

As shown in Figure 21-2 the test step can generate a feedback to the development of test criteria and to programming. If the test data does not contain the combinations to test the operations for which it was developed, then additional or different test data is required. The testing process will usually develop few changes in programming and file design. If the testing process indicates many changes in programming, file design, or detailed system design, then more careful management planning and control are needed for the design and programming process.

21.8 PARALLEL OPERATION

The parallel operation step is a continuation of the testing process but uses real data generated currently by the system. The full system may be operated in parallel or it may be desirable to execute all of the operations on only a portion of the system. As an example, one product at a time of the full product line may be processed in parallel. When parallel operation on the one product is proven correct, additional products can be added to the parallel test. As another example, if a company installs a system to perform route accounting, it may test in parallel using only eight or ten routes of the total number of routes. If the sample group of routes is handled correctly by the system, additional routes may be added to the test, or all the routes may then be converted to the new system. When only a portion of a system is to be operated in parallel, the selected portion should be as representative of the full system as possible.

During parallel operation the performance and outputs of the new system are compared with the performance and outputs of the existing system. These comparisons may indicate errors in the new system and cause feedback to previous steps as shown in Figure 21-2. If errors are detected, something (programming, file design, system design) must be changed to correct the condition. It is not unusual to detect some errors during parallel operation, but the cause of the error should be easily corrected. If the previous steps are well done and coordinated, serious errors or omissions will not be found during testing.

Although parallel operation is highly desirable for testing any system, several factors must be considered. Some of these are:

1. The new system usually produces outputs that the existing system does not, or could not, produce, thus making direct comparison difficult.

2. The inputs to the new system may be radically different from those of the existing system, requiring additional care in making comparisons. Because of the different inputs to the old and new systems, separate controls may have to be maintained and reconciled.

3. The cost of the parallel operation may be high since it is a duplicate effort.

4. Parallel operation should be continued for a limited time only. During parallel operation the operating personnel continue to depend upon the existing system. The availability of the existing system may discourage rapid conversion to the new system. Therefore, parallel operation should be continued only until some preset level of performance is attained.

21.9   CONVERSION TO THE NEW SYSTEM

The final step in the implementation stage is full conversion to the new system. This step may take days, weeks, or months. The required time is dependent upon:

1. The volume of existing records that must be converted to the new system.
2. The medium of the existing records. Converting punched-card records to magnetic tape or disk is normally not too difficult since the conversion can be performed by machines. However, converting from manual records to a computer medium can be an extensive task.
3. The people and equipment available to perform the conversion. Recording manual records in machine readable form may require additional personnel and equipment.
4. The need to convert the existing records. Management may decide that it is important only to place new records in the new system and convert the existing records slowly, or not at all. This approach minimizes or eliminates the conversion step.

The primary difficulty in converting is that business must continue while the conversion takes place. The records being converted must, customarily, be available to operating personnel. The most practical approach to conversion is to convert existing records in controllable units or groups which can be temporarily frozen while conversion takes place. Accounting controls on the conversion groups should be established to insure that they are correctly recorded in the new system. Special programs are usually required for validating the converted records before entering them into the files of the new system.

Personnel, customers, vendors, stockholders, and others who may be affected by the conversion of the existing records should be advised of the change. If the payroll application is being converted, employees should be notified of the change; if billing or accounts receivable records are being converted, customers should be notified; if purchasing or accounts payable records are being converted, vendors should be notified. Notification to affected parties may not always be necessary, but the value of such notification should be examined for each conversion.

The conversion schedule and procedures should be defined and agreed to early in the installation stage. If the volume of records to be converted is large, a special conversion team is desirable. The team can test existing files for completeness and, if the same data is available from one or more existing files, the team can recommend which data should be secured from which file.

If the existing files do not contain all the data desired for the new system (because the data for all new records entering the system has been expanded), a decision must be made as to the value of obtaining such data for the existing records. If the existing files are highly volatile, so that the life of a given record is short, then it may not be necessary to convert them at all.

Some companies have taken the approach of not converting any existing records until the new system is completely satisfactory using only new records as input. This approach is good if there is no relationship between new records and existing records, and if space and personnel permit two systems to be operating at the same time.

Regardless of the method used, conversion is usually a difficult task and often is not given enough consideration by the analysts or by management. Frequently, poor conversion techniques are the cause of dissatisfaction by employees, customers, and others who are affected by the new system.

21.10   STAGE 3: OPERATE, EVALUATE, MODIFY, AND MAINTAIN

The third stage—operate, evaluate, modify, maintain—in the life cycle of a business system is concerned with the day-to-day use of the system. Effective use of the system requires coordination amongst the many departments that participate in the system completely or partially.

Figure 21-3 shows the relationship of management, the computer department, and three operating departments labelled A, B, and C. The solid lines represent authority and control and the dotted lines represent coordination. The need for this coordination and the means by which it can be achieved is discussed in the following sections in conjunction with the more important details of each step in stage three.

21.11   SYSTEMS OPERATION: SCHEDULING

The operation of a computer-based system consists of the computer department functions plus the computer-related functions of the departments supplying input to the computer and using the output from the computer. The operation of the system should be considered as a production function. As in any production function, scheduling is of prime importance. Complete system scheduling consists of: (1) scheduling the computer and its related equipment, and (2) coordinating the computer room schedule with the work flow to and from the operating departments.

Scheduling within the computer room should begin with a monthly or weekly schedule showing the time of each unit of equipment necessary to achieve the processing required. When the system is first installed, this schedule can be developed from time estimates based on testing and parallel operation. The schedule can be refined as experience is gained in daily operation. It will usually require some day-by-day adjustment but a predetermined weekly or monthly schedule does establish a basic framework of equipment needs.

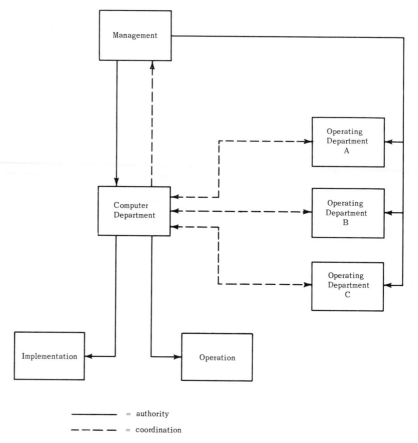

————— = authority

– – – – = coordination

Figure 21-3   Relationship of the computer department to management and the operating departments.

The schedule should include known periodic jobs which are performed only quarterly, semiannually, or annually. As an example, if the computer is being used for a payroll application, additional time will be needed each quarter and at year-end to prepare federal and state reports. If the computer is used for a sales analysis application, there may be several quarterly reports which must be prepared and the required time for preparing these reports should be recognized in the schedule.

The second factor in sound scheduling is coordination with the operating departments. When several departments supply data to the computer (and this is often the case), the scheduling of the receipt of data from the departments must be established and adhered to. The computer department cannot meet its own internal schedule if the data input schedule is not met.

Thus, if payroll checks are to be prepared by the computer on, say, Wednesday morning, all data for check preparation must be ready by that time. Input data, such as hours worked by each employee, rate changes, new hires, changes in deductions, and so on, must be proven and available at check-preparation time. If the system is such that this input data must be processed through one or more programs for proof and validation, then that processing should be scheduled sufficiently in advance to permit the results to be reviewed and corrected by the payroll department. Since the input data cannot be processed through the proof and validation programs until it is in machine-readable form, the conversion to machine medium must be completed according to schedule.

The best sequence of work flow which will facilitate meeting desired schedules can be established by the use of critical path techniques. Even an unsophisticated schedule network may reveal points of delay in the work flow and assist in making necessary changes. Whenever possible the overall schedule should allow some slack time for difficulties which may and do occur.

One method of encouraging proper coordination in scheduling between the computer department and the operating departments is to have the manager or supervisor of computer operations meet with the managers or supervisors of the operating departments to review the schedule for the coming week. Any anticipated delays by the operating departments or by the computer department can be discussed and adjustments in the schedule agreed to by all concerned. Management itself may be responsible for anticipated delays because it may choose to not close the period until certain transactions are recorded. Depending upon the structure of the system, considerable processing may be delayed until these transactions are processed.

As can be understood from this discussion, the proper scheduling of the operations of the system can be complex and may involve many departments. The dotted lines between the computer department and the operating departments, and between the computer department and management shown in Figure 21-3 represent the coordination needed to develop and attain desired schedules.

21.12   SYSTEMS OPERATION: PERSONNEL AND PROCEDURES

The basic personnel complement for computer room operations is one or more equipment operators. The total number of personnel needed depends upon the type and amount of equipment and the number of effective processing hours required. A system using a computer having only card input and card and printer output will usually require card sorters and collators. Operators are needed for the sorting and collating equipment as well as for the computer. A similar system using magnetic tape or disk files to accomplish the sorting and collating functions may require fewer operators. A one-shift operation will, of course, require less personnel than a two- or three-shift operation.

Standardized operating procedures should be defined for the equipment operators. The data-handling procedures for each program should be prepared in a format easily followed by the operators. A manual of instructions for data handling for each program is initially developed during the programming and documentation step of stage two. These instructions can be modified and amplified, if need be, by the manager or supervisor of computer operations. The equipment manufacturer can usually assist in the preparation of operating procedures by supplying forms designed for ease in recording such procedures.

An important part of the procedures for computer operations is the control system, which is established for checking computer output. In smaller installations the computer-room supervisor may maintain such controls. In larger installations one or more control clerks may be designated to perform this duty. In either case, the primary controls should be established by the operating department for whom the processing is performed. Thus, if the computer is used in an accounts receivable application, the total accounts receivable balance to which the statements prepared by the computer should agree can best be determined by the accounts receivable department.

When the computer total for a given report does not agree with the control established by the operating department, the reasons for the difference should be determined as soon as possible. Differences between the computer total and the operating department control may cause a delay in further processing of the data and thus cause exceptions to the predetermined schedule.

The coordination needed to facilitate balancing to established controls is expressed in Figure 21-3 by the dotted lines between the computer department and the operating departments.

21.13 EVALUATING AND MODIFYING THE SYSTEM

The evaluation of the system is performed by management, or by supervisory personnel who have day-to-day contact with the system, or by technical specialists who are effective systems auditors. Minor changes may be proposed that will significantly improve the efficiency of the system after it is in operation. Desired changes are made by the implementation or systems maintenance personnel. Extreme care is needed to be sure that changes which improve one portion of the system do not harm other portions. The efficiency analysis should continue over the life of the system until it is decided that the system needs to be replaced for economic or technical reasons.

Factors included in the evaluation of the system include cost, throughput speed, usefulness of output, and ability of the operating departments to work with the system. Minor changes in data flow or equipment may have a significant effect in reducing cost, and in improving throughput. Changes in report format may easily improve the usefulness of the output. Additional education and indoctrination of operating department personnel may improve their ability to work with the system. The system should not be drastically changed or abandoned until minor changes are made and their total effect evaluated.

21.14 MAINTAINING THE SYSTEM

Maintenance contributes significantly to the continued usefulness of the system. A system may be judged as operating poorly simply because it has not been properly maintained. The frequently heard comment, "The machine goofed," can usually be traced to lack of, or incorrect, system maintenance. For example, incorrect invoices may be prepared by the computer not because of any machine malfunction, but because the program was not changed to reflect a change in a sales tax rate. The change may have required only changing one constant in the program; but if it is not changed, or if it is changed improperly, all computations using this factor will be incorrect.

System maintenance is usually performed by assigned implementation or maintenance personnel who are thoroughly familiar with the system. Major system maintenance may require the assistance of additional programmers and complete testing to be sure that the changes are made accurately without disturbing the successful operation of the system.

Flexibility incorporated into the initial system design can greatly facilitate system maintenance. As an example, consider an application which includes the preparation of a sales analysis with a description of each product sold. The input to the program which produces the sales analysis report may contain only the code of each product and not the description. The description for each product can be obtained during the processing through the program from descriptions included in the program as constant information. Each time a new product is added, a change in the program must be made. If a table of product codes and descriptions is used in place of various constants, the table can be updated independently and the new product handled without any changes in the program itself.

Another important factor in facilitating system maintenance is proper program documentation. It is never known when a program may have to be changed to effect system maintenance. The time allotted for the change may be brief and even the programmer who originally wrote the program may have difficulty in locating the instructions or routine which should be changed. Good documentation will greatly assist in locating the area to be changed. If at the time of writing the original program it is known that changes will be required from time to time, then comments can be included in the program explaining how a change can be made.

System maintenance may also include the writing of new programs to prepare additional reports. A change in company policy, federal or state law, or in management personnel may make additional reports necessary. Thus, a new member of the sales or marketing staff may be well satisfied with existing reports but may also have definite and specific requirements for additional information from the system. The raw data may be available in the system with only one or two program modules required to prepare the desired additional report.

21.15   RETURN TO STAGE 1

A system that operates for any long period of time may be subjected to so many modifications and severe maintenance that Stage 1—study and design—in the life cycle of a business system should again be undertaken. The existing system must, of course, continue to operate during the new study and design stage. Fortunately, the experience gained during the life of the existing system will be of great value in determining the requirements of the next generation system. The life of a system can seldom be accurately predicted and the cycle of study and design, implement and install, operate, evaluate and maintain, study and design, and so on, continues indefinitely. Even if the organization is absorbed by another organization, the life cycle of the system will continue, if only as a subsystem of a larger system in the new organization.

SUMMARY

After the new system plan is approved, the normal course of events is to execute the implementation plan as originally developed by the analysts who designed the new system. The initial positive act on the part of the company is to sign a contract for the computer and related equipment. However, the responsibility for implementing, operating, and maintaining the system remains with the company. In the typical situation, it is company personnel who study the existing organization, design the new system, implement the system, operate the system, and maintain it.

The manufacturer of the equipment usually is able to provide test facilities, education in programming and computer operations, and general guidance. However, it takes a significant amount of time, effort, money, and ability in a company to install, operate, and maintain a computerized system for management or information-system processing.

During the implementation stage, documentation standards should be established, the system designed in detail, the files organized and laid out; there must be programming and documentation of the system, test data must be developed, and the system must be tested. This is followed by parallel operation and finally, conversion to the new system.

To put the new system in operation, new relationships have to be established between the affected operating departments and the computer department. Schedules have to be established for data inputs received from the operating departments and for the data outputs and reports to be sent to them. Cooperation and coordination are important ingredients in a successful system.

Eventually, the passage of time will have brought about so many changes that it will again be necessary to study the existing system and to design another one. Systems, like all aspects of nature, are born, serve a useful purpose for a while, and then die.

GLOSSARY

The technical vocabulary in the field of computers and data processing systems draws heavily on words that already exist in the English language, but often uses them with different meanings. Like the English language, the meanings are subject to change. A particular word may have one meaning in a certain place and at a certain time, but may have quite a different meaning at another place or another time. Even a group of people with similar interests may not be able to agree on the meaning of a word or term or on a method for defining the word or term.

Perhaps the most difficult problem for a noncomputer person reading a computer-related book is that some of the words and terms are defined by using expressions and concepts that are also not familiar. For this reason, some readers will find that they may have to return to certain parts of the book several times before they fully understand the technical jargon. To aid them, we present the following glossary; the reader should also refer to other sources noted in the bibliography that cover more extensively fields relating to computers. This glossary emphasizes words used in this book and defines them accordingly.

ACTIVITY   a logically related set of operations, usually self-contained with few ties to the surrounding environment; directed toward satisfying one or more fundamental business goals.

ACTIVITY REQUIREMENTS MODEL   a pictorial means of showing the relationship of required and imposed inputs, outputs, operations, and resources.

ACTIVITY SHEET   a diagram showing the flow of operations within a single activity and system characteristics such as volumes and times recorded in tabular form.

AFFECTABLE COSTS   the costs of a business which can be changed by a new system, for example, reduced personnel, waste reduction.

ALGORITHM   a set of rules, or steps pertaining to a constructive calculating process designed to lead to the solution of a problem in a finite number of steps.

ALGORITHMIC LANGUAGE   a language by which numerical procedures may be precisely presented to a computer in a standard form. The language is intended not only as a means of directly presenting any numerical procedure to any suitable computer for which a compiler exists, but also as a means of communicating numerical procedures among individuals.

ALPHAMERIC   a generic term for alphabetic letters, numerical digits, and special characters which are machine-processable. Synonymous with alphanumeric.

ANALOG COMPUTER   a computer which represents variables by physical analogies. Thus, any computer which solves problems by translating physical conditions such as flow, temperature, pressure, angular position, or voltage into related mechanical or electrical quantities and uses mechanical or electrical equivalent circuits as an analog for the physical phenomenon being investigated. In general, it is a computer which uses an analog for each variable and produces analogs as output. Thus an analog computer measures continuously whereas a digital computer counts discretely.

ANALOG DATA   data represented in a continuous form, as contrasted with digital data represented in a discrete (discontinuous) form. Analog data is usually represented by means of physical variables such as voltage, resistance, and rotation.

ANALYSIS   the breaking up of study subjects into manageable elements for individual evaluation.

ANALYST   a person skilled in the definition of problems and the development of algorithms and logical procedures for their solution, especially methods which may be implemented on a computer.

APPLICATION   the system or problem to which a computer is applied. Reference is often made to an application as being either of the computational type, wherein arithmetic computation predominates, or the data processing type, wherein data handling operations predominate.

ARGUMENT (1) an independent variable; e.g., in looking up a quantity in a table, the number or any of the numbers which identifies the location of the desired value; or in a mathematical function the variable which, when a certain value is substituted for it, determines the value of the function. (2) An operand in an operation on one or more variables.

ASSEMBLER a computer program which operates on symbolic input data to produce, from such data, machine instructions by carrying out such functions as: translation of symbolic operation codes into computer operating instructions; assigning locations in storage for successive instructions; or computation of absolute addresses from symbolic addresses. An assembler generally translates input symbolic codes into machine instructions item for item, and produces as output the same number of instructions or constants which were defined in the input symbolic codes.

AUDIT TRAIL a system of providing a means for tracing items of data from one processing step to the next, particularly from a machine produced report or other machine output back to the original source data.

AUTOMATION (1) the implementation of processes by automatic means; (2) the theory, art or technique of making a process more automatic; (3) the investigation, design, development, and application of methods of rendering processes automatic, self-moving, or self-controlling.

BATCH PROCESSING a systems approach to processing where a number of similar input items are grouped for processing during the same machine run.

BIT contraction of "binary digit," the smallest unit of information, which is dual-state (one or zero, on or off, mark or space).

BOOLEAN ALGEBRA a process of reasoning, or a deductive system of theorems using a symbolic logic, and dealing with classes, propositions, or on-off circuit elements. It employs symbols to represent operators such as AND, OR, NOT, EXCEPT, IF . . . THEN, etc. to permit mathematical calculation. Named after George Boole. See the bibliography for a reference to Boole.

BUFFER temporary storage; usual applications are for speed conversion or parallel/serial conversion between asynchronous units.

BUSINESS GOALS in addition to making a profit and providing employment, business goals are the special contributions a business makes to its environment, e.g., the primary goal of an appliance company is to manufacture and distribute appliances.

BYTE a group of bits handled as a unit; may be a character, a part of a word, or a word.

CENTRAL PROCESSING UNIT (CPU)   (1) the unit of a computer system which contains the main storage, arithmetic unit, logical unit, and special registers. (2) All that portion of a computer exclusive of the input, output, peripheral and in some instances, storage units.

CENTRALIZED DATA PROCESSING   data processing performed at a single, central location on data obtained from several geographical locations or managerial levels. Decentralized data processing involves processing at various managerial levels or geographical points throughout the organization.

CHARACTER   one symbol of a set of elementary symbols such as those corresponding to the keys on a typewriter. The symbols usually include the decimal digits 0 through 9, the letters A through Z, punctuation marks, operation symbols, and any other single symbols which a computer may read, store, or write.

CHECKPOINT   a point in a routine at which sufficient information can be stored to permit restarting the computation from that point.

COBOL   Co-mmon B-usiness O-riented L-anguage. (1) A data processing language that makes use of English-like statements. (2) Pertaining to a computer program which translates a Cobol language source program into a machine language object program.

CODE   a set of unique bit combinations assigned to represent characters.

COMMUNICATION   the process of transferring information from one point, person, or equipment to another.

COMPILER   a computer program more powerful than an assembler. In addition to its translating function which is generally the same process as that used in an assembler, it is able to replace certain items of input with routines. Thus, where most assemblers translate item for item, and produce as output the same number of instructions or constants which were put into them, compilers will do more than this. The program which results from compiling is a translated and expanded version of the original.

CONTROLLABLE UNIT   a set or group of existing records that are conveniently handled as a unit during conversion in such a way that conversion controls can be maintained and with minimal interruptions to the existing system.

CONVERSION   (1) the process of changing information from one form of representation to another; such as, from the language of one type of machine to that of another or from magnetic tape to the printed page. Synonymous with data conversion. (2) The process of changing from one data processing method to another or from one type of equipment to another; e.g., conversion from punch card equipment to magnetic tape equipment.

CPM (CRITICAL PATH METHOD)   is similar to, but differs technically from PERT. CPM is concerned primarily with time and cost and does not consider the problem of uncertainty of time for each activity. The terminology of CPM differs from PERT, as an event in PERT is a node in CPM, and an activity in PERT is a job in CPM. A critical path is the longest path through a network.

CYBERNETICS   the field of technology involved in the comparative study of the control and intracommunication of information handling machines and nervous systems of animals and man in order to understand and improve communication.

DATA   a general term used to denote any or all facts, numbers, letters and symbols, or facts that refer to or describe an object, idea, condition, situation, or other factors. It connotes basic elements of information which can be processed or produced by a computer. Sometimes data is considered to be expressible only in numerical form, while information is not so limited.

DATA PROCESSING   (1) the preparation of source media which contain data or basic elements of information, and the handling of such data according to precise rules of procedure to accomplish such operations as classifying, sorting, calculating, summarizing, and recording. (2) The production of records and reports.

DATA PROCESSING CENTER   a computer installation providing data processing service for others, sometimes called customers, on a reimbursable or nonreimbursable basis.

DATA PROCESSING SYSTEM   a network of machine components capable of accepting information, processing it according to a plan, and producing the desired results.

DEBUG   to detect, locate, and remove mistakes from a program or malfunctions from a computer.

DECISION TABLE   a graphical method for displaying the cause-and-effect relationship in systems logic. A means of relating conditions and actions through decision rules.

DETAIL FILE   a file of information which is relatively transient. This is contrasted with a master file which contains relatively more permanent information; e.g., in the case of weekly payroll for hourly employees, the detail file will contain employee number, the hours the employee has worked in a given week, both regular and overtime, and other such information that changes weekly. The master file will contain the employee's name, number, department, rate of pay, deduction specifications, and other information which regularly stays the same from week to week.

DIGITAL COMPUTER   a computer which processes information represented by combinations of discrete or discontinuous data as compared with an analog computer for continuous data. More specifically, it is a device for performing sequences of arithmetic and logical operations, not only on data but on its own program. Still more specifically it is a stored program digital computer capable of performing sequences of internally stored instructions, as opposed to calculators, on which the sequence is impressed manually.

DISK STORAGE   a storage device which uses magnetic recording on flat rotating disks.

DOCUMENT   (1) a form, voucher, or written evidence of a transaction; (2) to cite references; (3) to substantiate, as by listing of authorities.

DOCUMENTATION   the group of techniques necessary for the orderly presentation, organization, and communication of recorded specialized knowledge, in order to maintain a complete record of reasons for changes in variables. Documentation is necessary not so much to give maximum utility as to give an unquestionable historical reference record. Documentation records decision logic, program reference information, and data structure.

DRUM STORAGE   a storage device which uses magnetic recording on a rotating cylinder. A type of addressable storage associated with some computers.

ENVIRONMENT   that part of a business outside the scope of the study, but which influences the business. Included in the environment are items such as competitors, geographical considerations, market status, and customer attitudes.

EXPLOSION   a method in which required inputs, resources, and operations are defined from a statement of required outputs. The term is most frequently applied to computer programs that perform the parts requirements calculations in a manufacturing environment.

EXTERNAL STORAGE   a storage device outside the computer which can store information in a form acceptable to the computer, e.g., cards, tapes.

FEEDBACK   the part of a closed loop system which automatically brings back information about the condition of the variable being controlled.

FIELD   an assigned area in a record to be filled with information.

FILE   a collection of related records treated as a unit, e.g., in inventory control, one line of an invoice forms an item, a complete invoice forms a record, and a set of records forms a file. In general, an organized collection of information directed toward some purpose. The records may or may not be in sequence.

FILE MAINTENANCE   the processing or periodic modification of a file to effect changes in the file which occurred during a given period; for example, updating a master file.

FILE SHEET   a form used to support the operation sheet which describes a collection of messages or an information file.

FLOWCHART   a series of symbols connected by lines to demonstrate a sequence of events and decisions.

FORTRAN   For-mula Tran-slating System. A data processing language that closely resembles mathematical notation.

GANTT CHART   a method of showing scheduling requirements in chart form. The method was developed by Henry L. Gantt prior to World War I. In a typical Gantt chart the time required for completion of each step of a process is expressed as a bar across a sheet with the length of the bar denoting the total time required for the step. This method quickly shows overlapping steps. Prior to the development of PERT the Gantt chart was the basic method of expressing scheduling times. Gantt charts are still widely used in many ways.

GENERAL SECTION   this section of the phase I report describes the environment in which the business operates, and the position of the business in that environment.

GENERALIZED ROUTINE   a routine designed to process a large range of specific jobs within a given type of application.

GENERIC SYSTEM DESCRIPTION   the logical flow of information and the logical operations necessary to carry out a particular design without regard to equipment required to perform the task.

GOALS   those contributions (usually products or services) an organization wishes to make to its environment. Goals define the purpose and objectives of the organization.

HARDWARE   the physical equipment or devices forming a computer and peripheral units.

HIGH-SPEED PRINTER   a printer which operates at a speed more compatible with the speed of computation and data processing so that it may operate on-line. At the present time a printer operating at a speed of at least 600 lines per minute, with 100 characters per line is considered high speed.

IMPLEMENTATION   the process of taking a system design and making it perform the tasks specified in the design and meeting the measurement criteria.

IMPLEMENTATION PLAN   a description of the steps of installing the new system with cost and time schedules involved.

IMPROVEMENT STUDY   a study with the objective of strengthening an existing system by improving operating methods, providing better output from the system, and generally increasing the overall efficiency of the system.

INFORMATION   a collection of facts or other data especially as derived from the processing of data. Often used in a broader sense than data.

INFORMATION PROCESSING   a less restrictive term than data processing, encompassing the totality of scientific and business operations performed by a computer.

INFORMATION RETRIEVAL   the recovering of desired information or data from a collection of documents, or other records.

INLINE PROCESSING   the processing of data in random order, not subject to preliminary arranging, sorting, or batching.

INPUT   (1) information or data transferred or to be transferred from an external storage medium into the internal storage of the computer, (2) describing the routines which direct input as defined in (1) or the devices from which such information is available to the computer, (3) the device or collection of devices necessary for input as defined in (1).

INPUT-OUTPUT   a general term for the equipment used to provide information for, and accept it from, the computer. The actual data flowing into and out of a system.

INPUT-OUTPUT SHEET   a summary form used in Phase II to record the required input and output characteristics. Message sheets can be used for supporting material if more detail is required.

INQUIRY   a request for information from storage, e.g., a request for the number of available airline seats, or a machine statement to initiate a search of library documents.

INTEGRATED DATA PROCESSING   (1) a system that treats as a whole all data processing requirements to accomplish a sequence of data processing steps, or a number or related data processing sequences, and which strives to reduce or eliminate duplicating data entry or processing steps. (2) The processing of data by such a system.

ITERATE   to repeatedly execute a loop or series of steps, e.g., a loop in a program.

ITERATIVE PROCESS   a process for calculating a desired result by means of a repeating cycle of operations, which comes closer and closer to the desired result.

INTERFACE   a common boundary or physical connection between automatic data processing systems or parts of a single system. May also be used for program interrelationships.

KEY   (1) a group of characters which identifies or is part of a record or item; thus any entry in a record or item can be used as a key for collating or sorting purposes. (2) A marked lever manually operated for copying a character; e.g., a typewriter, paper tape perforator, card punch, manual keyboard, digitizer or manual word generator. (3) A lever or switch on a computer console for the purpose of manually altering computer action.

KEYPUNCH   (1) a special device to record information in cards or paper tape by punching holes in the cards or tape to represent letters, digits, and special characters; (2) to operate a device for punching holes in cards or tape.

LANGUAGE   a system for representing and communicating information or data between people, or between people and machines. Such a system consists of a carefully defined set of characters and rules for combining them into larger units, such as words or expressions, and rules for word arrangement or usage to achieve specific meanings.

LINEAR PROGRAMMING   a technique of mathematics used in operations research for solving certain kinds of problems involving many variables where a best value or set of best values is to be found. Linear programming is only feasible when the quantity to be optimized, sometimes called the objective function, can be stated as a mathematical expression in terms of the various activities within the system, and when this expression is simply proportional to the measure of the activities; i.e., is linear, and when all the restrictions are also linear.

LOGIC   (1) the science dealing with the criteria or formal principles of reasoning and thought. (2) The systematic scheme which defines the interactions of signals in the design of an automatic data processing system. (3) The basic principles and application of truth tables and interconnection between logical elements required for arithmetic computation in an automatic data processing system.

LOGICAL DECISION   the choice or ability to choose between alternatives. Basically this amounts to an ability to answer yes or no with respect to certain fundamental questions involving equality and relative magnitude; for example, in an inventory application, it is necessary to determine whether or not there has been an issue of a given stock item.

LOGICAL DESIGN   (1) the planning of a data processing system prior to its detailed engineering design. (2) The synthesizing of a network of logical elements to perform a specified function. (3) The result of (1) and (2), frequently called the logic of a computer or of a data processing system.

MAGNETIC DISK   a storage device on which information is recorded on the magnetizable surface of a rotating disk. A magnetic disk storage system is an array of such devices, with associated reading and writing heads which are mounted on movable arms.

MAIN FRAME   the main part of the computer, that is, the arithmetic or logic unit. The central processing unit.

MANAGEMENT ABSTRACT   a synopsis of the Stage 1 study for management evaluation, describing the proposal concisely but complete with background material on the current system and requirements for the new system.

MARK-SENSE   to mark a position on a punched card or other specially designed form with an electrically conductive pencil, for later sensing by machines.

MASTER DATA   a set of data which is altered infrequently and supplies basic data for processing operations. The data content of a master file. Examples include: names, badge numbers, or pay rates in personnel data; or stock numbers, stock descriptions, or units of measure in stock control data.

MASTER FILE   a file containing relatively permanent information.

MATHEMATICAL MODEL   a mathematical representation of a process, device, or concept.

MEASUREMENT   various criteria for evaluating system performance, such as time, reliability, accuracy, cost, efficiency, etc. comprise a means of system measurement. The way in which a future system is to be measured is established in Phase II before it is designed.

MECHANIZATION STUDY   a study in which the objective is to duplicate by machine certain operations that are being performed by other methods.

MESSAGE   (1) a group of words, variable in length, transported as a unit; (2) a transported item of information; (3) any communication of information, formal document, informal letter, or oral statement.

MESSAGE SHEET   a form used to support the operation sheet which provides information about system inputs and outputs.

METHODOLOGY   a science or method of accomplishing a specialized task.

MODEL   a representation of something to be made or already existing. A model may be physical, schematic, or mathematical. A mathematical model is a formula selected as a representation of a social or natural law. For business purposes, mathematical models are used to explain or predict changes in a system. Mathematical models are the foundation for simulating a system on a computer. Physical models include prototype machines, factory mock-ups, and so on. Schematic models include flow diagrams, PERT networks, systems flow-charts, and so on.

MODULE (1) an interchangeable plug-in item containing components, (2) an incremental block of storage or other building block for expanding the computer capacity, (3) the input to, or output from, a single execution of an assembler, compiler, or linkage editor; a source, object, or load module; hence, a program unit that is discrete and identifiable with respect to compiling, combining with other units, and loading.

MONTE CARLO METHOD any procedure that involves random sampling techniques in order to obtain a probabilistic approximation to the solution of a mathematical or physical problem.

MULTICOMPUTING two or more system control processors each operating as an independent computer system but with the capability of directly communicating between their respective memories; also called a shared-memory system.

MULTIPLEX the process of transferring data from several storage devices operating at relatively low transfer rates to one storage device operating at a high transfer rate in such a manner that the high-speed device is not obliged to wait for the low-speed devices.

MULTIPROCESSOR a system or machine complex with multiple arithmetic and logic units for simultaneous use.

MULTIPROGRAMMING multiple object programs, residing in a single system core memory, that are alternately executed by a processor to gain greater throughput through simultaneous input, output, and processor operations.

NETWORK a system of connected points—for example, terminals connected by communications channels and some form of exchange. Also used in CPM and PERT to describe the arrangements of tasks.

OFFLINE descriptive of a system and of the peripheral equipment or devices in a system in which the operation of peripheral equipment is not under the control of the central processing unit.

ONLINE descriptive of a system and of the peripheral equipment or devices in a system in which the operation of such equipment is under control of the central processing unit; online operation is required if information reflecting current activity is to be introduced into the data processing system as it occurs. Thus, inline processing requires online peripheral equipment.

OPERATION a related set of processes which, when initiated by a trigger, converts inputs to outputs utilizing resources. An activity contains multiple operations which in turn contain multiple processes.

OPERATION SHEET describes the processing steps which make up an operation and shows the inputs, resources, and outputs in relation to the processes.

OPERATIONAL SECTION this section of the Phase I report defines activities and relates them to the established framework of the business.

OPERATIONS LOGIC the means of transforming inputs to output; a definition of the cause and effect relationship between inputs and outputs.

OPERATIONS RESEARCH the use of analytic methods adapted from mathematics for solving operational or planning problems. The objective is to provide management with a logical, mathematical basis for making sound predictions and decisions. Among the common scientific techniques used in operations research are the following: linear programming, probability theory, information theory, game theory, Monte Carlo method, and queuing theory.

OPTICAL SCANNING a technique for machine recognition of characters by their visual images.

OUTPUT (1) the information transferred from the internal storage of a computer to secondary or external storage, or to any device outside of the computer; (2) the routines which direct (1); (3) the device or collective set of devices necessary for (1); (4) to transfer from internal storage onto external media.

OVERVIEW a broad-gauge, general description of a business.

PERIPHERAL EQUIPMENT the auxiliary machines which may be placed under the control of the central computer. Examples are card readers, card punches, magnetic tape units, and high speed printers. Peripheral equipment may be used online or offline depending upon computer design, job requirements, and economics.

PERT (PROGRAM EVALUATION AND REVIEW TECHNIQUE) a management information and control system used in the planning, control, and evaluation of progress of a project. It is time oriented and uses a network usually expressed in diagram form. The network consists of events which are connected by activities. PERT was developed by the U.S. Navy for the Polaris program. The first paper discussing PERT was published in September 1959.

PLOTTER a visual display or board in which one or more variables are graphed by an automatically controlled pen or pencil.

PROCESS one of the actions taking place within an operation. Uusually describable by a single statement, e.g., "Locate information in file." or "Compile report on scrap losses."

PROCESS CONTROL pertaining to systems whose purpose is to provide automation of complex physical operations. Usually relates to continuous processes like refining and paper manufacture. Sometimes called control systems.

PROGRAM (1) the complete plan for the solution of a problem, more specifically the complete sequence of machine instructions and routines necessary to solve a problem. (2) To plan the procedures for solving a problem. This may involve, among other things, the analysis of the problem; preparation of a flow diagram; preparing detailed code, and testing; allocation of storage locations; specification of input and output formats; and incorporating a particular computer run into a larger data processing system.

PROGRAMMER a person who prepares problem solving procedures and flowcharts and who may also write and debug routines.

PUNCHED CARD a heavy stiff paper of defined size and shape, suitable for punching in a pattern that has meaning, and for being handled mechanically. The punched holes are sensed electrically by wire brushes, mechanically by metal fingers, or photoelectrically by photocells.

QUEUING a study of the patterns involved and the time required for discrete units to move through channels, e.g., the elapsed time for auto traffic at a toll booth or employees in a cafeteria line.

RANDOM ACCESS pertaining to the process of obtaining data from or placing data into storage when there is no sequential relation governing the requests. Normally this is done on devices (like disks) where the access time to storage locations is not significantly dependent on sequential reading (as it would be on magnetic tape). Also called direct access.

RATING SCALES a means of establishing targets for measurement factors. Unacceptable, acceptable, and desirable ranges of performance may be placed on some linear or other scale for later evaluation of planned or actual performance.

REAL-TIME OPERATION the use of the computer as an element of a processing system in which the times of occurrence of data transmission are controlled by other portions of the system, or by physical events outside the system, and cannot be modified for convenience in computer programming. Such an operation either proceeds at the same speed as the events being simulated or at a sufficient speed to analyze or control external events happening concurrently. This is inline processing with immediate response. Data can be handled in a sufficiently rapid manner so that the results of the processing are usefully available at the data sources. Airlines reservations, information inquiry, bank teller operations, are examples of real-time systems.

RECORD (1) a group of related facts or fields of information treated as a unit, thus a listing of information, often in printed or printable form; (2) to put data into a storage device.

REGENERATION   the concept of computing answers on demand from decision logic rather than storing massive amounts of precomputed data.

REQUIRED OPERATIONS SHEET   a summary form used in Phase II to record input, outputs, processes, and frequency information of required operations.

RESOURCE   the means of performing operations, e.g., personnel, equipment and facilities, inventories and information.

RESOURCE SHEET   a summary form used in Phase II to record the logically necessary material and informational resources.

RESOURCE USAGE SHEET   a form which, when completed, shows the organization and cost by organizational component and by activity. A summary form developed in Phase I.

ROUTINE   a sequence of machine instructions which carry out a well defined function.

RUN   the performance of one program on a computer, thus the performance of one routine, or several routines linked so that they form an automatic operating unit, during which manual manipulations by the computer operator are minimal.

SCOPE AND BOUNDARY   a description of the operations performed by an activity and a description of what is not performed.

SIMULATION   Simulation in its general meaning is the act of assuming the mere appearance of something without the reality of the thing being studied. This can be done in many ways. (1) One can construct replicas of the thing to be studied. For example, if one is studying the pickling of heavy rolls of sheet steel, he can use small rolls of cellophane tape. He can simulate the huge machines and vats needed for the real process by using small models. For the passage of time, he can use speeded-up clocks so that an eight-hour shift might be run in one hour. This method is known as physical stimulation. (2) Another method is mathematical. In this method, the variables of the system are related by mathematical equations and the system is then analyzed by manipulating these mathematical symbols. However, it is very difficult to analyze complex systems in purely symbolic terms. Furthermore, the introduction of random variables complicates the equations and makes direct analytic solution far more difficult and often impossible. (3) A third method is heuristic or logical. In this method, the analyst draws upon his background and experience and then uses his best judgment and intuition in preparing a descriptive model that can predict the behavior of the system with the passage of time. (4) A fourth method is to use a computer to play a dominant role. In this method, the mathematical and logical relations are expressed in computer programs and the random variables are introduced on a probabilistic basis. Numeric data are entered and then the computer goes through simulation runs to predict expected system behavior.

The answers from each of these methods are typically only rough guides because real systems usually involve an extremely large number of variables and parameters, many of which cannot be measured. However, computer simulation is being refined, and this method has been found to provide excellent guides to management decisions in many situations where all other methods have failed.

SOFTWARE   the totality of programs and routines used to extend the capabilities of computers, such as compilers, assemblers, application programs, and subroutines.

SOURCE DATA AUTOMATION   the many methods of recording information in coded forms on paper tapes, punched cards, or tags that can be used over and over again to produce many other records without rewriting.

SOURCE PROGRAM   a computer program written in a language designed for ease of use by people to express certain problems or procedures.

STRUCTURAL SECTION   this section of the Phase I report amplifies the description of the business in terms of inputs, outputs, and resources.

SYNTHESIS   the combining of parts or elements into an entity, requiring logical reasoning in advancing from principles and propositions to conclusions.

SYSTEM   a set of methods and procedures utilizing a combination of personnel, equipment, and facilities working to produce outputs.

SYSTEMS ANALYSIS   the examination of an activity, procedure, method, technique, or a business to determine what must be accomplished and how the necessary operations may best be accomplished.

SYSTEMS PLANNER   responsible for creating, designing and implementing systems within a business. He must have insight, understanding, imagination, determination, and effective analysis and synthesis tools to successfully complete his tasks.

SYSTEM REQUIREMENTS SPECIFICATION   a series of information packets each of which describes requirements for one activity within the business which will satisfy a business goal.

TELETYPEWRITER   descriptive name for telegraph terminal equipment.

TERMINAL UNIT   equipment on a communication channel which may be used for either input or output.

TIME SHARING   the use of a device for two or more purposes during the same overall time interval, accomplished by interspersing component actions in very short time periods. Normally implies that the computer skips from job to job without regard to whether the first job has yet been completed.

TOTAL SYSTEM   a system designed to support the primary goals of a business and closely associated with them.

TRANSACTION DATA   a set of data in a data processing area, a record of occurrence of a new event or transaction, in which the incidence of the data is essentially random and unpredictable. Hours worked, quantities shipped, and amounts invoiced are examples from, representatively, the areas of payroll, accounts receivable, and accounts payable.

TRIGGER   any phenomenon, physical or otherwise, that sets an operation in motion. Triggers may fall in any of four categories: receipt of an input, a time or frequency per unit of time, receipt of multiple inputs, or a combination of inputs and times.

TURN-AROUND TIME   the total time from job request to job delivery.

UNIFIED SYSTEMS APPROACH   the business is treated as an entity, business goals are defined and refined, and an operating system is created to satisfy and further these goals. Oriented towards goals and activities which attain goals, and not toward personnel, equipment, or organization structure.

UNIT RECORD EQUIPMENT   the machines and equipment using punch cards. The group of equipment is often called tabulating equipment because the main function of installations of punch card machines for some years before the first automatic digital computer was to produce tabulations of information resulting from sorting, listing, selecting, and totaling data on punch cards.

BIBLIOGRAPHY

In the short history of electronic computers and their application to management, administration, and scientific problems, the amount of published material has become quite extensive. We felt we could provide the best service for the reader by preparing an annotated guide to:

1. Basic books
2. Bibliographies
3. Journals and magazines
4. Glossaries.

Since any list of specific references soon goes out of date, we feel that the reader will need to continually check a selected few of the reviews, digests, and journals cited below to keep abreast of current developments in the fields of management systems and computers.

Academy of Management Journal Graduate School of Business, Indiana University, Bloomington, Indiana. From the Journal we read, "The Academy of Management is dedicated to the search for truth and the advancement of learning through free discussion and research in the field of management. The interest of the Academy lies in the theory and practice of management, both administrative and operative." The articles are written primarily by academicians and usually cover topics that would appeal to management at all levels. The articles are not quantitative and do not pertain to systems, *per se,* but certainly are valuable contributions to people in fulfilling their managerial and operational functions.

American Standard Vocabulary for Information Processing   American Standards Association, 10 East 40th Street, New York, New York, 1966. This glossary, considered by many people to be the most authoritative of its kind, was developed by committee X3 of the American Standards Association and sponsored by the Business Equipment Manufacturers Association. It is interesting to note that the chairman of this committee is Mr. Charles A. Phillips, who was also chairman of the well-known Codasyl Committee that developed Cobol. The American Standards Association has published recommended standards on several other areas of computers and data processing including a code for information interchange, flowchart symbols, Fortran, bank magnetic ink characters, and so on.

Anthony, R. N., **Planning and Control Systems: A Framework for Analysis** Harvard Graduate School of Business Administration, Boston, Massachusetts 02163, 1965. This book is of value to those who study and use planning and control systems and to management personnel in general. The book establishes a framework intended to be useful in planning, control, and operational systems. It describes the distinguishing characteristics of the main elements of the framework, and shows how failure to make these distinctions has led to mistakes in designing and using systems.

Archibald, R. D. and R. L. Villoria, **Network Based Management Systems (PERT/CPM).**   New York: John Wiley and Sons, 1967. This book is a guide to the use of PERT and CPM. It is of use to the reader who merely seeks orientation in the subject as well as to the reader who wishes to apply these techniques. Case studies, some quite detailed, illustrate PERT and CPM applied to projects ranging from the introduction of a new product to the construction of an apartment house.

Automated Design Engineering: General Information Manual   (Form E 20-8151) International Business Machines Corporation, 112 East Post Road, White Plains, New York 10601. This manual is designed to provide management personnel with a general summary of the methodology of Automated Design Engineering (ADE). It covers the engineering design process, the use of computers in engineering, an automated system in operation, and the procedure in developing an ADE system. It would be an excellent supplement for the reader, especially in reading the new system plan for Butodale in Chapter 20.

Bibliography of Data Processing Techniques   (Form F 20-8172) International Business Machines Corporation, 112 East Post Road, White Plains, New York 10601. This bibliography and associated classification system provide a means to identify selected IBM publications which, either wholly or in part, document data processing *techniques* information. There are two parts: Part I of the bibliography lists publications alphabetically within major subject classification. Part II contains abstracts of the publications in form-number sequence only.

Bibliography for Records Managers General Services Administration, National Archives and Records Service, Office of Records Management, Washington, D. C. There are thousands of departments in the Federal Government that are carried on in a decentralized manner. Most of these have various configurations of data processing equipment. The General Services Administration has the responsibility of supervising and assisting all of these separate organizations with respect to data processing. A number of years ago it inaugurated its well-known source data automation program, which is aimed at mechanizing these separate operations. The goal is systems improvement, which, according to GSA, must be preceded by system study and design. To aid their work, GSA publishes an excellent set of handbooks, which would be valuable in any organization's library. The *Bibliography* covers a wide collection of references of direct interest to people concerned with systems.

Bibliography on Simulation   (Form 320-0924-0) International Business Machines Corporation, 112 East Post Road, White Plains, New York 10601. This bibliography provides the user with an extensive list of publications in the field of simulation. Anyone desiring to get a quick review of the literature concerning simulation would do well to search through this bibliography.

Boole, George, **The Laws of Thought** New York: Dover Publications, 1961. This is the first American printing of the 1854 edition of Boole's *An Interpretation of the Laws of Thought, on which are founded The Mathematical Theories and Probabilities.* For the reader interested in Boolean algebra, this book is basic. To anyone interested in analysis, this book represents a foundation of logical reasoning.

British Commercial Computer Digest Computer Consultants Limited. G.P.O. Box No. 8, 19, Roumania Drive, Llandudno, Caerns., Britain. This *Digest* contains a comprehensive survey, especially prepared for management personnel, of business computers and related products. The *Digest* covers the following types of information about computers: availability, prices, rentals, typical operating costs, characteristics, and names of users. A code representing the publisher's opinion of the equipment is also included. In addition to the *Digest,* Computer Consultants also publish a wide range of reports and memoranda which may be purchased from them. A "Current Publications" list may be requested from the above address. Beyond these publications, Computer Consultants provides a wide range of systems design, implementation, and other services relating to computers and their use in business, industry, and research.

Bross, Irwin J., **Design for Decision** New York: The Macmillan Company, 1953. Some years ago, Dr. Bross prepared this book so that the non-mathematician could understand the meaning of statistical decision making. The book has now become the classic in its field and is possibly the most widely referenced work of its kind. All management and systems people will benefit from reading this book, whatever their work. It explains in everyday language the same procedures for decision making that are being applied to the study, design, implementation, and operation of data processing systems. The topics cover the history and nature of decision, prediction, probability, values, rules for action, operating as a decision-maker, sequential decision, data, models, sampling, measurement, statistical inference, statistical techniques, and design for decision.

Business Automation   288 Park Avenue West, Elmhurst, Illinois 60126. The contents of this magazine will appeal primarily to people in the field of computers, data processing, and systems. Each issue usually contains articles covering data processing problems from the management and systems viewpoint. One feature of interest to the directors of computer departments is the annual data processing salary survey. The magazine usually contains advertisements for computer and related hardware. Of interest also are the descriptive reviews of recently-published books. For academicians, there is a special edition each quarter containing an "Automation Educator Section" devoted to articles and information for people in the field of education mainly at the university and college level.

Canning, Richard G., Installing Electronic Data Processing Systems   New York: John Wiley and Sons, 1957. This book is an excellent guide to organizations planning to install electronic computers. The book emphasizes the physical aspects of the installation.

Cases in Data Processing: Intercollegiate Bibliography   Intercollegiate Case Clearing House, Harvard Graduate School of Business Administration, Boston, Massachusetts 02163, 1965. This bibliography contains a listing of about 90 case studies in data processing grouped into the following divisions:

1. Preliminary study. Choice of equipment. Purchase or lease.
2. Systems. Flow of information. Data needed.
3. Introduction of data processing equipment. Conversion to its use.
4. Data processing center or company.
5. Mathematical programming.
6. Simulation.
7. Other techniques. Procedures.
8. Miscellaneous applications.

For each case there is an abstract, a listing of the course and subjects covered by the case, the setting of the case, the management positions involved by the case, and a method of identification of the case. These cases are available ($.35 each or $30 per set) by writing to the address given above. Upon request, the bibliography will be supplied from the same address.

Churchill, C. W., Russell Ackoff, and E. Leonard Arnoff, **Introduction to Operations Research** New York: Wiley and Sons, 1957. In many parts of our book we mentioned the methods of statistics, operations research, and management science. The book that is generally considered the classic in this field is the one cited above. Even though it was published many years ago, it still is basic. Furthermore, the reader should have no difficulty obtaining a copy as it has had a wide acceptance and most libraries will have it. The book provides a general introduction to linear programming, queuing theory, replacement theory, and similar areas that affect management. The authors cite case histories to illustrate many of the concepts.

Communications, Computing Reviews, and **Journal of the Association for Computing Machinery** 211 East 43rd Street, New York, New York 10017. The *Journal,* published quarterly, contains research articles on the mathematical aspects of computer science and data processing. The *Journal* is designed for scientists and mathematicians. The *Communications,* published monthly, covers more applied aspects of computer science and data processing. The basic aim of *Computing Reviews* is "to furnish computer oriented persons in mathematics, engineering, the natural and social sciences, the humanities, and other fields with critical information about all current publications in any area of the computing sciences." The seven major divisions of the reviews are (1) general topics and education, (2) computing milieu, (3) applications, (4) programming, (5) mathematics of computation, (6) design and construction, and (7) analog computers. Issues contain 50-100 pages of reviews. Many of these are technical or in fields of direct interest to various scientific specialities. However, the section on Management Data Processing Applications certainly is worthwhile for people who desire to keep current with the main literature in the area of systems. These three—*Journal, Communications,* and *Reviews*—play a significant role in the fields relating to computers.

Data Processing Digest Canning, Sisson, and Associates, 1140 South Robertson Boulevard, Los Angeles, California 90035. The *Digest,* published monthly, contains an analytical summary of the current major articles and books concerning computers and data processing. For its low cost, we recommend that any organization with a significant interest in management systems makes sure its computer department receives the *Digest.* Its summaries of the current books, articles, and happenings in the fields relating to computers provide a wealth of material that can be of considerable benefit to the organization.

Data Processing Magazine 134 North Thirteenth Street, Philadelphia, Pennsylvania 19107. This monthly magazine publishes material in the field of computers and information technology. It would be primarily of interest to people who are active in the area of systems and programming. The articles cover topics such as conversion, data transmission, estimating programming costs, information personnel, and management aspects of simulation. One feature that may interest the reader is the "Book Shelf" which provides a brief description of the latest books in the field of computers, data processing, systems, and information. There are also many advertisements for products and information in the field of computers.

Datamation   F. D. Thompson Publications, Inc., 35 Mason Street, Greenwich, Connecticut 06830. *Datamation* is published monthly and is aimed at management people in the area of computers, data processing, systems, information, and related areas. It usually contains about ten articles on timely subjects such as conversion problems or experiences, advances and trends in hardware and software, computing developments a decade hence, real time computing, tape and disk characteristics, and many other subjects relating to computers. Most of the articles are not technical in nature. In addition to the articles, there are several features including things such as: looking ahead, news items, new products, new literature, world-wide report, Washington report, books, people, and advertisements. The book review section is different from those in other publications of this type in that there is usually an interesting depth review of a single book. *Datamation* is probably the most widely-read single publication in the computer planning and programming field.

Decision Tables: A Systems Analysis and Documentation Technique   (Form F20-8102) International Business Machines Corporation, 112 East Post Road, White Plains, New York 10601. This manual describes the basic concepts of decision tables and a minimum set of conventions for their use in systems analysis, procedure design, and documentation. As we mentioned in the book, the purpose of such tables is to provide information in a concise format that is easy to read and understand. The tabular approach is used to express complex decision logic in a manner that encourages the analyst to reduce a problem to its simplest form by arranging and presenting logical alternatives under various conditions. The resultant tables present a system's logic in a concise manner that is easy to visualize and grasp. While the concepts are presented on an elementary level for easy comprehension, the methods are applicable by people at all levels of sophistication in a data processing environment.

Fisher, F. Peter and George F. Swindle, **Computer Programming Systems**   New York: Holt, Rinehart and Winston, 1964. This book explains the use of assembly and compiler languages including Algol, Fortran, and Cobol. The book also describes the steps by which an assembler or compiler translates a subject program into an object program. This book will give the reader a comparison of the difference between the meaning of the term "computer systems" (in its reference to the hardware and programs) as compared to the meaning of "management systems."

Flowcharting Techniques   (Form C20-8152) International Business Machines Corporation, 112 East Post Road, White Plains, New York 10601. For the reader who has little or no knowledge of flowcharting methods, this manual will serve as a good introduction. It describes in detail the preparation of system and program flowcharts. It stresses the fact that adherence to standard techniques for the preparation of flowcharts of data processing systems and procedures greatly increases effectiveness of communication between the programmer analyst and the many groups with whom he deals.

Glossary (0-682564) Superintendent of Documents, Government Printing Office, Washington, D. C. 20025. ($.40). This 62-page glossary covers the fields relating to computers. It was prepared by an Interdepartmental Glossary Task Force for use as an authoratative reference by all officials and employees of the Government. It is suggested that readers of our book obtain a copy of this Glossary for convenient reference.

Glossary for Information Processing (Form C20-8089) International Business Machines Corporation, 112 East Post Road, White Plains, New York 10601. This glossary contains definitions of over 1000 words, terms, concepts, and abbreviations. In addition to the many words originating within their own organization, the authors have referred to 40 other glossaries to insure completeness.

Hall, A. D., **A Methodology for Systems Engineering** New York: D. Van Nostrand Co., 1962. This book is widely-referenced as an excellent example of the concepts and philosophy of systems design and analysis.

Journal of Creative Behavior Creative Education Foundation. State University College at Buffalo, 1300 Elmwood Avenue, Buffalo, New York 14222. Throughout our book we have mentioned the importance of creativity on the part of analysts in studying and designing systems. In the opinion of many people, the major study of creativity is centered in the work of the Creative Education Foundation. The *Journal* provides a focus for the rapidly increasing interest and literature in creativity, intelligence, and problem-solving. This interdisciplinary subject touches on many areas of education and psychology, including related topics such as concept formation, cognitive functions, perception and language, and the thought process. It also bears directly on all levels, subjects, and types of education—in the arts, sciences, humanities, and the social sciences, as well as in the various professions, business, government, and industry.

Journal of Data Management Data Processing Management Association, 505 Busse Highway, Park Ridge, Illinois 60068. This journal is the official publication of the Data Processing Management Association, which is regarded by many people as the major organization representing the business and management use of computers. The association sponsors the Certificate in Data Processing. A study of the *Journal* will provide the reader with a good idea of the computer in its data processing function.

Journal of the American Statistical Association American Statistical Association, 1757 K Street, N.W., Washington, D. C. 20006. One of the major uses of computers is for statistical problems that arise in human activities of all kinds. The ASA is the oldest scientific society in America and is considered to be the classical parent body for all other societies dealing with quantitative methods.

Throughout our book we have referred to statistical methods. The *Journal* presents the articles containing the results of the current research in statistics. Many of these articles are of great importance in the area of systems.

Journal of the Operations Research Society of America   Mount Royal and Guilford Avenues, Baltimore, Maryland 21202. This journal, published bimonthly, would be of interest primarily to people with a good mathematical background. It, like *Management Science,* is aimed at the quantitative solution of management problems. It also has book reviews. Some of the topic areas include: information systems, Bayesian decision theory, linear programming, marketing models, critical path methods, economic order quantities, Markov chains, simulation, queuing, and life testing. In brief, this *Journal* would keep an organization up to date on the latest developments in this field.

Kemeny, John G., Arthur Schliefer, Jr., J. Laurie Snell, and Gerald L. Thompson, **Finite Mathematics with Business Applications**   Englewood Cliffs, New Jersey; Prentice-Hall, Inc. 1963. Topics in this book include decision trees, logical relations, sets and subsets, probability theory, vectors and matrices, mathematics of finance and accounting, linear programming, and theory of games. This book explains the need for, and uses of, logical problem solving techniques in business.

Management Science   the journal of The Institute of Management Sciences. Mount Royal and Guilford Avenues, Baltimore, Maryland 21202. T.I.M.S. is a professional association whose aim is to identify, extend, and unify scientific knowledge pertaining to management. The journal is prepared in three sections, A, B, C. Section A is primarily aimed at the scientific community. Section B is aimed primarily at management. Section C is primarily a bulletin for news and announcements. There are also some excellent book reviews. Although the tone of the book is quantitative, and would appeal mostly to people with a mathematical background, there are many articles that could be read profitably by systems people generally.

Management Services   American Institute of Certified Public Accountants. 666 Fifth Avenue, N.Y., N.Y. 10019. This periodical is the major publication in the area of accounting concentrating on planning, systems, and controls. It is published bimonthly. Its articles are for general managerial personnel. Representative titles are: "Decision Tables," "The Essence of Budgetary Control," and "Operations Research—The Basics." Of general interest are two other major departments in the magazine, (1) People, events, and techniques, and (2) What people are writing about. Both are devoted largely to topics involving computers. The second department is an excellent review section of books and articles of particular interest in the area of management systems.

McMillan, Claude and Richard F. Gonzalez, **Systems Analysis: A Computer Approach to Decision Models**   Homewood, Illinois: Richard D. Irwin, Inc., 1965. This book considers the use of the computer for simulation and includes discussions of inventory systems, Monte Carlo simulation, queuing concepts, management planning models, and a study in total systems simulation.

Morrison, Philip and Emily Morrison, (Eds.). **Charles Babbage and His Calculating Engines** New York: Dover Publications, 1961. This book contains selected writings by Charles Babbage and others. It explains the reasons for the development of, and the mechanics and logic of, Babbage's machines, including his idea for a large-scale computer. Not only is the book interesting for its coverage of the problems of computation in the early 1800s, it is also excellent for its discussion of management problems in developing advanced systems in backward surroundings.

Schmidt, Richard N. and William E. Meyers, **Electronic Business Data Processing** New York: Holt, Rinehart and Winston, 1963. This book is primarily a text to be used in teaching the principles of data processing from the management point of view. A review of this book will give the reader a good insight into the kind of work that is involved during the implementation stage of computer-based systems.

Schmidt, Richard N. and William E. Meyers, **Introduction to Computer Science and Data Processing** New York: Holt, Rinehart and Winston, 1965. This book is designed as a non-mathematical introduction to computers and their use. It would be of value to management or systems personnel who wish to obtain a basic understanding of the concept and operation of a stored program computer.

Schoderbek, Peter P., (Ed.), **Management Systems** New York: John Wiley and Sons, Inc., 1967. This book contains a set of 51 readings related to management and systems. The readings begin with an article by Kenneth E. Boulding, "General Systems Theory: The Skeleton of Science," to provide the theme for the book. The other articles cover the many and diverse fields with which this subject is concerned. The section on Models and Simulation opens with an article on "Models" by Irwin D. J. Bross and concludes with an article, "Management Control Systems" by Joel M. Kibbee. The final section of the book covers information retrieval. In summary, this book attempts to link the basic concepts employed in management systems to reveal their interrelationships.

Selected United States Government Publications Superintendent of Documents, Government Printing Office, Washington, D. C. 20402. Biweekly the Government Printing Office prepares a selected list of over 50 publications on a wide variety of subjects. Usually, each list contains one or more publications that are of importance and interest to management personnel. Occasionally, extremely valuable publications in the area of computers, data processing, and systems are on the list. The cost of most of the listed items is very low. When one considers that the Government is the world's largest organization using computers, and that it spends billions of dollars on systems of all kinds, the articles, booklets, and books it publishes in this area should be read with care by all interested people. The list is sent free biweekly to all who request that they be placed on the mailing list.

Systems and Procedures Journal Systems and Procedures Association, 7890

Brookside Drive, Cleveland, Ohio 44138. A person who desires to find out more about the kind of work done by systems and procedures people should examine this journal and the official book, *Business Systems,* published by the Association. Other publications of the association include: *Total Systems, Joint Man/ Machine Decisions, Profile of a Systems Man, Systems Film Catalog, An Annotated Bibliography for the Systems Professional, Ideas for Management,* and many others of interest to systems analysts.

Wiener, Norbert, **Cybernetics: or Control and Communication in the Animal and the Machine**   Massachusetts Institute of Technology Press, 2nd Edition, 1961. This book is the all-time classic on the theory of systems. It deals with a study of human control functions and the mechanical and electrical systems designed to replace the human being. It requires a certain level of mathematical maturity to benefit from its study. For those who do not have a mathematical background, Wiener's *Human Use of Human Beings* covers the same topics from a non-mathematical point of view.

QUESTIONS AND PROBLEMS

In this appendix are questions and problems designated for the 21 chapters of the book. They are numbered by chapter and then by number within the chapter For example, 1.3 would represent the third question of Chapter 1, and 8.7 would represent the seventh question of Chapter 8.

1.1   Obtain the dictionary definitions of organization, management, and system. (Use Webster's New Collegiate Dictionary if possible.) Discuss the similarities and differences in the definitions.

1.2   Figure 1-1 shows the three stages in the life of a system. On the basis of the steps listed for each stage, which is the most difficult stage and which is the easiest stage?

1.3   If every organization has a management system, why are so many organizations unable to achieve their desired goals?

1.4   Every management organization has a system. Every system has a management organization. Every management system has an organization. Discuss the above statements.

1.5   What are the objectives of each of the stages of the life of a business system?

1.6   The text states that business systems have matured considerably over the years. However, many organizations are operating today, and successfully, without modern systems. How can these organizations exist?

1.7   The text describes three phases for conducting a systems study. Rank the phases in order of importance in developing a successful system. Explain your reasons for the ranking.

1.8   What would the dangers be of going directly into the Stage 2 implementation of a system instead of carrying out a Stage 1 system study and design? Are there cases where you would skip Stage 1?

1.9   Would there be any reason to conduct a Stage 1 systems study and design without going through with implementation? Why?

1.10   Name five variables which help determine the range and scope for a business study.

1.11   What are the major stages in a system? How do they depend upon one another?

2.1   What is the purpose of each of the three phases in Stage 1?

2.2   Discuss the contents of the report which is prepared after Phase I is completed.

2.3   Figure 2-2 depicts a simplified model of a business system. Does this model really depict the system for any organization?

2.4   If Phase I defines the present system as it now exists, why is it necessary to determine systems requirements in Phase II? Are not the systems requirements defined in the Phase I study?

2.5   Let us assume that your reading and studying of this book can be defined as an "activity." Can such an activity be expressed in the structural form shown in Figure 2-4?

2.6   Discuss the contents of the "New System Plan."

2.7   Obtain definitions of the word "environment" from a dictionary. How can these definitions be applied to the environment of a management system?

2.8   Figure 2-5 depicts the general structure of an operation model. Let us assume that eating dinner is an operation. How can such an operation be described by the model in Figure 2-5?

2.9 Discuss the similarities and differences of activity, function, operation, department, system, and goals.

2.10 Discuss the concept of "activity formulation."

2.11 a) What two main questions arise in determining the requirements of a system?
b) How does one find out the answers to them?

2.12 Why is it necessary to sell the results of the study to management if the study team is already a part of the company?

2.13 Name five different types of resources that an organization possesses.

2.14 Name at least five different types of organizations. What criteria can be used to separate one organization from another for the purpose of examining goals and activities?

3.1 Why is it that the top executive of the company is so important to the success of a system?

3.2 State three ways in which the time schedule required for a study can be reduced.

3.3 What are ten steps which should be considered in determining the time schedule for a systems study?

3.4 In Figure 3-1 the amount of emphasis on documentation decreases from Phase I to Phase II to Phase III. Does this decrease seem reasonable?

3.5 Is it possible to have too much documentation during Phase I? Is it possible to have too little documentation?

3.6 Even though many systems are automated today, the text stresses the importance of proper announcement of the study and correct interviewing techniques. Since these are people-oriented problems, why be concerned about them in this automated world?

3.7 The text discusses three levels of languages in the study and design of systems—overview, systems view, and detail view. Discuss each of these languages in relation to:

    a. Time allotted for a systems study
    b. Complexity of the existing system

    c. Need in the design of a new system

    d. Cost of the study

3.8 Which type of reporting technique would be most applicable in presenting the results of a systems study to:

    a. The president and executive officers of an organization.

    b. The manager of a department whose functions were studied.

    c. An equipment manufacturer for the purpose of evaluating the type of equipment required.

3.9 Give two examples of pitfalls which can be encountered in conducting a system study.

3.10 What are management constraints? Why are they important in the design of a system?

4.1 What is the primary reason for studying the present business?

4.2 Describe some of the sources for general and structural data for a Phase I report.

4.3 What subjects should one or more members of a study team have knowledge of if the team is to study and design an information system for a telephone company?

4.4 What subjects should one or more members of a team have knowledge of if the team is to perform a major customer information systems study for a commercial bank?

4.5 Although direct interviews are a valuable source of data, what are some of the pitfalls of interviewing?

4.6 Describe two data collection methods designed to reduce the time requirements of a study.

4.7 Why might the analyst have difficulty in obtaining complete information about the existing system through interviews with supervisory personnel?

4.8 Would the report presenting the study team's findings during their study of the present business have any value for management of the organization concerned even if the study stopped there? Explain.

4.9 Why is a company dictionary important to systems study and implementation?

4.10 Define the following terms as they might appear in a company dictionary:

      a. hourly rated worker
      b. discount
      c. gross pay
      d. federal withholding tax
      e. employee
      f. charge account number
      g. net pay

5.1 What is the main purpose of the general section of the present business description?

5.2 What is the major purpose of the history and framework section of the general section of the present business description?

5.3 Summarize some potential sources of information for the industry background section of the present business description.

5.4 When studying a manufacturing process of a company it may be desirable to classify the tools used in the plant. What sources of data could be used for such classification?

5.5 Section 5.5 contains the policies and practices of the National Bank of Commerce. What information might these policies and practices envision for the bank's customers?

5.6 Section 5.2 of the text contains a selected statement of the history and framework of Butodale Electronics. Item number 3 in this example reads, "Opening of additional sales offices in Chicago and Fort Worth." Could the statement be changed to "Opened two additional sales offices"?

5.7 Government regulations vary from one industry to another. Classify the following industries as to the degree of government regulations a study team might encounter during a systems study. Use a classification system of very much, some, and little or none.

      a. Dairy
      b. Brewery
      c. Advertising agency
      d. Computer manufacturer
      e. Trucking company
      f. Stock broker

6.1 What are the three major elements of the structural aspects of a system?

6.2 What interest would management people have in the inputs of the organization?

6.3   What does the structural section of the present business description represent?

6.4   The text lists four categories of resources: finances, personnel, inventory, and facilities. Which category is the most valuable to an organization?

6.5   If the information presented in the report of the existing system is so valuable, why is it necessary to conduct a study to gather the data? Why does the company not maintain structural data on a current and continuing basis?

6.6   What might be the input pattern of the structure of a telephone company's business office, which is open from 8:30 A.M. to 5:30 P.M. ?

6.7   In the structural part of a manufacturing system, the term "family" may be applied to a group of parts with common geometrical or electrical characteristics such as shafts, printed circuits, motor laminations, brackets, and so on. If a team is studying the manufacturing process in a given company, what might be the team's source of data for establishing family groupings?

6.8   Many data processing departments assign an identification number to each report produced by the department, and maintain a description of the contents of each report and a list of recipients. Of what value would such information be during a systems study, especially where the structural aspects are concerned?

6.9   Structural data can be viewed from five levels:
      a.   Routine data
      b.   Control totals
      c.   Control ratios
      d.   Mathematical models
      e.   Mathematical models integrated with routine data
      Of what value is it to consider these five levels of data when studying the structural aspects of a system?

6.10 What are the main elements of the business model, and for what purpose is the model used?

7.1   Define an activity. How does an activity differ from a system?

7.2   Why is it impractical to structure an organization solely on the basis of activities?

7.3   Characterize the basic methods of activity formulation.

7.4   Explain the meaning of "area of application."

7.5   In formulating activities, systems analysts continually use the word "data." Explain its meaning.

7.6   During their activity formulation work, what are some areas that a team should examine when studying the information system for a telephone company?

7.7   During its activity formulation work, what might be the sub-team assignments of a team which is to study an information system for a telephone company?

7.8   A study team has been assigned the task of formulating the activities for the information processing system of a large university. Suggest areas which may be assigned to the members of the team for study as separate units. For each area list the data, documents, and reports which should be studied.

7.9   With reference to Figure 7-4:

        a) What do the points 12, 13, 14, etc., represent?
        b) In the cost file, what does the 4010 represent?
        c) What are the names of two information resources?

8.1   What primary purpose do the documentation forms serve?

8.2   Would it be of any value to management to have available a resource usage sheet (as shown in Figure 8-2) for each year, six months, or quarter?

8.3   Why is it that so many departments of a company can be interested in the same source document?

8.4   What might be the purpose of a company administrative blueprint?

8.5   Explain the difference between a routine document and a management report.

8.6   In addition to the message and file sheets described in the text, would a "field description sheet" be of any value? What information might such a sheet include?

8.7   How do the five documents described in this chapter together form a coherent description of the system?

8.8   In Figure 8-1 the arrow between the activity sheet and the resource usage sheet suggests that the data from the activity sheet flows into the resource usage sheet. Is this true?

8.9   Examine Figure 8-12. If Atlantic sells a quantity of 11 of a given item at $999.99 each, will the line item card be able to hold all the data?

8.10   Based on the information in Figure 8-12, what is the highest possible unit price for an item sold by Atlantic Distributors?

8.11   Based on the information contained in Figure 8-12, what is the greatest number of departments that the Atlantic Distributors could have?

8.12   On the average, how many active customers does Atlantic Distributors have?

9.1   What are the primary objectives of the present business description report?

9.2   The text states that the report of Phase I is useful in Phases II and III during which systems requirements are defined and a new system is designed. Which sections (general, structural, operational, appendix) would be most useful in Phase II? in Phase III?

9.3   Describe the key purposes of each of the sections of the present business description.

9.4   Briefly outline what might be in the various parts of a "present business description" of a major league baseball team.

10.1   Of what value would a present business description report, such as the Butodale report, be to organizations in their research for management personnel?

10.2   Use your local library or write to an appropriate brokerage house to obtain an annual report on three selected companies. See if you can obtain a history of one of the companies and its industry. Prepare a narrative description by following the format of the general section for Butodale.

10.3   There are many fine source books on certain basic industries such as insurance, banking, transportation, etc. Classify business and institutions into approximately 25 categories and identify source items which give industry history, government regulations, etc. for three of these categories.

10.4   Of what value would case studies, such as Butodale Phase I, be for introducing students to business?

10.5   What kind of frequency curve is suggested by the data for suppliers in Figure 10-1? Is this unexpected?

10.6   In Figure 10-13, is the selection of the words "provide product demand" reasonable to define the activity described by the phrase?

10.7   What is the average time for answering a quotation on a standard analog computer at Butodale? Why does it take so long if the product is standard?

10.8   What are some of the components that make up the miscellaneous costs in Figure 10-13?

10.9   What triggers the costing operation (630) shown in Figure 10-15?

10.10   In a system for Butodale how large a record will be needed to contain the information on a customer's request for a quotation? for a bid?

10.11   If one were to classify both message sheets and file sheets under a single name, what might be the term?

10.12   Figure 10-25 shows a blank form described on the message sheet in Figure 10-24. How could the analysts improve their reported information relative to this form?

10.13   What critical information is contained in file sheet number F-4010?

10.14   In file sheet F-4030, the analysts noted that the retention characteristic of the file is, "NEVER BEEN PURGED." What does this mean?

11.1   State three major kinds of goals that might apply to most organizations in general.

11.2   Public agencies often have a difficult time expressing their goals because they are not directly related to profit-making activities. For any three Federal, state, or community agencies which you select, state what you consider are their principal goals.

11.3   Identify and define activities related to the goals stated in response to Question 11.2.

11.4   In establishing goals, what are some considerations that should be recognized?

11.5   What might be the future goals of a quality control system for a manufacturing process?

11.6   What might be the goals a state might use for designing a welfare information system?

11.7   What might be the major files in a university information system set up after the activities of the university have been reformulated to accommodate an electronic system?

11.8   A study team has been requested to analyze the activities relative to order entry, billing, and accounts receivable. The team soon realizes that the organization has a very fine cost system for product costing but has no costs recorded which may be useful in analyzing activities during their reformulation. Why might this be?

11.9   What might be the goals the analysts might record for an information system involving the accounts payable activity of a company?

11.10   What might be some of the goals that analysts might record for a production control activity?

11.11   What may be considered as goals for the purchasing activity of a company?

11.12   What might be the goals of a team which is studying an information system for a telephone company?

11.13   What might some of the goals of a plant maintenance management system be?

12.1   What is the principal purpose of phase II?

12.2   Describe various ways in which information collected during phase I can be used in phase II.

12.3   In driving a car, what are some of the required inputs? What are the required outputs? Indicate some inputs and outputs which are not required. Indicate certain operations that must be performed or certain resources that must be used. Indicate some operations and resources which are optional.

12.4   What might be some of the questions that a study team should ask while defining an information retrieval system for an organization?

12.5   Prepare a narrative description of the operations involved in purchasing food from a supermarket. Cover all operations from entering the store until the groceries have been taken from the store. Show the same operation in flow chart form; use decision tables to express the decision logic used in making correct change.

12.6   The Slowburn Gas Company bills its customers according to the following rate schedule:

     First 500 cubic feet $1.00 minimum charge
     Next 3,050 cubic feet @ .125 per hundred cf.
     Next 35,000 cubic feet @ .120 per hundred cf.
     Next 125,000 cubic feet @ .110 per hundred cf.

Next 125,000 cubic feet @ .095 per hundred cf.
Next 425,000 cubic feet @ .0825 per hundred cf.
Any additional cubic feet @ .0735 per hundred cf.

Prepare a flowchart to show the steps in calculating a customer's bill.

12.7   An asset has a purchase price of X dollars and an estimated scrap value
of S dollars. Prepare a flowchart to show the steps in each of the following
procedures:

a. The asset is to be depreciated over Y years. Calculate the reserve for
depreciation and net value at the end of each year of the life of the
asset. Use the straight line depreciation method.
b. The asset is to be depreciated over Y years. Calculate the reserve for
depreciation and net value at the end of each year of the life of the
asset. Use the sum of the digits method of depreciation.

12.8   A study of a student information system for a university proposes that five
basic uses of student information are: counseling, admissions, academic,
general student data, and alumni. Prepare a list of the fields of information
which might be included in each record of such a file, and indicate for
each field which of the five uses listed above the information will serve. A
field may serve from one to five uses.

12.9   a. Prepare a flowchart to show the steps necessary to compute the value
of a principal amount P at the end of Y years if the principal earns
simple interest at the rate of X percent.
b. Prepare a flowchart to show the steps necessary to compute the value
of a principal amount P at the end of each year from 1 year through
Y years if a compound interest rate of X is used.

12.10   A study team has been requested to define the contents of a customer
record in a file of a public utility company. What information might the
team recommend be included in such a record?

12.11   Prepare a flowchart to show the steps necessary to calculate a twelve
month moving average for a set of sales data.

12.12   Assume that you are a member of a study team that is studying a system
for maintaining the customer records of a commercial bank. You are assigned the task of investigating and documenting the present file maintenance techniques. What steps should you follow in completing this task?

12.13   A study team is examining the overall operations of a credit bureau. As
one of the steps in the study the team wishes to define the prime purpose
for automating the credit bureau operations. What might their statement
be?

12.14 A large metropolitan hotel has decided to install a data processing system for recording all guest charges. What might be the inputs to such a system?

13.1 Establishing rating scales and setting values is a difficult task. To gain insight into a formal process quite analogous to this procedure, read a chapter from any of the standard personnel text books on position evaluation. This is a method for defining and rating the various positions within an organization. After reading about the method, point out 5 similarities and differences between the position clarification problem and the establishment of a rating procedure for a new management system. Note to instructor: As a group exercise you may wish to draw up position descriptions and rate them for various positions on a study team.

13.2 Identify and define briefly 5 measurement factors for local commercial enterprises like a drug store, restaurant, book store.

13.3 When are measurement factors and measurement scales established?

13.4 List ten major measurement categories and possible measurement factors.

13.5 What is the purpose of a rating scale?

13.6 Are measurement factors related to business goals?

13.7 What is the fundamental defect in simple business control ratios, which are often used as measuring factors?

13.8 What might be the goals in the design of a data processing system for work measurement?

13.9 Compare the concept of measuring the performance of a system to evaluating a new product which an organization is considering to replace an existing product.

13.10 From Figure 13-1,

    (a) What are the desirable and acceptable ranges?
    (b) Who sets and achieves the ranges in (a)?
    (c) How does the information revealed by the figure affect how the analysts plan their system?

13.11 For the information in Figure 13-3:

    (a) What is the smallest proportion of shipments under 6 hours that will permit the system to be classified as operating in the acceptable range?

(b) If 10% of the shipments had to wait 8 or more hours, what is the conclusion about the new system's performance?

(c) If less than 50% of the shipments under the new system had to wait less than 7 hours, how would one classify the system?

14.1   What is the purpose of the input-output sheet?

14.2   What does the required operations sheet summarize?

14.3   What does the resource sheet summarize?

14.4   How are inventories and files described on a resource sheet?

14.5   What is the prime determinant for system requirements?

14.6   What is the most important source of information for analysts when they try to establish the true requirements of a system?

14.7   How much freedom do the analysts have in designing the format of the customer record in the input-output sheet in Figure 14-4?

14.8   For how many days a year must the charge account activity of Associated Retailers be operational?

14.9   Explain the five types of processes the analysts have established for the "PREPARE BILLS" operation shown in Figure 14-5. How do they affect the system design?

14.10   In Figure 14-9 we see that management has imposed a unit record installation on the system. Comment.

15.1   According to Figure 15-1, what three tasks require the greatest amount of time of a study team designing a new system?

15.2   What does the general section of each activity packet of the system requirements specification describe?

15.3   What is included in the operations section of the system requirements specification?

15.4   What is the purpose of the summary section of the system requirements specification report?

15.5   What is the relationship between the information in Figure 15-1 and the implementation of the system once the new system plan is approved?

16.1   What functions are not included in Butodale's provide product demand activity?

16.2 What is not included in Butodale's provide end products activity?

16.3 Describe the scope and boundaries of Butodale's provide product demand activity.

16.4 What are the goals and objectives of Butodale's provide product demand activity?

16.5 What do "reference" and "symmetry" mean in relation to the appearance of Butodale's quotation bid?

16.6 From the Phase I report one would infer that all the major activities were going to be studied for possible conversion to the computer. In Phase II it appears that the scope of the study has been considerably reduced. Comment.

16.7 In Figure 16-1 we see six listed inputs. Are they all exclusive?

16.8 What freedom do the analysts have in designing the form on which to record the request for quotation or bid?

16.9 What is a *GPAC*?

16.10 In the Phase II report for Butodale, what appears to be the bulk of the work among the required operations? Of what value will be the computer for this work?

16.11 Comment on the four factors that Butodale management desires to use for measuring the effectiveness of the new system.

17.1 For the design phase, how can the data in the present files of a system be related, in tabular form, to the data in the files of the proposed system?

17.2 What problem may arise if a system is designed to merely work with mathematical models, with complete disregard for routine data processing?

17.3 What might be the contents of the data files of a mechanized plant maintenance system?

17.4 In most systems which include dynamic files some of the records become useless for various reasons. As an example, many payroll systems will carry an employee's record for one year after termination of employment and then delete the record from the file. This procedure is known as "purging" the file. As a member of a study team you have been asked to prepare a list of rules for purging the file of a credit bureau. List at least five applicable purging rules the study team might establish during the design phase of a system.

17.5   What are some factors an analyst must consider in the selection of a sequence key format for a customer information file for a commercial bank
when he designs a new system?

17.6   List five possible formats of a customer name and address in the customer
file of a commercial bank data processing application.

17.7   What are the basic questions to be answered in determining the file organization for an electronic data processing system?

17.8   Why is it common to split a manual record into more than one part to
form more than one master file?

17.9   Why do management personnel have difficulty in specifying the kind of
reports they desire?

17.10   As analysts design a system, how should they think about the following:
"As a commodity, information has two characteristics which can give
it monetary value—relevance and timeliness. To the extent that it is
relevant, it provides useful answers to specific questions, or supplies
data to selected individuals; to the extent that it is timely, it is available
at the time it is needed or usable. If either of these characteristics is
missing, the information is useless and the design of the system is
faulty."

17.11   What is the correct amount of data for a company to preserve in its data
bank?

17.12   What is meant by records retention?

17.13   Why is the government interested in records retention?

17.14   It has been stated that three axioms of business data are:

1. A company cannot afford to collect and process all the data that
   could be generated by it.
2. A company with an inadequate supply of business data is likely to
   fail.
3. A company should collect enough data at each stage of its existence
   to optimize its future earnings and return on investment.

Of what value are these three axioms to the study team during the design
phase of a new system?

17.15   Every manufacturing process has maintenance personnel and equipment
for performing maintenance on the plant and equipment. Effective manage-

ment of the maintenance activity is important to a company. What questions might a maintenance management system be expected to answer?

17.16 In an information system for a credit bureau the primary file may be referred to as the "subject file." This file contains all of the items of information pertaining to individuals' credit history and status. This file, although normally the largest and most important one, is by no means the only one used or maintained at a credit bureau. What might be some of the other files used and maintained by a credit bureau?

17.17 "Effective file maintenance rests upon a set of well-defined and consistent file audit rules." A credit bureau is designing a system for its subject file. What maintenance rules might the analysts set for this file.

17.18 A study of the inventory control system of a company reveals that the company is able to maintain a very small inventory merely by purchasing frequently and in small lots. Should the system be changed?

18.1 The credit manager for a certain department store makes frequent use of information from a credit bureau. The bureau is considering installing a data processing system. The bureau asks his opinion as to whether or not he would install a terminal in his offices so that he could have direct communication with the computer. As a systems analyst for the store, how would you advise the credit manager?

18.2 Visit a company that has a computer and prepare a report on the programming languages used by the company.

18.3 Distinguish between "hardware" and "software" with respect to a computer system.

18.4 What costs might a company reduce if it implements a system which will provide inventory control so that a smaller, but sufficient, inventory is maintained?

18.5 During a study you are assigned the task of gathering the costs associated with the purchasing activity of the company. What departments of the company should you consider as contributing to the total purchasing activity cost?

18.6 "A good system on a poor computer is better than a poor system on a good computer." Comment.

18.7 What is a waiting line?

18.8 Why does the computer play such an important role in simulation?

18.9   What is the relationship between the "Monte Carlo" method and simulation?

18.10   What is a deterministic model? a probabilistic model?

18.11   What are some major differences between Cobol, Algol, Fortran, and PL/I?

18.12   When establishing reorder points for items in an inventory control system, what factors should the analysts take into consideration?

18.13   It has been recommended that before a study of a distributor's salable products inventory system is begun, the following information about the inventory should be prepared:

1.   Distribution by value of items in sequence by dollar annual sales.
2.   Distribution by value of vendors in sequence by dollar annual sales.
3.   Distribution of items within vendor in sequence by dollar annual sales.

Of what value would this information be to the study team and to management?

18.14   Describe three factors for measuring the effectiveness of a newly designed system for the purchasing activity of a company.

18.15   List the fields of information, other than customer name and address, which may be included in an account record in a file of personal checking accounts in a commercial bank for which a new system is being designed.

18.16   What are some of the tangible advantages, other than cost, of an online data processing system for credit authorization in a department store?

19.1   Why have automated techniques not been developed for designing a new system?

19.2   What are two kinds of information which are generally included in the appraisal of systems value?

19.3   In the report describing the new system, what is included in:

a) management abstract
b) implementation plan?

19.4   What is one similarity between the system design process and the determination of system requirements?

19.5   A system has been designed to select from a skills inventory file those individuals who have given characteristics of education, product knowledge, specific field skill, and experience with product components. Prepare a Venn diagram to show the effect of such a combinatorial search. Would the diagram be of any value in the management abstract of the report for the proposed system?

19.6   What subjects are usually included in the appendix of the report describing the new system?

19.7   When an analyst begins the design phase for a new system, what two main kinds of information are important for his use? Where can the information be found?

19.8   Why is a management abstract needed in the "New System Plan" if all the information is in the rest of the report?

19.9   In Figure 19-3 we notice that the plan for the new system implies that more than 2 years will be needed for implementation. Why does it take so long to get a system into operation?

19.10   In Figure 19-4 we see the terms "OTC outputs" and "OTC inputs." What does OTC mean?

19.11   What would be the most significant aspect of the diagram in Figure 19-6 to management?

20.1   Prepare a flowchart in the format of the chart in Figure 20-2, to show the input data and output reports of the registration activity of a university. Assume that a student data master file, a student academic master file, and a course timetable master file are available for use.

20.2   A study team has determined that the primary purpose of a system to record and control customer information in a charge account file in a department store is to bill the customer and collect the monies due. When proposing such a system a study team could also include advantages which the system would have for:

   a) Credit promotion
   b) Sales promotion
   c) Bad debt analysis
   d) Account solicitation analysis
   e) Attorney effectiveness

What might the team include in its proposal as advantages for each of these areas?

20.3   A university may use a computer to process its data for a wide range of purposes. Prepare an overall flow diagram indicating the system that might be considered for student services, once the student is accepted.

20.4   Discuss some factors which indicate that an engineering design system should be automated.

20.5   Into what three major segments may a production control system be divided?

20.6   What type of information would be desirable from the material control phase of a production control system?

20.7   What type of information would be desirable from the manufacturing control phase of a production control system?

20.8   Prepare a flowchart to show the logic of the input edit and engineering design shown as operation 4 in Figure 20-2.

20.9   Prepare a flowchart to show the flow of the processes necessary to accomplish the verification and correction of input cards indicated as operation 3 in Figure 20-2.

20.10   Prepare a flowchart showing in more detail the flow of the processes in operations 1 and 2 in Figure 20-2.

20.11   Why is a letter of transmittal included in the phase III report for Butodale and not the previous two Butodale reports?

20.12   How does the model in Figure 20-1 help management understand the new system?

20.13   In Figure 20-2 how many computer runs are indicated? Will this be true in the actual system?

20.14   In Figure 20-3 we see a large difference between the purchase price and monthly rental of the proposed computer equipment. Should Butodale rent or purchase the equipment?

20.15   Why is there no cost shown for the two XYZ personnel in Figure 20-4?

20.16   How will the actual implementation differ from the plan in Figure 20-5?

20.17   The large changes in the cost figures among the departments in Figure 20-6 mean large personnel changes. How can this be done without demoralizing personnel?

21.1   If systems require study, design, and implementation on a continuing basis, how have many companies managed to survive as long as they have without constantly improving their systems?

21.2   What is the relationship between the implementation personnel and the operating personnel of the computer department?

21.3   Visit a company with a computer and report on the number and titles of the employees in the programming and operating sections of the computer department.

21.4   Suggest why a plan that calls for simultaneous conversion of all areas of a new system at one time is likely to encounter severe difficulties.

21.5   Why are standards necessary in programming and operating departments?

21.6   Why are accounting control totals important for conversion to the new system?

21.7   What is the difference between the people who install a system and the people who keep it going once it has been put into operation?

21.8   If a company signs a contract for a computer, should the computer manufacturer be responsible for getting the system to work?

21.9   Why is the selection of the senior person to install and operate the system so important?

21.10   Why do systems change during implementation? If the design had been done correctly the first time, should it not be suitable for implementation?

Index

425